T0375294

Book 4 of the ET 2041 Scenario Series

Cracking
the Twin
Global Reset
Code

These Twin Global Resets are Centered
Within the Soon Coming
Biblical 13 Year End Time Scenario

Philip R. Herron, a retired mathematician

authorHOUSE

AuthorHouse™
1663 Liberty Drive
Bloomington, IN 47403
www.authorhouse.com
Phone: 833-262-8899

Published by AuthorHouse 08/29/2024

ISBN: 979-8-8230-2725-0 (sc)
ISBN: 979-8-8230-2724-3 (e)

Library of Congress Control Number: 2024910544

Print information available on the last page.

Contents

Introduction

A coming global reset being planned by influential groups around the world is currently a hot topic of conversation within some circles. However, that reset is not a topic covered by this book. That reset is however possibly the first in the twin set of global resets separated by three and one half years that are extensively covered and well defined in the Biblical books of Daniel and Revelation. Those resets are also well covered in this book. What we will be doing is presenting several prophetic Biblical topics that make these twin resets, God's purpose for them, and the likely timeframe for the resets much easier to understand.

I used the words *soon coming* on the cover to describe the timing of the global resets in the same context that Jesus used these words in Rev 22 to describe his return to earth in the end times. In that context it means this; when it does occur it will take place very quickly and at a time when it is not being expected. However, the Bible also says that those who study such things should be able to recognize the signs that will take place indicating that the world is in the *season* of Jesus's return but that nobody will know the day or the hour of his return.

This book certainly reveals many, many signs that indicate that we are currently within that special season. It also reveals a specific timeframe which many of the Biblical signs seem to be pointing toward.

Ultimately, the major purpose for writing this book was to first seek out and then piece together the clues presented in the Bible about the end times so that we could identify all of the key events that take place in the end time scenario. Next we would analyze our clues to see if it appears that our generation is a good fit for fulfillment of God's 13 year end time scenario.

We will now transition to an introduction of the key discoveries that we made that enabled us to do the research that led to the writing of this four book series. Since the year 1844, there have been over a dozen very significant events that have taken place in the world, most of them involving the Jewish people and nation that were all prophesied in the Christian Bible to take place in the end-times. It turns out that most of these events have occurred in very precise mathematical patterns. The patterns turn out to involve the time spacing between events with similar themes tied to them. These event patterns can be projected back into history, and it turns out that in many instances, these patterns continue all the way back to the end of the seventh and final day of the biblical creation event. We have slowly been discovering these mathematically themed event patterns one by one since the year 2013. We have so far discovered well over one hundred of these patterns, and the majority of them are converging in our generation, with most in the fifty-year period from AD 2001 to 2051. The most amazing thing about the event patterns is that they all fit the end-times scenario presented in the Bible.

The second amazing thing about the event patterns is that as we tracked the patterns back into history, they hit nearly all the key events that have defined the history of both the Jewish people and the patriarchs of the Bible before them. The third most amazing thing is that specific patterns were predictive of events involving all the great periods of exiles, tribulations, judgments, destructions, new beginnings, great blessings, and so forth for the Jewish people. We ended up with a huge database of predictable events.

We now have six thousand years of repeating event patterns available for us to use if we want to try to take a peek into the likelihood of certain future years hosting events with now-predictable themes taking place on them. What is drastically different about our generation, however, is that nearly all the patterns are converging in one short time frame for the first time. What might this all mean? That is just what we are attempting to discover in this series of books. In particular, we are interested in investigating the likelihood of the end-time events taking place in our generation.

In fact, we have both the recorded history of the past and the Bible's prophecies of future end-time events to use in helping us take our peek into the future. We cannot with certainty know the specific details of events that will take place in certain years, but we can know the likely themes of those events.

This book is the fourth in a series of books that documents the discovery of the event patterns we are briefly describing here. The vast majority of the patterns are converging in the years AD 2041 to 2051, and we often refer to these books as the "2041 Scenario Series."

The discoveries that led to this series of books first began in 2013 when Jonathan Cahn's books about the Harbingers and Shemitah[1] years led us to conduct a search for the year when God told the Jewish people to first begin celebrating Jubilee years. We knew that if we could find that date, then we would likely find the original, real, and only fifty-year Jubilee pattern God intended for them to keep all their years. The real problem is that the Jews quit celebrating the Jubilee years at some time in the inter-testament period, the four hundred or so years between the Bible's Old and New Testament periods. It seems there was quite a controversy about when the celebration of Jubilee years stopped. We documented that search in a book we called *Commands* and taught to our Bible classes in 2014. In 2015 we decided to expand that book, and the process we went through led us to discover first the "tribulation" pattern and then the "exile" pattern. That led to the discovery of pattern after pattern to the extent that this went on for about seven years and what is now this series of four books.

I would next like to introduce myself, the author of these books. I am a retired mathematician and physicist who worked for thirty-eight years as a senior scientist, systems analyst, and manager in the defense industry. For the last thirty years, I have spent about one thousand hours a year studying, writing books and articles on the Christian Bible, and teaching the Bible with an emphasis on Bible prophecy. I have a prophecy website (Proofthruprophecy.com) that introduces me and my writings much more completely. It includes about four hundred pages of commentary, charts, and study aids for the book of Revelation along with books on God's plan for man, the kingdom parables of Matthew, and dozens of other topics for those wanting to study the end-times and what might be coming in the near future.

Let me now further introduce the four-book series. This series addresses one of today's most commonly asked questions: Could this be the generation that sees the coming of the end-times scenario painted in the Christian Bible? This scenario includes events referred to as the rapture of the saints, the great tribulation, the Second Coming of Jesus, and the start of the millennium. These books demonstrate that the Bible contains a very large series of datable events going all the way back to the fall of man. They also show that these events occur in a series of evenly spaced mathematical patterns that can be projected into our generation, and many of the patterns are grouped into similarly themed event groups occurring every two thousand years. Does our generation fit into this pattern?

Book one, *The Search for the Tribulation Code*, sets the stage for discovery by first presenting the author's gradual discovery of the way God has apparently been controlling the very nature and timing of key events in world history for his people in such a way that the ultimate end-times result will be achieved. By doing so, he is using a large set of event patterns hidden within the Christian Bible that span very long periods, generally spanning thousands of years. Each pattern has its unique theme for the events it contains. These may be events involving judgment, tribulation, exile, testing, reward, and so forth. This book contains all the basic information needed to conduct the event-pattern research as well as the most basic of the event patterns including the Jewish Jubilee pattern, the tribulation code pattern, and the exile pattern. Surprise! These event patterns all converge in our generation. Would you like to know more?

Book two, *God Is Cooking Up Something Incredible*, presents a series of plain-language interpretations of many of the key prophecies contained in the Bible and a discussion of whether they could see fulfillment in our current generation. It presents several other unique event patterns that seem to be converging in our generation as well as several special codes and a "skeleton key" that will open up an understanding of what may be coming for our generation. The messages provided by the event patterns presented in this book are so powerful that they could easily provide a potent antidote for anti-Semitism. This book contains far too many shocking and amazing discoveries to even begin to list here.

Book three, *The Angel of Death Super Code*, presents several incredible event patterns that again seem to be converging in our generation, including the ominous Angel of Death set of coded event patterns. Other major topics covered include a discussion of event patterns that are converging in the seventieth Jubilee period, which takes place in the years AD 2001–2051, event patterns that highlight man's wrestling match over the true identity of God and event patterns that help us unravel the understanding of end-time prophecy and the book of Revelation. The book concludes with the master template God seems to have been using all down through history to bring about his ultimate will for mankind.

This book, book four, *Cracking the Twin Global Reset Code*, presents both a summary and extension of the material presented in the first three books of this 2041 Scenario

Series. The material was simplified and written in a "mystery" format to make it easier and more compelling to read. Ultimately the book is about the coming end-times and whether they may occur in our generation. In the process, several hidden codes associated with the end-times were uncovered. These include a dual global reset code and several other codes that associate this pair of global resets to the end-times. These codes included the pandemic code, the Angel of Death code, and the dual great family reunion code. These codes are all simple mathematical event codes. Do these codes really associate our generation with the end-times? As we investigated these codes, we were looking for clues that might give us this answer. At the end of the book, we assembled all these clues and analyzed them to get our answer. Simply read the book to get the answer to where the clues led us.

The title of each of the four books in this series leads off with the phrase "the ET 2041 Scenario." We will explain why we used that phrase.

We will begin by revealing a very key finding in our research. The year 2041 turns out to be the key convergence point for many of the prophetic patterns we discovered in our research. It also turns out to be a very good fit for the end-times scenario pictured in the Bible in many places. The results of the research that led us to these startling conclusions are the main subject covered in these books. The *ET* in the phrase the "ET 2041 Scenario" has two equally correct applications: the end-times and extraterrestrials. We will not develop this topic fully until we get well into this book, *Cracking the Twin Global Reset Code*. So, we will hold our hats until we get there! The results of this research are very compelling. We call these four books the "ET 2041 Scenario Series."

These books reveal the gradual uncovering of an extremely important historical truth, mainly that an extensive number of historic events were preplanned and interconnected. The evidence presented is so overwhelming that it leads to the conclusion that some preeminent force outside of our human reality must have been the author of the events. If you would like to know more, you must read the books. A significant number of excerpts from each of the first three books in this series are included on my website, Proofthruprophecy.com.

A Further Keynote on How We Wrote These Books

We wrote these books in the general order of our discoveries. By the time we got to this book, we had found several better ways to phrase certain things or better symbols to use to distinguish pattern differences. As we did this, we *did not* go back and change the earlier books to reflect our better insights.

A Keynote on the Context of This Book

The information we will present largely focuses on the various forms of prophecies God used in the Christian Bible to let his people know what to expect in their future. In the Old Testament, God's focus was clearly on Abraham's descendants, who became the

Jewish people. Since most Bible prophecy is contained in the Old Testament, much of our focus is on the Jewish nations and people. This focus largely changed after Jesus came to earth, with the focus then being largely on both Jews and Gentiles who would accept and follow him. The Jewish people were in a timeout of sorts, a period of exile from God's focus and their homeland for the next eighteen hundred years after the destruction of their nation in AD 70.

A series of events starting in AD 1844 has resulted in the gradual return of the Jews from their exile and a gradual return to God's focus. This focus was largely on the Christians during these eighteen hundred years but is now being shared between Christians and Jews.

Another change in focus will take place sometime in the future when Jews and Christians will merge in unity under Jesus. This merger and the time of the merger will be one of our key focal points. This will take place at the time we refer to as "the twin global resets and twin family reunions."

Setting Our Perspective: Giving God the Proper Acknowledgment

After spending seven years writing this four-book series, I acknowledge much more certainly than ever before that God is really in charge and that he always has been. The clearly preplanned historical events that have always been and still are taking place in incredibly accurate mathematical patterns prove that beyond doubt. For that reason, I am acknowledging throughout this book that God is in charge and always has been in charge of the key events that take place in our world. For that reason, I consistently refer to these event patterns as "God's event patterns."

From the research I am presenting, it appears to me that God is influencing and controlling the key events in history that will influence how he brings about the fulfillment of his plan for mankind. Other events are being influenced by spiritual forces in the universe that are battling over the lives of all people on earth. It does seem that most events are "just happening," so to speak. These are those with no real influence on the eventual fulfillment of God's plan. In these books, we are studying the things God is using to bring about the purpose of his will for the people of earth and also for himself.

Thus, we see that there seem to be three major categories of events taking place on earth. First are the events that are key to God being able to fulfill the purpose of his will. God is clearly in sole control of these events. Second are events influenced by angelic forces for both good and evil. God is actually also in control of these, since he places limits on the forces of evil. He will allow them to go only so far. He will not allow them to interfere with his ability to eventually accomplish the purpose of his will. This is modeled in the book of Job. The third type of events are those that may be solely the product of the free will God gave humans. There is no real way we can be certain of how much outside forces are involved in these freewill decisions.

The equally spaced and similarly themed events that have been our major topics are principally about God's use of the first two types of events. God is clearly in control of these events. Thus, throughout this book, you will see us giving God credit for nearly all the events we are presenting. We hope this does not bother the reader, but we believe it is very important to recognize that God is the one in control.

Defining the Words *Code* and *Super Code* as We Will Be Using Them

A "code," as we use it, is a combination of numbers, items, techniques, and so forth. When properly applied or combined, a code can open up and reveal valuable things that have been hidden from view, often in some secret place. For example, a safe or safety deposit box is a place where we can safely store valuables to keep them from being lost, stolen, seen, or even known about. To be able to access these hidden valuables, a person must have the code that unlocks the safe or safety deposit box. In this case, the code is a combination of numbers that must be entered in a specific order. There may also be one or two other features to the code before the hiding place can be opened. For example, for a safety deposit box, a key available only to certain bank employees may also be required to access the box. We could thus say that this is a super code since it involves multiple persons and multiple keys, so to speak, to access the safety deposit box.

The codes we have been using are Bible codes, and scholars have discovered and documented several different types of these codes. Others are still hidden from view and have not as yet been discovered.

We can view those codes as the techniques God has used to hide his valuables and secrets, so to speak. God apparently keeps them hidden and does not reveal them to his people until the time is just right on his calendar. If we are truly in or approaching the end-times, then this may be the time God wants his people to discover them or in truth the time when he will reveal some of his hidden secrets to them. We have observed this taking place in prophecy circles in the last few years and in many really unforeseen ways. We believe God may have revealed several of them to us as well as we were writing our first three books in this series. In this book, we are summarizing them and revealing others we have only recently discovered.

In chapter 3 we will present one way God hides or codes things in the Bible. This is through prophetic models or types. In chapter 5 we will present the codes that have been our principal topic, event-pattern Strings. In chapter 7 we will present yet another type of code, Bible prophecies in which God has hidden secrets about future events, often end-time events. Then in chapters 8–9, we will delve into super codes, which are groups of codes all married together in a very large group to hide God's most valuable secrets. We will also discover and reveal the "master code," which is a set of seven super codes. These are the hardest codes to uncover, but we believe we may have found a couple of whoppers. As we uncover and reveal other specific codes and super codes in this book, we will define them in detail.

Introducing the Coming Twin Global Resets and Great Family Reunions

A Broad Outline for This Book

What We Are Trying to Accomplish in This Book

As we noted in the introduction, this is the fourth in a series of books that demonstrate that key events in history often occur in predictable patterns. The dates of these patterns are evenly spaced, and the key events in a given pattern all have similar themes associated with them. These themes often point to the future biblical end-times. This book will both summarize and then extend the topics associated with those themes. The most notable extension is that we will attempt to determine whether our generation is a good fit for the occurrence of particular types of thematic events associated with those end-times.

As we do that, we will search for patterns that point to the occurrence of four types of events that will be part of the end-time scenario:

1. A pair of global resets
2. A pair of great family reunions
3. The involvement of the Angel of Death and his secret companion
4. The occurrence of horrible plagues and pandemics with the ensuing chaos that will be produced

We will be searching for codes that are predictors of each of these types of events. If we find them, we will then try to determine whether there are times in the future when these codes will coincide in the same time frame. Will our generation be one of those convergence points? Our first three books ended up homing in on the years AD 2041 and 2051. Will those dates again turn out to be key focal points of our new research? We will reveal that answer as we continue.

We will now begin with a short discussion of the key topics we will be using. Is there mathematical evidence hidden in biblical prophecy along with religious and secular history that points us to the generation that will host the coming end-times? Might our generation be a good candidate?

What Are Global Resets and Family Reunions?

In our study of Bible prophecy—including books by Grant Jeffery, Chuck Missler, Hal Lindsey, David Reagan, Jonathan Cahn, John Hagee, Perry Stone, Ken Johnson, Gary Spearman, and others—we became aware that many prophetic topics in the Bible point to our generation as a possible and even likely candidate for the coming end-time scenario painted in the Bible. In our previous three books, we searched through one-third of the Bible that is prophetic in nature. We looked for clues, patterns, and codes that might lead us to the verification of our generation being a good candidate for the fulfillment of the end-time scenario. We were quite successful and discovered a number of hidden codes and event patterns that led to some incredible conclusions.

We have discovered that twin global resets are part of a grand plan God authored before the creation of the universe. We begin revealing that grand plan in chapter 2 and will slowly reveal more of the plan as we proceed.

The title of this book and the information shown on the back cover mention three of the means it seems God will use to bring the dual global resets about. These are largely hidden in the Bible, but we have discovered a way to uncover them. They are all part of hidden codes buried within the Bible, which we will reveal along with other secret codes we have discovered. These three means are what we call "the pandemic code," "the Angel of Death code," and "great family reunion code."

We hope and believe the reader will be enthralled with the adventure in discovery we present. We will be looking for and revealing clue after clue as we try to determine whether God has revealed enough in the Bible and secular history to allow us to find the time frame of his soon-coming twin global resets.

A close examination of the above topics quickly brings to mind five questions:

1. What are the soon-coming twin global resets, and are they associated with the end-times?
2. What are God's soon-coming great family reunions, and are they associated with the end-times?
3. What is the pandemic code?
4. Who is the Angel of Death, and what is the Angel of Death code?
5. Where are mysteries and secrets hidden in the Bible?

As we seek the answers to these five questions, we will answer the *five w's* associated with each of these questions: what, why, when, who, and where. We will also search for clues that these five topics and the biblical end-times might converge in our generation.

While we answer these five questions, we will also look for ways the topics of these five questions might be interrelated.

In the following chapters, we will present a simple discussion of our five topics and then go on to a detailed search for more complete information on those topics, along with answers to the questions posed above.

A Simple Discussion About the Twin Global Resets

The title of this book points out that there are twin global resets coming. "How can we know that?" one might ask. We have been deeply studying, writing books about Bible prophecy, and teaching that topic for about twenty-five years. The Bible clearly points out that there will be two global resets in the end-times and that they will be separated by three and a half years. The first is enacted by humans but seems to be inspired by spiritual forces opposed to the Christian God. The second is a supernatural reset God himself seems to have enacted in the person of Jesus, the second person in the Christian Trinity.

A human-inspired global reset seems to have had its birth in the 1960s, and the movement has spiraled upward since the early 2000s. At first, it was very much kept underground, but it has more openly revealed itself in the last few years. One question we will be addressing is this: Will this movement set the stage for the first of the twin global resets prophesied in the Bible? We certainly don't know, but it does seem quite plausible.

What we will be doing is gradually revealing the nature, scope, and details of the soon-coming, Bible-prophesied twin global resets.

A Simple Discussion About the Great Family Reunions

My wife and I were raised in West Virginia in the 1940s and '50s. During those years and for many years preceding and following them, family reunions were a very important part of family life. They took place each year during the summer months, generally on a weekend. During those occasions, the whole extended family—including grandparents, parents, siblings, aunts, uncles, cousins, and so forth—all gathered from near and far, often in one of West Virginia's many beautiful large state parks, to again see loved ones, enjoy good home-cooked food, play games, and swap memories and stories. We presume this tradition was carried out all across America. It was a very happy time families looked forward to.

These were often large gatherings, but the family reunions described in this book, our current topic, will be really large and include millions and millions of people from all over the world. It will again be a reunion of members of one very large family, the family of God. This reunion is presented in the third of the Christian Bible that is prophetic in nature. Since that is by far the least read and understood section of the Bible, very few Christians or people in general are familiar with the idea of a great family reunion coming in the future.

A pair of family reunions that are somewhat parallel to the one described above can be found in the Bible if we group together several specific future events described in Bible prophecy. We will attempt to do that in the following chapters and then answer the five *w's*.

A Simple Discussion About the Pandemic Code

An event took place in Matthew 24 just a few days before Jesus's death by crucifixion. That event may address this question. Here Jesus was having a very serious discussion with the apostles, who followed him through his ministry. For apparently the first time, he was getting very serious about giving them information about when he would return to earth in the end-times. One of their questions was about the signs that would appear in the period before his return. One of those signs could be interpreted to include things such as pandemics.

We went through a very serious worldwide pandemic in the period between late 2019 and 2022. We discovered several mathematical patterns in our first three books associated with God's punishment that converged in these very years. I refer to this set of event patterns as the "pandemic code." We will present details in later chapters.

A Simple Discussion About the Angel of Death

Even the simple use of the name "Angel of Death" sounds ominous and could bring chills to many people. An angel with this moniker is encountered near the end of the four-hundred-year period of slavery for the Israelites in Egypt, just before the exodus. He was the central figure in one of the plagues God sent on the Egyptians through Moses to convince the Egyptians to free the Israelites to leave Egypt. In this case, it was the key plague that convinced the Egyptians to do just that, free the slaves.

In this case, the Egyptians were told that if they didn't let the Israelites go, the Angel of Death would kill the firstborn of every Egyptian household. Meanwhile, the Israelites were told to perform a certain rite and place the blood of a lamb on the doorposts of their houses; then the Angel of Death would pass over them. Again, this worked, and the Israelites were freed. Thus, the Angel of Death is very ominous, and massive death accompanies him. We will see this event occurring again in the end-times. The details are fascinating. We will present them in later chapters.

A Simple Discussion of Mysteries and Secrets in the Bible

The Christian Bible can be very difficult for new readers to understand and even for theologians to properly interpret because it makes generous use of writing techniques that can be quite puzzling and mysterious to the reader. This is particularly true of the one-third of the Bible that is prophetic and of Jesus's parables, which all contain very symbolic language. These techniques are generally not obvious and are purposely hidden for many reasons, including to keep God's people interested over whole lifetimes as they are continuously looking for and often finding these hidden gems or golden nuggets, so to speak. Another reason is that the gems hidden in these techniques can "prove" to the reader that God is who he says he is.

These techniques are very mysterious and can reveal the secrets and codes deeply hidden in the Bible in various ways. Some of these techniques God uses are models, revelations or prophecies, hidden-event patterns, figurative language, parables or coded text, and God's use of spiritual warfare to punish or reward his people. We will reveal several of these as we proceed throughout this book. We could classify all these as falling in the category of mysteries and secrets.

Sometimes God tells us the theme of his mysteries but still leaves it up to us to search throughout the Bible to really understand the mystery. He gives us clues, and we must assemble them and put the puzzle together to better understand the mysterious topic. There are six of these mysteries presented in the book of Ephesians, which we call the "book of mysteries," and in chapter 1 and early chapter 2 of its sister book, Colossians. The six mysteries included in these books include the mystery of Christ in you, the mystery of God, the mystery of God's will, the mystery of Christ, a profound mystery (the future marriage between Christ and the church), and finally the mystery of the gospel. We conducted a deep dive into these books in 2017 when we seriously analyzed the books and wrote a commentary on them.

In the next chapter, we will disclose that the book of Ephesians presents the reason God created the world. He refers to this as "the purpose of his will." We will analyze the text of this book, and in doing so we will find seventeen means or vehicles God uses to bring about the purpose of his will. Two of these means or techniques are prominent in this book. We will be investigating various types of God's mysteries and secrets throughout this book.

Where do these preliminary discussions about our five topics leave us in our search for answers to our key questions?

1. We can visualize what a global reset might look like, but since spiritual entities including *God's will* are to be involved in the coming twin global resets, we have a lot to learn. Thus, we will be diligently seeking to discover what we can find hidden in the Bible that can help us understand the nature of these two resets.
2. We understand what a family reunion is in general, but we still need to search for answers to our key questions. We will do so throughout this book.
3. We will keep an eye out for clues to the pandemic code but will not address it until and unless we find possible references to this type of activity.
4. Likewise, we will keep an eye out for areas that could point to activity by the Angel of Death. Otherwise, we will not address it until we find these types of indications.
5. We now know the topical areas in the Bible where these mysteries and secrets are generally hidden, so we have our answer to that question. We will search diligently through each of these topical areas to find answers to the five *w's* for our basic questions.

We will also be diligently looking for interactions between each of these as we move forward.

We certainly hope that all these mysteries arouse your curiosity, that you enjoy mysteries and puzzles, and that you will join us as we reveal the answers to all these incredibly interesting and—as it turns out—very important excursions into the future as revealed by Bible prophecy.

A Preview That Unveils a Great Concern

As we open this book, we would like to first present a quick peek at one of the key discoveries we made in our first three books in this series. We do that in hopes of lessening the angst some readers might develop over the end-time events the Bible projects for the future of the world. Nobody knows the specific timing of those events, even though the Bible gives us multiple clues and scenarios about what they will be and even the themes of events that will precede them. Our preview will demonstrate that there have been large groups of similarly themed events that have occurred together in groups multiple times in the history of the world. So now we will proceed to present one of those groups of events and the concern it might cause to some individuals or groups.

First, we discovered that there are similarly themed events that occur over and over with the same exact time gap between them. For example, about thirty-five hundred years ago, God gave the Jewish people a set of rules he wanted them to live by and then told them he would judge them based on how well they were doing every fifty years. He even told them when he would start. We can track this event in history and see that it really did take place and in fact is still taking place. He also told them he would reward them handsomely if they kept his commands but also that he would punish them after a while if they weren't doing so. He even told them what the punishments would be and that he would administer them in evenly spaced and similarly themed patterns of events. Again, history shows this happening over and over. We discovered several similar patterns of this type that are taking place in the world even today.

God even revealed in the Bible that he would bring the world to a close sometime in the future and presented a complex scenario he would use in bringing this about. We will preview this later in the book. The incredible thing we found was that this end-time scenario of twelve or more events has already been previewed two times in the history of the world. In fact, we discovered that this preview of end-time events is occurring in exact multiples of two thousand years. This is hidden from general view, but we discovered a secret code hidden in the Bible that lets us see it and expose it. We discovered that this series of twelve or so events is taking place in the exact same order and time spacing between events. What could be scary about this is that the year AD 2041 is the six thousandth year since the end of the seventh day of creation, and the other two event previews took place around the 2000th and 4000th years. Thus, we see a spacing of two thousand years.

Prophecy scholars discovered that the series of events taking place surrounding the four thousandth year in AD 70 fits the end-time scenario so well that some have concluded that Jesus must have fulfilled the scenario presented in Revelation at that time. Thus, to them we are already in the one-thousand-year millennium, which in that case must last much longer than one thousand years. Despite the fact that some still hold to this view, neither I nor most other conservative Bible scholars hold to it.

We see this scenario of parallel events playing out again surrounding the six thousandth year in our generation. This time it does seem to fit the end-time scenario even better than that of the four thousandth year. However, *that does not mean it will actually take place in this generation.* What it does tell us, however, is that when it is actually fulfilled, it will likely take place in a two thousandth year. The Bible tells us we should get ready and stay ready because we do not know the day or time of Jesus's coming return. Thus, I see no real need to get anxious about all this. It may or may not take place in our generation.

One of the things we will do in this book is try to fit the events and patterns taking place in our generation to the Bible's postulated end-time scenario. We will do that over and over, always trying to show that what is happening in this generation fits the end-time scenario and fits it well—in fact, much better than even that of the previous two thousand years. The reader will be able to track this throughout this book.

As we said earlier in this chapter, one of the ways we will do this is by looking for clues about the time frame when the purpose of God's will is to be met, which includes the twin global resets and great family reunions.

Happy reading! And please stay calm. All things in the world will be vastly better after the end-time scenario is fulfilled, and all those who are ready will be vastly happier, healthier, wiser, and much more fulfilled.

A Broad Outline of How We Will Meet Our Stated Goals

We will use the following very broad outline to accomplish our goals:

- We will first identify God's stated purpose for his creation.
- We will next identify his stated plan for how he will accomplish that purpose.
- We will seek to find any secret codes leading to the identification of the master template God has been using to accomplish his plan.
- We will demonstrate that this master template relies on God using the event-pattern strings that have been a key focus of this four-book ET series.
- We will demonstrate that the seven master template patterns are all converging in our generation.
- We will identify the key elements of God's *end-time scenario*.
- We will seek to *determine whether our generation is a good fit for God's end-time scenario, which* will finally accomplish his ultimate purpose of creating the world.

Very Important Message and Revelation for the Reader

Will we be setting dates in this book? No! We do not know when Jesus will return to earth for his bride. However, we will attempt to see whether the event patterns shown in this book point to our generation being a good fit for the end-time scenario painted in the

Bible. The answer we will find for that question is a solid yes. However, we will also find and show that there is a pattern of over ten events that takes place every two thousand years; it is a good fit for the end-time scenario. It seems that our generation presents just such a time—in fact, the third two-thousand-year period since the end of the seventh day of creation.

We will present the whole end-time scenario painted in the Bible in chapter 10. When we do so, we will refer to it as our "speculated" end-time scenario based on the event patterns we discovered and the prophecies provided in the Christian Bible. Thus, for example, when we say that the Second Coming event date will take place in year xxxxx, we must understand that this date is based on patterns we have discovered, and uncertainty still exists in very ancient dates we have used to start the mathematical event patterns.

The fact that we will demonstrate that the end-time scenario fits very well into every two-thousandth-year period also places a great deal of uncertainty about the end-time scenario taking place in our generation since every two-thousandth-year period in the future would also qualify as a good fit for the end-times, all the way to eternity. Only God knows!

Again, as we are creating the fit for the end-times taking place in our generation, we will assign dates to each event. That only means the assigned dates match our assumptions and qualifications. Please do not take this as me saying that these dates are the absolutely correct dates for the end-time events.

The Purpose of God's Will and His Plan for Accomplishing It

Discovering God's Ultimate Purpose for His Creation and Seventeen Means He Uses to Accomplish It

What We Are Trying to Accomplish in This Chapter

In this chapter, we will show that God had a purpose in creating the universe and a plan for how he will fulfill that purpose. Throughout this book, we will demonstrate some of the unique methods God has apparently been using to interact with the people of the world to enact that plan. Over the last thirty years, we have gradually been becoming aware of one specific method God has been using to bring this about. To place this in its proper context, we must first describe what we believe the Bible says in general about God's purposes for his creation. We will try to summarize our understanding of this below.

One of the places in the Christian Bible that best describes this is the book of Ephesians, God's book of mysteries, by Paul, the apostle. Paul was a well-educated Jewish Pharisee and therefore a leader in the Jewish religious hierarchy. He and most of the other high-ranking Jews did not accept Jesus as their Messiah and God. In fact, Paul was likely the principal persecutor of Jews who accepted Jesus as their God, and he was responsible for the death of many believers. However, Paul had a supernatural encounter with Jesus that completely changed his perspective about who Jesus was. In this encounter, Jesus made a supernatural appearance to Paul after his death. This is all described in the book of Acts for those who are interested.

After this supernatural encounter, Paul went on to become the principal leader of a movement to make Jesus's teachings available to the world and in fact begin the process of starting many churches that would carry on this process. Paul wrote more Bible books than any other author. In his book of Ephesians, he described the reason God created the world and some of the techniques God would use to accomplish his purpose for creation. Very early in chapter 1, verses 7–10, Paul stated this purpose in a short, simple way as follows: "To bring everything in heaven and on earth together in unity under Jesus when time reaches its fulfillment."

That expresses the fact that God had a purpose for creating the universe. In Ephesians Paul also expressed at least seventeen different means or vehicles God would use to bring this purpose to its fulfillment. That means God had and still has a plan. *Our purpose for writing this chapter is to make us aware that God has a plan and that it has been in effect since the creation.*

Paul went on to say that much of this and how it would come about would be a "mystery" to the people of the world. Most will never understand it, and those who can at least partially understand it will be able to do so only with much study and under much hardship. However, in the end, all this study and hardship will be richly rewarded. We will now continue by listing several of the *means or vehicles Paul revealed in this book that God would use to bring about the purpose of his will.* We will present the chapter and verse in which these can be found. God will use the following:

1. Predestination, foreknowledge, and free will: God predestined us to adoption as his children through Jesus Christ in accordance with his will (plan). We can see predestination, the foreknowledge by God, and the free will by humans as all part of the narrative in verses 11–13 if we study them carefully. Paul presented these topics in several places in his books. Totally understanding the interaction between these three forces is beyond the realm of human understanding. However, we see in this passage that God uses them all—he works it all out in some way—to bring about the ultimate purpose of his will (1:5, 11–13).

2. Redemption: Jesus redeemed us from separation from God and enabled us to spend eternity in heaven with him through the forgiveness of our sins made possible by the blood he shed for us, all due to the grace of God the Father (1:6–8).

3. Revelations: God reveals things to us he wants us to know and do, especially concerning Jesus (1:10).

4. Mysteries: God presents things to us in mysteries but eventually reveals their meaning to us (1:10; 3:3–9; 5:32; 6:19).

5. Plans: God has plans he uses to bring about his purposes (1:10; 3:1–13).

6. Guarantees, warranties: God marks those who believe in Jesus with a sign, the indwelling of the Holy Spirit, who is a guarantee that we belong to him (1:13–14).

7. Building a dwelling place for himself: Christ builds the church, the body of believers, and Jesus himself is the chief Cornerstone; individual believers are also dwellings of Jesus through the Holy Spirit, and the collection of believers is the church (2:19–21).

8. Gifts and rewards: It is a gift provided through God's grace that we can be saved, and God also gives us gifts so we can do the good works he prepared for us to do even before creation (2:8–10; 6:18).

9. The church: God uses the church to reveal the purpose of God's will even to the highest angels in heaven (3:10).

10. Love: The love of God is beyond knowledge and understanding, and God uses that love to help us do the good work he gave us to do (3:18–19).

11. Promise of undeserved life in heaven: Jesus's death for our sins meant that in the three days between his death and resurrection, he could then take those in the Abraham's bosom section of Hades to heaven, thus giving living believers another great reason to follow him (4:7–10).

12. Instructions for Christian living: Paul gave us several instructions for how believers should live their lives (4:17–32; 5:1–32; 6:1–20).
13. Light: Jesus is the light of the world. He and his gospel reveal everything we do; nothing can be hidden. His light illuminates everything and brings about his eventual will (5:13–15).
14. Models including marriage: There are two forms of marriage, one physical and the other spiritual that are being modeled in this passage. Both are good and available to everyone in this life. One involves a human husband and wife, while the other involves the church being the bride of Jesus the Christ. This includes both the collective body of believers and the individual believer. Marriage involves unity, uniting two as one, and this helps to understand the purpose of God's will, to bring everything in heaven and earth together as one under Jesus (5:21–33).
15. Spiritual warfare: We are told to put on the "full armor of God" to protect us from the fiery arrows Satan and his angelic followers are constantly shooting at us. A battle is continuously taking place in heaven between God's angelic forces for good and Satan's angelic forces for evil. This is certainly one of the most important means God is using to choose who will and won't be part of the eternal bride of Christ. The armor we are told to use to help protect us in this battle includes truth, righteousness, the gospel of peace, faith, salvation, the Word of God, and prayer (6:10–18).
16. Answers to prayers of all kinds: We are told to pray all kinds of prayers and make requests to God on all occasions, to pray for all believers, and to stay alert (6:18).
17. The wrath of God: "The wrath of God" comes on those who are disobedient (5:6). Leviticus 26 says this wrath would include exiles, tribulations, loss of homeland, death, and so forth. Of course, these are the results of God's judgments, so God's judgments are obviously some of the most important—if not *the* most important—factors in God meeting the purpose of his will.

All the means God has been using to bring about the purpose of his will above were taken from a study of the book of Ephesians. We did a study of this book, wrote a commentary about it in 2017, and taught it to our Bible study classes.

It seems obvious that Paul, or God in reality, was presenting the ultimate purpose for the creation of the physical universe in this book and that he was also presenting several, at least seventeen, different means God would use to bring this ultimate purpose to reality at some future date. There certainly are other means God uses that are not specifically mentioned here, but a few others are at least hinted at.

One of these is the main subject of this book and the three books that preceded it. Two of the most curious means are mysteries and models. These are things hidden in some mysterious way but are still available to be discovered with serious study and observation. That is just the case for the main means that will be used in this book, namely God's use of equally spaced event patterns in the whole history of God's people on earth. This means principally applies to the Jewish people and their ancestors all the way back to the fall of man, but it also applies to the Gentile people group in their continuous interactions with the Jewish people, the people group God called his "chosen people." Again, that will be the principal topic of this book.

Background on the Use of Models and Symbols
in the Bible and Where We are Headed

So far, we have established that we believe the God of the Christian Bible created the whole of the universe and everything in it and that he had a grand purpose for that creation. We also know what that purpose was and a few of the means he used to bring that purpose to fruition. God also gave us many clues throughout the Bible about how he would use his means to accomplish his purpose. He did this within a series of models and prophecies that are scattered throughout both the Bible's Old Testament and New Testament. We will present several of those as we go forward. They include the following:

- There are models in Genesis of a wrestling match that summarizes the whole life of Israel as a people and nation, and offers a preview of the coming sacrifice of Jesus, which would lead to forgiveness of sins and provide an entryway into heaven.
- We find instructions for how the Israelites were to live their lives including details about how God would judge them and then correct them. This includes a list of the rewards he would provide if they followed the instructions and punishments he would administer if they did not. Also, there is a prophecy of how this would play out in the whole life of the people and nation of Israel and how this whole process would be completed in the end-times.
- There are many short and a few very detailed prophecies about how this whole process would play out, some with very detailed and specific timelines and others with more general details with less timeline specificity. In this category, we will present Daniel's seventy-sevens prophecy about the very year in which Jesus would be killed, Hosea's two-days-equal-two-thousand-years prophecy leading to the end-times, and a few others.
- There are very specific prophecies about the ways God would punish Israel and its people including very specific event details, the very specific number of years God would punish the Israelites, and a means to calculate when the prophecies would end. Guess when they will end? We will also present that topic. Will we then be able to determine the time frame of Jesus's return to earth? We will see as we go forward. Hold onto your hats for that.

It is quickly becoming quite apparent that God extensively uses both hidden mysteries and secrets in the Bible, especially when he is presenting prophetic topics. In this book, we are going to hone in on three special topics that fit into this category: the mysteries of the purpose of God's will, the twin global resets, and the coming great twin family reunions. Our premise and suspicion are that God buried clues in the Bible within the areas in which we seem to be seeing him hiding secrets. Those will help us to better understand these three topics. The clues we will be looking for are the codes that may unlock the means for solving his mysteries, his puzzles.

So then, just what will be our approach in this book to try to find these hidden codes and so forth? *We will systematically go through each of the categories of mysteries including models, revelations or prophecies, hidden-event patterns, figurative language, parables or coded text, and God's use of spiritual warfare in punishing and rewarding his people.* Some items on this list are called out separately in Ephesians, but all can also be classified as mysteries and secrets.

We begin our search in God's book of mysteries, the book of Ephesians, where we have found a long list of the means God uses to bring about the purpose of his will. We will then proceed to investigate the techniques that seem to both reveal and at the same time hide God's mysteries and puzzles. We will start with models and then proceed to prophecies, numerical event strings, and so forth.

We will be searching for clues as we go, and we will present a report card at the end of each chapter to document our progress. In some of our chapters we will be presenting several different major topics. At the end of the chapter we will present the clues from each topic individually. We will then analyze the clues to determine how they have helped us answer the five w's in each subject area and place them into our five w's report card. Our hope is that, at the end of our long search for answers to God's mysteries that are pertinent to our topic, we will be able to draw some conclusions. We will hope to have a much deeper understanding of the purpose of God's will and the coming great family reunion, possibly including some insights into their general time frames.

We are now about ready to present our first five w's report card but we first want to add a bit more information concerning our report cards. As we indicated at the end of chapter 1, we will focus our report cards on answering the five *w's* concerning our initial questions one and two. We basically answered question three in the first chapter, and we will answer questions about the pandemic code and the Angel of Death when we encounter them later in our book. However, we added a question to our basic set of questions, which we will address. That concerns answering the five *w's* about the "purpose of God's will, to bring everything in heaven and on earth into unity under Jesus when time reaches its fulfillment," from Eph 1:8-10. Our assumption is that the twin global resets and great family reunions will coincide with the time when the purpose of God's will reaches its fulfillment. Thus, we will be addressing the five *w's* on our report card concerning three questions only until the time we encounter the pandemic code and the Angel of Death super code. They will be added to our report card at that time.

Thus, when we get an answer to the five *w's* concerning the purpose of God's will, we will also have our answers concerning the twin global resets and family reunions.

Clues from God's book of mysteries can help us answer the five w's *associated with our subject questions. What are the coming twin global resets and family reunions, and how are they associated with God meeting the purpose of his will, bringing everything in heaven and earth together in unity under Jesus when times reach their fulfillment (the end-times, possibly in our generation)?*

Key Clues from the Book of Ephesians

- There are at least seventeen different means or techniques God is using to meet the purpose of his will.
- We now know God's key purpose for creating the universe and that it involves unity and Jesus.
- We also know marriage is another key factor in meeting his purpose and that it also involves unity and Jesus.
- Thus, we suspect that the marriage of Jesus to those who accept him and follow him is a key part of the purpose of God's will.
- We know that the purpose of God's will is to come to fruition when time reaches its fulfillment or in the end-times; thus, we now suspect that the marriage will take place in the end-times.
- These two events are great clues that are tied together, but they aren't specifically tied to the great family reunion in these events.

Thus, we can now fill out our initial Report Card.

The 5 W's Report Card :

CLUES FROM THE BOOK OF EPHESIANS THAT WILL HELP US BETTER UNDERSTAND END TIME EVENTS, THE UNIFICATION OF EVERYTHING UNDER JESUS, THE DUAL GLOBAL RESETS, DUAL FAMILY REUNIONS AND THEIR POSSIBLE TIE TO OUR GENERATION			
WHO	WHEN	WHERE	WHAT EVENT AND WHY
Jesus & church	End times	Heaven & on earth	**EPHESIANS MYSTERIES**: When the purpose of God's will is fulfilled both in heaven and on earth; this must be the end times; (WHY) To bring everything into unity under Jesus.
Jesus & church	End times		**EPHESIANS MYSTERIES:** The marriage of Jesus to the church, his bride, those who accept him; to unify Jesus and his bride as one.

3

God's Use of Prophetic Models

*A Demonstration of How God Used Prophetic Models
in the Bible to Bring About the Purpose of His Will*

What We Are Trying to Accomplish in This Chapter

In chapter 2 we went through Ephesians together and discovered the purpose God had for the original creation of the physical universe and mankind. *That was to bring everything in heaven and on earth into unity under Jesus when time reaches its fulfillment.* We found seventeen means God is using to bring all this to its eventual conclusion. In this chapter, we will begin concentrating on two of these means, models and mysteries that often seem to be tied together in their application. The topic of this book will primarily be on a particular type of model, equally spaced and similarly themed event patterns.

To be better able to understand that particular type of model, we will begin this chapter with several simple yet mysteriously hidden models presented throughout the Bible after first presenting some additional helpful information about the usage of models in the Bible. Thus, our purpose for writing this chapter is to investigate God's use of models in the Bible and to help us answer our basic questions and better understand God's overall purpose for his creation.

In this chapter, we will present seven unique prophetic models that demonstrate how God has used models to bring about the purpose of his will. In the Old Testament, God often presented models of far-distant or end-time events in symbolic language. When we find these hidden models, we can use them to better understand what God has planned for the far more important, real event even before it has taken place. Thus, we can use these models to help us anticipate the characteristics of future events being modeled. We will use these models to help us better understand both intermediate and coming end-time events.

Models: Their Usage in the Bible

I have had some questions from students about what I mean by the word *model*. It is a synonym for the word type, which has often been used in the past to describe this concept. The word *type* is a shortened use of the word *typical*. Thus, a type is something typical of something else. I like the word *model* better because it is more commonly used today in the scientific and everyday world.

For example, before building an expensive, new airplane or car, the designer and manufacturer first build a scale model of the airplane or car. The model looks just like how the real thing will look sometime in the future, but it is not the real thing. If it is a model airplane, it will have wings, a tail, a windshield, seats, propellers, and so forth. It can be put in a wind tunnel and tested to ensure it will perform as the designer thought it would. When most of us were young, models were built out of metal or plastic, while today they are generally built in computers as simulations. Then, even after the real thing is developed, the model can be displayed and used to teach others how the real thing works.

A Bible model is just like this. It has the same characteristics as the real thing, but it is not the real thing. It can be used to learn about what the real thing will be like before it becomes reality. Then, after the model becomes a reality, it can still be displayed and used to teach others about the real thing. The Old Testament is full of models I like to look for and teach others about. The fact that they are fulfilled in such a perfect way proves to me that God and his Son, Jesus, are just who they said they were and that the Bible is the inerrant Word of God. I hope that it does the same for you.

In the Bible, models are used to preview future key features and principles involved in certain God-centered events and persons. The fact that certain events in the lives of Isaac, Joseph, and Joshua modeled events in the future life of Jesus certainly does not mean or imply that all events in their lives modeled Jesus. Models were used to demonstrate and teach unvarying and universal godly truths and principles that would one day be lived out in the life and gospel of Jesus.

One of the things we will notice as we begin presenting several examples of biblical models below is that there is often a fairly lengthy list of features of the model that are very similar to key features of the very important future event being modeled. The features in the model are in the same order they will occur in the future fulfillment. They have the same themes associated with them, and sometimes the time gaps between the features are exactly the same as they will be in the future fulfillment. Sometimes a model may be repeated more than one time before the future fulfillment takes place, and there may even be multiple occurrences of these models before the final fulfillment takes place. These models may also occur in evenly spaced time gaps. In fact, all this makes the appearance of these models even more incredible.

Allegories and Figurative Language in the Bible

Apocalyptic Literature

These are books about events regarding the end of the world, including the beginning of the kingdom of heaven and the kingdom of God. In the Bible, this includes the book of Revelation.

Allegorical Interpretations of Scriptures

This means looking beyond the literal meaning of the text to find a second or hidden meaning. This method was widely used in the early church, but it is not used much today because of past abuses. This includes models, types, illustrations, and patterns. These types of hidden meanings in Old Testament events are mentioned many times in the New Testament. See ; Matthew 12:39–41; 13:36–43; Romans 5:12–14; Hebrews 8:3–5; 9:6–10, 23–24; 10:1; Colossians 2:16–17; Galatians 3:6–9; 2 Peter 2:6. This was particularly true of the parables; see Matthew 13:34–35, which fulfills Psalm 78:2. The mysteries spoken of so often in the New Testament generally involve allegorical interpretation. This includes the mystery of the gospel (Rom. 16:25–27), the mystery of the church (Eph. 3:2–6; 5:32), and the mystery of the Holy Spirit (Col. 1:24–29; John 14:15–21). Jesus entrusted us with these hidden things of God, and 1 Corinthians 4:1–2 says that for that reason, we must be faithful to him.

Figurative Interpretation

The Bible is full of figures of speech, and these should generally be interpreted symbolically rather than literally. A figure of speech is an expression that compares one thing to another to convey meaning or heighten the effect. In a figure of speech, one thing is used to represent something different. For example, Jesus is often referred to as a lamb or the Good Shepherd. In other places, believers are referred to as the temple of God (1 Cor. 3:16). In apocalyptic literature, the Bible often uses something akin to figurative language. We sometimes refer to this as coded text. The hidden meaning of the coded text is always found somewhere in the Bible, often in the Old Testament. For example, the four living creatures of Revelation 4:6–8 are revealed in Ezekiel 1:4–14 and 10:20–22 as well as Zechariah 1:7–11; 6:1–8.

Examples of Historical Biblical Events Being Prophetic of Jesus

- Israel being called out of Egypt was prophetic of Jesus being called out of Egypt. Compare Hosea 11:1–5 with Matthew 2:14–15.
- The children of Israel being killed in Ramah was prophetic of infants being killed in Bethlehem after Jesus's birth. Compare Jeremiah 31:15 with Matthew 2:16–18.
- The words reflecting the actions of prophets were sometimes prophetic of the actual words and deeds of Jesus. Compare Psalm 78:1–2 with Matthew 13:34–35.

Why Will These Models Help Us Meet Our Stated Goals?

In this chapter, we will be presenting "models" for the following reasons:

- The principal technique we are using in this four-book series to accomplish our stated goals is to identify God's event-pattern strings and analyze them to determine the message they contain individually and in sets that can help us answer the group of questions we have posed about the end-times and our generation.
- A secondary technique we will use similarly involves God's use of prophetic models or types. Like event-pattern strings, these models often feature a "string" of events in some historic event often involving key individuals that model a similarly themed set of events that will take place in some very important individual's life in the distant future, often in the end-times.
- These models may be easier to visualize than the event-pattern strings, so our hope is that they may help some of us in that visualization.
- The models themselves often model both intermediate and end-time events. The end-time features of the models may present us with some clues that will help us to answer our key questions about the end-times including the twin global resets and so forth. Of course, that is our main reason for presenting these models.

Presentation of Our Seven Models

We will begin with a model that demonstrates how the gospel was presented in advance to many of the patriarchs. Peter and others told us that the gospel was presented in the Old Testament (see 1 Peter 1:10–12; 4:6; Eph. 3:4–6). Paul told us in Galatians 3:6–9 that the gospel was presented in advance to Abraham. The following is one example of how this was done through the use of a model.

A Summary of the Parallels between the Sacrifices of Isaac in Genesis 22 and Jesus

1. The "only begotten" sons of both Abraham and God were involved in substitutionary sacrifices.
2. The preparation for both sacrifices involved two servants, a donkey, and wood.
3. Both Isaac and Jesus were "obedient unto death." Both were completely obedient to their fathers as lambs.
4. Neither provided a defense as to why he should not be sacrificed.
5. Both had to carry the means of sacrifice. Both were provided assistance.
6. Both were bound in preparation for the sacrifice.
7. Both sacrifices were on altars of wood.
8. The major points of both sacrifices involved substitution:
   - God provided a substitute lamb (ram or male sheep) for sacrifice to save Isaac (Isaac was to be the father of all Jews, so this substitute sacrifice saved all Jews).

- God provided a substitute lamb (Jesus) as a sacrifice of atonement for the sins of all mankind once for all! Jesus died for all sins—past, present, and future. No further sacrifice will ever be necessary. (This substitute sacrifice saved all mankind.)

9. Both were dead for three days, Isaac figuratively and Jesus bodily (see Heb. 11:17–19).
10. Both knew they would be resurrected after three days.
11. Both sacrifices may have been made on the same mountain just outside Jerusalem, and both may have been on the same day, Passover preparation day.
12. Isaac isn't mentioned as being bodily present again in Genesis until he comes for his bride, just as Jesus won't be bodily present on earth again until he comes for his bride at the rapture of the church.

Key Clues from This Model

Again we understand that the purpose of God's will is to bring everything in heaven and on earth to unity under Jesus in the end-times. The above model ends with both Isaac and Jesus coming for their bride. Neither is seen on earth again until they come for their bride. We will find this theme repeated in several Old Testament models. This ties into our keyword *unity* since in both cases the sacrifice of an innocent lamb precede the event where both Isaac and Jesus come for their bride.

Incidents in the Life of Joseph That Model the Life and Gospel of Jesus

Incidents in the life of Joseph are another example of how the gospel was presented in the Old Testament. I have heard that some scholars have counted over one hundred incidents in the life of Joseph that model the life and gospel of Jesus. The following are seventeen incidents Yacov Rambsel[2] mentioned in his book Yeshua. [1]

1. Jesus's brothers, the Jews, hated him just as Joseph's brothers hated him.
2. Jesus's brothers, the Jews, did not accept him just as Joseph's brothers did not accept him.
3. Jesus's bothers conspired to kill him just as Joseph's brothers conspired to kill him.
4. Jesus was killed so we might live just as a scapegoat was killed so Joseph might live.
5. Both Jesus and Joseph were taken to Egypt when they were young.
6. Both Jesus and Joseph were incarcerated with two thieves; in each case, one thief received life and the other received death.
7. Just as all bowed to Joseph, so too will all bow to Jesus.
8. Both the brothers of Jesus and Joseph were feeding their flocks in the wrong field (in the field of law rather than in the field of grace in Jesus's case; there is nothing wrong with the law as long as it leads one to Jesus).

9. Both Jesus and Joseph blessed their brothers and the Gentiles.
10. Both Jesus and Joseph had authority over those in prison (Sheol or Hades in Jesus's case).
11. Both Jesus and Joseph were destined to become rulers.
12. Just as everyone looked to Joseph for survival because of the greatest famine in history (seven years), so too will everyone look to Jesus for survival because of the greatest tribulation in history (seven years).
13. Each period of tribulation is preceded by many signs: Joseph's time of trouble and the birth pangs before the tribulation.
14. Both Jesus and Joseph were separated from their families for an extended period—Joseph for fifteen years and Jesus from AD 32 until the rapture.
15. Just as Joseph's brothers were made known to the ruler (Pharaoh), so too will Jesus's brothers, the Jews, eventually be made known to the ruler (Jesus himself).
16. Both forgave all the sins of their brothers.
17. Both were not recognized by their brothers; in each case they eventually revealed themselves to their brothers—Joseph when his brothers came to Egypt, seeking aid in saving them from their great tribulation, the famine; and Jesus when his brothers, the Jews, come to him, seeking him to save them from the great tribulation.

Key Clues from This Model

A couple of parallels in the above model confirm our understanding of God's ultimate purpose and how he will achieve it. Here we see both Joseph and Jesus becoming very high-ranking leaders, with both becoming key leaders after a terrible seven-year period. In Jesus's case, the seven-year period is the great tribulation period, and he will become King of Kings and Lord of Lords at the end of it, and it continues throughout the whole one-thousand-year millennium of Revelation 20.

Events in the Life of Joshua That Modeled Future Events

Joshua is the high priest in Zechariah 3:1–10 and 6:9–15. We know certain events in Joshua's life modeled future events because Zechariah 3:8 tells us Joshua and his associates were symbols of things to come. We will attempt to discover a few of those things modeled in Zechariah. First, we will analyze Zechariah 3:1–10.

1. In Zechariah 3:2, the Lord says, "Is not this man a burning stick snatched from the fire?" Joshua was a model of what Jesus would one day do for all persons who accepted him. He would snatch them from the danger of the fires of hell. John 15:6 says that anyone who does not remain in Jesus is like a dried-up branch that is picked up and thrown into a fire. By his substitutionary sacrifice of himself, Jesus

made it possible for people to escape the certain fires of hell and one day enter heaven. This idiom is looking forward to the first coming of Jesus.

2. Verses 3–5 say that Joshua was dressed in filthy clothes. These were taken off, and rich garments were put on him. Clothes in the Bible often symbolically stand for one of four things: (1) being "clothed in Jesus," as in Romans 13:14; (2) being clothed with our heavenly dwelling, likely meaning our resurrected body as in 2 Corinthians 5:2–5; (3) being clothed in love as in Colossians 3:12–14; and finally (4) being clothed in white robes, as in Revelation 3:4; 4:4; 6:11; 7:9; and other places. This likely means that his sins had been forgiven because the Branch would make his one-time sacrifice so that redeemed people of all ages might be seen as free from sin and made white and spotless in God's eyes. This idiom is looking forward in time to the death and resurrection of Jesus as the Branch.

3. When verse 4 says Jesus took away Joshua's sin, that may mean his sin nature, his natural body, would one day be taken away, and he would receive a sinless body, his resurrected body. It may further imply that he would be saved from his sin nature by the coming sacrifice of Jesus for him and all mankind.

4. The three things promised to Joshua above were conditional on Joshua following a command the Angel of the Lord gave him. This is presented in verses 6–7 as the Angel of the Lord, Jesus, made a conditional promise to Joshua to give him life in heaven if he would do what he was asked to do. It is clear from verse 6 that Jesus was speaking for God the Father. In verse 8, Jesus quoted God the Father, saying that he would send the Branch to make all this possible. We know this was a reference to the first coming of Jesus as the Branch of Jesse and David (Isa. 11:1).

5. God the Father went on to say in verse 9 that through the Branch he would remove the sins of the world in a day. The seven eyes on the one stone in front of Joshua represented Jesus being in the world through the Holy Spirit and being in the spirits of all his believers. Believers then became the eyes and light of Jesus to the world through the Spirit within them. Jesus is presented over and over in the Bible as being a rock or stone, the cornerstone in Ephesians 2:19–20 and 1 Peter 2:4–8 and in many other places. It is interesting that Isaiah 11:1–3, which presents a prophecy of the coming of Jesus as the Branch, also discusses the Holy Spirit being on Jesus and presents the seven characteristics of the Spirit. We looked at this as we studied the seven spirits of God in Revelation 1:4; 4:5; and 5:6.

6. In verse 9, God says he will engrave an inscription on the stone, representing Jesus. What is this inscription? It is described in Revelation 19:16 as being "KING OF KINGS AND LORD OF LORDS."

Next, we will analyze Zechariah 6:9–15, where we will see Joshua again presented as a model but as a different kind. Let's remember that Joshua was a high priest in Jerusalem as the temple was being rebuilt in 518–513 BC. Zerubbabel was the governor. In the model above, Joshua was representative of things Jesus would do during his first coming, while in this model he represented things Jesus would do in his Second Coming.

1. In verses 9–11, we see that Zechariah was instructed by God to take gold and silver that had been brought back to Jerusalem from Babylon and to make a crown out of it. He was told to then place the crown on Joshua, the high priest at the time.

2. In verse 12, we are told that Joshua represents the one whose name is the Branch. We know this to be Jesus. Joshua is called the branch, uncapitalized, because he was told that it was he who would branch out from his place and rebuild the temple in Jerusalem.

3. In verse 13, we see that Joshua would sit on the throne as both priest and king, in harmony. We also see that he would be clothed in majesty. That may give additional meaning to the discussion above about Joshua being clothed in rich garments (Zech. 3:3–5).

4. In verse 14, we see that the crown was then to be placed in the temple as a memorial. Some expect that this crown was really crafted for Jesus to wear on his return and that it will be found, along with the ark of the covenant, and that Jesus will use it during the millennium.

5. All this discussion about Joshua being both priest and king on the throne in Jerusalem will have its ultimate fulfillment when Jesus returns at his Second Coming. This is presented very clearly in the book of Revelation. We also know Jesus will build another temple in Israel outside of Jerusalem, as depicted in Ezekiel 45. This will be in a very large area and will be Jesus's dwelling place during the millennium. Here Jesus, the Branch, will reign on earth as both king and priest, as King of Kings and Lord of Lords.

Key Clues from This Model

We saw the same types of parallels in many of these Old Testament models. In this case, there are a couple of obvious parallels that confirm our understanding of how God will bring about the purpose of his will and just what that purpose is. Here we again see Jesus becoming King of Kings and Lord of Lords in the end-times and also building the millennial temple. Nearly all these models end up in the same time frame in the end-times, the seven-year period of the great tribulation and the one-thousand-year paradise that immediately follows it. All are confirming our interpretation of end-time prophecy. Thank God for that! He is so confirming in so many ways if we will just look for them.

An Old Testament Wrestling Match That Models the Whole Future Life of the Nation of Israel

Mankind's Eternal Wrestling Match with the Identity of God

Where in the world would we get the idea of a wrestling match between mankind and God? Well, the idea of using this in allegorical terms was God's idea. You see, in Genesis 32:24–30, we are presented with an incident involving Jacob, the father of the twelve sons, whose descendants became the twelve tribes of Israel, and someone who looked like a man but turned out to be God. This was likely the messenger from the Father who made dozens of appearances in the Old Testament and was mentioned over two hundred times. He visited Joshua before the Battle of Jericho with instructions, and Joshua knew it was God.

Nearly all Judges 6 is an incident between Gideon and the messenger from the Lord. Gideon made a sacrifice to him in this miraculous account and recognized it was God but not the Father he was speaking with. Jesus appeared to Zechariah just before the rebuilding of the temple started in about 518 BC and said he would return one day and live among the Jewish people. Again, he always looked like a man but was recognized as God. He allowed himself to be worshipped on one occasion, so he had to be God. Angels wouldn't allow this. It couldn't have been the Father, the Spirit, or an angel, so it must have been Jesus. There are many other clues to this being the case, so we conclude that Jacob was wrestling with Jesus.

In the wrestling match, Jacob clung to God all of the long nighttime and would not let go. Finally, at daybreak, God had to injure Jacob's hip to get him to let go. Jacob asked God to bless him after the wrestling match, and God did so. God then changed Jacob's name to Israel. This led to the future nation being called "Israel" and Jacob's descendants being called the "twelve tribes of Israel." Yet despite this, the Bible still referred to Jacob as Jacob and not Israel for the greater part.

If we look at Israel's history, we see that this wrestling match was an allegory about the future of the nation of Israel. They would cling to YHWH as their God and not let go, even as they accepted idol worship in large part in the Old Testament and rejected Jesus as their God in the New Testament. During all this time, the Jews wrestled with God's true identity. Prophecies in both testaments tell us that God will have to injure Israel in the coming seven-year tribulation period to get them to accept Jesus as their God. He will then come to live with them for one thousand years in their homeland as the King of Kings and Lord of Lords. This is akin to the Angel of the Lord's injuring Jacob's hip in the wrestling match. The Angel of the Lord was in essence saying to Jacob, "Stop wrestling with me and accept me as who I really am, your God and Savior."

Thus, we got the idea of picturing the history of God's interactions with man in terms of a colossal wrestling match. What a wrestling match it has been, as we will see. We will now move on with some further background before we tackle the wrestling match itself.

Ever since the creation of mankind, they have been in a wrestling match with God. The initial wrestling match is described in Genesis 2. The principals were God the Father; Jesus, the Son or Companion of the Father, who as the Tree of Life was the only one who could provide eternal life to created beings; Satan, who as the tree of the knowledge of good and evil was God's created force for evil; and the first two created humans, Adam and Eve. God's plan for his creation needed a counterforce to help bring about his intended, ultimate purpose, that of providing a future "bride" for his companion, the one we call Jesus.

As this wrestling match unfolded, God gave some clear behavioral instructions to Adam and Eve. Satan, the created force for evil and the father of lies in God's plan, went to the created humans and planted some seeds of doubt in their minds about what God's instructions really meant. Adam and Eve bought Satan's deception hook, line and sinker. They acted on it with the expected results. You see, humans must be and remain perfect to remain in heaven. Thus, God sent Adam and Eve into temporary exile in the physical section of the universe.

God then placed a barrier between the physical and spiritual dimensions of the mega verse. That barrier is described in Genesis 3:24 as a "flaming sword" going back and forth. What did this flaming sword represent in biblical terms? In Ephesians 6:17, it stands for the Word of God. John 1:1–2 says, "In the beginning was the Word, and the Word was with God, and the Word was God. He was with God in the beginning"—that is, when the universe was created. Verse 3 then says that the Word created the universe and everything in it. Colossians 1:16–17 says the same thing and even more. It says Jesus created everything, visible and invisible, both in heaven and on earth, and that all things hold together through him. It says he is the very image of the Father and that he has always existed.

John 1:14 then says the Word became flesh and lived with us on earth as a man. God, the Word, the flaming sword through whom all must go to get back into heaven, lived on earth for about thirty-three and a half years. John 1:10–11 says that even though God came to earth through Jesus, those he had created did not recognize him. This included the Jews, through whom he chose to be born in his incarnation.

Thus, we have another wrestling match taking place on earth. This wrestling match is in the minds of individuals and the collective minds of people groups regarding the true identity of God. They come up with many different answers including the following:

- There is no God.
- There are many gods.
- There is one God, but he is not YHWH, the God of the Jews.
- YHWH is God, but there are also other gods that must be appeased.
- YHWH is God, but Jesus is not God.
- YHWH, the Trinity of the Father, Jesus, and the Holy Spirit are the only God.
- Other variations of these six possibilities exist.

Thus, we have our wrestling match over which of these is true. It seems to be a universal match and affects everyone in some way. Some take the match very seriously, and some try to ignore it, but it is so pervasive that it cannot really be ignored.

Since this book is being written from an evangelical Christian perspective, let me go on with the wrestling match from that perspective.

We have seen that the Christian Bible presents YHWH as the Father God and Jesus as his companion, who created all things. We have also seen that the one called the Son of YHWH is presented as the only way in which humans can get back into heaven. Another verse that presents this clearly is John 14:6, where Jesus proclaims, "I am the Way, the Truth and the Life; no one comes to the Father except through me." But why would Jesus be the only way to heaven? I present a study of 1 John later in this chapter, which presents some real surprises and insights into John 14:6.

The answer to the above question is that God's requirement for getting into heaven is perfection, and Jesus is the only one who can provide that perfection. We recall that Adam and Eve were removed from heaven because they lost their perfection when they willingly sinned against God. Hebrews 10:1–22, especially verses 1, 14, and 22, say that those who believe in Jesus are made "perfect" in God's eyes through their acceptance of the sacrifice of Jesus on the cross for their sins. By their accepting that sacrifice, God sees their hearts, the mind of the spirits within them, being made perfect by being sprinkled with the blood of Jesus's sacrifice. Again, only those who accept this sacrifice of Jesus for the forgiveness of their sins and then try to follow his lifestyle will be granted acceptance into heaven at the time of their death. You see, the Bible presents Jesus as the flaming sword that guards the entrance into heaven and the only one who can grant access privileges.

Of course, nobody on earth is literally perfect, but the important thing is that God in heaven sees believers in Jesus as perfect in his eyes, from his perspective, because their sins have all been washed away by the blood of Jesus as the sacrificial Passover Lamb. He did for us what we cannot do for ourselves, and we must accept that. He lived the perfect life for us.

Three days after Jesus's death, he was resurrected back to life with an entirely new type of body, one the Bible calls a resurrected or glorified body. This body could function both in physical and spiritual dimensions. Philippians 3:10–11 and 20–21 say that believers will have a body just like this at the time of a future event, at the end of the wrestling match, when Jesus returns to claim his future bride for eternity. We call this the rapture event. Jesus's resurrection was primarily necessary to save mankind from their sins but also for several other reasons including (1) to prove he was God, (2) to confirm his teaching about his resurrection to his followers, and (3) to demonstrate the type of bodies we will one day possess if we believe in him. These resurrected bodies are essential to believers, or else they will not be able to realize the fulfillment of all the promises God made concerning them living on earth with Jesus during the millennium.

In addition, Jesus would have been a fraud if he had not been resurrected since he claimed he would die and then be resurrected in three days. When the Pharisees asked Jesus for a sign, his response to them was that he would give them only one, "the sign of Jonah." Jesus also told his disciples that his temple or body would be destroyed but that he would rebuild it in three days. In both of these figurative-language teachings, Jesus was saying that he would die and then rise on the third day. Paul says in 1 Corinthians 15 that if Jesus's death and resurrection did not occur, then we have no hope of ever getting to heaven and are to be pitied more than anyone else.

God designed this whole wrestling match scenario even before creation (Eph. 1:4; John 17:24; Rev. 13:8) and he is orchestrating its execution and completion. Jesus indeed gave us proof. It is the bedrock of the Christian faith.

We see the Bible beginning with the creation of the universe and mankind. In the third chapter of the Bible, we see man failing to meet God's requirements and being kicked out of heaven. A barrier is placed between earth and heaven so man cannot get back in by his own devices. The Bible ends after sixty-six books, with man finally getting back into heaven in the final four chapters of the last book, Revelation. All that is in between is a description of the wrestling match between God and man to decide who will and won't be let back into heaven. This is critical, because those who are let back in will be the eternal bride of Christ.

Key Clues from This Model

This was a wrestling match between Jesus in a pre-incarnate appearance on earth and Jacob, the father of the twelve tribes, who would become the father of the nation of Israel. Jacob was renamed "Israel" at the end of his wrestling match because he was representative of the future nation of Israel. Thus, this was an allegory. It is a mystery because the Bible never explains the meaning behind the wrestling match. It would have been a puzzle to the Jews because for a long time, the Jewish people had no idea that their whole lifetime would be very dark, even to the end-times. However, this turned out to be the case, and just like the wrestling match, the Jewish people will wrestle with the true identity of God until the very end. In that end, God will have to injure Israel very seriously and in a long-ago predicted way to finally get them to recognize who he really is—that Jesus is really their Messiah and God, and that he has always been their God as part of the Trinity that is God.

In the end, the Jews will finally join Jesus in unity, thus finally bringing the purpose of God's will to fruition.

Model of Jewish Wedding Customs Being a Model of the Church as the Bride of Christ

Jewish Wedding Customs as a Type or Model of the Church as the Bride of Christ

Introduction

I have discovered in my Bible study that there is a one-to-one correspondence between the relationship that exists between Jesus and his bride, the church, and the Jewish wedding customs of the biblical age. I find that every ceremony, ritual, and story in the Old Testament either hints at or prophesies the coming Messiah, or it is a model or type of the gospel story. Galatians 3:8 and several other New Testament scriptures tell us that the gospel was either announced in advance or in some way hidden in the Old Testament. There are literally hundreds of examples where Old Testament ceremonies, rituals, and stories are illustrations, types, models, or shadows of the gospel story. Now, I'd like to show you how the Jewish wedding customs were illustrations of the gospel of Christ. We'll look at the customs one by one in our study.

The feature of this model that is of most interest to us is that the Jewish wedding customs model the future rapture of the church, the seven-year tribulation period when the bride will be hidden away, and the Second Coming when the bridegroom will return to the home of the bride to show her off in her hometown. *This is one of several models in the Bible that are all in perfect lockstep with the depiction of the end-time scenario presented by pre-tribulational, pre-millennial theorists.*

We were first introduced to this topic in the teachings and writings of Chuck Missler of Koinonia House.[3] It is also presented in the Nelson New International Bible Dictionary,[4] 1995 under Weddings and in the book Zola Levitt, A Christian Love Story,1978.[5]

The Church Is the Bride of Christ

You may have already noticed many times in your Bible studies that Christ often referred to his relationship with believers in terms common to weddings. Let's look at some of these before we begin our comparison. The Bible teaches us in Ephesians 5:22–33 and other places (Rev. 19:7–9; 22:17; Rom. 7:1–4) that the church is the bride of Christ. Let's look at some of these scriptures.

Ephesians 5:22–23

Wives, submit to your husband's as to the Lord. For the husband is the head of the wife as Christ is the head of the church, his body, of which he is the Savior.

Ephesians 5:29–32

After all, no one ever hated his own body, but he feeds and cares for it, just as Christ does the church—for we are members of his body. "For this reason a man will leave his father and mother and be united to his wife, and the two will become one flesh. This is a profound mystery—but I am talking about Christ and the church."

Revelation 19:7

Let us rejoice and be glad and give him glory! For the wedding of the Lamb has come, and his bride has made herself ready.

The wedding of the Lamb refers to the wedding of Christ and his bride, the church. The church is made up of believers.

First Corinthians 6:15–17 tells us that when we are born again, we have spiritual oneness with Christ; just as the husband and wife become one flesh when they are married, a physical oneness occurs. Let's read this.

1 Corinthians 6:15–17

Do you not know that your bodies are members of Christ himself? Shall I then take the members of Christ and unite them with a prostitute? Never! Do you not know that he who unites himself with a prostitute is one with her in body? For it is said, "The two will become one flesh." *But he who unites himself with the Lord is one with him in spirit* (emphasis added).

These scriptures and others (including Acts 2:38) seem to tell us that when we are born again and baptized, it's almost as though our spirits become betrothed to Christ's Spirit. This is another confirmation of eternal security since Christ doesn't believe in divorce. As far as he is concerned, marriage is forever. He won't ever divorce us. When I watch a baptism ceremony, I see it as a betrothal ceremony, a betrothal of the believer to Christ. Also, every time we take communion, we are renewing our vows, as we shall see later.

The Principal Characters in the Wedding

So we see that the church will one day become the bride of Christ and that there will be a wedding and celebration in heaven. If there is to be a wedding, then there must be a whole cast of principal characters for the wedding. In fact, there are many references and hints in the Bible concerning who these principals will be. Let's look at who they will be according to things I have discovered in the Bible.

- Bridegroom: Jesus Christ (John 3:27–30; Matt. 9:15; 25:1–13; 2 Cor. 11:2)
- Bride: the church (Eph. 5:22–23; Rom. 7:1–4; 2 Cor. 11:2; Rev. 19:7–9; 22:17)
- Father of the Bridegroom: God the Father (John 3:16; Matt. 3:16–17; John 1:32–34)
- Mother of the Bridegroom: Israel (Jer. 31:31–34; Hos. 2:16–23; Matt. 12:48; Luke 11:27–28)
- Father of the Bride: Paul (2 Cor. 11:2)
- Mother of the Bride: the Holy Spirit (John 3:3–7; Rom. 8:9–10; Acts 1:8; 2:1–4). The church was born of the Holy Spirit at Pentecost. Everyone who is in the church of Jesus is born of the Spirit.
- Best Man: John the Baptist (John 3:27–29)
- Bridesmaids: Those waiting with the bride for the return of the Bridegroom. This includes all Gentiles Jesus took to heaven from Abraham's bosom upon his death (Luke 16:19–31; Eph. 4:7–10; Ps. 68:18).
- Guests: Jewish tradition says that the guests were friends of the bridegroom's father. This would have been the Old Testament saints but only those who accepted the invitation (Matt. 22:1–14; Luke 14:15–24; 2 Cor. 5:20).
- Those Turned Away from the Wedding Celebration: Those dressed in the wrong clothes (Matt. 22:1–14; Luke 14:15–24) and the bridesmaids who didn't have any oil for their lamps (the Holy Spirit; Matt. 25:1–13).

When will the wedding and celebration occur? Again, according to my interpretation, they will occur during the seven-year tribulation period. They will be held in heaven just after the rapture and before the Second Coming. However, we don't know the exact time they will occur (Matt. 25:1–13; 24:36–44).

Outline of the Principal Features of a Jewish Wedding

1. The son's father chose the mate for his son.
2. The father and son went to the home of the bride so a price could be negotiated.
3. A binding written agreement was signed, and the couple was considered betrothed.
4. The betrothal could be broken only by divorce.
5. During the betrothal period, the groom prepared a place in his father's house for the bride.
6. The father decided when the preparations were complete and set the wedding date.
7. Not knowing when the groom would return for her, the bride made herself ready and stayed ready. Her bridesmaids stayed with her and also had to remain ready.
8. During the betrothal period, the bride wore a veil so everyone knew she was spoken for and was considered "bought with a price."
9. On the day of the wedding, the groom and his friends, dressed in their finest clothes, went to the home of the bride, got the bride, and returned to the groom's father's house. The bridegroom and his friends made every attempt to surprise the bride. All Jewish brides were stolen away or abducted, so to speak, by the one who loved them so much. The groom and his party shouted warnings as signs that they were approaching the bride's house. They rejoiced and partied all the way home.
10. Once in the groom's father's home, the couple was ushered into the bridal chamber. The veil was removed from the bride and all her secrets revealed.
11. The marriage was consummated through sexual union. The best man stood outside the door to the wedding chamber, waiting for a signal from the groom that the wedding had been consummated, that they had become one.
12. Although the bride and groom became one in flesh, they remained under the authority of the bridegroom's father.
13. After the act was completed, a wedding celebration consisted of a feast and party that continued for seven days. The bride and groom appeared at the end of the week, and a marriage supper and reception were held.
14. After the seven-day wedding, the groom returned to the bride's hometown with the bride. The bride's veil had been removed, and now everyone could see who had been married.

Let's now begin our comparative study.

To view the table giving the details of how the relationship between Jesus and his bride, the church, corresponds to the Jewish wedding customs, go to my website,

Proofthruprophecy.com, and click on "proof through prophecy" on the website header. This model is one of several presented there.

There has been and still is much confusion about what the Bible says about the roles of the church and Israel in the coming age. Some believe and teach that the church replaced Israel in God's plan. That is not what I understand. Israel and the church each have distinct places in God's future plans. Isaiah 54:1–10 and Hosea 2, 3 are prophetic scriptures that deal with God's future plans for Israel. Israel is referred to as the unfaithful wife of the Lord, who prostituted herself with false gods but will be restored in the millennium. (In Hosea 2:21–23, Jezreel means "replanted Israel"; in other words, God will replant Israel in the land God gave her. In Hosea 3:5, David points to the son of David or the Messiah.)

Obviously, the Holy Spirit is behind every word, thought, and story in the Bible. When I discover an illustration of the gospel hidden in an Old Testament custom like marriage, I really enjoy looking for the scriptures that bring it to life and make everything fit together so well. The Holy Spirit did this type of structure and design on purpose. His fingerprints are on every page of the Bible. Examples like the Jewish wedding customs study can often help us decipher hard-to-understand concepts or prophecies. They also often give us a model or pattern of the end-times so we can understand them much better.

The marriage model we presented above is based on fitting ancient Jewish wedding customs to the coming wedding of the church to Jesus. We will next try to show how the scenario the Bible presents for the end-times also fits into our current wedding customs. To do that, we will try to match the features of end-time prophecy to our current wedding customs.

- We become engaged to Jesus when we become a believer in and follower of Jesus.
- We have dates with Jesus during our engagement period when we go to church, attend Christian music concerts, read our Bibles, go to Bible studies, engage in all sorts of works that benefit God's people and kingdom, and so forth.
- We contact Jesus and speak to him when we pray, simply thank him when we feel blessed, and so forth.
- We have a shower at the time of the rapture event when Jesus "showers" us with gifts during the trip to the Father's house in heaven; these gifts will include a new, resurrected, glorified body we will then have for all eternity.
- After our pre-wedding trip, we are in a paradise in a strange, new place where we will take tours, enjoy ourselves, meet with old relatives and friends, meet new friends, have a grand time meeting Jesus and his Father in person, and so forth.
- Near the end of the seven-year period, the wedding ceremony will occur, and the Wedding Supper of the Lamb will take place.
- At the end of the seven-year period, Jesus will take us back to earth, where we will watch as Jesus quickly prepares our new living quarters, where we will spend the next one thousand years with Jesus. He will prepare our new home

by first removing all evil from it. He will then restore the environment on earth to a paradise-like state, give us the new jobs that we will perform for the next one thousand years, and so forth.

- At the end of the one thousand years, we will finally get to the place where all the purposes of God's will can be completed. He will reunite heaven and earth in unity, and we will live with Jesus, the Father, and the Holy Spirit for eternity in a new, unified heaven and new earth.

Thus, we see how this model provides significant enlightenment for us as to how the purpose of God's will is to finally be recognized.

Key Clues from This Model

Ancient Jewish wedding customs are a model of the church; the bride of Jesus shows us in an overwhelming and invasive way that the idea or reality of believers one day becoming the bride of Christ is a certainty. This truth permeates the Bible cover to cover. It gives us clues about the family reunion, in that we see for certain that we will be members of the family of God as the bride of Christ. The great end-times family will be the family of God and Jesus; all those who belong to them will include all our earthly family and friends who were believers

This model also gives us a great clue about the setting or general time frame of the great family reunion; it will be in heaven during the seven-year period of tribulation on earth and then continue on earth for another six to seven years after the Second Coming of Jesus to earth at the end of the seven-year tribulation period.

Discovering the Supernatural Design Structure of the Epistle of 1 John and the Incredible Message It Reveals

An Amazing Pattern Hidden within the Text of 1 John That Reveals the Message of John 14:6 and Confirms Its Proper Interpretation

We will wrap this up with the revelation of a hidden mystery God gave me in late 2007. This was ten years after God had revealed the same truth to me in a supernatural vision.

This came to me as God was revealing new insights into John 14:6 to me. In this passage, Jesus says, "I am the way, the truth and the life; nobody comes to the Father except through me." This was late 2007, and I was preparing to write a commentary on the book of Revelation. Based on other commentaries I had read and studies I had attended, I was confused about the number, sequence, and timing of the judgments. God led me to another book John had written, the book of 1 John, for the answer. The answer was hidden in the design of the text John was writing. God also gave me two other supernatural witnesses to the truth I would find in 1 John, but we will not cover those here.

I will now present that study of the text of 1 John.

Patterns in 1 John That Reveal Jesus as the Only Way to Eternal Life: Developed from an Analysis of the Design Structure of 1 John

Introduction

♦ I studied 1 John, wrote a commentary for it, and taught it in 1995. In my study, I noticed that John seemed to be teaching the same basic theme three separate times using slightly different language but with repeated phrases. Twelve years later, in 2007, I began studying the book of Revelation (also written by John) and writing a commentary on it. As I began my study, the first thing I had to do was convince myself whether there were three sets of seven separate judgments presented in Revelation or one set of seven judgments presented three times using similar language yet with different features being emphasized. That is what led me to do this study. The results, along with several other clues in Revelation and elsewhere in the Bible, led me to conclude that the second case was in fact what was intended. I discovered that John did, in fact, write in repeating patterns in his Gospel, his letters, and Revelation.

♦ John said that he wrote 1 John so believers might *know for certain* they had eternal life (1 John 5:13). This book is John's proof to believers that they can be sure they have eternal life.

♦ John used several major arguments or topics to make his proofs. He presented each topic or argument over and over, each time in somewhat different language or in somewhat different contexts for emphasis. He used the word *know* in repeated phraseology in a very mathematically structured way to make his arguments. That structure will become evident as we go on.

♦ In fact, while revealing ways believers might know they have eternal life, John repeated the phrase "by this we know" seven times in this letter. This phrase is translated "this is how we know" in the NIV Bible. Each of these seven "by this we know" statements seems to be one of John's repetitive topics.

♦ In both the NIV and Greek versions of 1 John, we see *three sets of seven ways* John used "by this we know," "we know that," or other variations of "know" statements. In the attached table, I have ordered the verses that contain the phrase "by this we know" in the order they appear in 1 John. I discovered that the latter two sets of seven have a particular topic that amplifies one particular topic in the first set, which is the basic and most important one. It is interesting that in a few instances, the NIV doesn't literally translate the Greek. For that reason, the analysis and conclusions contained herein were made using the *Greek/English Interlinear Bible*.

♦ These three sets of seven variations of "know" statements from the Greek are shown in the following table.

♦ One of the interesting things I discovered in my analysis is that each of the "by this we know" statements somehow relates to God's New Testament command given in 1 John 3:23. "To believe in the name of his Son, Jesus Christ, and to love one another as he commanded us." Of course, that means each of the other "we know" statements also relates to this command in some way.

♦ Possibly the most amazing thing I discovered in this study was that when I ordered the topics in the same sequence that the "by this we know" topics appeared in 1 John, they seemed to be *ordered according to John's statement in John 14:6–7.* This statement tells us the only way we can *know* the Father. *"I am the way, and the truth and the life. No one comes to the Father except through me."* An analysis that shows this quite clearly is presented on the second page of the accompanying table.

♦ Another quite fascinating thing I discovered in this analysis is that each one of the seven topics presented has *an action* associated with it that is required for "knowing" that we have eternal life. Several *results are presented that are associated with each action.* These actions and results are also presented in the table. Another interesting discovery is that the actions required in all seven of the topics are all described by variations of two phrases: (1) to *obey* his commands and (2) to *love* as Jesus did. Of course, we can note that this goes right back to what is required of us in God's New Testament command as described above.

♦ As we outline and analyze 1 John in the accompanying tables, I believe that the mystical, repetitive writing style John used (as inspired by the Holy Spirit) will become obvious. It will require patience and considerable concentration to do this. So put on your thinking cap, read on, and enjoy the fruits of your study.

The Unique Design Structure of 1 John

- First, John contains three parallel teachings with each centering on how we can "know" for certain we have eternal life, with each involving "know" statements and with each of the three having seven related topics.
- Each of the seven topics has three key features: an act, a goal, and a result.
- Each of the seven topics amplifies John's key passage in his Gospel concerning Jesus being the "only way to heaven" (John 14:6). The obvious reason for this is that John's stated purpose for writing 1 John was to teach us "how we can know for sure that we are going to heaven."
- Just how do we get to heaven? It is only through Jesus. In each of these seven related topics, John tells us what our goals should be, what we must do to achieve those goals, and finally the results we achieve by meeting the goals. Each of the seven results gives us confidence that we have eternal life with God, with Jesus, in our future. John 14:6 says, "I am the way, the truth, the life. No one comes to the Father except through me."

The Seven "By This We Know" Verses in 1 John

- 1 John 2:2, "I Am"; Jesus, as the "I Am," takes away our sins.
- 1 John 2:5, "The way"; Jesus is the only way to God. We live in him; we are his children.
- 1 John 3:19, "The truth"; Jesus is the truth and the true God.

- 1 John 3:24, "The life"; he lives in us and gives us eternal life.
- 1 John 4:6, "No one comes"; there is an alternate path that leads to destruction; some choose death over life.
- 1 John 4:13, "To the Father"; The Father is love; love leads us to the Father.
- 1 John 5:2, "Except through me"; Jesus gave his life for us because he loves us; this enables us to get to heaven.

Isn't it interesting that all this intricate design is contained in 1 John, but it is essentially hidden from us unless we do as Paul told us and "eat" or "consume" God's Word.

The two charts we have been discussing will be presented on the following pages.

An Analysis of 1 John's Key Phrase, "By This We Know" Which He Used in Teaching Believers How they May Be Certain of Eternal Life

"BY THIS WE KNOW" Statements (7 of these; in the order written)	"WE KNOW THAT" Statements (7 of these)	OTHER "KNOW" STATEMENTS
2:2 HE IS the atoning sacrifice for our sins, and not only for our but for the sins of the whole world. 2:3 By this we know that we have come to know him: we OBEY his commands. 2:13 You have known the eternal Jesus. You have overcome the evil one. You have known the Father. 2:14 You have known the eternal Jesus. You have overcome the evil one. The word of God is in you.	5:18 We know that anyone born of god doesn't continue to sin, but HE WHO WAS BORN OF GOD protects him, and the evil one does not touch him.	3:5 You know that JESUS CAME to take away sins. In him there is no sin.
2:4 Whoever says "I know him" but does not keep his commands is a liar, and the truth is not in him. 2:5 By this we know that we live in him. If we OBEY his word God's LOVE is in us. If we live in jesus we walk as he did. 2:6 Whoever says he abides in him ought to walk in the same WAY in which he walks.	5:19 We know that we are CHILDREN OF GOD.	2:28 ABIDE IN HIM, so that when he appears we may have confidence and not shrink from him in shame at his coming. 2:29 You know that everyone who is righteous has been BORN OF GOD.

3:18 Little children, let us not *LOVE* in word or in talk but in deed and in TRUTH. 3:19 By this we know that we belong to the TRUTH.	5:20 And we know that that the Son of God has come and has given us understanding so that we may know him who is TRUE. We are in him who is TRUE. He is the TRUE God and eternal life.	2:21 I write this because you know the TRUTH and no lie comes from the TRUTH.
3:24 Those who *OBEY* his commands live in him and he in them. By this we know that he LIVES in us; we know by the spirit he gave us.	2:17 And the world is passing away along with its desires, but whoever does the will of God ABIDES forever. 2:18 We know that this is the last hour. The antichrist is coming.	5:12 He who has the Son has LIFE; he who does not have the Son of God does not have LIFE. 5:13 You may know that you have ETERNAL LIFE if you believe in Jesus.
4:2 By this you know the Spirit of God: Every spirit that acknowledges Jesus came in the flesh is from God; 4:3 but EVERY SPIRIT THAT DOES NOT ACKNOWLEDGE JESUS IS NOT FROM GOD. This is the spirit of the antichrist, which you have heard is coming and even now is already in the world. 4:6 By this we know the Spirit of truth and the spirit of falsehood: Whoever knows God LISTENs (OBEY's) to his word.	5:15 We know that he hears when we ask. We know we have what we asked for. 5:16 If anyone sees his brother committing a sin that does not lead to death, he shall ask, and God will give him life—to those who commit sins that do not lead to death. THERE IS SIN THAT LEADS TO DEATH; I do not say that one should pray for that.	4:7 everyone who loves has been born of God and knows God. 4:8 WHOEVER DOES NOT LOVE DOES NOT KNOW GOD for God IS LOVE.
4:12 No one has ever seen God; but if we *LOVE* one another, God (the FATHER) lives in us and his LOVE is made complete in us. 4:13 By this we know that we live in him and HE LIVES IN US. We know by the Spirit he gave us. 4:14 And we have seen and testify that the FATHER HAS SENT HIS SON TO BE THE SAVIOR OF THE WORLD.	3:1 See what kind of LOVE THE FATHER has given to us, that we should be called children of God, and so we are. The reason that the world does not know us is that it did not know him. 3:2 We know that when he appears we shall be like him for we will see him as he is. We are CHILDREN OF GOD	4:16 We have known and rely on love God has for us. God is LOVE. Whoever lives in love, LIVES IN GOD and God lives in him.
5:2 By this we know that we *LOVE* THE CHILDREN OF GOD: by LOVING God and keeping (OBEY) his commands.	3:14 We know that we have passed from death to life because we LOVE OUR BROTHERS. Anyone who does not LOVE remains in death. 3:15 We know that anyone who hates his brother is a murderer. A murderer (liar) has no eternal life.	3:16 By this we have known LOVE because HE GAVE HIS LIFE FOR US. we ought to lay down our lives for our brothers.

Love and Obey, for there's No Other Way

What ACT is required to satisfy this KNOW statement? LOVE OR OBEY	What are we trying to ACCOMPLISH by the action? What is the GOAL?	What is The RESULT of the action?	The ordered sequence of "by this we know" statements reveals a fulfillment of John 14:6 in perfect order: I am the way, the truth and the life. No one comes to the Father except through me.
OBEY his commands. [His commands are to LOVE]	To overcome sin and Satan To know Jesus. To know the Father	We know the I AM, the eternal Jesus. We know the Father. We have overcome Satan. The Word is in us. Our sins are taken away.	Jesus said :"I AM the way, the truth and the life." Jesus took away our sins to provide a WAY for us to get to heaven. There is no other WAY. We overcome evil through him. HE IS the I AM, the atoning sacrifice for our sins.
OBEY his Word. Live in LOVE. Live in Jesus Abide in Jesus	To live in Jesus. To be like him. To become righteous To have confidence in our salvation	God's love is in us. We live as he did. We will be children of God. God lives in us.	Jesus said :"I am the WAY, the truth and the life." Jesus provided the only WAY to heaven for us We must live and love as Jesus did. He was our model and our Savior.
LOVE with actions & in truth. [to love in action means to OBEY]	To put our faith into action. To be honest with our intentions to do good.	We belong to the truth (Jesus). We have understanding. We live in him.	Jesus said :"I am the way, the TRUTH and the life." Jesus is the TRUE God. He provides the only TRUE way to heaven. There are many false ways that lead only to destruction, We must accept and live in the TRUTH.
OBEY his commands.	To live in Jesus. /To live a holy life, To achieve eternal life	We live in God. God lives in us. Spirit lives in us. We have eternal life	Jesus said :"I am the way, the truth and the LIFE." Jesus said he was the LIFE and the only way to ETERNAL LIFE. We must :LIVE in him if he is to LIVE in us.

OBEY God's word. Listens to God's word Acknowledge that Jesus came as a man (and as God)	To reject false teaching. Knowledge of the Father, Son and Spirit The ability to distinguish spirits	We know the Spirit of God We can differentiate the Spirit of God from the spirit of the evil one. We know God We have been born of God God hears our prayers.	"**NO ONE COMES** to the Father except through me." Those who do not believe in Jesus and live in him have neither life nor eternal life. There are many antichrists in the world who present a false gospel. Those who follow these false beliefs are lost for eternity. NO ONE COMES to the Father in heaven except through him.
LOVE one another. LOVE as Jesus did. [To love in this way means to OBEY]	To live in love To become Spirit filled believers	We live in God God lives in us. Spirit lives in us. We are children of God. We completely reflect God's love.	"No one comes **TO THE FATHER** except through me." Jesus is the Savior of the world sent by the FATHER to make a way for us to get to him. We will one day be children of the FATHER and the bride of his Son if we OBEY his command to believe in his Son and follow his Son's command to love as he did, 1 John 3:23.
OBEY his commands. LOVING God. LOVE our brothers. (all three present Jesus' New Testament command)	To pass from death to life; obtain eternal life. To love the children of God.	We know and love God. We are born again. We receive eternal life.	"No one comes to the Father **EXCEPT THROUGH ME**." It is only through belief in Jesus and following his command to love that we can get to heaven. We are then born again and pass from death to an assurance of eternal life.

In this chapter, we present models that are buried within the Bible's text in mysterious ways. The book of 1 John is unique in that it presents a model hidden in a unique way. It is presented in a three-by-seven crossword puzzle. We did not realize this when we first did the research that resulted in this chart. However, as we have been writing this book and again pondering this model, we realized it could also be viewed as a crossword puzzle of sorts. The material presented in the chart was buried in the text of 1 John. But once you construct the chart that contains the key material in the book, something pops out at you. You have a three-columns-by-seven-rows chart that can be read either from top to bottom in each column or across the rows from left to right. In either case a clear message is being presented.

The message in either case is that Jesus is the only way to heaven. It tells us both who he is and what he can do. This represents another incredible method God uses in mysteriously placing key insights that totally validate who he is and what he does. In this case it involves one of the most important messages presented in the whole Bible.

We also discovered a similar but much more extensive set of material in the book of Revelation. It is a scene chart of the whole book of Revelation that contains five columns and 7x7=49 rows. We constructed this chart at about the same time we began writing this four-book series. A scene chart is something used in creating movies and television programs. It describes every scene that will be shot in great detail.

The extensive scene chart we constructed from the Revelation text presents a description, location, relative time frame of the scene within the seven-year period, and so forth for each of the forty-nine scenes. Since Revelation is so full of symbolic language, we also prepared a symbology dictionary for Revelation with about 140 different symbols defined and the source of the definitions. Revelation is full of clues to help avid researchers be able to unravel its mysterious language and put together a full picture that resembles what was originally intended.

We will not present that material here, but it is on our website (Proofthruprophecy.com) under the Revelation commentary header; it is called a "scene chart." We have about four hundred pages of commentary, charts, plain-language descriptions, summaries, and so forth for Revelation.

Revelation reveals some definite details about this end-times, seven-year period that help to answer our questions about the purpose of God's will, the coming family reunion, the time of the marriage between Jesus and his bride, who will be at the reunion, and so forth.

We will wait until later in the book to reveal much of this. However, this short discussion reveals that Revelation exemplifies God's use of mysteries, puzzles, figures of speech, symbology, and multidimensional concepts.

All this is very convincing evidence that says to me that YHWH is the creator God and that Jesus is the only way to heaven. If you don't know about Jesus, I suggest that you go to my website (Proofthruprophecy.com) and read the section on Jesus and his gospel. There is a section that reveals how anyone can accept him and his way to paradise in heaven. There is a clear possibility that the time may be short.

Key Clues from This Model

The book of 1 John is truly unique, like no other, since its very structure is modeled after one verse in the Bible: John 14:6. There Jesus says, "I am the way, the truth and the life. Nobody comes to the Father except through me." This is another marriage of a model and a mystery because it's not obvious at all in the text of 1 John, and the Bible doesn't tell us that is the case. In fact, it is hidden in the text three separate times. It is a model because the text is clearly modeled after this single verse, and that single verse may be one of the most important passages in the Bible.

This model helps us better understand the purpose of God's will, because it clearly presents the only way one can become part of the bride of Christ three separate times, and all three are hidden in a very curious way. Again, the purpose of God's will is to bring everything in heaven and on earth into unity under Jesus, and one of the ways that is accomplished is through the union or unity of Jesus with his future bride. This model teaches in no uncertain way on three separate occasions that the only way to get into this unity is through "marriage" to Jesus.

How the Details of the Battle of Jericho Model the Revelation Judgments

The battle of Jericho is described in Joshua 5. To reveal how the details of this battle model the Revelation judgments, we must first present an outline of the events taking place surrounding this battle. We will begin with a little background. This battle began not long after the Israelites had been allowed to cross the Jordan River and enter their Promised Land. It followed the exodus from Egypt and then a full forty years of wandering in a wilderness, waiting for God to allow them to cross the river. After they had crossed the river, Jesus made a pre-incarnate appearance to Joshua. He gave Joshua a plan for how they were to conquer the city of Jericho. This plan and its execution are the model of Revelation we have been promising. We will now go on with that short outline:

1. Jesus's plan included the whole scenario that would take place during a seven-day period.
2. Jesus gave Joshua details of the plan they should use to conquer the city of Jericho. This plan included first assembling their army, their leaders, and all their people, with the Ark of the Covenant prominently displayed; and marching around the city once a day for six days.
3. On the seventh day, they were to start by first marching around the city for six times in a row and then once more. After the seventh time, they were to blow their trumpets and give a loud shout. The walls would come tumbling down, with the defeat of the city in hand.

A careful study of Revelation shows the same scenario taking place. The seven seal judgments in Revelation fulfill the model of the plan Jesus gave Joshua. It was just a plan for what would take place, not the fulfillment of the plan. The scenario in Joshua lasted for seven days while the scenario in Revelation will last for seven years. The execution of the plan in the end-times will start with the trumpet judgments. These judgments span the whole seven-year period, with about one taking place per year. However, the effects of each may last for the rest of the seven-year period after it starts. In Revelation we see that the seventh trumpet judgment is not executed until the very end of the seven-year period. That is when Jesus becomes King of Kings. The first six trumpet judgments fulfill the Israelites marching around Jericho once a day for six days.

The seven bowl judgments of the end-times in Revelation are the first time a seventh judgment is executed. Just as on the seventh day in the Jericho scenario the Israelites marched around Jericho for a full seven times, so too during the seventh year of the end-time scenario we see all seven judgments being executed. The events we saw in the plan of the seal judgments, the execution of the seventh trumpet judgment, and the seventh bowl judgment all take place at the very end of the seventh year.

It is very revealing that a close study of the three sets of judgments in Revelation shows that the first seal and trumpet and bowl judgments all seem to be the same judgment with a little different emphasis revealed in the separate judgments. The same is true for all seven judgments. Thus, it almost seems that there is only one set of seven different horrible events taking place. There is a plan for these seven judgments; they are executed one at a time for six years, and then in the seventh year, they are all repeated in quick sequence, that being the greatest calamity in history, as Jesus said in Matthew 24.

As I have said, all this is explained much more thoroughly on my website. This summary is enough to fulfill our purposes in this book. The main purpose is to demonstrate once more that the models in the Bible are all fulfilled perfectly, and as we have seen again, they all seem to converge in the end-times at the great family reunion.

These are just a few of a very large number of parallels between the battle of Jericho and the Revelation judgments. If you are interested in a more detailed study of the parallels in this model, they are included in chapter 1 of the third book in this series, *The Angel of Death Supercode*, and on my website as a part of my Revelation commentary (Proofthruprophecy.com). The full list of parallels will likely amaze you.

Key Clues from This Model

We have clearly shown in the above discourse that this model again demonstrates how the purpose of God's will (to bring everything in heaven and on earth into unity under Jesus) is fulfilled. Bible prophecy shows this purpose being fulfilled in the end-times with the seven-year tribulation, the return of Jesus for his bride, and the one-thousand-year millennium. Here we see this model revealing the nature and execution of the Revelation judgments, with all this ending with the Second Coming of Jesus.

We could also make a case for the book of Revelation itself being another model in the same spirit as the other models we have been presenting. Revelation prophesies the last seven years before Jesus's Second Coming, which is when he returns to earth with his bride. In fact, Revelation 19 presents the Second Coming of Jesus, Revelation 20 reveals the events that will take place in the one thousand years six times in the first seven verses, and Revelation 21–22 presents the eternal order that follows the millennium. Just as the other models have been or are being fulfilled, so too will the Revelation model be fulfilled perfectly in due time.

We have just finished presenting seven different, detailed models presented in the Bible that lead us to a better and more complete understanding of the purpose of God's will. It is amazing to me that all these models spread across the whole of the Bible are so consistent in reaching the same conclusion. This fact is, this is just another example of the way God uses mysteries and puzzles in his Word. I would imagine very few are aware of this fact, since it is not at all obvious; and it seems that there would be few instances when anyone would be looking for such a set of parallels. God is emphasizing the same points to us over and over without us even knowing it.

Again, we have seen God using parallels in many different ways in the Bible in this set of four books. This confirms for us in many ways that God is who he says he is and that Jesus is our Savior.

Putting Models and Patterns into Proper Perspective

To place models and patterns in a proper perspective, we will first go to two key Bible passages to help us do so: John 14:6 and Revelation 13:8. John 14:6 tells us, "Jesus is the way, the truth and the life; nobody comes to the Father except through him," while Revelation 13:8 tells us, "Jesus was the Lamb slain even before the creation of the world."

In this chapter, we have been demonstrating how Old Testament models help us better understand the purpose of God's will and how it will be fulfilled. We will demonstrate how these two key passages are critical to understanding God's purpose.

We will begin with Revelation 13:8. Here we see that God had a plan even before he created the world. This plan was for Jesus to be slain as a Lamb even before he created the world. Why would God have such a plan, and what is the repetitive pattern or model connected to this? It was the repetitive slaying of innocent lambs and then sacrificing them to him. Why was this so important? We will explain.

We have already seen in several of the models we have presented that God had a plan to create a future "bride" for Jesus. He created the whole universe as the place in which he would bring this plan to fruition. He thus created humans and placed them on the place we call earth. He instructed them to multiply and let this multiplication process continue over several thousands of years.

He would need a selection algorithm to select who would and would not be selected to be a part of the bride. He created both forces for good and forces for evil to be part of this selection process. He gave humans free will and senses within them that would lead them to have a desire to participate in things both good and evil. Humans would turn out to be making many bad choices, and none of the humans could pass God's test for being part of the bride, which was perfection.

God knew even before creation that man would fail badly, so he needed a plan that could provide forgiveness for humans. That plan was for him to send Jesus to earth after about four thousand years to become a human for about thirty-three years. During these thirty-three years, Jesus lived the perfect life humans couldn't possibly live by themselves. He then allowed himself to be sacrificed as a perfect Lamb to provide forgiveness for the sins of humans if they would accept the reality of this and then become his followers.

We can now begin to see that this was the purpose of God's will, and the plan for accomplishing it was in place even before the creation of the world, as we saw in Revelation 13:8. This sacrifice by Jesus as a perfect Lamb was the original pattern or model that was to be repeated over and over by his people. At first, it was modeling an event that had not yet taken place, and after his death, it would then be a model of the real event.

The models we presented earlier in this chapter were thus modeled after the original pattern God had constructed in his mind. Again, the repetitive model we are presenting here is the sacrifice of lambs to God. So, just what were the details of the future pattern this was modeling?

Jesus died before the creation of the world as the Lamb who

- would be totally innocent;
- would always follow his Father's will without deviating;
- would be killed and sacrificed;
- and would be the Word, which was to be consumed.

Jesus followed the pattern the Father created and then returned to heaven to be with him once more.

If we do the same, we can also go to the Father in heaven after our lives on earth. That sounds impossible, so then how can we do these things?

- Since Jesus died for each of us so our sins could be forgiven, all we have to do to become totally innocent is to accept Jesus's sacrifice for us.
- We need to follow Jesus's three New Testament commands from 1 John 3:16.
- We need to love according to Jesus's commands, which require us to sacrifice our desires to meet the needs of those we love.
- We need to consume everything we can from the Bible about Jesus and make him an integral part of everything we do; we become what we eat, so to speak.

As in all our previous models or patterns, this one also leads us to a better understanding or confirmation of the ultimate purpose of God's will: to bring everything in heaven and on earth to unity under Jesus. It again leads us to be part of the bride of Christ, which takes place in the end-times when we will be in unity with Jesus and then head directly to the ultimate eternal state one thousand years later.

We will next go to our second Bible passage, John 14:6, and reconfirm for ourselves how it also helps us understand the purpose of God's will. Again, this passage says Jesus is the way, the truth, and the life; that nobody can get to the Father in heaven without going through him. We have already seen in the pattern above from Revelation 13:8 that the Father created the pattern Jesus was to follow in creating his bride. It is also true that Jesus then created the pattern or model we should follow if we want to become part of that bride.

The pattern we should follow is reflected in this same passage. The pattern we must follow is called "the way" Jesus provides. It is the only true way to the Father. Jesus's life is the life after which we must pattern our lives.

When Jesus asked the Father in the garden, on the evening before his crucifixion, if there was any other way for him to atone for the sins of mankind, the answer was no. This incident was really for our benefit because Jesus already knew the answer. He was in essence telling us that it would be very difficult for us to model our lives after his. Even his disciples, his closest followers, were sleeping. It was hard, even for them, to follow him.

In summary, we can see that from early in the lives of the nation of Israel, the Jews were following God's instructions to sacrifice innocent lambs in God's temple for the forgiveness of their sins. This was a model the Jews were to follow until the time their Messiah would come and fulfill this model, thus negating any reason for them to need to continue doing this. The problem was that this didn't work for the Jews since they rejected Jesus's fulfillment of the model. My understanding from Ezekiel is that this will be reestablished in the millennium as a reminder and remembrance of what Jesus did for them.

So then, what does this whole model story from beginning to end tell us about models in our generation? I believe it is just this. There are a whole host of models that are taking place in our generation that are hidden from our view unless we are either psychic or have studied God's use of numerical event patterns in great detail as God has been using them. These event patterns follow the exact model of the Jewish sacrifices and their ultimate fulfillment perfectly. These event patterns have been taking place since the creation of the world, but they will reach their fulfillment someday in the future, just as the Jewish patterns did.

The big question is this: when will this fulfillment take place? We know the answer since it is presented in Bible prophecy, and the patterns each have an obvious fulfillment point. There are periodic convergences of these patterns as we have seen in our first three books in this series. One of those is in our generation. Will this be the convergence point that brings the fulfillment of God's prophetic promises? We will see as we go on. Thus, the big new question we are faced with is this.

Will the great pattern convergence of our generation result in the fulfillment of the purpose of God's will and thus be the time for the twin global resets and the great family reunions to take place?

We will attempt to answer that new question as we proceed in our book.

Clues from seven prophetic Biblical models can help us answer the five w's associated with our subject questions. What are the coming twin global resets and family reunions, and how are they associated with God meeting the purpose of his will, bringing everything in heaven and earth together in unity under Jesus when time reaches its fulfillment (the end-times, possibly in our generation)?

Key Clues from Seven Biblical Models

- We know from the model of Abraham's sacrifice of Isaac that Jesus's sacrifice of himself was necessary for him to be able to one day claim his bride.
- We also know Jesus will not bodily return to earth until the time he comes to claim his bride.
- We learned from the Joseph model that Jesus will become a very high-ranking leader on earth after a seven-year period of tribulation on earth.

- In the model of Joshua in the book of Zechariah, we see Joshua modeling Jesus as both king and high priest who would rebuild the temple in Israel.

- We learn in the wrestling match over the true identity of God between Jesus and Jacob, who models Israel, that Israel will wrestle with God over his true identity through the whole nighttime of its existence. We also learn that God will need to seriously injure Israel to get them to acknowledge the true trinitarian nature of his existence. Thus, we see this will be in the end-times.

- The model of ancient Jewish wedding customs being a model of the church as the bride of Jesus shows us in an overwhelming and invasive way that the idea or reality of believers one day becoming the bride of Christ is a certainty. This permeates the Bible cover to cover. This gives us clues about the family reunion, in that we see for certain that we will be a member of the family of God as the bride of Christ. The great end-times family will be the family of God and of Jesus; all those who belong to them will include all our earthly family and friends who were believers.

- There is a truly unique model hidden in the book of 1 John. It is unique because the whole book models one single verse in the Gospel of John, one in which Jesus says, "I am the way, the truth and the life; nobody comes to the Father except through me." Thus, it says that if we want to go to heaven, the only way to get there is to become a member of the bride of Christ.

- The battle of Jericho is an incredible model of the seven Revelation judgments. It reveals the only way to enter God's Promised Land, a renewed paradise like earth, in the end-time millennium. Just as the Israelites were able to enter their Promised Land after winning the battle of Jericho and after completing forty years of exile in a wilderness, so too will the Jews finally be able to enter the whole of the land long ago promised to their ancestors. This will be the first time they have had everything promised to Abraham; this time will be after another forty-year exile, only this time will be a period of forty years multiplied by fifty for a grand total of two thousand years. This was an exile not only from their land and nation but also from God, since they had refused to honor and accept Jesus, their Messiah, as their God. In essence, this was a Jubilee of exile periods. Jesus proclaimed this as a series of woe judgments in Matthew 23. The seven trips around Jericho by the army of Israelites perfectly model the Revelation judgments taking place over a seven days'=seven years' timeframe, ending up with a passage into the Promised Land. The model is likely pointing to the seven-year tribulation period, which is the subject of Revelation. This is presented in much more detail in our third book in this series, *The Angel of Death Super-code*.

The 5 W's Report Card :

CLUES FROM GOD'S PROPHETIC MODELS THAT WILL HELP US BETTER UNDERSTAND END TIME EVENTS, THE UNIFICATION OF EVERYTHING UNDER JESUS, THE DUAL GLOBAL RESETS, DUAL FAMILY REUNIONS AND THEIR POSSIBLE TIE TO OUR GENERATION			
WHO	**WHEN**	**WHERE**	**WHAT AND WHY**
Jesus			**MODEL: ABRAHAM'S SACRIFICE OF ISAAC:** Jesus sacrifice was necessary for him to one day be able to claim his bride.
Jesus			Jesus will not be on earth again until he comes to claim his bride.
Jesus	End times post trib		**MODEL: JOSEPH:** Jesus will become a very high ranking leader on earth after a 7 year period of tribulation.
Jesus		Israel	**MODEL: JOSHUA:** Jesus will one day oversee rebuilding of the temple in Israel as both king and high priest
Jesus & Israel	End times		**MODEL: WRESTLING MATCH:** In the end times Israel will finally acknowledge Jesus as Messiah and God.
Jesus & church			**MODEL: JEWISH WEDDING CUSTOMS:** They model the church as the bride of Christ: Thus we see the whole family of God, of Jesus, including all of our family and friends who are or were believers in Jesus all being a part of the GREAT FAMILY REUNION of the end times.
Jesus & church			**MODEL: JOHN 14:6 BURIED IN 1 JOHN;** 1 John emphasizes over and over that the only way to heaven is thru becoming a part of the bride of Christ.
Jesus & bride	End times	Israel	**MODEL: BATTLE OF JERICHO AS A MODEL OF REVELATION:** Just as winning this battle provided passage into the Promised Land for the Israelites so to do the Revelation judgments take us to the new Promised Land, also in Israel.

Were We Successful in Meeting Our Purpose for This Chapter?

In this chapter, we set out to investigate God's use of models in the Bible to see whether these models would give us clues to help us answer our key questions and be able to better understand God's plan. We found a whole host of clues (shown above) that helped us greatly in this endeavor. Thus, we were successful.

CHAPTER

4

The Ongoing Battle Between Order and Chaos

Chaos, a Principal Means for Accomplishing the Ultimate Purpose of God's Will

What We Are Trying to Accomplish in This Chapter

Our topic in this chapter is chaos. When I asked Siri on my IPAD to give me a definition of the word chaos her response was simply this; "complete disorder and confusion." In contrast, God is the God of perfect order. That is obvious from the intricate design of everything in creation. This order goes to extremes that scientists are still discovering even today. However, even within God's intricate order, there are often "collisions" between orderly realms that can cause great disorder and chaos. Collisions of huge galaxies are one example. Another example is collisions that occur between extremely orderly patterns that God is and always has been using to bring about the order of his will.

What we are thinking about are collisions between extremely orderly patterns in historic event spacing's and themes. When these patterns collide or converge, they can result in great chaos, even to the point of massive death. We present these event patterns in the next two chapters, but before we do that, we want to present some discussion about, and background of, how God uses chaos to suit his purposes and bring about his will. Since this book is in large part for and about the Jewish people, we want to start with some discussion about how chaos has been such a huge part of the history of the Jewish people and nations.

Chaos and the Jewish People and Nations

One of the principal topics of this series of books is the Jewish people along with their nation and how they fit into God's plan to accomplish the purpose of his will. One thing that is most obvious about the Jewish people and nation is how often they have been involved in long periods of tribulation and exile of various types. One of the major characteristics of all these difficult situations is how often they involve chaos. We will point out a few of them.

- The event that sparked the very birth of the nation took place in the seven years surrounding the year 1863 BC. There was a massive drought in Israel and its neighboring countries. Jacob, the father of the twelve tribes of Israel, took his whole family to Egypt that year, seeking to buy grain to get them through the drought. This is chronicled in Genesis and is also included in our first book in this series. This situation led them to be slaves in Egypt for four hundred years. This whole period and the thirty years preceding it were all characterized by very trying, chaotic times for the Israelites. Through this chaotic ordeal, the small family of Jacob ended up becoming a group of about 1.5 million people by the end of the four hundred years. Thus, they essentially became a nation amid chaos.

- The events surrounding the exodus of the Israelites from Egypt involved a series of chaos-invoking plagues. Thus, a time of great chaos characterized the time of their escape from slavery.
- Their entrance into the Promised Land forty years later involved the Jews inducing a chaotic event for the city of Jericho and its people.
- The early life of King David was plagued by a horrible series of chaotic events as King Saul sought to kill him. This is obvious in the writings of David.
- The destruction of all three Jewish nations, first Israel and then Judah followed by Judea, all took place in periods of great tribulation followed by the exile of their people from their land. All involved a huge amount of chaos and death.
- The Jewish rejection of Jesus as their Messiah and God resulted in them losing their nation and being exiled from their homeland for over eighteen hundred years. During these eighteen hundred years, the Jewish people were expelled from one country after another, were called Christ killers, and were harassed and killed by the millions. The whole six hundred years of the Catholic Inquisition was a period of intense chaos for the Jewish people, as evidenced by the event patterns we have presented in this series of books.
- Even in our generation, we have seen the Jewish people undergoing one period of chaos after the other including the horrible Holocaust and the numerous wars with their neighboring countries.

If we go to the king's scroll, which will be shown in the next chapter, we can see that God prophesied that all this would happen. It was because of their rejection of God's three great rules of living in large part. The first of those rules involved loving God and would include Jesus. The second involved protecting their environment and honoring God's sanctuary. The third involved keeping God's rules for living. God told them very plainly that he would punish them including eventually taking their land away from them and exiling them to nations who would treat them horribly.

However, the good news is that God said he would finally return to them in the end-times when they returned to him, that he would restore them to their land and bless them once more. We are right now in that final period. The Jews have been restored to their homeland. Jews all around the world are finally returning to God in small numbers, and the stage is being set to create the situation that will result in the Jews finally accepting Jesus in mass numbers.

We presented the above discussion to make it abundantly clear that great chaos has been following the Jewish people no matter where they have been for all their days on earth. There will be one more period of the greatest chaos in the whole history of the world. It will be centered on the Jewish people, followed immediately by Jesus returning to earth to live in Israel for one thousand years among the then-Jesus-loving Jewish people.

Thus, our objective in this chapter is to make us even more aware of how God has been using chaos to bring about the purpose of his will. We will show that chaos is a key ingredient in the event patterns we have been presenting in this book. We should also be able to recognize that chaos will be a key ingredient in the signs God said he would use to make his people aware that his end-time scenario was on the horizon.

It turns out that chaos is a factor God uses in most of his punishment-event patterns and also in many of the means he will use in the coming seven-year period of huge tribulation that is coming on the earth in the end-times. Thus, it will certainly be a factor in bringing about the purpose of God's will including the twin global resets and great family reunions. That is why we are presenting that topic here.

As a physicist, mathematician, astronomer, and self-taught theologian, I have created a model I believe unifies scientific discoveries with the Word of God. I will present it briefly here and show how it relates to the ongoing battle between the forces for good and the forces for evil, between chaos and order.

Thoughts on God's Creation

In trying to understand all the complex forces in the universe and how they work together, physicists have developed a theory that seems to help greatly in this endeavor. It is called "string theory," and for it to hold together, the universe must apparently contain at least ten to eleven dimensions. Of course, that also means it could contain twelve dimensions. It seems to me that if the universe does in fact have twelve dimensions, that fact would help us understand the way the Bible describes the universe. "How so?" one might ask.

Let me explain. The universe presented in the Bible has both physical and spiritual dimensions, and one cannot pass from one to the other without direct intervention from God in some way. Paul, the apostle, claimed to have been taken up to the third heaven. That was the dimension in which God seems to have his throne and control center. The apostle John was also taken to this place and presented word pictures of it in Revelation 4 and 5. Those pictures seem to be three-dimensional areas. That would lead us to expect that if there are four levels to the universe, one the physical and the other three in the heavenly areas, all four would likely have three dimensions each for a total of twelve dimensions.

Another set of circumstances presented in the Bible involves God kicking the leader of the forces of evil in the universe, Satan, down in dimension a total of up to four times. The first took place after Satan led the first humans God created to disobey him and commit the first sin. This led to God placing barriers between the various three-dimensional spaces. Mankind was confined to earth, and Satan was thrown out of the third level of heaven down to the area of earth. However, despite this fall, Satan cannot be physically seen on earth. That would lead one to suspect that this fall was to the first level of heaven or the three-dimensional space directly above earth, so to speak.

We also see from Bible prophecy that Satan will also have three other falls of sorts that are still coming. The first of these happens in the middle of the seven-year period of tribulation when he is thrown down to the physical earth. The fourth fall takes place after the Second Coming of Jesus at the end of the seven-year tribulation period. Here Satan is sent to a place called the "Abyss" for one thousand years. At the end of the one thousand years, Satan has his fifth and final fall, this one into the lake of fire for all eternity. We obviously don't know in which dimension these places exist, but the Bible's language seems to indicate that they are below the earth or inside the earth in some way.

We are describing this to set the stage for our discussion of the interactions between order and chaos.

In both the first three chapters of the Bible and its last two chapters, Genesis 1-3 and Revelation 21–22, we see that the universe seems to be unified. That would obviously mean that all twelve dimensions were together and that there were no barriers between the four three-dimensional spaces. In fact, this would likely be one twelve-dimensional space. In Genesis 3, we see God, mankind, and the angelic being called Satan living together in a paradise. Genesis 3 presents a description of a barrier being created between the area where God lived and the physical earth on which mankind would live as a result of their sin. In Isaiah 14, we see the first fall of Satan being described.

At the end of the sixty-six books in the Bible, in Revelation 20, we see Satan's final fall, this one to his final end in the lake of fire. Then in Revelation 21, we see that after the end of the one-thousand-year millennial paradise, mankind will once more be living with God, including Jesus, the Holy Spirit, and all believers of all ages again in a unified new heaven and earth once more, this time for eternity. The Bible clearly identifies this existence as being both on earth and in heaven, with both being unified as one. This also fits precisely with the purpose of God's will described in Ephesians 1 as finally being reached. We remember from chapter 2 that the purpose of God's will is "to bring everything in heaven and on earth together in unity, as one, under Jesus."

We will now go on to describe this unification process and how it seems God brings it about a bit more completely.

We can infer from the Bible that God created beings that would be forces for good and others that would become forces for evil, all to bring about the purpose of his will. These forces of evil would be in the angelic realm. These beings cannot procreate, so they cannot add other angels to their number. Apparently, God created one-third of the angels to have a propensity to want to be godlike. He created one who would be quite special, in that he would turn out to be the most beautiful, most talented, and most prideful of all the created beings. That led to his fall, and he convinced one-third of the angels to follow him in their desire to become rulers themselves, with Satan as the chief. Before his fall, he held a very high position in God's heavenly government. He appeared to be in charge of the heavenly music program. This is described in Isaiah 14 and Ezekiel 28. We see that Satan was, and in fact still is, the leader of the forces of evil in the universe. In the Bible, he is called the "father of lies" and the "god of this world," among other things.

Even though Satan and his forces are very powerful, we see that God places limits on them as we see from the book of Job when Satan had to go to God for permission to tempt Job in serious ways.

It certainly seems as though God uses these forces for his ultimate purpose. We can infer from Jeremiah and Zechariah that he called Nebuchadnezzar, the king of the evil Babylonians, his "servant." God used him and his forces to punish the nation of Judah for what Ezekiel implied were 390 years of idol worship and for not honoring God's temple. Nebuchadnezzar still had free will in what he did since we see that God said in Zechariah that he had to punish his servant Nebuchadnezzar because he went too far in punishing and destroying Judah. Thus, we can see that God may use forces for evil to bring about the purpose of his will. God did this by bringing about chaos through wars, killings, plagues, and so forth to bring about the change and new order he desired. The new order could be either good or bad from a human perspective, but it would be whatever God needed to bring about the purpose of his will.

How God Used Pride to Help Accomplish the Purpose of His Will

We would like to next attempt to more completely explain our understanding of how forces for evil came about and how God can use them. One of our main theses is that *pride* was a key factor in bringing about and then sustaining the forces of evil in the universe.

First, many if not most theologians do not believe God could or did create evil. However, God knew that to accomplish his purposes, he would need to have forces for evil in the universe. It seems that his solution was to create a set of beings with so much pride that they would eventually develop a desire to become like God. They would then use the free will that God gave them to create a counterculture of sorts that would oppose the things of God. They would rule this counterculture as opponents of God. We call this counterculture "evil" and those who use it "forces of evil."

However, within this counterculture God would place boundaries on the forces of evil. There would be limits on what he would permit the forces of evil to do. The book of Job in the Bible is a primer or model of how God uses these extremely prideful beings to help him accomplish his will.

One of those who became a part of the forces for evil must have had much more pride than any of the other forces for evil. This being was the one the Bible calls Satan. These beings were part of the group of created beings the Bible calls "angels." One-third of this group also had very prideful genes within them, and they would eventually choose to follow the "beautiful" one, Satan, and become partners in his legion of forces of evil in the universe.

The battle modeled in Job has been playing out on the earth ever since the time of creation. In this set of four books, we have discovered that God has broken this contest into equally spaced periods. A football contest, with four equally spaced quarters, is a good example of this. God has a key means he uses to bring each of his periods to a close or time of reset. That means is "chaos." He is apparently also using two other means to bring this chaos about. These means are "exiles" and "tribulations" of various types. God has been inserting these means into his interactions with his people since the fall of man in 4070 BC.

One of the possible ways God may do this is to lessen his boundaries on these forces forty years after judgments when he needs to punish his people. At these judgments, Satan and his forces are given a certain amount of time to accomplish their purposes to get God's people to follow them, to do their will with an expectation that they can reach their goal of being able to get these people to become permanent followers of them and their own ground rules.

These periods of punishment have started at multiple times in history, but a very curious thing is about to take place. All these periods of punishment of various types are all expiring at the same time, in the same fifty-year period, in the seventieth Jubilee period from 2002 until 2051!

That means we should expect a great amount of chaos for one thing. That has certainly already started with the terrible COVID-19 pandemic. If we are really going into the early part of the end-times, we should next expect chaos within the church, with many turning away from Jesus's ground rules for living. Again, that seems to be picking up momentum already. How about fear of things approaching in the heavens? Ever heard of Apophis? There is a big force in the world that is pushing for a one-world government. Anyone who is paying attention should be aware of this. The next thing would be the rapture of the church. We keep hearing nationally known prophecy scholars telling us they believe it will take place in the next few years, and they all have reasons for their predictions. I have heard 2026, 2029, 2031, and so forth. Our patterns seem to indicate it would be several years farther in the future or even another two thousand years or more. Nobody really knows, but we should keep watching for the signs to keep being fulfilled, in our opinion.

Another very key technique God uses to bring about the purpose of his will is the use of *mathematics to bring about order*. Examples of this abound in everyday life. For example, the study of biology, chemistry, physics, architecture, auto mechanics, economics, food preparation, sports, gaming or gambling, quilting, crafts, computer science, and so forth. All show that nearly everything organized in some way involves numbers, mathematics, and patterns, often repeating patterns.

My personal field of work involved rocket science, in particular modeling the flight of rockets on computers and then analyzing the results using mathematical techniques. This relies completely on computer science, which relies on mathematical coding and so forth. Success in any field nearly always involves creating some sort of order, often involving mathematical order as we have shown.

Thus, we would expect God, as creator and sustainer of the universe, to use mathematics in doing so. This finally brings us to the point of all this discussion of mathematics and patterns.

That is why we would certainly expect the architect and ruler of the universe to use complex mathematical patterns to control the events that are and have always been taking place in the world he has created for one particular purpose: to bring about the purpose of his will.

In fact, we have historically seen that in all the events in which God has had to punish the Jewish people and nation, which have included the destruction of their cities and their temple and the loss of their homeland for extremely long periods, he has followed this destruction up with very long periods of exile in foreign nations. These long periods of exile have always included persecution, tribulations of all sorts, death, hatred, jealousy, and so forth, which have produced severe chaos for the Jewish people. All this chaos has always eventually resulted in a new order of some sort for the Jewish people. Bible prophecy says there is one more gigantic period of chaos still coming for the Jewish people, and this one will result in twin global resets.

In the next two chapters, we will present the mathematically themed event patterns God has been clearly using to control the process of bringing about the eventual final purpose of his will. Several of these patterns involve themes that always result in some sort of chaos for the people of the world as we will see.

Clues from the ongoing battle between order and chaos can help us answer the five w's associated with our subject questions. What are the coming twin global resets and family reunions, and how are they associated with God meeting the purpose of his will in bringing everything in heaven and earth together in unity under Jesus when time reaches its fulfillment (the end-times, possibly in our generation)?

Key Clues from the Ongoing Battle between Order and Chaos

- God often seems to use chaos of all sorts to bring about the order that will be required to eventually accomplish the purpose of his will.
- This chaos is often the by-product of some of the means God uses to achieve the purpose of his will.
- Bible prophecy seems to indicate that there is one more period of great chaos coming for the Jewish people and nation and that it will occur during the seven-year period of great tribulation during the end-times.
- Our generation has had several periods hosting great chaos and death. Could these events possibly point to the end-times taking place in our generation?

The 5 W's Report Card:

CLUES FROM EVENTS INVOLVING CHAOS THAT WILL HELP US BETTER UNDERSTAND END TIME EVENTS, THE UNIFICATION OF EVERYTHING UNDER JESUS, THE DUAL GLOBAL RESETS, DUAL FAMILY REUNIONS AND THEIR POSSIBLE TIE TO OUR GENERATION			
WHO	WHEN	WHERE	WHAT EVENT AND WHY
		On earth	**CHAOS AND TRIBULATION**: Chaos often accompanies events used by God to bring about the purpose of his will.
Jewish people	7 yr trib period	Israel, world	The 7 year tribulation period creates great chaos and death which will aid in bringing about the final redemption of the Jewish people. We have had several events in our generation that have hosted great chaos and death. Might this point to our generation being a good fit for the end time scenario?

Basic Event-Pattern Strings and the King's Scroll

How God Uses Them to Bring about the Ultimate Purpose of His Will

What We Are Trying to Accomplish in This Chapter

In this chapter, we will introduce a very different type of pattern, equally spaced and similarly themed event patterns or event-pattern strings that are mathematical in nature. They exhibit gaps between key events in history that project into the future. They are based on the mathematics God consistently uses in the Bible. It turns out that these patterns come in long strings of events. These event-pattern strings come in two basic types, which we will call "basic event-pattern strings" and "special purpose pattern strings." The basic pattern strings fall into two groups we will refer to as "Gentile pattern strings" and "chosen people pattern strings." The chosen people will migrate from the patriarchs to the Jewish people to the Christian people, with the transition taking place in successive two-thousand-year periods. We will present this later in the master template in chapter 9.

These basic event-pattern strings have their origin at the fall of man in 4070.5 and 4060.65 BC with the Gentile pattern strings starting in 4070.5 and the chosen people pattern strings starting in 4060.65 BC. The special-purpose event-pattern strings have their origins at key events in history according to God's needs as he interacts with his people.

These event-pattern strings have the following characteristics:

- They involve time gaps of the following double-digit integers—30, 40, 50, 60, 70, 80, and 90 years—plus 100, 200, and 66.666 years. They also include 7x, 10x, and 13x multiples of each of these time gaps. When we use the letter x in this way it is simply the mathematical symbol that denotes "times" or "multiplied by."
- Each of these time gaps has a specific God- or Bible-defined theme associated with it, which we will present later in this chapter.
- For example, the theme of the forty-year time gap is associated with exiles in some wilderness experience for God's people. History has shown that all major exiles of the Jewish people have taken place in the string of forty-year periods that started in the year 4070.5, which means that God always uses the Gentiles to punish his people and does so in the Gentile-pattern strings. The punishment

would be some multiple of forty years and would end in some future Gentile year that is a multiple of ten and forty.

- There is a hidden code God uses to hide these dates from his people, so it is extremely difficult for them to recognize the patterns he is using. This code derives from the fact that God seems to always count his time on a 360-year calendar. Thus, a 200-year punishment would last for only 197.13 years on a 365.24-year calendar.

- We will further define this process a little later in this chapter and much more completely when we present God's master template in chapter 9.

- The special-purpose pattern strings always start at some key event that has taken place in one of God's basic pattern-string events. An example is God's use of punishment- patterns strings for his people. He may deem that they need to endure seventy periods of forty years of exile away from their homeland for long periods of idol worship. This punishment decision would be made in some fifty-year Jewish Jubilee year judgment event and then be administered forty years later in a Gentile fiftieth-year period. This was just the case for Israel in 719 BC when the Assyrians destroyed the northern kingdom of Israel. God punished them for 70x40 periods totaling 2,800 years. When we convert this to 365-day years, we see the punishment would be for 2,730 years. It would start in 719 BC and end in AD 2041.

We see that the vast majority of these special-purpose event-pattern strings, most consisting of punishment periods for the Jewish people, are nearly all ending in our generation. These are in what we call the seventieth Jubilee period for the Jews that stretches from AD 2001 to 2051. Might this be a good indication that the end-times might be a good fit for our generation? That is another clue we will add to the long string of clues we are accumulating as we go through this book.

It will be quite interesting to speculate on whether we expect these patterns to be confirming, contradictory, or noncommittal in terms of their agreement with the clues we have found in the mysteries and models we have already presented. What would be your guess?

We will now continue our investigation of our quest to better understand the purpose of God's will for the universe and the nature and time frame of the soon-coming twin global resets and great family reunions as we further investigate God's use of equally spaced and similarly themed event patterns. That will be quite an adventure. Buckle your seat belts for this.

A Further Introduction to the Characteristics of the Event Patterns That Will Be Presented in This Book

The first three books in this 2041 series discussed my gradual discovery of a large series of patterns involving the spacing and theme of key events over the last six thousand years. We wrote those books in the general order in which we discovered the event patterns over a seven-year period. The event patterns seemed to be supernatural for the following reasons:

1. They have continued for thousands of years.
2. Events with similar themes take place in precise mathematical patterns.
3. The spacing between similarly themed events agrees perfectly with how the Christian Bible consistently presents these periods.
4. Large numbers of the patterns converge in the very year in which the most important events took place.
5. The theme of the key event hosting the event-pattern convergence agrees precisely with the themes of the event patterns converging in that year.
6. The dates and themes of these key events agree quite well with Bible prophecies made hundreds or thousands of years before events took place.

The three books contain over one hundred different individual patterns of this type.

The sheer number and makeup of the patterns seem to clearly infer that the patterns must have been preplanned and then executed or overseen by some much higher-order entity. Again, the details are presented in the first three books of this series.

In this book, an attempt will be made to keep things simple and easy to understand. The patterns will be presented one at a time in overview form with many of the details left out.

An Introduction to the Basic Numerical Time Gaps between Key Events God Uses in His Interactions with His People

Very early in the first book of the Christian Bible, God revealed the basic duration periods of and time gaps between the key events he would use for the whole time of the existence of the physical universe. He also introduced us to the key people group he would choose to use during this whole period, those he called his "chosen people" and the patriarchs of that people group. That nation would eventually be called "Israel," and its patriarchs would be Noah and his son Shem, who went through the great flood on the ark, and then Abraham and his son Isaac and grandson Jacob. God would eventually change Jacob's name to Israel, and Jacob's twelve sons would become the twelve tribes of Israel, whose descendants would become the nation of Israel.

This nation would be formed during a long period of exile in the nation of Egypt. The length of that period of exile will be our first introduction to one of God's very key time gaps, which he would continue to use all down through the history of the Israelites, who would later become known as the Jewish people. That number is four hundred, and it is given to us in Genesis 15:13. That four-hundred-year period is said to last for four generations in Genesis 15:16. That would mean that a generation in this case would last for one hundred years, and the four-hundred-year period would consist of four equally spaced periods of one hundred years. They would all involve an exile, and so we could conclude that these periods were similarly themed. Thus, we have our first evidence of an equally spaced and similarly themed event pattern.

Our second and third examples took place soon after the end of the four-hundred-year period of exile, which would take place in 1438 BC. God chose an Israelite named Moses to lead the escape or exodus from Egypt. Just a couple of months after the exodus, God called Moses to meet him on a mountain clothed in a cloud to give him the Ten Commandments and other instructions the Israelites were to follow during their long future. Not long after this meeting with God, the Israelites disobeyed the instructions God had given them, so he instituted another period of exile for the Israelites, which would take place before he would allow them to enter the land he had earlier promised he would give them. This land is referred to in the Bible as the Promised Land, and it was in the area the Jewish people still occupy today.

That additional period of exile was for forty years, one-tenth of their original exile in Egypt. Thus, we now have our second key number God will use, and we see that it was related to their original exile period. The original exile was a multiple of ten times the second exile. We find that this was a multiplier factor, the number ten, that God would often use as he was dealing with the Israelites as he interacted with them. We will see that God often used periods of forty and four hundred years in exiling the Jews throughout their long history. The number four hundred would include ten equally spaced and similarly themed periods of forty years.

Our third encounter with an equally spaced and similarly themed pattern would begin at the end of the forty years of exile in a wilderness when they entered their Promised Land. This was originally presented to Moses on the mountain when God gave him his instructions for living for the Israelites. Moses spent forty days up on the mountain with God, and during this time he gave Moses the material Moses would use to write the first five books of the Old Testament, which is called the Torah or five books of Moses. In chapter 25 of the third book, called the book of Leviticus, we find God's instructions to the Israelites for how they were to preserve their environment—in this case, the land they farmed to provide for their food supply. We will next explain how God told them to do this.

God told the Israelites that in every seventh year of their crop planting and harvesting cycle, they were to neither plant nor harvest. They were to give their land a full year of rest, and the growth in their fields would provide nourishment for the land since it had been plowed under. That would provide nourishment for the land for the next six years, and then in the next seventh year, they were to repeat this process of neither planting nor harvesting. This process was to be continued for seven periods, totaling forty-nine years; and after that year they were to repeat the process of neither planting nor harvesting for a second year in a row. That would be two years in a row of rest and re-nourishing for the land. This would take place in the fiftieth year. God would call this year a "Jubilee year."

The Jubilee year or the fiftieth year would be a very special year for the Israelites. Why would that be? It was because God told the Jewish people that he would "judge" them in that year, starting in 1399–1400 BC and continuing in every following fiftieth year for the whole of their existence. God gave them a list of ten wonderful rewards he would give them if they kept three specific commands he gave them, as recorded in Leviticus 26.

He also gave them a list of seven terrible punishments, which would gradually increase in intensity if they didn't keep his three great commands. At the end of this list, he told them he knew they would fail and that he would need to punish them. He further said that this would be repeated multiple times, but at the end of a long period, they would return to following his commands; and at that time, he would also return to them and restore them and their nation.

One key feature of this list of seven punishments was that God said that after he had to go to the second punishment, he would multiply what they deserved in punishment by a factor of seven; and he would continue to do so for all of the last six of the punishments. We can track this throughout the long history of the Israelite nations, even up to our generation. In fact, many of the long sentences for the Israelites are ending in our generation, and they had been multiples of seven punishment periods.

God had Moses greatly expand the information he had given him in Leviticus 26 into the whole book of Deuteronomy. In fact, in Deuteronomy 17 God told Moses that after the Israelites got to the time when they would choose to have kings who would rule them, the king was to produce a scroll of his key instructions, largely given in Leviticus 26, and read it repeatedly himself and make it known to the people. I have written something I refer to as the "king's scroll" of Deuteronomy 17, and it is presented on the following page. We will often refer to that since it contains God's three great commands and the lists of rewards and punishments he would use.

Thus, we now see one-third of our key equally spaced and similarly themed patterns, one of fifty years in this case. It will turn out to be the most significant of all the many patterns God gave the Israelites.

This fifty-year Jubilee judgment pattern is an excellent demonstration of how God uses his equally spaced, similarly themed event-pattern strings in his interactions with his people on earth. We see that it was

- equally spaced, in that the events are separated by exactly fifty years;
- similarly themed, in that there is a judgment every fiftieth year;
- a pattern string, in that the same pattern was strung together like a string or chain with many links, and it had clearly defined starting and ending points.

THE KING'S SCROLL OF DEUTERONOMY 17

(A SUMMARY OF LEV 26)

DEUT 17:18 When he (the king you choose) takes the throne of his kingdom, he is to write for himself on a scroll a copy of this law taken from the Levitical priests. 19 It is to be with him, and he is to read it all the days of his life, so that he may learn to revere the LORD his God and follow carefully all the words of his law and these decrees.

DEUT 31:11 When all Israel comes to appear before the LORD your God at the place he will choose, you shall read this law before them in their hearing.

GOD'S REQUIREMENTS AND PROMISES OF LEVITICUS 26:1-46 (GIVEN TO MOSES IN ~1438 BC)
GOD'S UNCONDITIONAL REQUIREMENTS OF LEV 26:1-3

1. **Love God with all of your heart, mind and soul; do not create or worship false gods**
2. **Observe God's Sabbaths(days and years) and have reverence for his Sanctuary**
3. **Follow God's decrees and keep his commands**

GOD'S CONDITIONAL PROMISE 1 OF LEV 26:4-13; 10 GREAT REWARDS FOR THE JEWS *IF* THEY KEEP THESE 3 REQUIREMENTS

1. **Plentiful rain, crops and fruit**
2. **Live in safety in their land**
3. **Peace in their land without fear**
4. **No wild animals in their land (could be fierce animals, angels, or men who act like wild beasts)**
5. **No war within their land**
6. **Victory in wars with their enemies outside of their land**
7. **A growing population**
8. **God will honor his covenants with them**
9. **A year round harvest**
10. **God will live among them and they will be his people**

GOD'S CONDITIONAL PROMISE 2 OF LEV 26:14-39; 7 JUDGMENTS, 7 PUNISHMENTS FOR THE JEWS *IF* THEY DO NOT MEET HIS LEV 26 REQUIREMENTS

Punishments are progressive; as soon as the Jews listen to God, accept his correction, begin to follow his commands & decrees he will forgive them and restore them; otherwise the punishments progress from one to the next to the next, with a multiplier of 7 being applied to each punishment after the first, etc.

Punishment number	Where Applied?	Multiplier Factor	God's Punishment
1	Land	1	SICKNESS; Sudden terror, wasting diseases, fevers
2	Land	7	SEVERE DROUGHT, hard ground
3	Land	7	PESTS , Living creatures; could be wild animals, angels, humans acting like beasts
4	Land	7	PLAGUES, INVADING NATIONS, God will personally send enemy nations into their land to destroy them
5	Land/ Exile	7	ENEMY SIEGE during which they act as cannibals to live; he will destroy all signs of their idols & high places
6	Land/ Exile	7	LAND LAID WASTE, EXILED to the nations, God will have them KILLED while in exile
7	Exile	7	EXTREMELY FEARFUL while they are in exile; many will perish before and during the exile

GOD'S UNCONDITIONAL PROMISE 3 OF LEV 26:40-46; GOD WILL NOT FORGET THE JEWS OR THEIR LAND; HE WILL FORGIVE THEM AND RESTORE THEM WHEN THEY CONFESS THEIR SINS AND RETURN TO HIM

1. God tells them why he will punish them so severely in the future; it will be due to their unfaithfulness and hostility to him, because they will reject his laws and abhor his decrees, and because they will not give the land its Sabbath rests.
2. After their hearts have been humbled and they have paid for their sins God will then remember the covenants that he made with their ancestors and will remember their land. A remnant will finally be saved.

We learned in the research leading to this series of four books that the material presented in Leviticus 26 and summarized in outline form on our king's scroll would be extremely important in the whole history of the Jewish people. In fact, it is the guide or template God used in dealing with Israel and its people over and over—in fact, going all the way back to the birth of Noah in 3025 BC, six hundred years before the flood. We recall that Abraham and the Jews descended from Shem, Noah' son. History shows that God used this outline, this scenario, all the way back to the fall of man.

We have included copies of this in all four of our books, since it is so key to understanding the way God has always dealt with his people on earth. This will become clearer and clearer the farther we get in this book. A much more extensive discussion of this scroll and this topic is included in our book *The Search for the Tribulation Code* for those who are interested.

Key Clues from the King's Scroll

The king's scroll is a huge help in finding answers to our key questions. It gives us five very important clues as follows:

- We learn that God indeed has a plan for his chosen people and that it will involve a long period of successes and failures by the Jewish people.
- It will involve both punishments and rewards for his people, and they will be judged every fifty years to determine the outcome.
- This fifty-year period is called a "Jubilee judgment period," and it will continue for the whole lifetime of the Jewish nation, starting at the time the Israelites entered the Promised Land. These periods will be strung together, and thus we have our first equally spaced and similarly themed event pattern or event-pattern string.
- The Israelites will fail miserably from time to time, and God will need to punish them. If he has to punish them for the same offense two or more times, he will multiply these punishment periods by a factor of seven. Thus, we also now have our first punishment period multiplier.
- Might we also expect God to multiply the Jubilee period itself by seven, resulting in event patterns lasting 7x50=350 years? We will be looking for that later.

This is the first example we have found of God using equally spaced and similarly themed event patterns. We were digging for clues to help us answer our key questions in the above king's scroll, and we not only found a few very important clues but in actuality struck a gold mine!

We will follow the chart of the king's scroll with another chart, this one a "cheat sheet" for understanding equally spaced and similarly themed event-pattern strings. We thought we would keep these two charts together because readers might often want to refer back to one or both of them as they go through this book, which makes extensive use of these types of patterns. Before presenting that chart, we would first like to provide a further discussion of some of the basics of these pattern strings and why God used them.

God had a purpose for the creation of the world and an ultimate purpose for the humans he created to populate it. He apparently chose to use numerical patterns in his interactions with humans to bring that plan to completion. He apparently chose to have these interactions take place in events separated by ten years. If we started at the fall of man and circled every tenth year on a calendar, we would come up with six hundred dates in the years from the fall to the apparent six thousandth year in AD 2041. It turns out that the vast majority of key events in the history of God's people take place in these tenth years. There are about one hundred very key events for God's people in history, and nearly every one of them has taken place on one of these six hundred dates. The reason we have not noticed this pattern is that God has been counting off his years on a 360-day-per-year calendar. That was to keep us from being able to look ahead and see his plan for us. Below is a chart that explains these event patterns much more completely.

We will next explain why we use the term *strings* to describe these patterns. If we think of these strings as a chain of links strung together, this will help our understanding. If we imagine a necklace of chained links with twenty links in the necklace, with all links being white except for every fourth link being black, we would have a chain-link necklace with the black links being equally spaced and having a similar theme, with the common theme being that they are all black. This represents a good model of our forty-year event-pattern string if we think of the links being "years," the four being "forty," the black theme being "exile," and the length of the chain being two thousand years instead of twenty links.

If we created a second necklace that had every fifth link red and then laid the two necklaces side by side, we would see that the only place the black and red links were side by side was the twentieth link in each necklace. That would be a convergence of the black and red links. This explains the convergences in our event-pattern strings. In our pattern strings, the fortieth- and fiftieth-year event patterns converge every two hundred years. That is because 4x50=5x40 or 200 years.

We are now ready to present our cheat sheet.

A *Cheat Sheet* for Understanding Equally Spaced, Similarly Themed Event-Pattern Strings

Term Being Addressed	Definition of the Term Being Addressed In this dialogue the word "God" refers to the God of the Christian Bible
Event	A key event that has either taken place or is prophesied to take place at some time in the whole history or future of God's people on earth, from the fall of man in 4070 BC to the end of the millennium projected to be in AD 3037. God's witnesses would be the Patriarchs in the 1st 2000 years, the Israelites in the 2nd 2000 years and the Christians in the 3rd 2000 years.
Event-Pattern	A sequence of key events that always take place in a mathematical pattern. In this case the pattern involves the time gap or spacing between key events. These event-pattern dates are always presented on a 360 day/year calendar.
Equally Spaced	In these patterns the time gaps or spacing's between key events are always multiples of the same time gap i.e. if the time gaps in the pattern involves multiples of 40 years then the individual time gaps in the pattern could be 1x40, 2x40, 3x40 to x times 40 years. There would be no time gaps that would not be multiples of 40 years.
Similarly Themed	Every event within a pattern must involve the same topical theme. These themes were derived from the ways that God used the individual numbers in the Bible, i.e. 40 for exiles, 50 for judgments, 66.666 for tribulations, 70 for testing, completeness, 200 for convergences of multiple patterns, which thus multiplies the intensity of the pattern, etc.
Event-Pattern Multipliers	God often uses event pattern multipliers of 7, 10 or 13 to enhance the effects of his patterns. Thus he might use a pattern of 10x40=400 years to enhance the effects of his periods of exile when necessary to accomplish his purposes.
Pattern String	An event pattern that contains a large number of events with a similar theme associated with them. For example, the 50 year Jubilee pattern string contains at least 38 individual key events that we have found.
Abbreviations	The full name of the pattern strings is "equally spaced, similarly themed event pattern strings." We often abbreviate these to simply pattern strings, event pattern strings or event patterns.
King's Scroll Interactions	The King's Scroll is our compilation of God's basic rules for living from Lev 26 and his rewards or punishments for either keeping or not keeping his rules. It shows the patterns that God will use if he must punish his people. A large number of our event patterns result from use of this chart.
Pairs of Event Patterns	There is a pair of event pattern strings that travel together all down through history separated by exactly 10 years. The first is associated with God's Witness groups and the second with Gentile people groups. These two patterns started at the fall of man and then 10 years later.

The Necklace Symbolization of Pattern Convergences

	1	2	3	4	5	6	6.6	7	8	9	10	11	12	13	13.2	14	15	16	17	18	19	20
4				Ex					Ex				Ex					Ex				Ex
x5				Ju							Ju						Ju					Ju
6.6							Tr								Tr							Tr

A Simplified Version of God's Mathematics Template

An Introduction to How God Uses Numbers in the Bible

In 2013, we discovered the first of many equally spaced and similarly themed event patterns hidden in the Bible. Discovering these patterns required first using the genealogies and time gaps given in the Bible between events to produce a table of event dates. Incredibly these genealogies and time gaps between events were presented so completely in the Bible that we could go all the way from the first century AD back to the fall of man. We have included our event date database in Appendix A.

We soon found that these time gaps between events fit into a large series of equally spaced and similarly themed event patterns. We eventually found that there were event patterns with spacing's of 30, 40, 50, 60, 66.666, 70, 80, 90, 200, 360, and so forth years. We also found that the topics presented in every one of the patterns fit the exact meaning of the time spacing used in the Bible. For example, events in time gap patterns of forty or four hundred years always fell on dates associated with exiles for God's people. All the exiles presented in the Bible lasted for multiples of either forty or four hundred years in duration. The trick we had to learn before doing all this study was that God always presented the material in the Bible in 360-day years, so we had to convert all the biblical data into 365.24- day years.

A Short Summary of God's Mathematics Template

Before I present the incredible patterns, it is necessary to present the meaning of the time gaps that will be used in the pattern. They reflect periods involving the following topics:

30	The Jerusalem temple and/or a major new leader coming to power
40	Going into or coming out of an exile of some sort that produces chaos, often in a wilderness experience
50	A Jubilee judgment period; it may result in either reward or punishment; God often used Gentiles to administer the punishment in a separate fifty-year pattern, which we call the "Gentile 50," which occurs exactly forty years after the Jubilee judgment.
60	The number of man, his inherent characteristics, sin
66.666	Going into or coming out of a period of tribulation for man that produces chaos, the number of the Antichrist
70	Perfection, completeness, a period of testing; the product of God's two key event pattern multipliers, 7x10=70; the ever-present pattern that results in redemption
80	A new beginning
90	A full season
200	A time of convergence or coming together; the place where three worlds collide, the worlds of 40 (exile), 50 (judgment), and 66.666 (tribulation)
7x360=2520	God years, God's perfect and complete punishment period for repetitive sin, especially worshipping idols or other gods
2000	The super collider, where event patterns of 400, 500, and 666.66 collide or converge
6000	The monster collider, with not only all the collisions of the 2000 pattern but also the 600 and dozens of other special-event patterns
7, 10, 13	God's three pattern multiplier; 13 is connected with death.

For a much more complete definition of the numbers along with a much more extensive list of God's numbers, see our first book in this series, *The Search for the Tribulation Code*.

Further Defining Event-Pattern Strings

What I have referred to as equally spaced patterns in the first three books in this series were really "event-pattern strings." We will refer to them as such in this book. In the numerical pattern strings we used in our first three books, the numbers in the patterns always reflected the way God originally used those numbers in the Bible.

Thus, the Bible used the number forty to represent periods or time gaps of forty years, which always involved *an exile away from the norm in some way*. Thus, the way the number forty was used was the original model or pattern and long strings of these patterns put together in long sequences became a *string of forty-year patterns* or a pattern string of periods of exiles. A good example of this in the Bible is reflected in Daniel's seventy-sevens prophecy of Daniel 9:24–27. Here we see that after a well-defined starting event, it would be a long string of sixty-nine periods of a seven-year pattern until another key well-defined event would take place—in this case, the death or sacrifice of Jesus.

We began this book by presenting "the purpose of God's will" from Ephesians. We found seventeen different means or vehicles God uses to bring that purpose to fruition. We are homing in on two of these models and mysteries. We find that one way God uses these models and mysteries is through what we call "equally spaced and similarly themed event patterns." We are shortening that moniker in this book to "xx-year event-pattern strings," where "xx" stands for 40, 50, 60, and so forth periods that reflect the pattern-spacing gap between events.

In this book (and in fact all four books in this series), we will demonstrate how the event-pattern strings help enlighten us to and eventually lead us to the "purpose of God's will" in the coming end-times.

Presenting a Basic Example of How God Uses Event-Pattern Strings in the Bible

We will next present a good simple example of how God uses his event-pattern strings in the Christian Bible to prove who he is and what he requires of us. This is the world-famous seventy-sevens prophecy of Daniel 9:24–27. It is the first such pattern I became aware of in my study of prophecy. That was from Chuck Missler in the mid-1990s. He acknowledged Sir Robert Anderson of Scotland Yard fame as being the first to unravel this mystery. He did so in his book *The Coming Prince* written in the 1890s. This is an incredible prophecy, as you will see.

We will next present a very short summary of that prophecy. It is a very simple yet multifaceted event pattern. It is multifaceted in that I have discovered there are multiple possible ways to interpret this prophecy. All seem to have incredibly enlightening messages associated with them. Each interpretation points to a separate time when Jesus will be visiting earth—either his First Coming or his Second Coming in some way. We will go into this in detail in chapter 7.

We will next present the basic interpretation as a formula and then show how it fits the definition of a simple event-pattern string.

The original basic formula is as follows: If we start at the time of a specific decree (444 BC) and then go 7x7 years, we come to the time of the completion of a rebuilt city (395 BC). If we then go another 7x62 years, we come to the time of Jesus's death (AD 32). If we then go another undefined sequence of seven years, we come to Jesus's Second Coming in a final seven-year period.

Next we will show how this fits the definition of a basic-pattern string.

- It contains a long sequence of equally spaced events separated by seven years.
- The event-pattern string has a well-defined starting event.

- The pattern has a well-defined final convergence point.
- Multiple key events will take place in the pattern sequence.
- Key events in this pattern take place after sequences of seven, then sixty-two, and finally another undefined period of seven-year time gaps.
- This pattern is special in that it has a major concluding event that will last seven years in the end-times.

That is exactly how event patterns work. There may be any number of sequences of one of God's well-defined pattern gaps within a pattern. All the key events-pattern dates then fall within this sequence of evenly spaced time gaps. There are often many, even as many as thirty-five, key events in the case of the fifty-year Jubilee year pattern.

Key Clues from Daniel's Seventy-Sevens Prophecy (Some from the Expanded Topic Presented in Chapter 7)

Daniel's seventy-sevens event pattern again gives us a whole wealth of clues to help us in our search for answers to our key questions. Some of the key clues we have uncovered in this event pattern include the following:

- Both Jesus's First and Second Comings are addressed in this prophetic pattern. In fact, we are given a formula with which we can calculate the event dates for both. The first is very clear and has already been authenticated, while the second is rather murky. It will require much more digging to unearth it.
- It gives us details about the final seven-year period of tribulation leading up to the Second Coming of Jesus.
- At the end of the seven-year period, Jesus will be anointed King of Kings on earth.
- The end of the seven-year period also begins a time of righteous living and an end to sin. This implies that most of those on earth at that time will be the resurrected saints of all ages, who will no longer be capable of sinning.

The Basic Two-Hundred-Year Family of Event-Pattern Strings That Span the Whole Period from Creation to the Eternal State

A Further Introduction to God's Event-Pattern Strings

Equally spaced and similarly themed event patterns (shortened to "event-pattern strings"), as we said earlier, were the principal topic in our first three books in this 2041 series of now four books. You can go to those three books for a much more complete presentation on these event patterns and how God seemed to use them. Again, in this book we are simply presenting a much simpler, much shorter summary of those patterns. We also present a short summary of the mathematics God seems to be using in these patterns earlier in this chapter.

The first patterns we discovered in our research, in the order we discovered them, were the fifty-year Jewish judgment pattern, the 66.666-year tribulation pattern, the forty-year exile pattern, and finally the two-hundred-year convergence pattern. These seem to be the most basic and most used event-pattern strings in God's interactions with his people on earth to bring about the purpose of his will. That may be the key reason these were the first event-pattern strings we discovered.

As we said at the beginning of this chapter, we were already quite familiar with the Bible's use of prophecy, especially end-time prophecy, models, mysteries, allegories, mathematics, and so forth, before we began this series of books in about 2015. We had studied those topics quite extensively, written a dozen books on them, and taught them to our two Bible classes. However, we certainly were not ready for or expecting what we would find as we researched and wrote these four books. The results were really quite mind numbing!

We will next present an allegory we created about the way God seems to be using these incredible event-pattern strings.

An Allegory of How God Seems to Use His Event Patterns

As we have clearly seen, God has apparently placed special meaning on certain numbers. We can see this by close observation of the way he used specific numbers in the Christian Bible. We discussed this topic extensively in chapter 6 of our first book in this series. The way God has been using equally spaced and similarly themed event patterns throughout the history of man has also made it obvious that God has been using numbers in his own unique way.

This likely means God's plan for mankind at the time of creation already included use of these patterns. Since God had an ultimate goal for his creation, a goal that would be reached at some predetermined time, reaching the goal would require God's intervention in the affairs of man on a regularly scheduled basis. He apparently decided to place those interventions at predetermined, equally spaced, and similarly themed event dates. Having multiple patterns converging in the manner we have seen would give God the flexibility to allow man's free will to determine how he would apply his ingredients associated with each pattern. What a plan! *The coalescing of man's free will and God's supreme judicial authority would determine the outcome of the events associated with these predetermined pattern events.*

Again, in God's plan for mankind, he is cooking up something very important to him. In my mind, I view all mankind being poured into a monstrous pressure cooker. This pressure cooker was placed on God's stove top at the time of man's creation. There was a very well-defined recipe for preparing the ultimate "dish" God has been cooking. That dish would be an eternal companion, a bride, so to speak, for his Son, Jesus the Christ. This would result in meeting the purpose of God's will: to bring everything in heaven and on earth together in unity under Jesus.

The ingredients God has added at regularly scheduled times include wonderful, joyous rewards of all types. God lists ten of these rewards in Leviticus 26. We presented these in the king's scroll early in this chapter. As opposed to the rewards, some of the ingredients are horrible curses and plagues of all kinds. The king's scroll also lists seven of these curses, again from Leviticus 26. God places the ingredients in the pressure cooker at his scheduled times based on how man has performed in keeping his three great commands also listed in the king's scroll. Thus, we see that how man exercises his free will in keeping God's very clear instructions to him affects how God determines which and how much of each ingredient he will place into the pressure cooker at the prescribed times.

Unfortunately for mankind, God is judging us as both individuals and as composite members of very large groups. Thus, we so often see that both good and bad people, so to speak, may all be adversely affected by the ingredients God sometimes places in the pressure cooker. Once in the pressure cooker, the newly added ingredients spread throughout all the ingredients in the pressure cooker. Individuals have an effect on the outcome. Sometimes God dips his spoon or ladle into the pot and removes some part of the cooker's contents, either permanently or often for just a little while, before placing it back in the cooker. As the contents are cooking, some of it boils down, so to speak. It boils off or evaporates. This represents those who become vapor or spirits and go to either heaven or Hades before the final dish is ready to serve.

That is how I see God using the patterns. This seems to me to be part of the grand scenario he developed to bring about his ultimate goal of providing a bride for Christ. Thus, every forty years, God may add a time of exile to the pot. Every fifty years, he may add some amount of reward or joy. Every 66.666 years, he may add some tribulation and so forth. In multiples of these years, the strength and amount of the ingredient added may be increased significantly. God may greatly vary the amount of the ingredients added at each event depending on his judgment concerning what mankind needs and deserves at that particular time.

God may also turn the amount of heat being applied to the pressure cooker either up or down, depending on what he deems is needed or deserved. Likewise, the amount of pressure within the cooker may be turned either up or down to get the desired results. God will really increase the pressure on Israel at the future event we call the seven-year period of tribulation. Revelation makes this abundantly clear.

We can examine history and see that the results are often extremely obvious, while at other times they are not obvious at all. God may dump in any amount of ingredients—a lot, a moderate amount, or very little, depending on what is needed and deserved in his judgment.

The Way God Seems to Be Using His Four Basic Event-Pattern Strings

Again, God's basic pattern strings seem to be those featuring time gaps between events of 40, 50, 66.666, and 200 years. As we also said previously, God also seems to be using pattern multipliers to enhance the effect of the results of the pattern topics—in other words, exiles, tribulations, and so forth. These multipliers are seven, ten, and thirteen. He principally uses seven for multiplying his punishment periods, thirteen if large-scale death is associated with the punishment pattern, and ten as his basic, general pattern result multiplier. Thus, we quickly discover that events that hosted pattern convergences in multiples of ten were the most significant of all the patterns we found. We will present some examples below.

- 10x40=400 years for periods of enhanced exiles
- 10x50=500 years for more significant judgments
- 10x66.6666=666.66 years for enhanced tribulations
- 10x200=2,000 years for significantly enhanced effects of all the basic event-pattern strings in the same event year

We also found that if we further multiply these enhanced event-pattern strings by a second pattern multiplier, the effect is again significantly enhanced. We again demonstrate this.

- 7x40=280 and then 10x280=2,800 years
- 7x50=350 and then 10x350=3,500 years
- 7x200=1,400 and then 1400x10=14,000 years, the total number of years from creation until the eternal state, as we will show in our master template later in this book
- 13x66.666=866.666 years

In our event-pattern research we also found that the basic starting years for the event patterns were at the times of either the fall of man in 4070.5 or the end of the seventh one-thousand-year day of creation in 3873.4 BC. We also found that God started patterns we will define as "Gentile patterns" at these two dates while he began the patterns for those we will call God's "witnesses" exactly ten years later in both cases. These will be in the years 4060.6 and 3863.5 BC. We will define these two people groups as follows:

God's "witnesses" on earth:

First 2,000 years after the fall: the patriarchs
Second 2,000 years after the fall: the Jews
Third 2,000 years after the fall: Christians
Next 1,000 years: then unified Christians/Jews

Gentiles:
All people groups on earth not in the above categories in each period

We will define these people groups much more completely when we present our master template later in chapter 9.

We will demonstrate several of these in the first chart we will present and others later in this book. We are now ready to present our first chart of event-pattern strings. We will discuss each of the pattern strings after presenting the chart. Happy studying!

Very Important Note to the Reader

Throughout the remainder of this book and especially in the master template, we will discover that the fifty-, two-hundred-, five-hundred-, and two-thousand-year event-pattern strings seem to be the most important event-pattern strings God has used to bring about the purpose of his will. We will see that there is a set of these event-pattern strings that are separated by exactly ten years and flow together down through history, with one assigned to the Gentiles and the other to the people group God is then using as his *witness* group on earth. The *witness* events always follow the Gentile events by exactly ten years. The Gentile set began at the fall of man, and the witness set began ten years later.

The Basic 200 Year Family of Event-Pattern Strings that Span the Whole Period from Creation to the Eternal State

Key Event Years	50 7x50= 350 Jubilee Judgment Witness	50, 500 1000 3000 5000 Enforce Gentile	40, 400 Exile Gentile	66.666 666.66 Trib-Ulation Gentile	200 2000 4/6000 Monster Converg Gentile	Description of the events taking place in the specified years
10,773		1000				God's BIG BANG; start of creation
9787.3		1000				End day 1: create heavens, earth, light
8801.6		1000				End day 2: create water, clouds
7816.0		1000				End day 3: create seas, land, vegetation
6830.3		1000				End day 4: earth/moon/ solar system align
5844.7		1000				End day 5: create fish, birds
4859.0		1000				End day 6: create animals, mankind
4070.5		50	40	66.666	200	Fall of man: 800th year of day 7, rest
4060.6	50					Start chosen people 200 yr pattern set
3873.4		1000 500/50	40	666.66 66.666	2000/ 200	End day 7: start 7 1000 yr days of man
3863.5	50					Start Witness 2000 year pattern set
3025.6	50					Birth of Noah
2434.3	350/50					Great flood
2296.3		50	400/ 40	66.666	200	Start of Tower of Babel event
2286.5	50					End Tower event; confuse languages
2148.5		50				Abraham born
2138.6	50		40			Sarah born, Abraham's wife, Isaac's mother
2099.2		50	40	66.666	200	Exactly 2000 years after the fall
2089.3	350/50					Death of Noah
2049.9		50				Birth of Isaac
2040.1	50					Shem 500 years old
1990.8	50					Birth of Jacob
1941.5	50		40			Shem dies at age 600
1902.1		1000/50	400/40	666.66	2000/ 200	Joseph born; leads to Jewish nation
1892.2	50					Jacob wrestles with Jesus, renamed Israel
1862.7			40			Jacob and family come to Egypt to buy grain

1842.9	50					New Pharaoh who knew not Joseph
1836.4-1833.1				66.666		Period of events leading to the 400 year exile in Egypt
1793.7	50					Death of Joseph at age 110
1507.8		50	400/40	66.666	200	New Pharaoh, unkind to Israelites
1442.1 1438.8				66.666		Period of events that led to the Exodus from Egypt
1409.2		500/50				Gentile 50 pattern
1399.4	350/50					Jews enter Promised Land; start 50 year Jubilee celebrations
1350.1	50		40			Joshua dies; start period of judges
1054.4	350/50					Jubilee; start period of kings
1005.1	50					David captures Jerusalem, now in Israel
965.7		50				Solomon's temple construction starts
916.4		3000/50	40	66.666	200	Rehoboam dies
758.7	50		40			Jubilee warning; harbingers coming
719.3		50	400/40	66.666	200	Assyrians destroy, exile Israel
709.4	350/50					Only dateable Jubilee in Bible; God supernaturally saves Judah
709.4	350/50					Only dateable Jubilee in Bible; God supernaturally saves Judah
610.9	50					Babylonians conquer Assyrians
587.9-586.3				666.66		Period from siege to destruction of Jerusalem, Temple by Babylonians
561.6	50		40			Nebuchadnezzar dies
522.2		50	40	66.666	200	Darius becomes Persian king, issues edict
512.3	50					1st Jubilee after temple rebuild
463.0	50					Artaxerxes becomes Persian king, will issue edict allowing rebuilding of city, walls
443.3			40			City walls rebuilt; start last Babylonian 360 year fixed term punishment patterns
423.6		500/50				End of O.T. Exact mid of 7000 yrs
325.0		50	400/40	66.666	200	Greeks take control of Judea
167.3	50		40			Hanukkah event
127.9		50	40	66.666	200	Starts God's 200+70 period of exile/tribultn
118.1	50					Last Jubilee celebrated in Judea?
68.77	50					Pharisees take greater temple role
62.2				66.666		Romans take control of Judea
29.33		50				Romans conquer Greeks
19.5 BC	350/50					Herod's temple upgrade begins in Jubilee yr

4.52 AD				66.666		Judea loses ruling authority
30.8	50		40			Start 30th Jubilee in 3rd yr of Jesus' ministry
70.2		1000 500/50	400/40	666.66 66/666	4000/200	Roman destruction of Jerusalem, Temple, with death and exile of huge no. of Jews
80.1	50					Vesuvius destroys 4 idolic temples
129.36	50					Jubilee year; start of Bar Kokhba revolt
135.9				66.666		Romans end Bar Kokhba revolt
326.4	350/50					Counsel of Nicea, creed, Canon
622.2	50		40			Muhammad's Hegira to Medina
858.7		50	400/40	66.666	200	Pope Nicholas Bull; Jews register, etc.
1055.9		5000/50	40	66.666	200	Great Schism in Church
1253.0		50	400/40	66.666	200	Pope Innocent Bull; torture Jews
1262.9	50					Muslims capture Jerusalem
1302.3		50				Pope Boniface issues Unam Sanctum bull declaring papal supremacy over nations
1351.6		50				Jews blamed for Black Plague in Europe
1450.1		50	40	66.666	200	Cardinal requires Jews register, etc.
1607.8	50		40			Jamestown, in future Jewish sanctuary
1647.2		50	400/40	66.666	200	Polish massacre of near 100,000 Jews
1657.1	50					England readmits Jews
1844.4		50	40	66.666	200	Ottoman Turk decree of toleration
1903.53	50					End of 2nd Aliya
1943.0		50				Peak of Holocaust, the Final Solution
1952.8	50					1st Jubilee after rebirth of Israel
1962.7			40			1st nuclear reactor in Israel
1992.2		50				Oslo 2, Jericho & Gaza to PLO; NO PEACE
2002.1	50		40			9/11 event starting 70th Jubilee period
2041.5		1000 500/50	400/40	666.66 66.666	6000 2000/200	By far the date with the most pattern convergences
2051.4	350/50					Ends 70th Jubilee year. Possible major forgiveness coming; anoint Millen. Temple?
3027.2		1000/50	40	66.666	200	Ends 7000th and 7200th years of man
3037.0	50					Eternal state of Rev 21-22????
Total no. patterns	50 – 38 350 - 8	50 - 30	40 – 33 400 - 10	66.6 - 26	200 - 20	

Discussion of the Basic Two-Hundred and Two-Thousand-Year Family of Event-Pattern Strings

We now begin our discussion of the most basic event-pattern string set. We realize this discussion will be somewhat incomplete because this pattern set interacts in many ways with a complementary set of pattern strings, the thirty-, sixty-, or ninety-year pattern set, the whole punishment pattern set, and several other prophetic pattern sets. However, to keep things simple, we must start with this basic pattern set.

As we said earlier, the first basic, equally spaced, and similarly themed pattern we became familiar with in our research was the fifty-year Jubilee judgment pattern. We began our search for that pattern just to satisfy our curiosity about which of the several possibilities we had read about might be the true Jubilee-year pattern.

We were aware of one event in the Old Testament that sounded like a Jubilee-year event. It involved Isaiah, King Hezekiah, and the Assyrian army, which had surrounded Jerusalem with the intent of conquering it. This event was ten years after the Assyrians had destroyed Israel and King Hezekiah, and the city residents were terrified. God miraculously saved them. All the details of this event are included in our first book, *The Search for the Tribulation Code*, so we won't repeat them here.

Our way to confirm this was really God's intended Jubilee pattern was to again continue the pattern both backward and forward in history to make certain it hit the proper key event dates. As we did this, we found that it hit the most important date of all to confirm our suspicions; that being the year 1399 or 1400 BC, a generally accepted date for the year the Israelites first entered the Promised Land and the year God told them to start keeping his Jubilee-year requirements. As we see from the chart above, it hit thirty-eight key event dates in history overall. Quite a pattern!

We also wanted to find the real starting year for the fifty-year pattern overall. In that regard, we found that it hit the event year for the great flood in 2434 BC and the birth date for Noah in 3025 BC. However, we later discovered that it originally started ten years after the fall of man in 4060.64 BC and also hit the year 3863.5 BC at the end of the seventh one-thousand-year day of creation as we saw earlier in this chapter.

Immediately after finding this pattern and the event years it converged with, we began wondering whether God might have other similar event patterns. Our first thought was to investigate whether there might be a pattern set that would connect the event years in which God had destroyed the nations of Israel, Judah, and Judea. We began by checking on the time gap between the destruction of Israel in 719.29 BC and Judah in 587.87 BC. We found the gap to be 131.42 years. That was initially a big disappointment for us. We also tried dividing it by two, three, and four with no apparent success. Our next thought was that maybe we should convert these gaps to 360-day years. The initial gap of 131.42 became 133.33. When we tried dividing it by two, we hit the jackpot. The result was 66.666! From our familiarity with Bible prophecy and especially the book of Revelation, we recognized this number would be tied to the number of the Antichrist, or 666, from Revelation 13.

Our next thought was to check to see whether it also hit the year of the destruction of Judea in AD 70.23. Guess what? It hit it precisely. Not only that, but it also hit the year of the defeat of the Bar Kokhba revolt in AD 135.9. From there we sent our big IPAD calculator to whirl back and forth in history. We hit tribulation event after tribulation event. We can see from the tally at the bottom of the previous chart that we hit twenty-six events total that might have some tie to tribulation for the Jewish people or nation. Wow!

We found the likely starting date for this event pattern to be either the fall of man event or the end of the seventh day of creation. They turned out to be exactly two hundred years apart, meaning that the 66.666-year pattern would hit all two-hundred-year events that started at the same initial historic event. It turns out that there are three 66.666-year periods in two hundred years. We also noticed that fifty and forty also divide evenly into two hundred years, meaning that patterns of 40, 50, and 66.666 would all converge every two hundred years if they all started in the same-event year.

Our next target was the forty-year event pattern. As we began researching this pattern, we soon noticed that it was in the same two-hundred-year pattern as the 66.666-year pattern but in a different two-hundred-year pattern than the fifty-year Jubilee-year event pattern. This led us to discover that there was indeed a second fifty-year pattern that fell into the two-hundred-year pattern with the forty- and the 66.666-year patterns. Thus, we will present that fifty-year pattern after we complete presenting the forty-year pattern.

The forty-year pattern did indeed turn out to be a pattern of exile for the Jewish people all throughout their long history. Like the 66.666-year event-pattern string, we found that it began at the fall of man and again hit the end of the seventh day of creation. We found that it hit at least thirty-three key event dates in history, with most having something to do with an exile theme.

The second fifty-year event-pattern string did in fact converge every two hundred years with the forty- and the 66.666-year event-pattern strings. It turned out to hit thirty-three key event dates in history. We found that the two fifty-year patterns tracked each other all down through history separated by ten years with the Jewish Jubilee fifty-year event following the two-hundred-year convergence fifty-year pattern. That would also mean that they would be separated by forty years on the other end of the patterns with the Jubilee year being forty years ahead of the second fifty-year pattern.

This forty-year separation turned out to be by far the most significant. We discovered in our research that when God needed to punish the Jews because of one of his Jewish fifty-year Jubilee judgments, as shown in the king's scroll, that he typically used the Gentile nations to do the punishing for him. This punishment would often start in the Gentile fifty-year event that would come forty years after the judgment. As a result of this discovery, we began calling the two-hundred-year event pattern, as well as the forty-, fifty-, and 66.666-year patterns that converged with it, "Gentile event-pattern strings." This can be easily seen in the basic event-pattern string chart we just presented. There are thirty of these fifty-year Gentile events shown on the chart.

Other than the fifty-year Jubilee judgments with their consequences, the most significant of the patterns by far were the two-hundred-year convergence event patterns. There were an incredible twenty of these long-time gap pattern events, which turned out to host very important events for the Jewish people. In fact, it was the multiples of these patterns that paint the really significant story of Jewish history. We will next take a look at these event-pattern multiples.

As we noted in the presentation of God's mathematics early in this chapter, there are pattern multipliers God seems to use to significantly enhance the impact of his pattern themes. These multipliers are seven, ten, and thirteen. The seven and thirteen are used most often in the punishment-pattern strings, while the multiplier ten is the general-purpose multiplier used for all the key event time gaps. We will take a brief look at a couple of these and then concentrate on the multiples of two hundred years, which are extremely significant.

The 10x40=400-year event-pattern gap is a very good example to use. This pattern started at the Tower of Babel event in about 2296 BC and continues for forty-four hundred years. There are twelve key events in this pattern, all separated by gaps of four hundred years, and a full ten of them are very significant to God's people. All ten seem to involve exile of some sort. That is incredible. It sounds totally impossible, but it is historically accurate. It seems to end in our generation in the year 2041, the year that was the major theme of our first three books in this series.

The real whopper in all this is that the 10x40, 10x50, and 10x66.666 event-pattern strings all converge every two thousand years in the years 1903 BC, AD 70, and AD 2041. These are the two thousandth, four thousandth, and six thousandth years since the year of the end of the seventh day of creation. Very significant events that involve a large amount of death, long periods of exile, and great tribulation over and over accompanied the first two of these two-thousand-year events. The third such event is quickly approaching us in the year AD 2041. Will the same types of horrible events occur again?

As we saw in our first three books and will see again later in this book, the year AD 2041 has far more event-pattern strings falling on it than any other single year in all recorded history! Stay tuned for much more on this. We will keep searching for our clues.

As we showed on the chart, the three thousandth and five thousandth years also hosted important events, but they were much less impactful in the big picture. Most of our recent discussion has been about the Gentile-event patterns used in enforcing God's judgments against the Jews, primarily for idol worship and not recognizing God's true identity. Therefore, we will now switch our focus to the Jewish event-pattern strings and focus on the fifty-year Jewish Jubilee year event-pattern string and multiples of this pattern in particular. The most significant of these uses God's multipliers of both seven and ten. This is the 350-year event pattern. It is a multiple of 7x50=350. This pattern really starts at the flood, and after three periods of 350 years, it hits the year 1399, when the Israelites first entered the Promised Land and started counting off God's Jubilee judgment periods of fifty years. It was then another ten periods of 350 years until the seventieth Jubilee period ends in AD 2051. Those ten periods cover thirty-five hundred years, and a prophecy we will discuss later will reveal that it could be a very significant time for the Jewish people and in fact the whole world. The year 2051 also has a very large number of significant event-pattern strings that are going to converge in it. One of these is a pattern string of thirteen times 350 years, one of the Angel of Death patterns. This pattern is the combination of the three plus ten times 350 patterns mentioned just above. We will present the other patterns later as we discuss the punishment-event pattern strings.

There is one final thing we would like to reveal about this chart. We began the chart with what we believe could be a valid representation of God's seven days of creation. We presented the days as depicted in Genesis 1 in the Christian Bible, with the one exception that it shows each day lasting one thousand earth years. The Bible says in two specific places, in Psalms and 2 Peter, that a day can be like a thousand years to God and a thousand years can be as a day. Thus, this doesn't contradict the Bible, in our opinion.

I took a two-semester higher-level physics class that centered on Einstein's theory of relativity. That theory paints time as being a variable that changes as one approaches the speed of light. This could bring a meeting of the minds as to the age of the universe between conservative theologians and more liberal scientists. When we consider the time compression Einstein expressed, it seems possible that something akin to ten to fourteen billion years could be compressed into the seven days and/or seven thousand years of creation according to the Bible. That aligns the Bible with what seems to be the apparent age of the universe.

Many theologians believe God created the universe with "apparent" age, while many scientists consider this to be foolish thinking. The real answer to this question won't be settled until we meet Jesus at the Second Coming. We can then ask him since he was the original creator, according to Colossians 1.

My principal reason for wanting to present this was to show that if my presentation is correct, the universe will be thirteen thousand years old in AD 2041, the real target year in this four-book series. The possible significance of that lies in that it can also be expressed as 13x1000 years. The multiplier of thirteen means this could be ominous as we will see in our presentation of God's judgment-pattern strings.

That is all we will say right now about these basic patterns, except to say that the other event-pattern types we will present later will significantly magnify the importance of these patterns and their convergences.

We will now present the clues we picked up concerning our key questions next.

Key Clues from the Basic Two-Hundred-Year Family of Event-Pattern Strings

- We know from the basic family of two-hundred-year event-pattern strings that a very large number of patterns will converge in the years AD 2041 and 2051, and that the themes of the patterns will be great judgment, exile, and tribulation. We don't yet know whether these events will involve the beginning or ending of the patterns and what types of judgments will be taking place.
- The Gentile fifty-year judgment application or enforcement pattern, the 66.666-year tribulation, and the forty-year exile-event pattern strings as well as the 10x version of these pattern strings, the five-hundred-, 666.66-, and four-hundred-year Gentile patterns, the super code patterns all converge in the year AD 2041. That

could be pointing to this being a year with especially ominous events. Could this be the end-time year the prophets, including Daniel, pointed to?

- The year AD 2041 may also be the 13x1000 or thirteen thousandth year since the beginning of the creation process. Thirteen is God's pattern multiplier pointing to serious punishment events, possibly including the great amount of death we found in the 13x Angel of Death event-pattern set. Could AD 2041 be such a year?

- The year AD 2051 may also be a very significant year for the Jewish people since it is their seventieth Jubilee judgment period since they first entered their Promised Land in 1399 BC. Might there be a clear tie between the events of 2041 and the judgments made in this year?

- There seems to be a thematic tie between events taking place every two thousand years. The events of those years led to tribulation and exile for the Jewish people. Might the year 2041 host another set of this type of events? Could it also be pointing to the end of such events for the Jewish people and nation?

- Might all the above convergences be pointing to the year 2041 and our generation hosting the end-time events? We could then call this set of patterns a super code, since they are a set of multiple patterns or codes that are all part of a single set of patterns pointing to the same potentially massive event.

We will keep these clues in mind as we continue to see whether we can find other clues that will help us answer these questions and show whether they involve meeting the purpose of God's will and the soon-coming twin global resets and the great family reunions.

Event-Pattern Strings That Are Complementary to the Basic Two-Hundred-Year Family of Event-Pattern Strings

God's Thirty- and Sixty-Year Event-Pattern Strings

The thirty-, sixty- and ninety-year event-pattern strings are event patterns we consider complementary to the basic set of event-pattern strings. A chart depicting the thirty and sixty sequential year date patterns is presented on the following page. We now suggest that you examine the chart to see what trends and clues you might find. We will present what our analysis revealed to us on the pages after the chart.

The 30/60 Year Pattern of Events Critical to Either

(1) The Future of God's Temple or
(2) The Future of the Jewish People Based Upon Actions Precipitated by Key World Leaders Called and Used by God to do His Will

God's Use of 30 (29.57) & 60 (59.139- see ♦) Year Patterns

Year: Starts 4070.5	Involves Either Temple or World Leader	EVENTS: All of the sequential date patterns seem to involve fixed time periods of testing followed by some mix of blessing and curse. The 30 year pattern generally seems to involve the 2nd of the 3 Lev 26 commands; namely to revere God's Temple. The blessing or curse is administered by some key influential national leader.
♦4070.5 BC	Pre Israel	Fall of Adam & Eve
♦2887.7	Pre-Israel	End of 1st 1000 year day
♦2296.3	Pre Israel LEADER	languages confused at the Tower of Babel; Nimrod was the arrogant leader who was behind this
2148.5	LEADER	Birth of Abraham, father of the Jewish nation
1438.8	BOTH	Exodus; Moses leads people out of Egypt; plans for Tabernacle given
♦1350.1	LEADER	Period of judges begins for Israel; Joshua is the first judge
♦1054.4	LEADER	7th Jubilee; leads to period of kings; Saul is first king 3-4 years later
965.7	BOTH	Construction of first Jewish Temple begins under King Solomon
611.0	LEADER	Babylonian Empire conquers Assyria under King Nebuchadnezzar
♦522.2	BOTH	Darius becomes King of Persia; issues edict allowing temple rebuild
♦463.0	BOTH	Artaxerxes becomes Persian king; 20 yrs later issues edict allowing rebuilding of Jerusalem and its walls; temple worship then begins
♦167.3	BOTH	Seleucid King Antiochus Epiphanies commits abomination of desolation in temple followed by cleansing resulting in Hanukkah
19.5 BC	BOTH	Roman King Herod begins program of greatly expanding and beautifying the temple in Jerusalem
♦11.0 AD	BOTH	Jesus goes to the temple at age 12 with his parents
♦70.2	BOTH	Romans under future Emperor Titus destroy the city of Jerusalem and the temple in the 4000th year of man on earth
♦129.4	BOTH	Last Jubilee year before Bar Kokhba revolt leading to the Romans plowing the Temple Mount, renaming the area Palestine and exiling the Jews remaining in the land, all under Emperor Hadrian
632.1	LEADER	Muhammad, founder of Islam dies; they will become the arch enemy of the Jews until the end times
♦1253.0	LEADER	Papal bull of Pope Innocent allowing torture of Jews in the Inquisition
♦1607.8	LEADER	Founding of Jamestown in America, future refuge for the Jews
♦1844.4	LEADER	Ottoman Empire releases edict of tolerance for Jewish exiles
♦1903.5	LEADER	End of 67th Jubilee cycle; Zionist Aliya, immigration to their original Holy Land; receive support from British and others
♦1962.6	LEADER	First nuclear reactor in Israel; PM David Ben-Gurian
♦2021.8	BOTH	A few world leaders agree that Temple could be built on Temple Mount; Major Temple plans completed; Red heifer discovered
2051.4	BOTH	70th Jubilee; Prophecy calls for Jesus to anoint Millennial Temple
♦3027.2 AD	LEADER	End of 7th 1000 year day; 7200 God years after fall of man

All the sequential year-date patterns seem to involve fixed periods of testing of God's people followed by some mix of blessings and curses for them based on his judgment of the results. For the most part, the thirty-year pattern seems to involve the second of the three Leviticus 26 commands, namely "to revere God's temple." You can go back to the study of Leviticus 26 and the king's scroll if you want to review these three commands. The blessing or curse associated with the thirty-year judgments seems to be administered by some key influential, identifiable national leader. We concluded that the pattern tied closely to the temple because when we examined the dates identified with the thirty-year pattern, we found that eleven of the nineteen dates involving Israel were associated with the temple. I have identified what I consider to be ten total periods in Jewish history with significant identifiable events involving the temple. They are as follows:

1. 1438.8 BC, the year God gave Moses detailed instructions for building the portable tabernacle
2. 966–959 BC, the building of Solomon's temple
3. 587–586 BC, the Babylonian destruction of Solomon's temple
4. 522–513 BC, the period of approval for, and reconstruction of, the temple
5. 464–443 BC, the edict allowing the rebuilding of the city and walls leading to the temple being used again because people could feel safe there
6. 168–163 BC, the Hanukkah event involving the abomination and subsequent cleansing of the temple
7. 20–19 BC, the year Herod's temple expansion began
8. AD 11, the year Jesus went to the temple with his parents at age twelve
9. AD 70, the year the temple was destroyed again
10. AD 129–136; the last Jubilee in Judah, the period of the plowing of the Temple Mount after the Bar Kokhba Revolt

As you can see on the chart depicting the thirty sequential year-date patterns, key dates involving the temple fall within all ten of these short periods. That is astounding and unbelievable. That is why we associate this thirty-year pattern with the temple in Jerusalem. Likewise, seven of the ten fall in the sixty-year pattern.

The other key association we made with the thirty-year pattern was the fact that very key identifiable leaders could be associated with all nineteen events. These were nearly always kings, emperors, or at least very high-level national leaders. Again, this is rather astounding. Several scriptures tell us it is God who appoints our kings and national rulers; these include Romans 13:1; John 19:10–11; Daniel 2:21; and Proverbs 8:15. It seems that God may often make these decisions in years that are in the thirty sequential year-date pattern. Our presidential election cycle in 2020–21 fell within this thirty-year pattern.

Obviously, many of these thirty-year pattern dates would also fall within the sixty-year pattern dates. Again, we see something quite incredible if we examine this closely. We have identified ten dates within the period going from the time God gave Moses the instructions for how to build the portable tabernacle until the year 2022 that fall into the thirty-year pattern. What we found is that eight of these ten dates also fall within the sixty sequential year-date pattern. What is the significance of this? What it means is that God is applying not only his thirty-year judgments to these dates but also his sixty-year judgments. This covers the last two thousand years plus. So what is the sixty-year judgment all about?

Well, the sixty-year judgment patterns are compounded with the thirty-year judgments. Just what compounding effects do they add? We found the number sixty to be associated with a time of slavery to sin, the will of Satan, and a time of needing to work extremely hard just to subsist. The Jews have certainly had to deal with this for about eighteen hundred of the last two thousand years since they have been exiled in nations that are unfriendly to them. However, we also see in God's plan that after six days of hard work, there comes a day of rest. According to my research, man will reach the end of his sixth one-thousand-year day in the year 2041.5. Will that mean that a one-thousand-year day of rest will begin at that time? Maybe not since the thirty- or sixty-year pattern hits in the year AD 2051, not the year 2041.

As we move forward, we will find that the years 2021 and 2051 may indeed be associated with the temple in a very important way.

A Final Word on the Sixty-Year Event-Pattern String

Before moving on, we would like to present a final word on the sixty-year event pattern. The sixty-year pattern is a 10x pattern for the integer six. As we recall from God's mathematics presented earlier in this chapter and in chapter 6 of book one in this series, God uses the number six to represent man. In the sixty-year chart, we noticed that the number six was sometimes associated with God's temple. That might make one wonder why God would make this association between man and His temple.

The sixty-year pattern hits most of the beginnings and endings for God's Jewish temple. The Bible shows the Spirit living in either the portable tabernacle or Solomon's temple for hundreds of years until shortly before the temple was destroyed in about 587–86 BC. There is no indication that he ever returned to the Jewish temple after that year. However, God's mathematics has a solution to this dilemma. First Corinthians 3:16–17 says believers are now the temple of God and that he lives within that temple for all those who are believers in and followers of Jesus. Man, whose number in Revelation 13 is said to be six, is now the temple of God and the residing place of the Spirit. This began in June of AD 32 at the time of Pentecost and continues to this day.

The Ninety-Year Event-Pattern String

The ninety-year event-pattern strings typically represent events that mark the end of seasons of some sort or the other. They are a subset of much larger event-pattern strings that also represent seasons. These would be the nine-hundred- and eighteen-hundred-year event- pattern strings. These all began at the fall of man in 4070.5 BC and run until the apparent end of the millennium in AD 3027. For the eighteen-hundred-year pattern, the four seasons represent the apparent way God has divided the whole history and future of mankind on earth into four equal-length seasons leading to the prophesied eternal state of Revelation 21–22. The four gigantic eighteen-hundred-year seasons are as follows:

4070 BC–2296 BC
This was from the fall, which was a massive punishment for man for disobeying God, until the Tower of Babel when God had to make a new start for mankind because he was conspiring against him. He did this by confusing the languages in such a way that it would be much more difficult for humans in different areas or countries to communicate with each other and conspire against God in sinful activities.

2296 BC–522 BC
This was from the Tower of Babel, which involved punishment for disobeying God's will, until Persian King Darius's decree allowed the Israelites to rebuild their temple. This was during the Jewish exile the Babylonians administered after destroying Jerusalem and the temple in 587–586 BC. It was also exactly one ninety-year season since the Babylonians had conquered the Assyrians, leading directly to their conquering the nation of Judah. Just as the first season ended with God needing to punish his people in a major way, so too would the end of this second season end with an event that would lead to God again administering a very long sentence of exile on his people. The Israelites did rebuild their temple but would not use it after finishing it due to fear of what their neighbors might do to them if they congregated in a large group in a single place. Thus, God administered a punishment period lasting 7x360 years involving exiles and tribulations of many sorts. This was an accruement of punishment for their idol worship over a period of about 780 years after the exodus. Check out book two in this series for all the details.

522 BC–AD 1252–53
This is from Darius's decree, which ultimately led to punishment for idol worship and not honoring God's temple as directed on the king's scroll, until the papal bull allowed torture of the Jewish people if they didn't become Christians during the six-hundred-year Catholic Inquisition period. The Jews were also expelled from France during this year, 1252–53. The torture and series of expulsions from first one country and then the other, featuring all sorts of tribulations for the Jews, including the massive killing of Jews, often reached well over one hundred thousand people in a short period. This lasted until about the year AD 1844 when the Ottoman Turks issued their Edict of Toleration for the Jews.

AD 1252–53–AD 3027
This is from the papal bull allowing the torture of the Jews until the end of the millennium and the start of the eternal state. This again began with God's punishment for the Jewish people, with this one being instituted in AD 1252–53, and it will again end with a punishment. However, this time the punishment will be for all people of all ages who aren't followers of God and Jesus. This will be the Great White Throne Judgment of Revelation 20. In great contrast to the first three, this season will end with a huge reward for all those who have been followers of God and Jesus. After the end of this period, there will

be no more sorrow, tears, death, grieving, and so forth, since everyone will now have a glorious, new resurrected body and will be living with God, Jesus, and the Holy Spirit in a new heaven and new earth for eternity in an absolute paradise.

So, what are our conclusions from this presentation? We will list a few:

1. All four began with an edict either from God or a major world leader.
2. All four began with God needing to punish his people for not keeping one or more of God's Leviticus 26 commands over and over for a long period without repentance.
3. All four also ended with a serious punishment from God, with the last of the four having a quite different conclusion. In contrast to the first three, this punishment was for all people of all ages past who had not been followers of God, keepers of his commands, whose sins had not been forgiven by accepting Jesus's sacrifice of himself for their sins.
4. All four periods contain twenty periods each of ninety-year sub-seasons, so to speak. Several of these either open or close mini seasons, as we will see later when we introduce the master template, which God has apparently been using since before the creation of the world.

We will close this discussion about the ninety-year season event-pattern string by presenting a notable ninety-year pattern.

It will be exactly 7x7 periods of ninety-year season-event periods from the Tower of Babel event in 2296 BC until the year AD 2051. Might this then be the year when punishment for God's people will end? It will be the end of the perfect and complete ninetieth season pattern since God's first punishment after the great flood. Might that spark the start of the millennium?

Key Clues from the Thirty-, Sixty-, and Ninety- Year Set of Complementary Pattern Strings

- Ten key dates in our database involve God's temple in the period from the exodus in 1438 BC until the Jubilee year leading to the plowing of the Temple Mount in AD 129. All ten are in the thirty-year event-pattern string. Also, seven of these ten dates are in the sixty-year pattern. In addition, a key world leader could be identified with every one of these events.
- In the mathematics God uses in his event-pattern strings we presented earlier in this chapter, we found seventy to be God's basic testing pattern. In the king's scroll, we discovered that God was using a fifty-year event-pattern string for judging the Jewish people and nation and that this was to begin in 1399 BC. The seventieth such pattern hits the year AD 2051. We also found that it was exactly 7x7=49 season periods of ninety years from the Tower of Babel incident until the seventieth Jubilee year in AD 2051. Could it be that the new season that begins

this year might be the start of the millennium and that the association with the temple might involve Jesus's anointing of the new millennial temple? We will keep an eye out for that as we go forward.

Thus, we have discovered other major clues that our generation might be a good fit for the coming end-time scenario.

Clues from God's basic event-pattern strings and the king's scroll can help us answer the five w's *associated with our subject questions. What are the coming twin global resets and family reunions, and how are they associated with God meeting the purpose of his will, bringing everything in heaven and earth together in unity under Jesus when time reaches its fulfillment (the end-times, possibly in our generation)?*

Key Clues from Daniel's Seventy-Sevens Prophecy

- Both Jesus's First and Second Comings are addressed in this prophetic pattern. In fact, we are given a formula by which we can calculate the event dates for both. The first was in AD 32 and has already been authenticated while the second is rather murky. It will require much more digging to unearth it.
- It gives us details about the final seven-year period of tribulation leading up to the Second Coming of Jesus.
- At the end of the seven-year period, Jesus will be anointed King of Kings on earth.
- The end of the seven-year period also begins a time of righteous living and an end to sin. This implies that most of those on earth at that time will be the resurrected saints of all ages, who will no longer be capable of sinning.

Key Clues from the Basic Two-Hundred-Year Family of Event-Pattern Strings

- We know from the basic family of two-hundred-year event-pattern strings that a very large number of patterns will converge in the years 2041 and 2051, and that the themes of the patterns will be great judgment, exile, and tribulation. We do not yet know whether these events will involve the beginning or ending of the patterns and what types of judgments will be taking place.
- These patterns have major convergences in our generation. This could mean our generation would be a good fit for the end-time scenario.

Key Clues from the Thirty-, Sixty- and Ninety-Year Set of Complementary Pattern Strings

- There are ten key dates in our database involving God's temple in the period from the exodus in 1438 BC until the Jubilee year leading to the plowing of the Temple Mount in AD 129. All ten are in the thirty-year event-pattern string. Also, seven of these ten dates are in the sixty-year pattern. In addition, a key world leader could be identified with every one of these events.
- In the mathematics God uses in his event-pattern strings, which we presented earlier in this chapter, we found seventy to be God's basic testing pattern. In the king's scroll, we discovered that God was using a fifty-year event-pattern string for judging the Jewish people and nation and that this was to begin in 1399 BC. The seventieth such pattern hits the year AD 2051.
- Thus, we have discovered other major clues that our generation might be a good fit for the coming end-time scenario.

Key Clues from the King's Scroll

- We learn that God indeed has a plan for his chosen people and that it will involve a long period of successes and failures by the Jewish people.
- God instituted a fifty-year period for the Jews that is called a "Jubilee judgment period," and it will continue for the whole lifetime of the Jewish nation starting at the time the Israelites entered the Promised Land. These periods will be strung together, and thus we have our first equally spaced and similarly themed event pattern or event-pattern string.
- The Israelites will fail miserably from time to time, and God will need to punish them. If he has to punish them for the same offense two or more times, he will multiply these punishment periods by a factor of seven. Thus, we also now have our first punishment-period multiplier.
- Might we also expect God to multiply the Jubilee period itself by seven, resulting in event patterns lasting 7x50=350 years? We will be looking for that later.

Overall Key Clues from This Set of Patterns

- Many of the patterns presented above are converging in our generation, especially in 2041 and 2051, as shown above. They could be a good fit for the end-time scenario. Thus, we have discovered other major clues that our generation might be a good fit for the coming end-time scenario.

The 5 W's Report Card:

CLUES FROM EVENT PATTERN STINGS AND THE KINGS SCROLL THAT WILL HELP US BETTER UNDERSTAND END TIME EVENTS, THE UNIFICATION OF EVERYTHING UNDER JESUS, THE DUAL GLOBAL RESETS, DUAL FAMILY REUNIONS AND THEIR POSSIBLE TIE TO OUR GENERATION			
WHO	WHEN	WHERE	WHAT AND WHY
Jesus, All believers	In end times	Whole world	**DANIEL'S 70 7'S:** Daniel gives us a formula for calculating the year of Jesus Second Coming to earth. Daniel's clues lead us to believe that the Second Coming will be closely followed by the 1000 year millennium.
Jews, all people	2041, 2051?	Israel, whole world	**BASIC 200/2000 EVENT PATTERN STRING:** These patterns involve great chaos for the Jewish people as a result of exiles, tribulations, terror, etc. They all will end in a whopper of an end time event.
Jews, whole world?	2041	Israel, whole world?	Both basic and mega event pattern strings of 50 and 500 year judgment enforcement, 40 and 400 year exile and 66.666 and 666.66 tribulation all converge in the year 2041. Could this forebode a period of serious end time chaos?
	2041		The year 2041 may also be the 13x1000 or 13,000th year since the beginning of the creation process. 13 is God's pattern multiplier pointing to serious punishment events. Could this be such a year?
Jews	2051	Israel, all over world	The year 2051 may also be a very significant year for the Jewish people since it is their 70th Jubilee judgment period since they first entered their Promised Land in 1399 BC. Might there be a clear tie between the events of 2041 and the judgments made in this year?
	3027 AD	Whole world	**COMPLEMENTARY 30/60/90 EVENT PATTTERN STRINGS:** The super season that covers the whole period from the fall to the eternal state contains 20x90=1800 years. It may end with the eternal state in 3027 AD after 4 full seasons.
Jews	2051?	On earth	**THE KING'S SCROLL:** This scroll introduces us to our first event pattern string; a judgment string that will converge for the 70th time in the year 2051.
Jews		In the nations	The Jews will fail God's tests miserably and he will exile them to the nations, which will involve great chaos for them. He will re-gather them one day in a great family reunion.

God's Punishment Event-Pattern Strings

Historical Evidence of God's Use of These Pattern Strings to Bring about the Ultimate Purpose of His Will

What We Are Trying to Accomplish in This Chapter

So far in this book, we have established that God has given us a glance at the plan he had for the universe that he created and the coming twin global resets and great family reunions that will occur when that plan reaches its fulfillment. We are searching the Bible in various ways to try to find clues that will help us better understand both the plan and the accompanying global resets and family reunions and when they might occur. We have searched through several of the Bible's prophetic models to try to find some of the mysteries and secret codes often hidden in them. We had some success and next began searching through another type of means God uses to hide these mysteries and secret codes. This means was God's use of his basic event-pattern strings. Again, we had some success and found some interesting clues that might lead us to some answers.

We will continue that search in this chapter by looking at a very special type of event-pattern strings. These are the event patterns that involve God punishing his people for violating his Leviticus 26 and king's scroll commands over a very long period, totaling hundreds of years. We will again be interested in finding out whether the punishment patterns are converging in our generation and whether they fit the end-time scenario.

The patterns we found and the message they contain are truly mind boggling. As you will see, these patterns match the historical event data extremely precisely. They also perfectly match the prophetic promises God had given them many hundreds of years prior to him having to carry them out to their conclusion. We will next go through this in some detail, but we will try to keep it as simple as possible and fairly easy to understand. We will leave the intricate details of our previous three books in this series for those who want to dig a little deeper.

A Brief History of the Jewish Nations

The Jewish people have had their nations completely destroyed and their people exiled to other nations three times in history. There have been only three Jewish nations in history up to the re-founding of Israel once more in 1948. Israel was founded as a nation and had a land of their own for the first time forty years after the exodus, in the year 1400–1399 BC. This nation split into two nations after the death of Solomon in 931 BC largely over a squabble about paying large taxes to pay for Solomon's huge building program. These nations were the northern kingdom of Israel and the southern kingdom of Judah.

Abraham's grandson Jacob and his whole family of sixty or so people all ended up in Egypt in 1863 BC when trying to buy grain as the result of a seven-year drought. Jacob's son Joseph had already been in Egypt for about twenty-five years, and a series of events found him as second in command to Pharaoh, so they all settled in Egypt. An ugly situation thirty years later under a new Pharaoh landed the whole family into a situation where they became slaves. They spent the next four hundred years as slaves in Egypt, but in the process, they grew to be a people group of over a million. A very interesting series of events, ultimately involving the Angel of Death, led to them being able to escape Egypt in 1438 BC.

Likely the worst thing that happened to the Israelites while in Egypt was that they became very aware of the idols the Egyptians worshipped. The Israelites continued to hold onto YHWH as their God but began to wonder in their minds whether the gods of Egypt might also be valid gods. Thus, when the Israelites escaped Egypt, they were already worshipping both YHWH and idols. God seriously warned them about this idolatry in Leviticus 26, Deuteronomy, and the king's scroll, which we presented earlier in this book. He also told them about the consequences of this idol worship. As you can see again, on the king's scroll God told them precisely what their punishments would be and told them he knew ahead of time that they would fail, that he would need to seriously punish them, take their land away from them, and exile them to the nations of the world for many, many years. Thank goodness, he also told them that after many years, they would return to him, and he would also return to them, restore them in their land, and so forth. We will be documenting this long, complicated process in the coming pages.

Solomon was the third king of Israel, following David and Saul. Solomon was obviously an avid follower of YHWH, as we can see from his writings, including Proverbs. However, he also seriously violated God's clear directions to future kings in the book of Deuteronomy when he took six hundred different wives along with three hundred concubines. Solomon was likely the richest man on earth and was widely admired for his accomplishments. That led all the surrounding countries to have a deep desire for Solomon to marry one of their princesses. He did so to the extreme. But guess what? When they moved to Israel, they brought their idols with them. Very bad! Solomon's son Jeroboam became king at his death, and he was a serious idol worshipper. Israel continued idol worship until God allowed the Assyrians to destroy their country and exile their people to the nations in 720–719 BC.

God's Use of the Assyrians to Punish Israel

God would have detected the type and duration of Israel's punishment at the Jubilee judgment of 759 BC. God made known to the prophet Isaiah that he was enacting his nine harbingers against Israel as warnings for them to return to him. These are recorded in Isaiah 8–10, and Isaiah wrote these chapters in the 750's BC. Despite the warnings, things apparently didn't change, so God enacted his judgment through the Assyrians in 720–719 BC. The Assyrians destroyed their capital city of Samaria, killed huge numbers of Israelites, and exiled everyone they could round up to other nations that they had captured or were ruling over. However, a large number of Israelites escaped and went to live in the southern kingdom of Judea. God's punishment still applied to them, however, and it would be enacted later when they were in Judea.

How long would this exile last? When would the Israelites be forgiven? Well, the only clue we have in the king's scroll is that whatever it was, it would be multiplied by seven because they had been sufficiently warned many times before. We have a huge clue in Ezekiel 4, however. That wouldn't be made known until Ezekiel wrote it about 130 years later in around 592 BC. Here God told Ezekiel that Israel was due a punishment of 390 years and Judah forty years.

If we multiply the 390 years by seven, convert the result to 360-day years, and begin in 719 BC, we come to the year AD 1972. God was adding another seventy years to his punishment periods as additional periods of testing. Thus, the punishment would end, and the Israelites would be forgiven in the year AD 2041. The details of how God was doing this are included in Ezekiel 4–5; and the way God would be using the seventy-year periods is given in Jeremiah 25, 29. We have been seeing the year 2041 cropping up several times before in our searches of God's other means for hiding his mysteries and secrets.

God's Use of the Babylonians to Punish Judah

The Babylonian destruction of Judah is much more complicated and detailed to present. We will keep it as simple as we can with the understanding that all the details are presented in book two of this series, *God Is Cooking Up Something Incredible*.

The script for the Babylonian destruction and exile of Judah began to be written in about 611 BC when the Babylonians overthrew the Assyrian Empire. They overthrew Judah in about 606 BC and took a number of young Israelites back to Babylon, including Daniel, the one who would become the famous prophet of God. Nebuchadnezzar, king of the Babylonians, told the king of Israel they could live in peace under Babylon if they would pay homage and taxes to Babylon. The youngsters they had taken were hostages of a sort. But of course, the Judeans wouldn't cooperate, and the Babylonians kept changing out the kings of Israel and taking other groups of exiles to Babylon. Ezekiel was in the second wave of exiles in 597 BC. He was allowed to live in a house and continued to have many freedoms, including writing his book, having counseling sessions with Judah's leaders, and so forth.

However, the continued failure of Judah's leaders to cooperate with Nebuchadnezzar finally persuaded the Babylonians to destroy Judah. They began a siege of Jerusalem in 587 and ended up destroying the city and temple in 586 BC. They killed many thousands and took a huge number of exiles back to Babylon with them, along with the valuables from the temple, and so forth. Now, how would this exile play out? We have attached a couple of charts to help us tell the story. Again the details are in our book two.

The first chart presents all the key dates and events that took place over the Babylonian exile and then later the Persian exile period from 606 until 443 BC. Again, God was punishing the Judeans just as he had punished the Israelites, principally for idol worship. The extent of the idol worship is described in Ezekiel 8–11. It had reached extreme proportions. Men were visiting the temple early in the morning to worship the sun god. The Judeans had statues of idols in the temple and pictures of idols painted all over the temple walls. God was extremely upset by this. In these same chapters, we see the Spirit of God departing the temple and hovering nearby since he was so unhappy about having to leave, about what had been going on, and so forth. He apparently never again inhabited a Jewish temple and now resides in a new sort of temple, the body of all those who believe in and worship Jesus as God.

We will next describe the ways God enacted his punishment, the different type of exile that would be enacted, when it would all end, and so forth.

Again, Ezekiel and Jeremiah were the principal prophets at the time when the Babylonian destruction and exile of Judah took place. Jeremiah prophesied that the initial exiles would last for seventy years, and Ezekiel revealed in chapter 4 that God's punishments would be 390 years for Israel and 40 years for Judah. The total would be for 430 years. Ezekiel said in chapter 5 that God would enact it in three separate ways, and we know from Leviticus 26 that the punishment periods would be multiplied by seven. I first came across this interpretation in a 1997 book by Grant Jeffrey, *Armageddon, Earth's Last Stand*.[6] What I teach and write is like what is presented in that book, but I have significantly expanded the interpretation based on the findings in my event-pattern string research. That is what I present in my books, including this book.

We will start our presentation by showing that God apparently enacted his punishment in three separate periods, with one of God's punishments in each section tied to a violation of one of the three Leviticus 26 commands as follows:

Period 1: 605–536 BC—command 3
　　　　Keep God's commands.
Period 2: 586–517 BC—command 1
　　　　Love God; do not worship idols or false gods.
Period 3: 512–443 BC—command 2
　　　　Revere God's sanctuary; keep the Jubilee commands.

When we analyze the information we have available to us, along with our knowledge of how God seems to use his event-pattern strings, we come to the following as a possible conclusion.

God apparently wants us to take the 390- and 40-year punishment periods for Israel and Judah as the periods he would multiply by seven to get to the ultimate end of the punishment. We will explain the following:

We have already explained the Assyrian punishment period as being 7x390 years with one seventy-year period of testing at the end, taking us to the year AD 2041. We could have also used the numbers 70x40=2,800 years, added that to the year 719 BC, and come up to the same year, AD 2041.

Now, how about the Israelites who escaped from the Assyrians and settled back into Judah? They still had the 7x390 years of punishment due them. How might God have applied his punishments to them since they were then in the country of Judah?

Let us try using the formula Daniel gave us for reaching the end-times in Daniel 9:24–27, which indicated that it would be 7+62+1=70 periods until the end-times. We already saw earlier that this formula takes us to the very day of Jesus's death if we start in 444.6 BC, the time of Artaxerxes's decree. The formula has one additional seven-year period at the end, which is presumed to be the seven-year tribulation period. We are not told explicitly how to get from AD 32 to the time of the last seven years. We have an idea that could be a possibility. We will explain.

This formula fits the case of the Israelites who escaped to Judah perfectly. Do you suppose that is the way God expected to use Daniel's formula to get to the end-times? Your guess is as good as mine. The formula works out like this:

We start in 719.29.

719+(7x40=280) takes us to 443.3 BC, and from there 443.3+(62x40=2480) takes us to the start of the seventieth Jubilee period in AD 2002.1. Finally, adding one more forty-year period from Daniel's formula takes us to the year 2041.53 once more.

Now what about the people of Judah? We have only one forty-year period to deal with, but we still must multiply it by seven, getting us to 280 years of punishment for these people. Next, we see that 443.3 BC+280 years takes us to the year 167 BC, the same year the Seleucid king Antiocchus Epiphanes committed the abomination of desolation in the temple in Jerusalem. This so infuriated the Jews that they had an uprising under the Maccabeans and overthrew the Seleucids, thus gaining their freedom and self-rule once more.

However, this lasted only until 62 BC when the Romans captured Jerusalem and the Jews were once more living under another powerful and oppressive regime.

Before we leave the destruction patterns God apparently used in punishing Israel and Judah, we would like to present a couple of additional charts that summarize the whole scenario and present us with a couple of incredible clues we can use in answering our subject questions. After presenting the charts, we will discuss the additional information we have presented. The charts are somewhat self-explanatory, so we would like the reader to study them a bit before going on to our conclusions.

Chronology of the Events Associated with God's Lev 26 Punishment of Israel and Judah in the Assyrian and Babylonian Captivities, Destructions and Exiles

Year BC Ending in	Prophet	Scripture	Event
	Moses	Lev 26	God gave Moses a summary of the whole future of the nation of Israel in Lev 26; He prophesied the whole future of the Israelites based upon his foreknowledge of how they would fare in keeping these Lev 26 instructions
1399.4	Moses	Deut	Deut is a large expansion of Lev 26 presented to the Israelites by Moses in the year before they entered the Promised Land; whole future of Israel repeated. Israel was incredibly well warned of consequences for disobedience
1399.4	Joshua	Lev 25	Year when Israelites were to begin counting the 50 (49.2825) year Jubilee cycle
965.7			Start date for construction of Solomon's Temple in Jerusalem
758.7	Isaiah	Isa 8-10	Jubilee judgment when God instituted 7 harbingers as warnings to Israel
719.29	Isaiah		Year the Assyrians destroyed Israel and exiled people to other nations Isaiah had been warning them about this for about 28 years; see Isa 9 harbingers
610.9	Jeremiah	Jer 25:4-14, 29:10	A Jubilee year and the year in which the Babylonians conquered the Assyrians. About the year that Jeremiah prophesied that Judah would be overtaken by Babylon and face destruction, death and an exile which would last for 70 /69 years
605.4	Jeremiah	Dan 1	Babylon takes over Judah; Nebuchadnezzar takes Daniel in first wave of exiles
597	Ezekiel		Second wave of exiles taken to Babylon, including Ezekiel
592	Ezekiel	Ezek 4-5	God reveals to Ezekiel the means, the reasons and the extent of the punishment that he is inflicting on Judah
590	Ezekiel	Ezek 20	Elders in exile visit Ezekiel, also in exile, seeking reasons for God's severe punishment on them; he repeats the message of Lev 26 and Deut to them
587.9 586.3	Ezekiel	Ezek 8-11	The Holy Spirit leaves the temple sometime between 590-588. The siege of Jerusalem begins in 587.9 and the city and temple are destroyed on 9 Av 586; thousands are killed and the third wave of exiles is taken to Babylon
561.6	Daniel		A Jubilee year. King Nebuchadnezzar dies, beginning wave of instability in rulers of Babylon
539-538	Daniel		Cyrus and Persians conquer the Babylonian empire
536.4	Daniel		Cyrus gives Judean exiles freedom to return home after 50-70 years in exile; some return and some choose to stay in Babylon.; initial work on temple begins
522.2	Zechariah		Darius becomes king and provides edict allowing temple construction to resume
520-516	Zechariah	Zechariah 1-4	Angel of the Lord, Jesus, visits Zechariah the priest and others on earth and gives them instructions and prophesies, Zech 1:12 confirms that it had been 70 years since the temple had been destroyed; this was the 2nd 70 year exile/testing period
517.3	Zechariah	Ezra 1-6	Construction of replacement temple finally begins in Jerusalem, taking 3 ½ yrs for completion; this was the precise end of the 2nd 70 year exile/testing period
512.3			The 18th Jubilee year: the 3rd 70 year punishment was enacted for failure to keep the 2nd Lev 26 command resulting in a final 70 year period of testing
463.0	Ezra		A Jubilee year: Artaxerxes Longimano becomes king of Persia; will be friend to Judah's remaining exiles
457-456	Ezra, Nehemiah	Ezra 7:8	In 7th year of Artaxerxes, he gave Ezra a letter allowing him and other Judeans to return to Judah, set up self-rule, take temple treasures with them, etc.
443.3	Ezra Nehemiah	Ezra 6-10, Nehemiah	End of testing periods for Judeans, displaced Israelites; final sentence of 7 x 360 years imposed which well end in 2041 AD

Amazing Proof that God is in Control of World Events Through Repetition of the Babylonian Captivity Event Patterns After 7 X 360 or 2520 (2483.8) Years Exactly as He Prophesied (All Jews of All Tribes May Have a New Beginning in 2041.5)

God's Supernatural End Time Fulfillment of the Babylonian Punishment Pattern						
3 Phases of Punishment, Ezek 5. Each started with 70 years testing, then 7x360 = 2520/2483.84 yrs exile from Ezek 4-5, Lev 25-26, Dan 9, and Jer 25, 29.						Description of the events which took place in each year, for both the original and final fulfillment periods
Babylonian Exile Phase 1		Babylonian Exile Phase 2		Babylonian Exile Phase 3		God appeared to break up each 70 yr testing period into 50/20 yr segments for both original & fulfillment periods
Origin BC	Fulfill AD	Origin BC	Fulfill AD	Origin BC	Fulfill AD	
605						Babylon seizes Judah; exile begins, Daniel
	1879					Exile ends; Jews begin return to Palestine
586		586				End of Jewish nation; destroy city, temple
	1898		1898			Birth of Zionism; goal to restore Israel
		567				War: Nebuchadnezzar defeated in Egypt
			1917-8			War: WWI, British take Jerusalem
536						Judah reborn; exiles allowed to return
	1948					Israel reborn; mass immigration begins
		517				Temple rebuilding begins on Temple Mt.
			1967			Temple Mt. captured in Six Day War
				512.3		Jubilee; fear, decision to not use temple
					1972.5	Fear; decision to not use Temple Mount
				463.0		Key new leader comes to power in empire
					2021.8	Key new world leader comes to power???
				443.3		Start of God's final long term punishment
					2041.5	End of God's final long term punishment

God's Supernatural End Time Fulfillment of the Assyrian Punishment Pattern		
7x390=2730/2690.8 yrs. 719.3 − 2690.8 = 1972.5 + 70 (69) = 2041.5.		Description of the events which took place in each year, for both the original and final fulfillment periods
Assyrian Exile		God began all three phases of the Babylonian punishment periods with a 70/69 year period of testing as we saw above. It appears that he will end the Assyrian punishment period with a 70 year period of testing and again break it into ~50/20 year segments.
Origin, BC	Fulfill, AD	
719.3	1972.5 2021-22 2041.5	Assyria conquered & destroyed Samaria & Israel and exiled the Jewish people in 719 BC. 2041.5 may mark the end of 7x390 years of punishment for the northern kingdom Jews, after God added another 70/69 years of testing. Thus all twelve tribes of Israel will finally be free in 2041.5. Will God be satisfied or will there be even more tribulation in store for the Jews? If the patterns hold, a key new world leader may take power in 2021-22. We may not initially know his identity.

The king's scroll, which we presented earlier in this book, shows that God specifically told the Israelites what their punishments and the durations of their punishments would be if they didn't keep his three key commands. He also told them he would warn them over and over if they didn't follow him and would eventually begin to punish them in seven different ways with ever-increasing consequences until they returned to him. He also said that after his first such punishment, he would multiply any additional punishments that were needed by seven. Our patterns show that God did this very thing several times.

The first of the two charts we just presented is simply a presentation of all the key events and dates associated with both the Assyrian and Babylonian destructions and exiles of first Israel and then Judah. The really interesting thing about these event dates is that there is an incredible set of event-pattern strings hidden within them. What makes them a secret and mystery of sorts is that it is nearly impossible to pick them out. Why would that be? Well, as we said before in the discussion of God's mathematics, he bases all of his dates, genealogies, time gaps and so forth on a 360-day year. You can simply multiply the dates in the chart by 1.01455, and you will come up with God's calendar dates. Then the patterns are quite easy to pick out. We will present a few examples.

- 200 years between 719 and 522
- 610, 561, 512, and 463 are all Jubilee years and fifty years apart.
- The dates in the three Babylonian exile periods are all separated by exactly seventy years.
- 280 years from 719 to 443, the total period of the combined Assyrian and Babylonian event periods
- Both 7x360=2,520 and 63x40=2,520 years are the gaps between the parallel events in the Babylonian prophetic event period and the fulfillment events in our generation. Wow!

Key Clues from the Babylonian and Assyrian Punishment Patterns

- Punishment for all northern kingdom Israelites for 390 years of idol worship will end in AD 2041.
- Punishment for those of the southern kingdom of Judah was in two phases enacted in two phases. The first phase ended during the Hanukkah event in 167 BC. The second phase took place after the Romans overtook and ultimately destroyed them. Their punishment was apparently for two thousand years and will end in 2041.

Warning!

You Have Just Entered the Twilight Zone!

What we have just presented and will present next is "otherworldly." It had to come from the spiritual world in which God resides. It involves the fact that world "history" tells us that the nine key events in the Babylonian punishment and exile period all have parallel events that have occurred or are occurring in our generation. This seems insane. Eight of the nine have already been fulfilled, and the ninth thus seems very likely to take place. We ask readers to go through these events once more and ponder the likelihood that this could be happening. What does this tell us about who is in charge of world events?

Since we have just entered the twilight zone, let's stay within it for a short period to see whether we can find some additional clues that might help us solve the mysteries and secrets about God's plan for the world and the coming dual global resets and great family reunions. To do that, we would like to go back to the basic two-hundred- or two-thousand-year event-pattern strings we presented in the previous chapter. Of course, what we present next is also supernatural and again seems to be statistically impossible. Thus, it is the stuff of the twilight zone.

The supernatural thing we discovered about the Babylonian punishment pattern was that at least nine of the key events that occurred in the original historical event period had parallel events matching the theme of the original event, which was exactly 2,520 years after the original events. The events in our generation are only different in that they involve forgiveness themes that reflect the original theme. For example, if the original event theme involved losing their land, then the fulfillment theme in our generation would reflect an event that would result in them getting their original land returned to them.

Our next topic will involve a very similar type of thing happening once again, but it will involve parallel themes between a whole series of at least eleven events that have parallels taking place every 2,000 years instead of every 2,520 years; and the events will take place over a 200+70 year period surrounding the two thousandth, four thousandth, and six thousandth years after the end of the seventh day of creation. So, let's go and check it out!

Parallel Events Surrounding the Three Two-Thousand-Year Periods in the History of the World That Demonstrate They Must Have Been Preplanned

We also created another set of charts to reinforce the points we are trying to make. Those points are that something supernatural is taking place in the spacing and themes of events in both secular and biblical history. In this set of charts, we examine the *events taking place* surrounding the three two thousand years of man and look for unexpected corollaries between events and their date spacing. What we found was that there is a uniquely similar pattern in the series of events taking place in these three periods in history. This pattern shows that there is a repeating theme within the event patterns, and the thematically similar patterns are always separated by exactly two thousand years in all three periods. There are at least eleven events taking place within the patterns in all three two-thousand-year periods that are thematically similar in nature and separated by exactly two thousand years. That is crazy and impossible. It cannot be happening unless some supernatural force or being has been making it happen. We know the identity of that being, and we identified him several times in our first three books in this series.

Before presenting the complete set of charts, we will present a summary showing what we have found. The dates of the three two-thousand-year events are 1903 BC, AD 70, and AD 2041. Each set of dates is separated by exactly two thousand years. We will follow the dates with our interpretation of the similar theme shown in each of the three dates.

A Quick Peek at the Parallel Events in the 200+70-Year Periods Surrounding the Three Two-Thousand-Year Events and in the Four Hundredth and Eight Hundredth Years before Each Two Hundredth Year

2690 BC, 719 BC, AD 1253: 2x400 years before the two-thousandth-year event dates. All dates involved soon start of exile and/or tribulation. Four hundred years later in each case, we see the following:

2296 BC, 325 BC, AD 1647: Four hundred years before the two-thousandth-year event dates. All dates involved soon start of exile and/or tribulation. Four hundred years later in each case, we see the following:

2099 BC, 127 BC, AD 1844: Start of the 270-year period in the two-thousandth year after the fall in 4070 BC and encompasses the two-thousandth year after the end of the seventh day of creation two hundred years later. This period will play a key role in God revealing himself. Sixty years later in each period, we see the following:

2040 BC, 68 BC, AD 1903: Jubilee year that started the 210-year period. All dates in some manner involve a birth of some sort. Fifty years later in each period, we see the following:

2000 BC, 29 BC, AD 1943: Event that took place exactly one hundred years before the two thousandth year. Dates involved a very serious event that would lead to a major change in the status of the Jewish people and nation.

1990 BC, 19 BC, AD 1952: Jubilee year marking birth of Jacob/Israel, Herod's temple, and the rebirth of Israel. Twenty years later in each period, we see the following:

1971 BC, AD 1.23, AD 1972: Entering new seventy-year testing period leading to the two thousandth year. It marks time for leaving exiles, Jesus from Egypt, and the Jews from the long Assyrian punishment period. Thirty years later in each period, we see the following:

1941 BC, AD 30.8, AD 2002.1: Jubilee year with apparent major exile/tribulation judgments made. Each date may mark the start of a new era, post-flood era, Christian era, and possibly the end-time era. Forty years later in each period, we see the following:

1902 BC, AD 70, AD 2041: The three two-thousandth-year days of man. All seem to reflect events that led to great tribulation and exile for the Jewish people. Ten years later in each period, we see the following:

1892 BC, AD 79–80, AD 2051: Jubilee year that would usher in a time of great change for the Jewish people and nation. Each event seems to involve a payback of some sort. Fifty years later in each period, we see the following:

1842 BC, AD 129, AD 2100: Last Jubilee year before a new form of exile begins for the Jewish people. First in slavery, then in the nations, and finally in ?

1833 BC, AD 139, AD 2110: Seventy years after 2041 and 210 years after AD 1902. This is the year when a long period of exile began in each case.

Below is the detailed pair of charts from which we summarized the above information. We believe the above summary clearly shows the supernatural nature of the parallel events in the three two-thousand-year periods. The first of the following charts presents a summary of the events taking place in each of the three eleven sets of parallel events. The second chart is quite similar to the first chart but reflects the commonality between the three events in each of the eleven sets of parallel events. The second chart is somewhat redundant with the previous page but this is a quite complicated topic and we felt that it might be a bit easier to understand in the chart format.

Short Description of the Specific Themes in the Parallel Events in and Surrounding the 2000th Year Periods

Parallel Event Dates in the 2000th, 4000th, and 6000th Years All Separated by 2000 Years				Description of the Events Taking Place in the Specified Event Dates
2000th yr 1902.1 BC	4000th yr 70.23 AD	6000th yr 2041.53 AD	Gap to 2000th yr	
2690.6?? BC	719.29 BC	1253.01 AD	800	2x400 years before the 2000 year event date All dates involved soon start of exile, tribulation
2296.33?	325.03	1647.3	400	400 years before the 2000 year event date All dates involved soon start of exile, tribulation
2099.2	127.9	1844.4	200	Starts Gentile 200 year period ending in 2000th year Seemingly insignificant event is really important
2040.1??	68.77	1903.53	140	Jubilee starts Jewish 210 year period in 2000th years 2040.1; 500TH birthday for Shem. Time Abraham took Isaac up on future Temple Mt modeling Jesus 68.77; 2400 years post flood: Start of new role for Pharisees in Sanhedrin, Judicial body met in Temple 1903.5; 4400 years post flood. 3rd Aliya to reclaim original Promised Land and Temple Mount site
2000.6	29.3	1943.0	100	100 years before the 2000th year: 2000?? Unknown event 29.3; Romans take over the Greek empire 1943; the terrible Holocaust of Jewish people
1990.79	19.49 BC	1952.81	90	90 years before 2000th year; represents 1 season 1990.79; birth of Israel, originally named Jacob 19.49 BC; birth of Herod's Temple in Jerusalem 1952.8; birth of Israel in original homeland
1971.1??	1.23 AD	1972.53	70	Middle 70 ear testing period in 3x70=210 years 1.23 AD; Jesus/family return from exile in Egypt 1972.5; End of 2730 year Assyrian exile
1941.5??	30.8	2002.1	40	Jubilee years: major exile/trib judgments made 1941.5; start of post flood era at Shem's death 30.8; Start of Christian era in Jesus' Jubilee 2002.1; 70th Jubilee may usher in Millennial era
1902.07	70.23	2041.53	Yr 6000 In Gentile pattern	2000 year days of man; Entering a time of great tribulation, exile 40 years after Jubilee judgment 1902.1 BC; Joseph's birth, great exile coming 70 AD; Romans destroy city, temple, exile starts 2041.5; possibly mid-trib, involving Temple; 3 ½ years exile??
1892.25?	80.09	2051.39	10 Yr 6000 in Witness pattern	Jubilee year that would involve the perpetual Jewish struggle over God's true identity 1892.2; Jacob's wrestling match with God that is prophetic of future struggle with God's identity 80.09 AD; Mt Vesuvius erupts destroying 4 temples to idols in Pompeii as God repays Romans for destroying Jewish Temple 2051.4; Jesus anoints Millennial Temple as all living Jews finally accept Jesus as their true God
1842.9	129.3	2100.6 ??	60	Last Jubilee before new form of exile begins
1833.07 BC	139.23 AD	2110.53?? AD	70	1833.07 BC; Israelites enter 400 year slavery in Egypt 139.23 AD; Jews enter 1800 year exile in nations 2110.53; unsaved enter 1000 years in Hades??

Short Description of the Commonality within Themes in the
Parallel Events in and Surrounding the 2000ᵗʰ Year Periods

2000ᵗʰ yr 1902.1 BC	4000ᵗʰ yr 70.23 AD	6000ᵗʰ yr 2041.53 AD	Gap to 2000ᵗʰ yr	Description of the Events Taking Place in the Specified Event Dates
				Parallel Event Dates in the 2000ᵗʰ, 4000ᵗʰ, and 6000ᵗʰ Years All Separated by 2000 Years
2690.6?? BC	719.29 BC	1253.01 AD	800	2x400 years before the 2000 year event date. All dates involved soon start of exile, tribulation, death.
2296.33?	325.03	1647.3	400	All dates involved tribulation, death, and exile of some sort for the Jewish people.
2099.2	127.9	1844.4	200	Seemingly insignificant event is really important. Each event involved wrestling over true identity of God.
2040.1??	68.77	1903.53	140	Events involved birth or start of some new roll for Gods leaders.
2000.6	29.3	1943.0	100	Dates involve a very serious event that would lead to a major change in the status of the Jewish people and Nation.
1990.79	19.49 BC	1952.81	90	Jubilee year marking the birth of Jacob, the birth of Herod's temple in Jerusalem, and the rebirth of agriculture in Israel with refurbishment of the land and the planting of a huge number of trees.
1971.1??	1.23 AD	1972.53	70	Events mark the return from a period of exile of some sort. Jesus and his family returned to Israel from self-exile in Egypt. The end of a 2800 year exile as a result of the Assyrian destruction of Israel in 719 BC.
1941.5??	30.8	2002.1	40	Jubilee year when major judgments involving exiles and tribulations are made.
1902.07	70.23	2041.53	Yr 6000 In Gentile pattern	2000 year which seems to usher in a period involving major exile and tribulation for the Jewish people.
1892.25?	80.09	2051.39	10 Yr 6000 in Witness pattern	Jubilee years that usher in a time of great change for the Jewish people and nation. Each event seems to involve payback of some sort.
1842.9	129.3	2100.6 ??	60	Last Jubilee before new form of exile begins for the Jewish people. First in slavery, then in the nations and finally in a new promise land.
1833.07 BC	139.23 AD	2110.53?? AD	70	70 years after 2041 and 210 years after 1902 AD. The year when a long period of exile of some sort began.

Key Clues from the Eleven Parallel Events in the Three Two-Thousandth-Year Periods in History

- There are eleven events in a 270-year period surrounding the two thousandth, four thousandth, and six thousandth years in history that are parallel, with all eleven pairs separated by exactly two thousand years and with all pairs thematically tied together. These events all culminate in 2041, the six thousandth year, and all involve exile and great persecution for the Jewish people.
- These events also parallel the theme of end-time events from Bible prophecy.

Demonstrating That the Major Mileposts and Key Events in History Often Occur in Thematically Similar Patterns

We have just finished demonstrating that God seemed to be bringing about his eventual purpose for creating the universe by interacting with his people on earth in a very precise pattern of equally spaced events. What we showed above was only one of a whole myriad of different patterns God has been using. What we would like to demonstrate next is a chart that presents clear evidence that historical events have been intelligently preplanned. We will do so by showing that the mileposts and key events in history have often occurred in evenly spaced time gap patterns with the events having the same topical themes.

We will start our chart with a discussion of how God describes the events that took place in what he calls the "seven days of creation." We have presumed these to be days lasting one thousand years each, since the Bible tells us in two places that one of God's days may last for one thousand years. This led us to presume that God might follow these seven one-thousand-year days of creation with seven one-thousand-year days for man on earth as God brings about his will and purpose for creation. We did notice that the pattern of events taking place led us to believe that the fall of man occurred in the eight hundredth year of the seventh one-thousand-year day of creation. We have thus seen that man's time on earth seems to be divided into patterns lasting both seventy-two hundred and seven thousand years. It seems that the seven-thousand-year patterns start exactly two hundred years after the start of the seventy-two-hundred-year patterns. The following chart reflects both of these two patterns.

We will use five different very long time-gap patterns in our chart that we wouldn't expect to be composed of events that are thematically tied together. We will next present and discuss the five patterns.

1. In the first pattern, we took the seventy-two-hundred-year period from the fall of man until what we might expect to be the start of the eternal state and broke it up into a pattern of four equally spaced periods of eighteen hundred years. This would be four quarters or four seasons for mankind, so to speak. We have often found that God used ninety- or nine-hundred-year periods as seasons. Thus, each eighteen-hundred-year season would be composed of two nine-hundred-year half

seasons. We see that every eighteen-hundred-year event in history signaled a key edict from a supreme leader. In this case, these leaders were God, the Persian King Darius, and the pope. The events all involved a thematically similar action taking place.

2. In the second pattern, we broke the 7,000 years of man into four equal sections of 1,750 years, again representing four seasons for man. This 7,000-year period started at the end of the seventh one-thousand-year day of creation in the year 3873 BC. We see that the 1,750-year events all involved some very key religious leader or religious movement. We noted on the chart that the number 1750 is equal to five periods of 350 years. We also noted that a pattern of 350 years is composed of patterns of both 5x70 and 7x50 years. Thus, the 1750-year pattern would be a super conjunction of patterns of judgment and testing. The 1750-year pattern ends at the very end of the millennium in AD 3027. This is the seven thousandth year of man. Might this pattern be an indication that it would host the mega judgment event referred to in Revelation 20 as the Great White Throne Judgment of all unbelievers of all ages? Since the 350-year pattern that started at the year when the Jewish people first entered the Promised Land in 1399 BC converges in AD 2051, shortly after the six thousandth year of man, could that mean that this might also host a mega judgment for the Jewish people? Might this be the judgment referred to in Daniel 12? Might this judgment end at the start of the soon-coming great family reunion? According to the meanings of the patterns, these would be perfect and complete judgments taking place after extremely long periods of testing.

3. Our third pattern is the two-thousand-year pattern that is within the Gentile two-hundred-year extended family. We have included the five-hundred and one-thousand-year patterns with it since they all seem to reflect God using them for similarly themed purposes. Those purposes involve the birth, death, end of, or breakup of very major religious nations, institutions, leaders, or large periods of influence.

4. The fourth pattern is the incredible four-hundred-year Gentile exile pattern. We included this event pattern in this chart because it is one of God's key punishment patterns, which are the theme of this chapter. This four-hundred-year pattern is within the two-hundred-year Gentile pattern, but it involves the exile of Jewish peoples and nations. The really incredible thing about this pattern is that there are eleven four-hundred-year periods in the forty-four-hundred-year period between the Tower of Babel event in 2296 BC and AD 2041, the year of great tribulation forecast in our patterns, and a full nine of them involve exiles of some sort for God's people.

5. The fifth and final pattern is the Jewish tribulation pattern. We again include this pattern in our chart because it is another one of God's punishment patterns. It is again in the Gentile two-hundred pattern but always involves the Gentiles inflicting the tribulations on the Jews. Tribulation has always been a key part of the lives of the Jewish people. Their very nation came about during a four-hundred-year

period of slavery in Egypt. The tribulation pattern is one of 66.666 or 666.66 years. Every third 66.666 years, the pattern converges with the two-hundred-year pattern, and every third 666.66 years the pattern converges with the two-thousand-year pattern. There are twenty-three event dates in this pattern, and every one involves tribulation of some sort for the Jewish people. The vast number involve going into or continuing periods of tribulation, and a few involve actually coming out of periods of tribulation.

We will now present the chart. We suggest that readers ponder the chart a bit and verify to themselves the comments we make as we introduce the chart. Since we present our analysis of the chart as we are introducing it, we now move on to our next topic.

Demonstrating Clear Evidence That Key Historical Events Have Been Intelligently Pre-Planned by Showing That the Mile-Posts and Key Events Have Often Occurred in Evenly Spaced Time Gap Patterns With the Patterns and Events Having the Same Topical Themes

Key Yrs	1800 Yr: 4 Double 900 Year Seasons, (Major Edicts)	1750 Yr: Start New Season 5x350	2000, 1000, 500, 50G Year Gentile Converge	400 Yr Gentile Exile	666.66 66.66 Yr Tribul-ation	Description of the Events Taking Place in the Specified Years
10,773			1000			God's big BANG; start of creation
9787.3			1000			End day 1: create heavens, earth, light
8801.6			1000			End day 2: create water, clouds
7816.0			1000			End day 3: create seas, land, vegetatn
6830.3			1000			End day 4: earth/moon/solar syst align
5844.7			1000			End day 5: create fish, birds
4859.0			1000			End day 6: create animals, mankind
4070.5	1800		50			Fall of man: 800th year of day 7, rest
3873.4		1750	2000/50	400	666.66	End day 7: start 7 1000 yr days of man
2296.3	1800		50	400	66.666	Start of Tower of Babel event
2148.5		1750	50			Abraham born
1902.1			2000/50	400	666.66	Joseph born; leads to Israelite nation
1836.4					66.666	Tribulation begins for Israelites
1442.1					66.666	Plagues begin in Egypt
1409.2			500/50			Gentile 50 pattern
916.4			1000/50		66.666	Rehoboam dies
719.3			50	400	66.666	Assyrians conquer Israel, exile to nations
587.9					666.66	Babylon destroys City/Temple, Exile people
522.2	1800		50		66.666	King Darius edict allows temple to be rebuilt
423.6		1750	500/50			End of O.T. Exact middle of 7000 yrs
325.0			50	400	66.666	Greeks take control of Judea
62.2					66.666	Romans take control of Judea
4.52 AD					66.666	Judea loses ruling authority
70.2			2000/50	400	666.66	Romans destroy city, Temple; exile people
135.9					66.666	Romans end Bar Kokhba revolt
858.7			50	400	66.666	Pope Nicholas Bull; Jews register, etc.
1055.9			1000/50		66.666	Great Schism in Church
1253.0	1800		50	400	66.666	Pope Innocent Bull allows torture of Jews
1302.3		1750	50			Pope Boniface issues Unam Sanctum bull declaring papal supremacy over national leaders
1450.1			50		66.666	Cardinal requires Jews register, etc.
1647.2			50	400	66.666	Polish massacre of near 100,000 Jews
1844.4			50		66.666	Ottoman Turk decree of toleration for Jews
1975.9					66.666	Massive Russian immigration to Israel
2041.5			2000/50	400	666.66	Patterns may show this being Mid tribulation; all punishment sentences end
2051.4		350				Ends 70th Jubilee year; patterns may show Jesus anointing Millennial Temple
3027.2	1800	1750	1000/50	200	66.666	Ends 7000th and 7200th years of man
3037.0		50				Eternal state of Rev 21-22????

Key Clues from the Demonstration That Mile-stones in History Often Occur in Parallel Events

1. The mega four-hundred-year exile event-pattern strings and 666/66-year tribulation event-pattern strings are both punishment patterns, and both converge in 2041. This confirms our many other clues that point to this year being a very important year in the end-time scenario.

Returning to Earth from the Twilight Zone

We got trapped in the twilight zone for a while, but we finally escaped, so we will get back to our discussion of the history of the Jewish nations and the way all the Jewish nations were destroyed and exiled. The last destruction was the destruction of Judea, and the ensuing exile has just ended in this generation after over eighteen hundred years. We covered the first two destructions of Jewish nations but got stuck in the twilight zone before we got to the third destruction. Thus, we will now get back on track.

Continuing Our Brief History of the Nation of Israel

We started this chapter with a brief description of the history of the Jewish nations and quickly found that Israel began as a united nation called "Israel" after the exodus and began conquering a land inhabited by seven different people groups after a forty-year period of wandering in a wilderness of sorts. After conquering the seven people groups, they remained united until the death of Solomon in 931 BC when they divided overpaying taxes to fund Solomon's building program. Thus, they became two separate nations, Israel in the north and Judah in the south, with Jerusalem being in the southern kingdom.

Israel quickly became enamored with the idols they had learned about to the extent that God allowed the Assyrians to destroy their nation and exile the people, with many escaping to Judah. Judah remained loyal to God for much longer and to a greater extent but eventually became much too friendly with the idols God abhorred, so he also had to destroy their nation. He used the Babylonians to do this. We covered all this in some detail earlier in this chapter.

Judah finally recovered, was punished for 7x40=280 years, ending in 167 BC when the Maccabean revolt resulted in Judah again gaining self-control of their country. They held it until the Romans took control of their country in about 62 BC. That takes us to the time of the next destruction of Jerusalem, the third destruction of a Jewish country, this time Judea, since the Greeks had renamed the country Judea after conquering the Persians in about 325 BC.

God's Use of the Romans to Destroy Judea
and Punish and Exile the Judeans

After the Romans took control of Judea, they became quite oppressive to the extent that in the AD 60s, the Judeans began attempting to regain control of their country. This ended up in disaster as a seven-year war ensued in the years AD 66 to 73, with the city of Jerusalem and the temple being destroyed in AD 70. About a million Jews were killed in the war, and over one hundred thousand were exiled, many back to Rome. The Jews were miserable, and in 129 the Jews revolted against the Romans again under Bar Kokhba. The revolt ended in AD 135–136 with the Romans plowing the Temple Mount, building a temple to Jupiter, and renaming the area Palestine.

We covered most of the key events in this destruction period in the above charts, which described the parallel events between the two thousandth, four thousandth, and six thousandth years after the end of the seventh day of creation. We suggest that the reader go back and review them a bit. The year AD 70, in which the Romans destroyed Jerusalem and the temple, turned out to be the year 4000 since the end of the seventh day of creation. That means the events of this year will be a parallel of events we should expect to take place in the coming year 2041. We would expect that to be the case since all the previous events in the chart that have parallels in our generation have already been fulfilled in an incredible way.

After the nation of Judea ceased to exist in AD 135, the Jewish people eventually ended up living in nations all over the Middle East and Europe. Everywhere they went, the prophecies presented on the king's scroll from Leviticus 26 and Deuteronomy were fulfilled to the utmost detail. The Jews became the most hated people in the world, and they were persecuted over and over in one nation after another for the whole of the eighteen hundred years. Their principal persecutors were the leaders of the Catholic Church all over Europe, both long before and all during the six-hundred-year Catholic Inquisition, which didn't end until the 1800s. Muslim leaders joined them in their hatred. The Jews were kicked out of one country after another, were called "Christ killers," were forced to wear badges to identify themselves, and were often killed in Holocaust events, often involving tens or one hundreds of thousands of people in short periods. Much of this is described in some detail in the charts that contain the 66.666- and two-hundred-year events in history. It is covered much more extensively in the first three books of this series.

How the Events in the Four Thousandth Year
Model End-Time Prophecy from the Bible

Again, in the previous section, we showed how the events in the three two-thousandth-year periods parallel each other in incredible ways. Something we have not yet revealed about these three periods is that they also parallel the events forecast for the end-times in Bible prophecy. The book of Revelation, the last of the sixty-six books in the Bible, is all about the final seven-year period just preceding the Second Coming of Jesus. This is by far the most complete picture of the end-time seven-year tribulation period, but clues to the end-time period are given throughout the Bible, both Old and New Testaments. Many of Jesus's parables were about this period.

The key point we want to make about all this is that the events in the three two-thousand-year periods all follow this model in incredible ways. In fact, the events surrounding the four thousandth year in AD 70 mimic the end-time events so well that many prophetic scholars over the years have concluded that the end-time events were fulfilled in the events surrounding the year AD 70. Many people still believe this, and this theory is called *preterism*. We discussed all the major views of the end-times on our website, Proofthruprophecy.com. I have friends who still apparently hold this viewpoint.

The main point I want to make with this discussion is that if the events surrounding the four thousandth year mirrored the end-time events of Bible prophecy, then the same can be said of the events surrounding the year 6000, which is the year 2041. In fact, my research shows me that the events surrounding the year 2041 mirror the end-time prophecy much more completely than those of the first century.

However, that doesn't necessarily mean Jesus will return in the events surrounding the year 2000 or 2041. It could mean the likelihood that his return will be in some year whose events are in a cycle of two thousand years; then it will have a good probability of being that year. That could be in the eight thousandth, ten thousandth, and so forth year. Late in our research that resulted in this book, we discovered another three possible periods that could host the end-times. These three also host eerily similar sets of parallel events. The incredible thing is that all six sets of events last for periods of 200+70 years. We discovered these patterns when we were trying to develop something we called "God's master template." That is a series of incredible "master patterns" that all span the whole period from the fall of man until the eternal state.

Thus, we will wait until we get to the chapter on the master template to present those master patterns.

Key Clues from the Roman Destruction of Judea in the Four Thousandth Year

- This is the two-thousandth-year period when Jesus's first coming to earth took place. The Jewish people had corporately rejected him as their Messiah and God. Jesus apparently enacted a two-thousand-year judgment of 50x40 years on them in AD 32 from Matthew 23, which started in AD 70 and will end in AD 2041.

Clues from God's punishment event pattern strings can help us answer the five w's associated with our subject questions. What are the coming twin global resets and family reunions, and how are they associated with God meeting the purpose of his will, bringing everything in heaven and earth together in unity under Jesus when time reaches its fulfillment (the end-times, possibly in our generation)?

Clues from God's Punishment-Pattern Strings

Key Clues from the Babylonian and Assyrian Punishment Patterns

- Punishment for all northern kingdom Israelites for 390 years of idol worship will end in AD 2041.
- Punishment for those of the southern kingdom of Judah was enacted in two phases. The first phase ended in the Hanukkah event in 167 BC. The second phase took place after the Romans overtook and ultimately destroyed them. Their punishment was apparently for two thousand years and will end in AD 2041.

Key Clues from the Eleven Parallel Events in the Three Two-Thousandth-Year Periods in History

- There are eleven events in a 270-year period surrounding the two thousandth, four thousandth, and six thousandth years in history that are parallel, with all eleven pairs separated by exactly two thousand years and with all pairs thematically tied together. These events all culminate in 2041, the six thousandth year, and all involve exile and great persecution for the Jewish people.
- These events also parallel the theme of end-time events from Bible prophecy.

Key Clues from the Demonstration That Mile-stones in History Often Occur in Parallel Events

- The mega four-hundred-year exile and 666/66-year tribulations are both punishment patterns, and both converge in 2041.

Key Clues from the Roman Destruction of Judea in the Four Thousandth Year

- This is the two-thousandth-year period when Jesus's first coming to earth took place. The Jewish people had corporately rejected him as their Messiah and God. Jesus apparently enacted a two-thousand-year judgment of 50x40 years on them in AD 32 from Matthew 23, which started in AD 70 and will end in AD 2041.

Key Clues Overall from This Set of Patterns

- Many of the patterns presented above are converging in our generation, especially in AD 2041 and 2051, as shown above. Could this be pointing to our generation being a good fit for the end-time scenario? The clues we find in each of our search areas certainly seem to point in that direction.

The 5 W's Report Card :

CLUES FROM PUNISHMENT EVENT PATTERN STRINGS THAT WILL HELP US BETTER UNDERSTAND END TIME EVENTS, THE UNIFICATION OF EVERYTHING UNDER JESUS, THE DUAL GLOBAL RESETS, DUAL FAMILY REUNIONS AND THEIR POSSIBLE TIE TO OUR GENERATION			
WHO	**WHEN**	**WHERE**	**WHAT EVENT AND WHY**
Israel, Northern Kingdom	Ends in 2041	Israel	**ASSYRIAN PUNISHMENT PATTERN**: Punishment for all Northern Kingdom Israelites for 390 years of idol worship will end in 2041 AD.
Judah, Southern Kingdom	167 BC, Ends in 2041 AD	Israel	**BABYLONIAN PUNISHMENT PATTERN**: Punishment for those of the southern kingdom of Judah was enacted in two phases. A first phase ending in the Hanukkah event in 167 BC. The second phase took place after they were overtaken by the Romans and ultimately destroyed. Their punishment was apparently for 2000 years and will end in 2041.
Israel	Ends in 6000th year, 2041	Baries with years, ends in Israel	**11 PARALLEL EVENTS IN THE 3 2000TH YEAR PERIODS:** There are 11 events in a 270 year period surrounding the 2000th, 4000th and 6000th years in history that are parallel, with all 11 pairs separated by exactly 2000 years and with all pairs thematically tied together. These events all culminate in 2041, the 6000th year, and all involve exile and great persecution for the Jewish people.
Israel	End Times	Israel	These events also parallel the theme of end time events from Bible prophecy.
Israel	Ends in 2041 AD	Israel	**PARALLEL EVENTS IN KEY MILESTONE YEARS:** The maga-400 year exile and 666/66 year tribulations are both punishment patterns and both converge in 2041.
Israel	Ends in 2041 AD	Israel	**ROMAN DESTRUCION OF JUDEA PATTERN:** This is the 4000th year, when Jesus first coming to earth took place. The Jewish people had corporately rejected him as their Messiah and God. Jesus apparently enacted a 2000 year judgment of 50x40 years on them in 32 AD from Matt 23 which started in 70 AD and will end in 2041.

End-Time Prophetic Codes that are Revealed in Hosea, Daniel and the Kingdom Parables that will Bring About the Purpose of God's Will

What We Are Trying to Accomplish in This Chapter

In this chapter, we focus on several of the most incredible end-time prophecies presented in the Bible. We begin with an incredible prophecy Hosea made almost two hundred years before Daniel. Hosea gave us a prophecy of the whole future history of both Israel and Judah that proceeds all the way into the end-times. We next go to three specific end-time prophecies Daniel the prophet made and go into a few possible applications of those prophecies, which may be tied to some of our basic event-pattern strings.

Jesus cited Daniel in Matthew 24 and thus gave his prophecies significant credibility. Daniel was a high-profile youngster in the first wave of exiles of Jews to Babylon in about 605 BC. He became a very high-ranking official in the governments of Babylon for many years up to and including the reign of Cyrus in the 530s BC. Daniel was the Old Testament prophet and historian, and John the apostle was the New Testament prophet and historian who made us aware that God always uses a 360-day-per-year calendar throughout the whole of the Bible. This is critical for the proper understanding and interpreting of the dating of events and periods in the Bible, including all genealogies, time gaps, and so forth.

Finally, we will turn to eighteen prophetic end-time prophecies Jesus made in the book of Matthew. In Matthew 13, Jesus told his disciples and thus us as well how to interpret his parables. He explained that all his parables made extensive use of figures of speech or symbolic language. He gave the disciples, and thus us again, examples of how he did this and how to interpret them. Despite knowing they can still be difficult to understand without significant background in the right biblical topics, Jesus gives us many clues about the specific end-time events including the rapture, the Second Coming, the seven-year tribulation period, the end-time judgments, and so forth. We will now begin this exploratory adventure into Hosea's end-time prophecies.

We have been seeing the year AD 2041 crop up in an alarming number of the models, event-pattern strings, and so forth, which we have been investigating in our search for clues concerning the nature, themes, and timing of end-time events. Will we continue to find this as we investigate a few more key end-time prophecies in this chapter? If the years surrounding 2041 keep appearing, that will give us significant evidence that our generation is a very good candidate for fulfilling the end-time prophetic scenario.

We will now begin our search for clues in those prophecies, starting with a study of Hosea's two-days-equal-two-thousand-years prophecy.

Section 1

Hosea's Two-Days-Equal-Two-Thousand-Years End-Time Prophetic Pattern Leading to the Year AD 2041.5

Hosea was an Old Testament prophet in the period of about 785–720 BC. In the book of Hosea, God expresses his ultimate desire for his people. He tells them that they have abandoned him to pursue idol worship. He tells them that very serious consequences await them if they do not return to him. These consequences include their destruction, loss of their land and a long period in exile among the nations. This warning includes both Judah and Israel. God further reveals a prophetic word to them about Jesus's First and Second Comings, about his return to heaven after his First Coming, and finally about the events and circumstances surrounding their eventual return to him. We will present and analyze Hosea 5:13–6:6 so we can get the full context.

- When Ephraim saw his sickness, and Judah his sores, then Ephraim turned to Assyria, and sent to the great king for help. But he is not able to cure you, not able to heal your sores. For I will be like a lion to Ephraim, like a great lion to Judah. I will tear them to pieces and go away; I will carry them off, with no one to rescue them. Then I will return to my lair until they have borne their guilt and seek my face—in their misery they will earnestly seek me. (Hos. 5:13–15)
- Come, let us return to the Lord. He has torn us to pieces but he will heal us; he has injured us but he will bind up our wounds. *After two days he will revive us; on the third day he will restore us, that we may live in his presence.* Let us acknowledge the Lord; let us press on to acknowledge him. As surely as the sun rises, he will appear; he will come to us like the winter rains, like the spring rains that water the earth. What can I do with you, Ephraim? What can I do with you, Judah? Your love is like the morning mist, like the early dew that disappears. Therefore I cut you in pieces with my prophets, I killed you with the words of my mouth— then my judgments go forth like the sun. For I desire mercy, not sacrifice, and acknowledgment of God rather than burnt offerings. As at Adam they have broken the covenant; they were unfaithful to me there. (Hos. 6:1–7 emphasis added)

This passage had both historical and prophetic implications for the Jewish people. Historically, it was a warning to the Jews about what was soon going to happen to them because of their unfaithfulness to God. Prophetically speaking, its ultimate fulfillment will be in the end-time tribulation, the Second Coming of Jesus, and the millennium. This passage was written shortly before the Assyrians conquered Israel in 719 BC and carried them away into captivity. They were essentially scattered among the nations and wouldn't exist as a nation called Israel again until the year AD 1948. In this passage, we see the following prophetic message:

1. Both Israel and Judah would be conquered and the people scattered among the nations.

2. Jesus, the lion of the tribe of Judah, would be responsible for enacting this judgment against the Jews for their unfaithfulness in both cases.

3. After Jesus accomplished his mission on earth, many years later during his first coming as a suffering servant for man, he would go away; he would return to his lair, to his home in heaven with the Father.

4. Jesus will then remain in heaven until the Jews admit their guilt and earnestly seek him as their Savior.

5. In the latter stages of the end-time tribulation, when the Jews finally recognize that Jesus is the only one who can save them, they finally call on him as their Messiah and Savior. See Matthew 23:39 and Psalm 118:26 from the tabernacles celebration. Also see Zechariah 12:10; 13:9.

6. Jesus will wait for two days, then return to save them from total destruction on the third day, modeling his death and resurrection.

7. Jesus will restore the Jews to their Promised Land and live on earth with them during the one thousand years of the millennium (Rev. 20:1–7).

8. Just as surely as the summer and winter rains meet the needs of the earth's crops, so too will Jesus meet the needs of those he has planted. They will produce a bountiful harvest, this time a soul harvest.

9. I interpret Hosea 6:6 to be telling us that Jesus wants the following of the Jews and us:

Jesus's real interest is not in sacrifices and burnt offerings in and of themselves. His real interest is in having us express our love for him through (1) our faithfulness to him; (2) our loving-kindness and goodness to our family, friends, and neighbors; and (3) our honoring him through acknowledging our remembrance of and thankfulness for what he did for us through our belief in him, through acknowledging that he is the one and only God of the universe, and by placing him above everything else.

Jesus quoted this passage, Hosea 6:6, in Matthew 12:7 during his encounter with the Pharisees, in which he accused them of committing the unpardonable sin. He basically told them that if they understood this Hosea passage, they would recognize that he was their Messiah, their God. He told them in somewhat veiled terms that this was an old covenant prophecy of his first coming to earth. He was the fulfillment of this prophecy.

Prophetic passages such as this often have double or multiple fulfillments. The obvious fulfillment concerning 6:2 is that Jesus will return at his Second Coming during the Feast of Tabernacles when the Jews finally accept him as their Savior and Messiah when they call for him, Jesus, to come to earth to save them as they repeat Psalm 118:26, "Blessed is he who comes in the name of the Lord," as Jesus prophesied in Matthew 23:39.

However, there is also a second possible interpretation, a second fulfillment if you will, of this passage in Hosea 6:2. That fulfillment involves the fifth and sixth one-thousand-year days of man. You will recall from our study of the one thousand sequential year date pattern that there are exactly six one-thousand-year periods from 3873.37 BC to AD 2041.5. You will also recall that the fourth one-thousand-year day ended in AD 70.2 with the destruction of Jerusalem and the temple. Going back to Matthew 23 and continuing into Matthew 24, where Jesus prophesied that he would return to save the Jews when they repeated Psalm 118:26, we see the context being a prophecy by Jesus that the generation of that time would live to see the destruction taking place in AD 66–73. That destruction is one of the most important events in all Jewish history. Again, it marked the end of the fourth one-thousand-year day of man.

We know Jesus was aware that this passage in Hosea 5–6 was a prophecy of his coming to earth from Matthew 12:7, where he tells the Pharisees that if they understood this passage, they would know he was the Messiah. So we have Jesus's personal confirmation of what this passage is all about. Now let's go back to the second fulfillment. Hosea and Jesus may also be referring to the two days as two-thousand-year days and the third day as another thousand-year day. In that case, we see the following:

1. Jesus would return after two one-thousand-year days. That would be in the year ending in AD 2041.5. Hosea 6:2 says, "After two days he will revive us; on the third day he will restore us, that we may live in his presence." That might be saying that after two thousand years Jesus would *revive the Jews*, meaning that they would *return from spiritual death* in that they would finally become believers in him and *receive his Spirit within them*.

2. Then on the third day, they would *be restored*, in that they would be in his physical presence again. This day would start in AD 2041.5 and would include the one thousand years we refer to as "the millennium." Revelation 20 tells us six different times, once each in verses 2–7, that this lasts for one thousand years.

3. This interpretation is hugely confirmed by the punishment patterns we presented in chapter 6. There we saw that all the punishment sentences God had given each of his nations—Israel, Judah, and Judea—will be ending in the two-hundred-year period from AD 1844 to AD 2041. We recall that Israel's punishment was for 2,800 years, Judah's for 2,520 years, and Judea's for 2,000 years; and all these finally end in the year AD 2041. The last punishment was exactly two thousand years or two days in God's timetable, since to him both Isaiah and Peter tell us that two days to God can be like two thousand years to man. We recall in Hosea 5:15, which we quoted above, that God said Jesus would return to his lair, his home in heaven, until the Jews had borne their guilt. When will the Jews have finally borne all their guilt according to this? It will be in the period surrounding the year AD 2041.

Something else that is so compelling about this interpretation is that it merges with an extraordinary number of other patterns and prophecies in the year 2041.5. A final compelling argument is that exactly one thousand years later, in the year 3027.2, there is another huge confluence of patterns merging, and that is also the year of convergence of the seventh one-thousand-year day of man and the seventy-two hundredth year after the fall of man.

We will now present a chart that shows a possible way in which the key first-century dates might be repeated in our generation, with each of the events being separated by exactly two thousand God years.

Projecting the End Time Scenario onto Parallel Events
Surrounding the 4000th and 6000th Years

Original Event Date	Original Key First Century Events	Original Event Dates (+1971.3 Yrs)	Series Of Prophetic End Time Events Which Precisely Fit the 2000 Year Pattern Convergence Taking Place in our Generation
	HISTORICAL SCENARIO 1		PROPHETIC SCENARIO 1
66.7	Start 7 yr Roman/Jewish war. Judean groups attack Roman sites in north Galilee due to harsh treatment by the new Roman Emperor. The Romans retaliate starting the Roman/Jewish war, a 7 year period of Tribulation for the Jews.	2038.0	Start 7 yr end time tribulation. Christmas season; Rapture?? End time encounters start?? Pattern fits precisely but it may be just another intermediate fit (every 2000 yrs?).
3.30 BC + 69= 66.7 1.23 AD +65.71= 66.7	The Roman/Jewish war starts 70 yrs after Jesus conception and 66.66 years after Jesus and his family returned from self-exile in Egypt in 1.23 AD.	1969 AD +69= 2038.0 1972.5+ 65.71= 2038.0	1968-69 started the Hong-Kong worldwide pandemic. If 2038 finally starts the end time scenario, a war would erupt and then the Antichrist would enact a 7 year peace treaty between Israel and her attackers.
66.7+ 3.45= 70.2 Yr 4000	At the mid- point of the 7 year Roman-Jewish war the siege of Jerusalem begins. Nero is a type of antichrist.	2038.0+ 3.45= 2041.5 Yr 6000	At the mid- point of the 7 year tribulation; the antichrist takes control, seizes Jerusalem?
70.23 + 5 mo = 70.6	Time of the destruction of the temple and city of Jerusalem. The abomination of desolation takes place in the temple on the 9th of Av.	2041.5+ 5 mo = 2041.9	Time of the fifth trumpet judgment which involves death, resurrection and rapture of the two witnesses and tribulation saints. Killing of all believers is akin to destroying God's spiritual temple.
70.23+ 3.45= 73.7	Siege of Masada by the Roman army begins. Fall of last Jewish stronghold and of Masada, ends the 7 year Roman-Jewish war.	2041.5+ 3.45= 2046.0	Satan and antichrist mobilize a huge army in attempt to destroy Israel. If the pattern holds, then 2nd Coming, Armageddon, defeat of Satan and his followers takes place.
73.7+ 2300 days= 80.1 Jubilee	End of 30th Jubilee, 2300 days after the end of the 7 yr war; first Jubilee without a temple. Eruption of Mt. Vesuvius destroys idol worshipping temples.	2045.0+ 2300 days= 2051.4 Jubilee	Millennium beginning 75 days later in 2045.19, Dan 12. End of 70th Jubilee 2300 days later. First Jubilee in new temple in the millennium? Temple anointed?

If we use the first-century seven-year tribulation as a model, we see that 70.23 was the exact middle of the seven-year period. Starting at the exact end of the seven-year period, we see that is 3.45 years after 70.23, and if we go forward exactly 6.9 years, we come to the exact time of the next Jubilee year or AD 80.07. There are exactly twenty-three hundred days between these two events. Likewise, if we go exactly 3.45 after 2041.53, we come to 2044.98, which is exactly twenty-three hundred days before the next Jubilee year, 2051.39. We will see much more on these twenty-three hundred days in the next topic.

The tribulation period will last exactly seven years, according to Daniel 9 and 12. Thus, the Second Coming would be included in the seven-year period. It would very likely be the last event in the seven-year period. However, there are still several events that must take place before the millennium begins, including the sheep-goat judgment of Matthew 25:31–46. Daniel 12 says there is another seventy-five-day period at the exact end of the seven-year period. He further says that a very blessed event will take place at the end of this seventy-five-day period. The events within the seventy-five-day period would likely include the soul harvest of Revelation 14 and the sheep-goat judgment. The event at the end of the seventy-five-day period would likely be the start of the one-thousand-year millennial kingdom of Revelation 20.

Again, as in the first-century model, there would be exactly twenty-three hundred days between the end of the seven-year tribulation period and the next Jubilee year. This works out perfectly on the calendar in both cases. This twenty-three-hundred-day period was prophesied in Daniel 8:13–14. *It is certainly possible that any first-century parallel events taking place between 2038 and 2051 may simply involve another punishment for Israel for not accepting Jesus as their Messiah. This would not necessarily involve the Second Coming and the start of the millennium.* Mathematically speaking, there are similar parallel patterns every two thousand years, and those key events may still be far in the future.

Might Hosea's Two-Days-Equal-Two-Thousand-Years End-Time Prophetic Pattern End in Our Generation in 2041?

Perhaps we should consider this prophetic pattern to be a bit speculative on our part. However, it does fit with so many of the other end-time prophetic patterns that it is difficult for us to dismiss it. It could certainly be coincidental, but there are too many of these types of patterns for them to be mere coincidence. Again, we see the year 2041 being closely associated with the end date in our scenario. In this case, it fits the midpoint of the end-time seven-year tribulation period perfectly. We also see that it provides a perfect fit for the twenty-three-hundred-days prophecy of Daniel 8:14.

Thus, the answer to our question concerning 2041 is a resounding yes!

Might All This Speculation Lead Us to the First Possible Dates for the Coming Twin Global Resets and Family Reunions?

We may have finally found our first candidates for the times of the twin global resets and family reunions. The family reunions may be at the time of the rapture when there will be a reunion in heaven of all past and then present believers in Jesus. This will be the family of God and the coming bride of Jesus. The second will be at the time of the seventieth Jubilee. All saints will come back to earth at the Second Coming at Armageddon. The reason for the family reunion, as we will see in our next topic, is that Jesus will apparently be anointing the millennial temple at that time, and all saints will be required to be there, according to Zechariah 14.

The time for the global resets could be at the time when the Antichrist declares himself to be God and the ruler of the whole earth in the middle of the seven-year period. This will be an evil-inspired kingdom of unbelievers in Jesus. The second global reset will be at the time of the Second Coming of Jesus when he becomes King of Kings over the whole earth and starts reigning for one thousand years on earth. We will continue to look for possible confirmation of these events and their time frames as we move forward.

Clues from Hosea's Prophetic Topics:

- If we are properly interpreting the symbolic language used in Hosea's prophecy, we can see that Israel would be destroyed because of the sins of the Jewish people, principally for not accepting Jesus, and that he would basically abandon them for two days before he returned to save them. If these two days are two thousand years of abandonment from God, starting in the seven years surrounding AD 70, then that means Jesus will return in the seven-year period surrounding AD 2041. In the scenario painted, that would be at the end of the year AD 2044. We will see in coming prophecies that this greatly aids in answering our three key questions.
- If we project the six key events taking place, starting with the beginning of the seven-year Roman/Jewish war surrounding AD 70.23 and ending in the Jubilee year ten years later onto our generation two thousand years later, we can come up with a perfect fit for the prophesied end-time scenario. This also leads us to discover a possibility for all three of our great family reunions. They would occur at the rapture, shortly after the end of the seven-year period and at the seventieth Jubilee celebration in 2051. More later.

Section 2

Cracking Daniel's Three Amazing End-Time Prophecy Codes

Daniel is the sixth century BC prophet who gave us three incredible, yet seemingly impossible to interpret, formulas that would apparently lead to the dates of three very important end time events if we could properly interpret them. The huge problem is that the formulas are easy enough to understand but we do not know where to start in applying them. These three formulas and the events that they lead us to are as follows:

1. The 2300 days prophecy that leads to the anointing of the millennial temple in Israel,
2. the 7+62+1 prophecy that leads to the mid-point of the end time seven year period of tribulation, and
3. the 1260+1260+30+45 prophecy that leads to the start of the millennium.

The problem in solving all three prophetic formulas or codes is that there seems to be one or more missing pieces of information that would be necessary to properly use the formulas. However, we may have hit the jackpot. In this four book ET 2041 series we have discovered a huge database of incredible equally-spaced similarly-themed event patterns that along with a huge database of applicable event dates that when taken together may allow us to finally crack Daniel's end-time code. We will present our research and conclusions in this section. There will be some redundancy since we wanted to make our points in multiple ways to add some credibility to our speculations. Thus we should call these code-breaking efforts a bit speculative.

Our first investigation will center on Daniel's twenty-three-hundred-days prophecy in Daniel 8. We will then proceed to a possible alternate way to interpret the Daniel 9:24–27 prophecy, which leads to both the date of the crucifixion of Jesus during his first coming and the time of the seven-year period of tribulation, which will host his Second Coming to earth.

Daniel's Prophetic Topic 1

The End-Time Twenty-Three-Hundred-Days Prophetic Pattern

We discovered years ago that it's extremely difficult to correctly understand and interpret the twenty-three-hundred-days prophecy of Daniel 8:14. However, during our recent date pattern studies, we finally found a possible fit. It is a precise fit, as you will see in the scenario we will discuss below. I have tried several times over the last few years to find a fit for the twenty-three-hundred-days prophecy of the end-times but with no success. Many prophecy scholars have tried using these twenty-three hundred days as years. I have not seen any proposed fulfillment that looked compelling to me, so I have kept looking. I believe the end-time date patterns we have discovered may possibly lead us to the correct answer.

I believe this might be *the rest of the story for the twenty-three-hundred-days prophecy.* It occurred to me that I should try fitting the twenty-three hundred days into the end of the two-days-equal-two-thousand-years prophecy of Hosea 5:14—6:3 as I had interpreted it earlier. I had been puzzling for over a year about the significance of the ten-year period between the key dates of 2041.53 and 2051.39. I had certainly observed that there was another pair of dates exactly ten years apart and separated from these dates by one thousand years. There was a large number of sequential year date patterns converging on all four of these dates, 2041.53–2051.39 and 3027.18–3037.04. Again, the first dates in these pairs are the sixth and seventh one-thousand-year days of man.

I could easily understand a possible scenario with the second set being the end of the millennium, with ten years at the end, during which Satan will be freed on earth for a short period followed by the final judgments, with the eternal state beginning in 3037.0. This fits the scenario painted in Revelation 20–22 quite nicely. The first set of dates was a little harder to conceive, but I had an idea. The millennium will need to start sometime early during the ten-year period, and there will need to be some time for several events that seem to take place or at least start shortly after the Second Coming. These are the sheep-goat judgment of Matthew 25:31–46, the renewal of the earth's environment after the terrible tribulation events, the dividing and allocating of the Promised Land to God's people, and the building of the city and temple of Ezekiel 40–48. After the temple is completed, there will be an anointing, as mentioned in Daniel 8:14. Then there will be a requirement for people from all over the world to come to Israel for a celebration. Zechariah 14:16 mentions this. My guess is that the anointing and first millennial celebration will take place in 2050–51, which is a Jubilee year. All this activity could certainly fill up the time frame between 2045 and 2051.

I could easily see the seventy-five days of Daniel 12 taking place immediately after the Second Coming and including the very important sheep-goat judgment. This will be necessary for Jesus to determine whom he will allow to enter the millennium. This could certainly be included within the twenty-three-hundred-day period and could even start the twenty-three-hundred-day period.

My big discovery was that it is exactly twenty-three hundred days or 6.39 years between 2044.98 and 2051.39, with exactly 3.45 years preceding this in the period between 2044.98 and 2041.53, our target date. That is exactly one-half of the 7- or 6.9-year tribulation period. Could that mean that 2041.53 will be the exact middle of the tribulation period? This is the exact time when Daniel 9:24–27 says the Antichrist will go into the newly rebuilt temple in Jerusalem, declare he is God (2 Thess. 2:4), and begin attacking the Jewish people to completely exterminate them. This well-documented Bible prophecy is included on my website (Proofthruprophecy.com) under the topic of Revelation.

If all this mathematics involving dates is a coincidence, it is quite a coincidence. Again, we have already presented this information on a chart in the pattern concerning two thousand years representing two days as a fulfillment of the Hosea prophecy mentioned above. In that chart, we showed the twenty-three-hundred-day gap with no discussion. Also, if you go back to that chart, you can easily see there are six events in the pattern. You can also see that the sequence of times between the events matches the biblical prophecies to the very month. This is astounding, but the really astounding thing is that this is happening over and over, pattern after pattern. Something is going on here!

So we see that we have identified a twenty-three-hundred-day gap in our end-time scenario. However, does it fit the time gap identified in Daniel? In Daniel 8, verses 17 and 25 make it clear that the vision being presented concerns the end-times. This passage in Daniel seems to say that these twenty-three hundred days go from Armageddon and the

Second Coming up to the time of the dedication of the millennial temple. This fits the period from 2044.98 to 2051.39 perfectly. It is then 3.45 years back to 2041.5. This is half of the 7- or 6.9-year period and fits the exact time of the temple abomination from Daniel 9:24–27. This places the peace treaty negotiated by the Antichrist three and a half years earlier in 2038.08.

That leaves us with the question: "What peace treaty?" The prophecy in Ezekiel 38 presents an attack on Israel shortly before the start of the tribulation period.

In the chart in the previously presented two-days-equal-two-thousand-years pattern, we can also see that this scenario also fits the seven-year tribulation the Jews underwent in the Roman-Jewish War of AD 66–73. In fact, that scenario is likely a model for and precursor of the final end-time tribulation period. We have presented one possible take on that model in the chart. The dates we show for the events in the first-century Roman-Jewish war seem to match the historical accounts fairly well. The gaps between the dates in the end-time scenario model what we see presented in Bible prophecy. This model seems to fit much too well to be a coincidence. All the dates are precisely two thousand God years apart.

We have noted that it is apparently twenty-three hundred days from Armageddon to the dedication and anointing of the millennial temple. If we divide the twenty-three hundred days by 360 to get the exact number of years in the time gap, we get the following number of God years in twenty-three hundred days: 6.3888888888 years.

The string of *8s* running into infinity may signal that this event represents a new beginning for God's people.

Might Daniel's Twenty-Three-Hundred-Days End-Time Prophetic Pattern Be Associated with Our Generation and 2041?

We presented this in the previous topic, Hosea's two-days-equal-two-thousand-years end-time prophecy. We saw there as well as in this topic that if the year 2041.5 is the mid-point of the seven-year tribulation period, then there is a twenty-three-hundred-day gap from the end of the seven-year period until the end of the seventieth Jubilee year period in 2051.4. Thus, we again see 2041 being a very key date in another of our patterns. This time it is not the end of the pattern, but it is closely associated with the pattern.

Thus, the answer to our question concerning 2041 is a resounding yes!

Daniel's Prophetic Topic 2

Daniel's 9:24–27 Prophetic 7+62+1 7's Pattern; God's Multi-use Pattern Which May Lead to Both the First Coming of Jesus and the End-time Seven Year Period

The incredible prophetic book of Daniel may be the book that finally leads to a clear understanding of the end-times that the world is approaching. Daniel was a first-hand observer of much of the Babylonian captivity pattern as it was unfolding. He observed most of it from Babylon, since he was part of the first exile of Judeans to Babylon. This took place in 606–605 BC as part of the initial conquering of Judah by Nebuchadnezzar and the Babylonians.

Daniel was a contemporary of both Jeremiah and Ezekiel, two other key prophets during the Babylonian crisis. Jeremiah was the prophet who forecasted that the first exile would last seventy years, and he did so before it began. He lived in Jerusalem as Nebuchadnezzar and the Babylonians conquered the city and nation. He observed it all and prophesied many of the events that would happen and the reason for them. He was never exiled to Babylon, but he was left behind. He eventually moved to Egypt, where he spent several years in self-imposed exile, so to speak. His book is a compelling read.

Ezekiel was the other key prophet of this period of exile in Babylon. He was part of the second wave of exiles to Babylon in 597 BC. He wrote his complete book while in exile in Babylon. He is the one who prophesied the destruction of Jerusalem and the temple. He was also the key prophet who told us that God would punish the Judeans in three separate ways, and God gave him a formula, which, together with Leviticus 26, can be used to calculate how long each punishment would last. These are in his chapters 4–5.

Daniel also wrote his complete book while he was in exile in Babylon, but circumstances described in his book tell us he didn't remain an exile for long. You see, he did some spectacular things for King Nebuchadnezzar that led to Daniel becoming second in command in Babylon. He essentially remained in a very high position for nearly all his approximately seventy-five years in Babylon.

Daniel is the prophet who gave us three of the most incredible and unbelievable prophecies in the Bible. The first of these was a prophecy of every major kingdom that would dominate the world throughout its future history. He gave so many details of these future kingdoms that critics and scholars have tried unsuccessfully to prove Daniel could not have written them. He also gave us a formula in Daniel 9:24–27 that forecast the coming of the Messiah and the exact date when he would be killed (April, AD 32). Of course, it was accurate to the very month. We will next present an analysis of the details of that incredible prophecy.

Analysis of Daniel's Seventy-Sevens

Daniel was written near the end of Israel's seventy-year Babylonian captivity in the sixth century BC. The angel Gabriel gave Daniel several prophecies, which would not be fulfilled at the end of the seventy-year captivity but after a future seven-times-seventy-year period. The prophecies involved Daniel's people and holy city, the Israelites, and Jerusalem.

Daniel's seventy-sevens prophecy in Daniel 9:24–27 is an excellent place to begin presenting God's patterns that use time gaps in years between key events God specifically presented in the Bible. This example gives us a prophetic outline of the history of Judah (Israel) and Jerusalem. This outline goes from about 444 BC, when the decree to rebuild Jerusalem was issued, until Jesus returned at the end to destroy sin and establish everlasting righteousness. This outline is the key to understanding end-time prophecy.

Details of the end-times are given throughout the rest of the Bible with a little given here, a little there, as Isaiah says (Isa. 28:10–13). It remains for prophecy scholars to fill these details into their proper places on Daniel's timeline. This is very difficult to do since the prophecies are so extensive, so spread out, and at times so cryptic. God did this on purpose so there would be some mystery to it and to keep us interested and ready for his return. Another result is that not all scholars agree on the interpretation. We'll concentrate on the interpretation I consider most likely to be correct. We will present the prophecy verse by verse and then provide our commentary on that verse.

Daniel 9:24 says, "Seventy 'sevens' are decreed for your people and your holy city to finish transgression, to put an end to sin, to atone for wickedness, to bring in everlasting righteousness, to seal up vision and prophecy and to anoint the most holy place."

In this model, the term "seventy sevens" represents 490 years. It says that at the end of the 490 years, several things would be different: (1) There would be no more transgression against God, (2) there would be no more sin, (3) the price for all past wickedness would already have been paid, (4) there would be eternal righteousness, (5) there would no longer be a need for visions and prophecies, and (6) Jesus would be anointed king. This is a description of the beginning of the millennial kingdom right after the Second Coming at the end of the seven-year period of great tribulation. In summary, this verse says that the Jewish people will have seventy periods of seven years each, or 490 years total, to fellowship with God before the millennial kingdom begins.

Daniel 9:25 says, "Know and understand this: From the issuing of the decree to restore and rebuild Jerusalem until the Anointed One, the ruler, comes, there will be seven 'sevens,' and sixty-two 'sevens.' It will be rebuilt with streets and a trench, but in times of trouble."

This verse gives the prophesied date when the ruler, the messiah, would first come to earth. The date is described as being at the end of a time interval. The interval starts with the decree to rebuild Jerusalem and lasts for seven and sixty-two sevens or 483 years. Let's look back in history to see when this decree was issued. The issuing of the decree to rebuild Jerusalem is described in Nehemiah 2:1–8, 17. Nehemiah tells us that the decree was issued in the month of Nisan in the twentieth year of King Artaxerxes, king of Persia. This would have been in March 444 BC.

Let's look at a little more background to help put things in perspective. Babylon, which was then the dominant kingdom on earth, conquered Judah in 606 BC. The Babylonian conquest of Judah continued until Jerusalem and the temple were destroyed in 586 BC. The Jews were carried away to exile in Babylon in waves, with Daniel apparently being in the first wave in 606 BC. The exile lasted for seventy years, as Jeremiah prophesied in Jeremiah 25:11–12. Persia later conquered Babylon under Cyrus the Great in 539–538 BC, as both Jeremiah and Daniel prophesied. Daniel was on the court of Cyrus and had his confidence. Cyrus decreed that the temple in Jerusalem could be rebuilt, as described in Ezra 1–7. He also decreed that the seventy-year Jewish captivity be ended (Ezra 1).

Only about fifty thousand Jews returned to their homes since many were very happy with the lives they had developed during their seventy years in Babylon. In fact, Daniel stayed in Babylon and continued serving on the court of Cyrus. The Jewish exiles returned to their land in four waves: (1) In 537 BC under Sheshbazzar, who was made governor of Judah, when rebuilding of the temple began; (2) in 525 BC under Zerubbabel and Joshua, the high priest discussed in Zechariah; (3) in approximately 456 BC when

Ezra returned with exiles and royal authority to renew religious practices in Jerusalem; and (4) in 444 BC when Nehemiah returned with King Artaxerxes's blessings and the means to rebuild the walls of Jerusalem and the city itself. It's obvious from a reading of Nehemiah and Ezra that the rebuilding was done in a "time of trouble" since they had much resistance and trouble during the work period.

The prophecy further says that the ruler would come in seven-plus sixty-two periods of seven years after the decree to restore Jerusalem. We know from the above that this decree was issued on 1 Nisan or March 14, 444 BC on our calendar. In those days, important events were reckoned on the first of the month. In the accompanying definitions, we see that sixty-nine periods of seven years after the decree would end on April 6, AD 32. This is the very day Jesus was declared King of the Jews on Palm Sunday. This has to be one of the most amazing prophecies in the Bible.

Daniel 9:26 says, "After the sixty-two 'sevens,' the Anointed One will be cut off and will have nothing. The people of the ruler who will come will destroy the city and the sanctuary. The end will come like a flood: War will continue until the end, and desolations have been decreed."

Daniel went on to prophesy that the Anointed One (Jesus the Messiah) would be cut off (killed) and would have nothing, possibly meaning that he wouldn't have any of his legal rights and/or earthly possessions. We know his legal rights were violated repeatedly during his trials and execution. Despite the unfairness of this, he did not defend himself. He was guilty in that he was standing in for us, paying the penalty for the sins of all mankind past, present, and future. We also know he had no earthly possessions, in that his clothing was taken by casting lots (Ps. 22:18; Matt. 27:35). Philippians 2:7 also says Jesus made himself nothing and became a servant man for us.

Starting on this very Palm Sunday, the Jewish nation was put into timeout again (Luke 19:42–44) as they had been a couple of times in the Old Testament. When this happened, God seemed to ignore the Jews until they returned to him. He even quit counting these years when he made prophecies of coming events involving Israel. This happened again in Daniel's prophecy of the future of Israel. God apparently quit counting them in his prophetic timetable and won't start again until the beginning of the final seven years, during which Israel will finally accept Jesus as their Savior.

Jesus and Paul spoke of the Jews being blinded during this time. Paul spent a lot of time on this subject, especially in the book of Romans. This gap has now reached over two thousand years (360-day years), and we are still counting. The Jewish nation won't be back on God's clock until the final seven years begin, at which time their blindness will be removed. We know this because if God is counting their time in his prophetic timetable, he has renewed his fellowship with them. Revelation 7 and 14 speak of the one hundred forty-four thousand Jews who will become believers in Jesus and have God's seal placed on them during this period. These one hundred forty-four thousand may become soul winners for Jesus. Despite the fact that their blindness will be removed, it will still take several years for many Jews to accept Jesus for who he is. It is three days from the end before they finally call on Jesus to return and save them from their enemies

(Hos. 5:14—6:2). Paul told us that their blindness will be removed when God is satisfied with the number of Gentiles who have become believers (Rom. 11:25).

However, Daniel made one additional prophecy concerning Israel that would be fulfilled before the final seven years. This concerns the destruction of Jerusalem and the temple, which occurred in AD 70. This involved Titus and the Roman army completely destroying the city and temple as Jesus prophesied in Luke 19:41–44. In fact, Jesus said the reason for the destruction was because the Jews hadn't recognized Daniel's prophecies and hadn't recognized who he was. Daniel even said who would do the destruction, "the people of the ruler to come." The people were the Romans, which implies that the coming ruler or Antichrist will come from the remains of the Roman Empire.

Daniel now jumps to the end-times and says the end will come like a flood. What do you suppose this means? How fast and completely can people be overcome by a flood? Jesus and Paul told us repeatedly to stay ready because the end could come at any time. The end will involve wars and complete desolations, as Daniel told us. Many chapters and pages in the Old Testament books of prophecy detail these wars and who will be involved in them. Let's move on to the end of Daniel's prophecy.

Daniel 9:27 says, "He will confirm a covenant with many for one 'seven.' In the middle of the 'seven' he will put an end to sacrifice and offering. And on a wing he will set up an abomination that causes desolation, until the end that is decreed is poured out on him."

Daniel said that at the beginning of the final seven-year period before the millennium, the ruler or Antichrist, as he is sometimes referred to, will establish a peace treaty with Israel and others. However, this will last only three and a half years. At that time, he will force the Jews to stop worshipping God in their temple and worship him there instead (2 Thess. 2:3–4). This means the temple in Jerusalem must be rebuilt before this can happen. My understanding is that plans are in place for this rebuilding, and the implements of worship have largely been collected. We are awaiting the arrival of this world ruler, who will declare peace and provide means for the rebuilding of the temple.

We know that the ruler would require that false gods be worshipped in the temple, since that is the historical meaning of the term "an abomination that causes desolation." This happened in 167 BC when Antiochus Epiphanes, the ruler of the northern Greek kingdom, sacrificed a pig on the altar of the temple in Jerusalem. This resulted in the Maccabean revolt when Judas Maccabeus and his brothers led a successful revolt and recaptured the city and temple. The temple was rededicated, and the date is still celebrated today as Hanukkah. The Maccabees continued to rule in Judea from 163 to 37 BC, although the area came under Roman dominance in 63/62 BC. Another abomination of desolation occurred in AD 70 (Luke 21:5–7, 20–22) when the Romans under Titus destroyed the city and temple.

This is the basic outline of end-time prophecy as Daniel provided. Jesus gave this prophecy credibility in Matthew 24:15. The one very major event Daniel didn't discuss was the rapture. That's because it involves the church, which was a hidden mystery in the Old Testament.

This prophecy God gave to Daniel was truly supernatural. Daniel was given a prophecy of a time gap between key future events. The starting event in the pattern would take

---

place about eighty-five years after the death of Daniel, and the closing event in the pattern would be seven times sixty-nine years after the starting event. This took place precisely according to the prophecy, even to the very day. The fulfillment of this prophecy has been a life changer for many people.

Summary Chart of Daniel's Seventy Weeks Prophecy

DANIEL'S TIMELINE

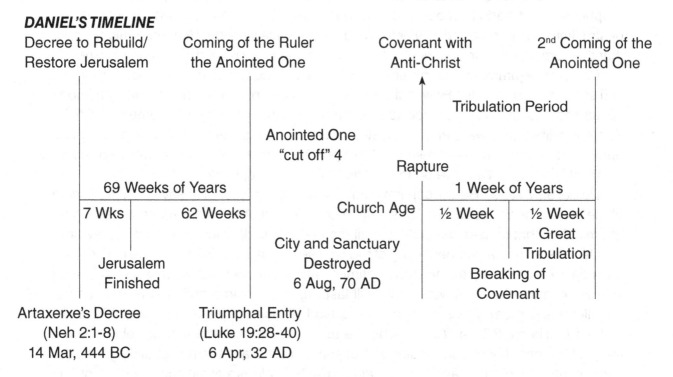

Something else very critical that we learned in studying this prophecy is that God always uses 360-day years in his prophecies and in fact in all his dealings with people of earth. We find that this prophecy works out only if we use 360-day years in our mathematics. We can see in both the books of Daniel and Revelation that God always uses 360-day years. He points this out in the text of these two books over and over in several ways. In both books, God points out that there are 360 days in a year, 1,260 days in 3.5 years or forty-two months and there are 2,520 days in seven years, and so forth. Every one of these leads us to the only conclusion possible: there are thirty days in a month, twelve months in a year, and thirty times twelve or 360 days in a year. That means we must convert all biblical references from 360-day years to 365-day years to conform to our calendar.

As we continue our investigation into Daniel's seventy-sevens, we will next study several aspects of Daniel's seventy-sevens prophecy including its ties to the Assyrian/Babylonian destruction patterns, the seventieth Jubilee period in our generation, and most importantly, whether this prophecy may also lead us to the time of Jesus's return. This will be a very revealing investigation.

Daniel's seventy-sevens prophecy of Daniel 9:24–27 leads us to the very day and month of Jesus's crucifixion. Daniel's prophecy was a prophecy that would lead to both the exact date of the coming crucifixion of Jesus as well as the time of his Second Coming to earth. The prophecy said that from Artaxerxes's decree to allow the Jews to rebuild the walls of their city until the time of the death of the coming Messiah would be a period of 7+62 seven-year periods. Daniel's prophecy also contained one more seven-year period for Israel during their existence until the end-time tribulation would come. Thus, Israel has a total of 62+7+1=70 seven-year periods before the end-time tribulation. Does this mean God wasn't counting their time in punishment and exile? We have seen that the time in exile associated with the Assyrian/Babylonian punishment periods doesn't end until 2041.5. Could Daniel's seventy- sevens in conjunction with the Assyrian/Babylonian captivity pattern possibly lead us to this same date? Let us examine a possibility.

In our analysis, we noticed that it was exactly sixty-three periods of forty years from 443.3 BC until the year AD 2041.5. When we discovered that, we began to wonder where we would end up if we counted back in history for a period of seven forties from the same starting date of 443.3 BC. That would give us a formula of 7+63 or possibly even 7+62+1 forty-year periods. Surprise! Seven forties or 280 God years led us back to the year 719.29 BC and the year of the Assyrian destruction of Israel. Thus, we found that if we started at the destruction of Israel in 719.29 BC and used Daniel's 7+62+1 formula for getting to the end-time tribulation period, we would come to the years 443.3 BC, AD 2002.1, and AD 2041.53. Thus, we hit the year of the rebuilding of the city walls, the start of the seventieth Jubilee cycle, and the year 2041. Wow!

The way we used Daniel's formula would take us to the end of the tribulation. How can we know that? Well, Daniel 9:24 says that the end of the seventy-sevens takes us to the time when the following would be accomplished for the Jewish people and the city of Jerusalem:

1. There would be no more transgression.
2. There would be no more sin.
3. All wickedness would be atoned for.
4. Everlasting righteousness would be brought in.
5. The time of visions and prophecies would end.
6. And Jesus and his holy temple in Jerusalem would be anointed.

It seems that all this will be accomplished in the short time frame when Jesus returns at his Second Coming, when the Jews finally accept him as their Messiah and Savior, and when Jesus then sets up his rule on earth as King of Kings with an iron scepter for a period of one thousand years.

The final seven will begin with a peace treaty negotiated by the Antichrist. In the middle of the seven years, he will go into the temple and commit an abomination that causes desolation. He will be destroyed at the end of the seven.

So, it seems that we are a bit conflicted about whether 2041.5 would most likely be at the middle or end of the tribulation. We will study on to see where all this leads us.

We briefly introduced the possibility that Daniel's 9:24–27 prophecy may lead us to the end-times above. We will explore this much more completely in our next topic.

Might Daniel's Seventy-Sevens Prophecy Be Associated with Our Generation and 2041?

Daniel's seventy-sevens prophecy of 7+62+1 years leads us to our generation and AD 2041 if we start the pattern in 719.29 BC and use a multiplier of forty years, as we will see below.

Daniel's Prophetic Topic 3

How Associating the 7+62+1 Pattern with a Forty-Year Exile Pattern May Lead Us to the End-Times and 2041

In this section, we will expand on what we discovered near the end of the last section concerning how Daniel's 7+62+1 prophecy may lead us to the end-times. We will now begin that expansion:

1. Daniel's seventy-sevens is in a pattern of 7+62+1 periods of seven years, starts in 444.6, and takes us to the time of Jesus's death.
2. A similar pattern, this one a pattern of forty years, could lead us to the final or seventieth seven. It starts with the destruction of Israel in 719 BC. A period of seven forties takes us to the year 443.3 BC. A further period of sixty-two forties takes us to the start of the seventieth Jubilee period in AD 2002.1. A final period of one forty takes us to the year AD 2041.53. Could this year be associated with the final seven? This forty-year pattern of Jewish exile began with the very first destructive punishment God inflicted on Israel/Judah for a long-term violation of his three Leviticus 26 commands. It then hits the date of the very last year of the extended Assyrian/Babylonian punishment judgment period and is directly followed by the last of the extended periods of Jewish exile. This period went from 443.3 BC to AD 2041.5 and lasted exactly 7x360=2,520 or (62x40)+(1x40)=2,520 years. Incredibly both of these hit the year 2041.5. This may be saying that God used the very same mathematical pattern to prophesy the year of Jesus's death and the year of his return during the last days. We recall from our study of the Assyrian and Babylonian captivity patterns that both punishment periods finally end in the very same year, 2041.5.
3. In the above pattern, the pattern of forties hits the year 30.8, which is the Jubilee year in Jesus's ministry. There were twelve forties from 443.3 to 30.8. In God's mathematics, the number twelve is associated with governments. Could this represent the fact that Jesus would bring in a new form of government for his

people? This would be a spiritual kingdom with Jesus reigning as King in the hearts of those belonging to him. This spiritual kingdom would then last until Jesus sets up a physical kingdom on earth, where he will reign as king of kings for a period of one thousand years. The last few years just before the setting up of this physical kingdom will include the rapture of Jesus's bride, the seven-year period of tribulation, and the Second Coming.

4. We saw above that the Assyrian destruction began in 719.29 BC. It was then two further periods of 66.666 God years until the Babylonian destruction started in 587.87 BC. The Babylonian destruction and exile of Judah that started at this date lasted all the way to the year AD 2041.53. Incredibly, this was also a period of a tribulation of exiles or 66.666 periods of forty years from the destruction of Judah in 587.87 BC until AD 2041.53. That also means it was an exile of tribulations or forty periods of 66.666 years in this same period. That is certainly supernatural, to say the least. Could this mean that 2041.53 might bring an end to tribulation and exile for the Jewish people and also possibly the rest of the world as well?

5. A pattern of sixty God years starting in 443.3 BC also hits the year 30.8 in Jesus's ministry as well as the year AD 2041.53. It was a Jubilee of sixty-year periods from the death of the first seriously idol-worshipping king of Israel in 916.4 BC until the year AD 2041.53. That could mean that this whole period was a judgment of judgments of the Jews for their serious idol worship.

6. It was eleven periods of 360, or ninety-nine periods of forty God years from the time Jacob and his sons first entered Egypt in 1863.6 BC until the year AD 2041.53. This pattern also hit the key date of 443.3 BC. It was then seven periods of 360 years until AD 2041.53. Would this year then be the perfect year to bring completion to God's plan to create his final bride for Christ? This would represent the end of the fourth ninety-year season at the end of the seventh pattern of completeness. Whew!

7. How do all these dates align with the three two-thousandth-year dates in history? We have seen that there are very key dates in nearly all these patterns that are in the two-thousand-year periods. We won't repeat them again.

We could go on and on with this, but we believe we have made our point. This is all clearly supernatural, and only the creator God of the universe could be bringing all these patterns together in this incredible way.

Might Daniel's 7+62+1 Prophecy Be Associated with Our Generation and 2041?

In this investigation, we found that it was an exile of tribulations or forty periods of 66.666 years from 587.87 BC until AD 2041.53. We also found that it was a Jubilee of sixty-year periods from the death of the first seriously idol-worshiping king of Israel in 916.4 BC until the year AD 2041.53. That could mean this whole period was a judgment of judgments of the Jews for their serious idol worship. We also found that it was eleven periods of

360 God years from the time Jacob and his sons first entered Egypt in 1863.6 BC until the year AD 2041.53. This pattern also hit the key date of 443.3 BC. It was then seven periods of 360 years until AD 2041.53. Would this year then be the perfect year to bring completion to God's plan to create his final bride for Christ? This would represent the end of the fourth ninety-year season at the end of the seventh pattern of completeness.

Daniel's Prophetic Topic 4

How We Can Tie the Final Seven in Daniel's 7+62+1 Prophecy to the Forty- Year Exile Pattern, the Three Jewish Temple Destruction Events, the End-Time Tribulation Period, and to the Year 2041

Let us take another possible track on when Daniel's final seven will take place. It is difficult to understand why God considered the Jews in timeout, so to speak, a period of two-thousand years when they would be partially blinded to the truth of Jesus's identity. It seems that they have been blinded, for the most part, to the real truth about the fact that Jesus is their Messiah, their God, their creator.

Why would this be the case? What happened in AD 32 that caused God to quit counting them in Daniel's prophetic timetable, his 70+62+1 prophecy for the next two-thousand years? One of the two things that I can think of is their rejection of Jesus as their Messiah and God. If that is the case, then God won't begin counting them in his prophetic timetable again until the seven-year period, during which they will finally accept Jesus as who he really is: their Messiah and God. In this discussion I have been thinking of the period of the blinding of the Jews (in part), which Paul described in Romans 11. That blinding will end during Daniel's seven-year tribulation. The second possible reason for the blinding of the Jews during this long period is also mentioned by Paul in Romans 11. That is because this blinding will lead to the acceptance of Jesus as their savior and God by a huge number of Gentiles. That will eventually lead to the formation of the bride for Christ that will lead to the fulfillment of the ultimate purpose of God's will that we have been highlighting throughout this book.

In Matthew 23 and the early part of Matthew 24, Jesus was forecasting what would take place during the next generation after his death. He was forecasting a generation of tribulation for the Jewish people that would end with their city and temple being destroyed. This was all accomplished within forty years of Jesus's death. Could it be that God will begin counting again at the beginning of the seven-year tribulation when millions of Jews finally become believers in Jesus because of the work of the two witnesses, the one hundred forty-four thousand sealed Jews, and the Revelation 14 witnessing angel? And could it also be true that God won't begin counting until the Jews begin building their temple on the Temple Mount soon after the seven-year period begins? These all happen in the seven-year tribulation period according to Bible prophecy. We do see three periods of lengthy exile for the Jews, all beginning at the time of the destruction of their temples. Each period will likely last for a period that is a multiple of forty years. Let us check it out.

Temple destroyed in Samaria, capital of Israel in 719.3 BC

719.3−.98565 (70x40=2800)=2041.5

Temple destroyed in Jerusalem; siege began in 587.9 BC

587.9−.98565 (66.666x40)=2041.5

Temple destroyed in Jerusalem; siege began in AD 70.2

70.2+.98565 (50x40)=2041.5

That is absolutely astounding. There is a multiplier of forty, the number for exiles, that takes us from the exact time of the destruction of the three Jewish temples to the exact year AD 2041.5. What are those three multipliers, and what do they mean in God's mathematics?

- 70, God's super multiplier for determining periods of *punishment* for his people and also for periods of *testing* his people
- 66.666, God's multiplier for periods of *tribulation*
- 50, God's number for periods of *judgment*

These are exactly the three numbers you would expect God to use. All three temples were destroyed as the result of God punishing the Jews after judging them and placing them in periods of tribulation. Based on the years we have been encountering over and over, just which year would you expect these three periods of punishment to converge on? If you said AD 2041.5, you are both paying attention and very insightful and correct. Wow! And again I say, Wow!

Now, since these three formulas all involve the temple and possibly the seven-year tribulation period, just what part of the seven-year period would you expect 2041.5 to represent? I would say the exact middle since Revelation 11:1–2 indicates that the temple will have been completed and have worshippers there in the exact middle of the seven-year period of tribulation. My guess is that the temple will be built in the first three and a half years of the tribulation as a result of the peace treaty the Antichrist negotiated. This strongly suggests that 2041 will be at the exact middle of the tribulation. We will continue to study until we have a clear preponderance of evidence one way or the other.

That completes our research into the ways the Assyrian and Babylonian captivity patterns conjunct with Daniel's seventy-sevens, the two-thousand-year sequential year-date pattern, and the year AD 2041.5. Whew! We will continue our research by studying a couple of other patterns associated with Daniel's end-time prophecies and AD 2041.

Might the Pattern of Forty-Year Exiles That Hits All Three Jewish Temple Destructions Be Tied to Our Generation and 2041?

Patterns of seventy 40s from Israel's temple destruction in 719.29 BC, 66.666 40s from Judah's temple destruction in 587.87 BC and 50 40s from Judea's temple destruction in AD 70 all hit the year 2041.53 in our generation. Thus, there will be a convergence of judgment, tribulation, and exile for Israel's temples all converging in AD 2041.53. Will 2041.53 thus likely be a key date in the reconstruction of a new temple in Jerusalem?

Daniel's Prophetic Topic 5

The Multiple Fulfillments of the Daniel Chapter 12 Seven-Year End-Time Prophecy and How They Tie to the Year 2041

Daniel also gave us prophecies in chapter 12 about the coming seven-year period of tribulation and again possibly the date when it will take place. We will later see if it is being properly interpreted. You often cannot tell for certain until after the events have taken place. We will go to that prophecy next. Let's begin by outlining what we see in chapter 12.

1. The angel Gabriel gives Daniel a final end-time prophecy from God.
2. We see that we are in the end-times when the angel Michael will once more become prominent in the Bible. This is described in Revelation 12 as the time when Michael and his fellow angels will war with Satan and his angels. They prevail and will throw them out of heaven and down to earth. This will occur just before the middle of the seven-year tribulation, as I interpret the seal and trumpet judgments.
3. We also see that this is the time when all the Jews who have been believers will be resurrected and raptured to heaven. So we have two witnesses that these events are at the time of the end-time tribulation period.
4. There are at least two resurrections and raptures in the tribulation period. One is very early, one is at least five months to a year or so past mid-tribulation, and there may also possibly be a special resurrection of Jews right after the Second Coming of Jesus.
5. Daniel is told to seal up the scroll he has been writing because it will not be understood until the time of the end when a knowledge explosion takes place. We seem to currently be in such an explosion.
6. Gabriel is asked when these things will take place. He says it will be three and a half years until the "power of the holy people will be broken." This sounds like the middle of the seven-year tribulation when the Antichrist will go into God's temple, declare himself to be God, demand to be worshipped, and declare war on Israel.
7. Daniel is confused and asks for further explanation. Gabriel tells him that even in the end-times, only the wise will understand the words of the scroll.
8. Daniel is next told that from the middle of the seven-year period when the Antichrist performs the abomination of desolation, there will be another 1,290 days. This takes us to thirty days past the seven years of tribulation.
9. Gabriel then finishes by saying, "Blessed is he who reaches the end of the 1335 days." This takes us another forty-five days past the end of the seven-year period. Thus, Gabriel is describing a period of seven years and seventy-five days total.

These seven years and seventy-five days or 7.2 calendar years are what we have used previously in describing the tribulation period. However, we know from experience in studying Bible prophecies that God often has multiple meanings or messages in his prophecies. With that in mind, we began looking for a second possible fulfillment of this prophecy that might use years instead of days and therefore might lead us to the exact dates for the end-times. We may have hit the jackpot and found something. A better way to say this is that the Spirit may have led us to something quite incredible. We will explain.

Daniel was writing the end of his scroll, or book as we know it, in about the year 535 BC or so. The Persians under Cyrus the Great had already conquered the Babylonians. Cyrus had already written his edict, allowing Jews to return to Judah. Cyrus had likely already given permission to begin rebuilding the temple. However, several complications ended up delaying the start of the rebuilding of the temple until 517.3 BC, according to the patterns we discovered in the Babylonian destruction and exile period. This was precisely seventy (sixty-nine) years after the final destruction of the original temple in 586 BC.

We will next apply the pattern of Daniel 12 to the starting date of 517.3 BC and assume the days in this case are also meant to be interpreted as years. We will go forward 1260+1260=2520 (2,483.84) years. We will next add thirty and then forty-five days (years this time) to the result to see where it takes us.

517.3 BC−2483.8=AD 1967.5—This is the year Israel captured the Temple Mount, Old City, West Bank and so forth during the Six-Day War.
1967.5+30 (29.6)=1997.1—This is the year when Israel gave part of the West Bank to the Palestinians as part of a land-for-peace accord.
1997.1+45 (44.4)=2041.5—This is our target date, which we keep hitting over and over.

So we see there may be two valid interpretations of the Daniel 12 prophecy, one using days when it describes the seven-year tribulation period and the other using years when it is pointing us to the time of the end.

Now, what exactly did Daniel say this was pointing toward? Gabriel made the following statement about the 1,335 days: "Blessed is he who reaches the end of the 1335 days." So, what conclusion can we reach about the 1,335 years? We can certainly say that those who reach the year 2041.5 will be blessed. However, this context doesn't match many other patterns we have discovered concerning 2041.5. This result would have the Second Coming and Armageddon in 2041.5. This might be a good fit in a couple of ways, however. The millennium starting on the sixth day of man would certainly make sense. It would require the rapture to be seven years earlier in about 2034.5. Only God knows if either of these will really be his time for beginning his end-time scenario.

We also might add that the Assyrian/Babylonian captivity punishments in conjunction with Daniel's seventy-sevens also can be interpreted with 2041.5 being either the middle or end of the seven-year tribulation. Maybe God doesn't want us to know which, if either, is more likely.

It is also quite possible that we started at the wrong date. Let us examine that. There is another very good possibility. The temple rebuilding was begun in 517.3 BC and finished three and a half years later in 513.8. Let us try starting with that date and see where it takes us. That starting date would seem to make more common sense anyway since the temple would then be ready for use once more. We will go through the same process we used above.

513.8 BC–2483.8=AD 1971.0—This is the year the rabbinical council met and voted to prohibit use of the Temple Mount, even though they now had control of it.

1971.0+30 (29.6)=2000.6—This is the year of the Camp David retreat with another round of land-for-peace talks with the Palestinians. This effort failed.

2000.6+45 (44.4)=2045.0—This is the point that is twenty-three hundred days before the end of the seventieth Jubilee year.

This would then signify the Second Coming just after all still-living Jews have come to Jesus, Armageddon, and the start of the millennium. The Jewish judgment of Daniel 12 could also occur in this time frame.

This scenario fits quite well with all the scenarios "this generation" patterns seem to be taking us toward.

Might the Daniel 12 End-Time Tribulation Prophecy of a Tribulation of 1260+1260+30+45 Days Be Associated with Our Generation and 2041?

Hosea's two-days-equal-two-thousand-years prophecy led us to the year AD 2045.0. A pattern assuming the 1260+1260+30+45 days from Daniel 12 can be interpreted as years also leads us to the year AD 2045.0 if we start at the time of the completion of the rebuilt temple in 513.8 BC. This date is twenty-three hundred days before AD 2051.4.

Daniel's Prophetic Topic 6

God's Possible Use of the Daniel 9 (7+62+1) Prophecy to Lead Us to the End-Time Tribulation Period and His Promised Great Family Reunion

We first discovered a possible way in which God might be using Daniel's chapter 9 7+62+1 prophecy when we were writing the commentary on this topic and the Assyrian/ Babylonian destruction of the Jewish nations in our second book in this series, *God Is Cooking Up Something Incredible*. In doing so, we noticed that it was exactly 7x40=280 years from the destruction of Israel in 719 BC by the Assyrians and the year when God instituted his punishment on Judah in 443 BC. According to Ezekiel, Judah was due a punishment of 7x40 years at that time. However, while the original inhabitants of Judah were only due a punishment of 7x40 years, those who had escaped from Israel when it was being destroyed and came to Judah still had the balance of their 7x390-year sentence to serve, from Ezekiel 4. That would be another 62+1 periods of forty years or another 7x360 years. They had already served a sentence of 7x30=210+70=280 years in exile. This was an exile from their original homeland in the former northern kingdom of Israel. This is complicated, but I assure you as a mathematician that this works out perfectly. God things always do.

Well, that is how I discovered the possible application of Daniel's end-time prophecy. However, in writing this book, I discovered something even more incredible. It is this.

There is a whole series of patterns of 7+62+1 applications for this prophecy. And guess what? All of them converge in the year 2041. Incredible. We will next present a chart that depicts those possible prophetic applications. We will then give some possible interpretation about what this might indicate in terms of God's plan to reach fulfillment of the purpose for his will.

Speculation on How God May be Using 4 Event-Pattern Strings in the 2000 Year Family to Fulfill Daniel's 9:24-27 Formula of (7+62+1)X7 For Reaching the End Times

Pattern & Origin Date	7x Pat Gap Date	(7+62)X Pat Gap Date	(7+62+1)X Pat Gap Date	Description of the Events Taking Place in Each of the Prophetic Start, Intermediate and Concluding Event Dates
40 YEAR 719 BC	443 BC	2001 AD	2041 AD	719 BC – Assyrians destroy Israel, exile to nations 443 BC – Start God's punishment, exile of Judah 2001 AD-Start 70th Jubilee period since 1399 BC 2041 AD- 6000th year of man; may be associated with great tribulation for whole world
50 YEAR 1399 BC	1054 BC	1992 AD	2041 AD	1399 BC- Jews enter Promised Land; Jubilees begin 1054 BC- Israel begins using Kings to rule over them 1992 AD- Oslo transfers Jericho, Gaza to PLO 2041 AD- Same as above
60 YEAR 2099 BC	1685 BC	1982 AD	2041 AD	2099 BC – 2000th year after fall of man in 4070 BC 1685 BC – Near middle of Israelite time in Egypt 1982 AD – PLO declares Palestinian state 2041 AD- Same as above
66.66 YR 2559 BC	2099 BC	1975 AD	2041 AD	2559 BC – In Gentile trib pattern; 4 periods to Babel and 20 periods after end of 7th day, 3873 2099 BC – Same as above 1975 AD – massive immigration from Russia to Israel 2041 AD – Same as above

An Explanation of What These Interpretations Might Be Telling Us

We will next present our interpretation of one way God might be using each of these four prophetic patterns. That would fit very well into the end-time prophecy presented over and over in the Bible.

- 40 pattern: This is God's exile pattern. We have seen earlier that all three historic Jewish nations—Israel, Judah, and Judea—are all currently in a period of exile from God. We have seen that all three are apparently ending in AD 2041. This fits the narrative of the prophecy in the king's scroll from Leviticus 26 that says in the end-times the Jews will return to God and that he will also return to them.

- 50 pattern: This is the Jubilee judgment pattern gap, and it was always during these fiftieth-year judgments that God would pronounce their punishments for violating his three Leviticus 26 commands. God always seemed to use Gentiles to carry out his punishments and to do so in Gentile pattern strings. The year AD 2041 is the seventieth Gentile fifty-year period since the twin fifty Gentile/Jewish pattern string began in 1409/1399 BC. Seventy is the number God uses for testing his people in ways destined to bring about redemption. Will the Gentile-initiated event that will bring ultimate redemption to the Jews take place in this year? It certainly fits the Bible's end-time prophetic scenarios.

- 60 pattern: The sixty-year event-pattern string involves sinful mankind. Will this be the year of the event that will result in the ultimate forgiveness of the sins that led to their exile from God, in large part according to Paul in Romans? It is the one hundredth anniversary of the sixty event-pattern string, the year 6000 since the end of the seventh day of creation. In Genesis God said that man should work for six days and then rest on the seventh day, just as he did in the creation process. Could that mean man's day of rest, a 1000-year day, will start in the events surrounding the year AD 2041? That would be the one-thousand-year period prophesied in six verses in a row, verses 2–7, in Revelation 20. That would, of course, be the millennium, when Jesus will reign on earth as King of Kings and Lord of Lords according to Revelation. Again it certainly fits the Bible's end-time prophetic scenario.

- 66.666 pattern: The description in the forty-year pattern above also fits this 66.666 pattern to a T. If you simply substitute 66.666 in for the forty above, it fits quite well. If we again go back to the king's scroll, we can see in the seven penalties that God said he would give to the Jews if they didn't keep his commands; we can see that tribulation is associated with all seven punishments in some way or the other, with the severity of the tribulation growing significantly as we proceed from punishment to punishment. The year AD 2041 is in the ominous 666.66-year pattern; in other words, it means greatly multiplied tribulation. If we go back through Jewish history, we can certainly see this. In recent history, the whole of the six-hundred-year Catholic Inquisition, which ended in the mid-1800s, proves this. The Jews were killed by the millions, kicked out of one country after the other, tortured, blamed for all sorts of maladies that struck the world in general, and so forth. Will all this horrible treatment of the Jews finally end in the events surrounding the year 2041?

This is all covered much more completely in the first three books of this 2041 series. We left out most of the details in the above discussion, but we hope we have said enough to make the point. 2041 seems to be pointed to again and again in God's use of mathematical patterns he is using to bring about the ultimate purpose of his will.

However, we must be careful about jumping to conclusions too soon, since we will present a pattern later in this book that could explain all these convergences in our pattern strings, but still show that the end-times could still be in the distant future.

We will later paint a scenario that shows all this to be true, but the end-times may not be right around the corner, so to speak.

We would like to emphasize that we aren't date setters. We aren't creating anything, other than a presentation of things, including dates God has hidden in the Bible in his models, prophecies, patterns, genealogies, time gaps between events, and so forth. We are simply a God-loving, Bible-loving, self-taught theologian who worked as a mathematician and senior scientist, who has a passion for digging through the Bible both quite deeply and also very broadly, looking for the things God has hidden in his mysteries, parables, models, history, and so forth in the Bible. I find it indisputable from the evidence we are presenting that God has a plan and that it is extremely detailed yet still quite simple, and the details can be dug out of the Bible if we can find the codes hidden in the Bible and use them to diligently seek out the plan. That is exactly what we have been doing for the last twenty-five or so years.

God is the date setter, and when we find many of the clues and codes he has been hiding, we must be careful not to jump to conclusions. The same applies to the reader of our books, including this book. There is so very much we can find and understand, but there is still more we may not clearly understand until time reaches its fulfillment.

Clues from Daniel's Prophetic Topics

The Twenty-Three-Hundred-Days Prophecy

- We now know the exact time between two of the key events in the end-times, the Second Coming and the anointing of the millennial temple in Israel. The second date would be the time of a great family reunion on earth for God's family and thus the families of believers in Jesus.

The 7+62+1 Years to the End-Times Prophecy

- Daniel's 7+62+1 sevens prophecy leads us to both the First and Second Comings of Jesus to earth, with the first being very specific and the second being much more mysterious. We found several ways to use this formula that would lead us to not only the end-times but also the year 2041.

The Daniel 12 End-Time Prophecies

- We found an interpretation of the 1260+1260+30+45=2595 days prophecy, which leads us to the Second Coming in 2045, which matches the other prophecies in Daniel precisely.

Section 3

A Study of the Eighteen Prophetic Kingdom Parables of Matthew

Matthew often uses the terms "kingdom of heaven" and "kingdom of God" in his gospel account. The parables of Jesus that Matthew includes in his book nearly all seem to reflect some aspect of the kingdom of heaven. They are often called "kingdom parables." We will next begin a study of all the kingdom parables included in the book of Matthew, but before doing that we would first like to say a bit about parables.

We could call all of these parables codes. That is because they are basically impossible to understand and interpret without knowing the codes. Jesus revealed the codes to his disciples in Matthew 13 but we still find in John 15, near the end of Jesus's ministry, that they still did not understand them. These parables are dual intertwined in a miraculous way such that they all have a very valuable life's lesson attached to them but it appears that Jesus also attached a much more important meaning to them. This meaning was encoded in mysteries, figures of speech and symbology, all with a prophetic implication attached to them. They were explaining the deeper things of God, things that only those who intensely studied the whole council of God could fully understand. This includes the one third of the Bible that is prophetic in nature.

Matthew says that Jesus never spoke to the crowds without speaking to them in parables. This is likely one of the things about him that led to him attracting huge crowds when he spoke. The people would leave amazed and talking to each other about the meaning of the mysteries and puzzles that he presented to them. Many of us are familiar with the valuable life's lessons attached to these parables because we hear them from Sunday to Sunday as we attend church services. However, few hear about the ultimately even more valuable lessons presented in the hidden text of the parables. That is what we are presenting in this section.

Jesus begins using parables extensively in Matthew's account in chapter 13. There are seven parables in Matthew 13, and they are all kingdom parables.

Jesus explains to the disciples why he speaks to the people in parables in Matthew 13:10–16. I will quote verses 10–13: "The disciples came to him and asked, 'Why do you speak to the people in parables?' He replied, '*The knowledge of the secrets of the kingdom of heaven have been given to you, but not to them.*' Whoever has will be given more, and he will have an abundance. Whoever does not have, even what he has will be taken from him. This is why I speak in parables" (emphasis added).

Jesus then goes on to say that this fulfills a prophecy from Isaiah 6:9–10. This prophecy says, "They [the Jews] will be ever hearing, but never understanding; be ever seeing, but never perceiving. This people's heart has become calloused; they hardly hear with their ears, and they have closed their eyes."

Verse 12 may be saying that whoever has the Spirit within him or her will be given more (eternal life and the associated rewards). Whoever does not have the Spirit within him or her will lose everything (including his life; he will spend eternity in the lake of fire). The Jews are forever hearing the Word of God, but they never see and perceive the truth in that word; Jesus is the Messiah and Savior. They have become calloused and stubbornly refuse to listen to and see the truth, the gospel of Jesus.

What are the secrets or mysteries Jesus referred to that have been given to the disciples and believers that others do not have? What allows believers to understand these secrets? I would say that it is the ability to understand the Word of God, the will of God, and the things of God through the help of the Holy Spirit, who has been given only to believers. Believers have been given the "mind" of Christ (1 Cor. 2:11, 16). This seems to say that the Holy Spirit puts the thoughts of Jesus into the spirits (hearts) of those who belong to him. These thoughts or insights from Jesus through the Holy Spirit enable believers to understand the things of God that others cannot even begin to comprehend.

One mystery that seems to have particular application to the kingdom of heaven is given in Ephesians 1:8–10. "He lavished on us all wisdom and understanding. And he made known to us the mystery of his will according to his good pleasure, which he purposed in Christ, to be put into effect when the times have reached their fulfillment – to bring all things in heaven and on earth together under one head, even Christ."

This passage clearly teaches that the literal, physical phase of the kingdom of heaven begins when all things in heaven and on earth are placed under one head, Jesus. This can only be at the Second Coming when Satan is bound and thrown into the Abyss for one thousand years. Before that time, Satan is the ruler of the earth (John 12:31; 2 Cor. 4:4; Eph. 2:2; Matt. 4:8–9). Revelation 10:7 confirms that the prophecy described in Ephesians 1:8–10 is accomplished at the Second Coming of Jesus.

In Matthew 13:18–23, 36–43, Jesus taught the disciples how to interpret the kingdom parables by example. He very clearly interpreted two of the parables for them. We can use these examples to help us interpret the other sixteen kingdom parables in Matthew. We have attempted to do just that.

We will now move on to our study of the kingdom parables of Matthew. As we study, we will note that nearly every parable presents a division of some sort, with most focusing on the separation of believers in Jesus from unbelievers in some interesting way.

1. **The Sower and the Seed (Matt. 13:1–9, 18–23)**
2. **The Weeds among the Wheat (Matt. 13:24–30, 36–43)**
3. **The Mustard Seed (Matt. 13:31–32)**
4. **The Yeast (Matt. 13:33)**
5. **The Hidden Treasure (Matt. 13:44)**
6. **The Pearl of Great Value (Matt. 13:45)**
7. **The Dragnet (Matt. 13:47–51)**
8. **Forgiveness, Settling Accounts (Matt. 18:23–35)**
9. **The Vineyard Workers (Matt. 20:1–16)**
10. **The Two Sons (Matt. 21:28–32)**
11. **The Landowner and the Rented Vineyard (Matt. 21:33–40)**
12. **The Wedding Banquet (Matt. 22:1–14)**
13. **The Fig Tree Parables (Matt. 24:32–35)**
14. **The Fig Tree Parables (Matt. 21:18–22)**
15. **The Thief in the Night (Matt. 24:42–44)**
16. **Caring for the Flock While the Master Is Away (Matt. 24:45–51)**
17. **The Ten Virgins (Matt. 25:1–13)**
18. **The Talents (Matt. 25:14–30)**

Recurring Themes in the Kingdom Parables of Matthew
(The number of parables in which they are presented is in parenthesis.)

1. (18) The eighteen kingdom parables in Matthew all present some characteristic of the kingdom of heaven and/or kingdom of God.
2. The kingdom has both spiritual (16) and physical (8) phases. Sixteen parables deal with phase one of the kingdom of heaven, eight with phase two, and three with the kingdom of God.
3. (18) All the parables in some way or another address who will be in heaven and who will not. All deal with actual or implied separation or division of some sort. They generally present separation of believers from unbelievers, with believers being rewarded in heaven and unbelievers being sent to the lake of fire or outer darkness. This is figuratively or symbolically expressed in various ways in the parables, including separation of the wheat from the chaff, the good fish from the bad fish, false doctrine from the church, those who forgive from those who do not, the humble from the exalted, the Jews from their land, the invited from the uninvited, those who bear fruit from those who do not, teachers of false doctrine from teachers of true doctrine, the wise from the foolish, those who use their talents for God from those who do not, and so forth. Jesus said in Luke 12:51, "Do you think I came to bring peace on earth? No, I tell you, but division." He went on to say that even families would divide over belief in him: father against son, son against father, mother against daughter, and so forth.
4. (7) Many are called, but few are chosen. Only those who hear the Word, understand it, and produce fruit for the kingdom will be part of the kingdom.

5. (7) The wicked, the enemies of God, face severe punishment for eternity. They will be cast into the lake of fire (hell) and sent to outer darkness forever. Nobody who rejects Jesus and refuses to follow him will enter heaven.

6. (6) The kingdom will be taken from the Jews and given to another people, the Gentiles.

7. (5) God will severely punish the Jewish leaders and Jewish people for rejecting Jesus. The leaders will be punished for leading the flock astray. The punishment will last for a long time. This has been fulfilled for the last two thousand years and is still being fulfilled.

8. (5) It is very important for believers to produce fruit for the kingdom. Salvation depends on belief in Jesus and becoming a follower of his. Being a follower involves producing fruit for the kingdom.

9. (5) Many in the church will be caught by surprise at the harvest. Many of those in the church will not go to heaven.

10. (3) There will be a harvest at the end of the age. Those in the harvest will be divided into those who are believers and those who are unbelievers. Believers in Jesus will all go to heaven for eternity, while unbelievers all face an eternity in the lake of fire and outer darkness.

11. (3) The last will be first, and the first will be last in heaven. Leaders will be judged more harshly; more is expected of them. We usually think of the servant as being the least or last, so to speak. However, in the kingdom those who are servants of Jesus, those who do everything he asks as best they can, will be first. Who will be last? It is those who lead God's servants astray. The leaders of all the false religions, who promote notions such as, "There are many paths to heaven, not just one through Jesus," "God is not the creator," "Jesus is not God," and so forth will be last. It would be better for them if they had a millstone placed around their necks and they were thrown into the sea.

12. (3) Sin and false doctrine will permeate the church until the end-time.

13. (3) Jesus will be away a long time before he returns.

14. (3) Believers must stay ready for Jesus's return and not be caught by surprise. Nobody knows the day or hour of Jesus's return.

15. (2) Jesus loves and greatly values his bride, the church. He was willing to pay a great price for her.

Jesus's Message In the Kingdom Parables Was Not Politically Correct

One of the reasons Jesus taught in parables was to keep his message, which was not politically correct with the first-century leaders, from getting him and his disciples killed before the proper time. The chief priests and Pharisees eventually understood enough of the parables to know Jesus was referring to them in ways that made them very uncomfortable. Matthew 21:45–46 tells us that because of this, they looked for a way to arrest him.

This may also explain Jesus's instructions to the twelve in Matthew 10:5–16, when he sent them out to preach the message "The kingdom of heaven is near." Jesus said he was sending them out like sheep among wolves. Therefore, when they preached the message of the kingdom, they were told to be as shrewd as snakes and as innocent as doves. They were told to be on their guard against men, who would hand them over to the local councils and flog them in their synagogues.

Jesus's Message in the Kingdom Parables Is Still Not Politically Correct

Jesus's message in these parables is also not politically correct in our society today and is becoming less politically correct year after year. Look again at the themes in the parables listed above. It is not politically correct today to say that anyone is going to hell. It is not politically correct to say that orthodox or reformed Jews are going to hell, as Jesus made very clear. It is not politically correct to say that only those who believe in and follow Jesus are going to heaven. We are told that saying such things offends many people and that we must be sensitive to their feelings. Many in both the Protestant and Catholic churches today espouse such doctrines and believe them. As Jesus said in three of the kingdom parables in Matthew, sin and false doctrine will permeate the church until the time of the end. We must all pray for the church.

Possibly the most politically incorrect one of the kingdom parables is one I was able to pair with a parable in Mark to possibly arrive at a date for the coming rapture of believers to heaven. This parable is one of the eighteen kingdom parables of Matthew. We will now present that study and give the reader an example of how these parables can be interpreted. This is the only parable for which we will present a complete interpretation in this book. If the reader would like to go deeper into the other kingdom parables, he or she can go to our website under the heading "Answering the complex Bible questions"; and under that the topic, look for "The Kingdom of Heaven." We will next present that study.

What Did Jesus Mean When He Said He Would Be Gone for a Long Time?

Luke 20:9–16

The parable in Luke 20:9–16 figuratively stands for the period from 4070.5 BC to AD 32. In this parable the vineyard stands for the earth. God created mankind and placed them on earth to produce a soul harvest for him. People initially knew God intimately and knew what he required of them. After "a long time," it became necessary for God to begin sending godly messengers to earth to reaffirm his requirements of them concerning his harvest expectations. God sent a particular messenger to earth during four separate periods in the 4,100-year period covered in this parable, each time with messages about God's harvest requirements. The first three messengers were the Angel of the Lord. During the fourth, it was God's Son, Jesus. In fact, since the Angel of the Lord was Jesus, the messenger in each of the four periods was Jesus. From the time of the fall in 4070.5 BC until 2064 BC, there were no specific visits recorded in the Bible. The four periods of visitation were the following:

1. 2064 to the mid-1800s BC—the time of Hagar/Ishmael's birth, Abraham, Isaac, and Jacob. (This is the period when the seeds for Israel were being planted.)
2. 1440 to about 700 BC—the time of Moses and the birth of Israel until its destruction by the Assyrians. (Israel—this is the period from birth to death in the Promised Land.)
3. Mid-600s to mid-400s BC—the time just before, during, and after the destruction of Judah, the exile of its people, their return from exile, and the rebuilding of Jerusalem and the temple. (Judah—this is the period of its death, exile, return, and rebuilding.)
4. 2 BC to AD 32—the time of Jesus's life on earth. (God was physically on earth.)

There are over two hundred appearances of a visitor from heaven to earth that can be translated as the "theophanic" angel recorded in the Bible during the first three of these periods. This messenger from heaven can be clearly proven to be God in several of the appearances. He looked like a man but acted and spoke like God. There are three persons in the Godhead, and we can easily show that this is neither the Father God nor the Spirit God. Thus, we draw the conclusion that these must be pre-incarnational appearances of Jesus. In fact, one of the clearest proofs that this visitor is in fact Jesus himself is in Zechariah 2:10, where the Angel of the Lord was speaking to Zechariah and told him he would return to earth and live among men.

This scenario matches that of the parable; four times messengers from the vineyard owner were sent to the vineyard, and four times the messengers were severely mistreated and their messages ignored. In the fourth visit, the messenger was the Son of the vineyard owner. He was treated likewise and even killed, with the vineyard turned over to others.

Verse 16 says God will take the vineyard from the tenants and give it to another people. In AD 135, the Romans ended their destruction of Judea, exiled many of the remaining Jews, and renamed the area "Palestine." God had finally completely taken the Promised Land from the Jewish people and would not return it to them until 1948. Verse 19 was completely fulfilled in AD 313 when the Roman Empire collapsed and the Hasmonean Dynasty assumed control of the Holy Land.

It was a period of about 2,006 years from the time of the fall of man in 4070.5 BC until the next recorded appearance of God on earth. This was when Abraham was eighty-six years old, which was at the time of Ishmael's birth to Hagar in 2064 BC. The 2,006-year period of absence of God from earth was called a "long time" in verse 9. The same phrase was used in Matthew 25:19 concerning the time Jesus would be gone from earth, a period from his ascension until his return at the rapture. We will now go to that parable.

Matthew 25:14–30

The parable in Matthew 25:14–30 about the talents is a kingdom parable sandwiched between a parable about the rapture and a description of the sheep-goat judgment right after the Second Coming at the end of the seven-year period of tribulation. The parable about the rapture concerns ten bridesmaids/virgins waiting for the bridegroom to return for them at an unknown hour to "snatch" them from their home and take them to his father's house for the wedding.

This parable about the talents concerns the whole time from Jesus's ascension to his return for his bride (all believers) at some unknown future time when he will "snatch" then up to his Father's home in heaven for the wedding. The talents are all about the time between the two events when decisions will be made about who will be and who will not be part of the bride based on what each person has done with the part of the Master's wealth entrusted to him or her. The Master's wealth was his salvation plan for man. This evaluation period goes from the time the bridegroom became engaged to the bride and left earth to go to his father's home to prepare a place for him and his bride to live until the time he will return for his bride at the future rapture event. This translated to the time from Jesus's ascension to the future rapture of his bride to heaven.

Verse 19 says that this will be a "long time," meaning the time before Jesus's return for his bride. This same term was used in the parable about the workers caring for the Father's vineyard In Luke 20:9–16. There the long time was about 2,006 years. That may give us a gross expectation for what God might have in mind for the period before he sends Jesus back to earth for his bride. The first-century apostles and followers of Jesus must have not understood this parable. In the time just before Jesus's death and during the forty days after his resurrection, Jesus spent a great deal of time relating end-time prophecy to the disciples.

We know from Matthew 13 that the disciples were very puzzled by his parables. Jesus gave them the key for understanding them, but they apparently still missed some part of what they meant in the big picture. The church today still has the same problem. Both Peter and Paul understood the critical importance of Jesus's prophetic message, and they began their first sermons recorded in Acts with Bible prophecy. Paul and the author of Hebrews both began their initial introduction of the gospel of Jesus with prophecy. They called it "elementary." I wish it was still elementary today! I expect that God is very displeased with us because of this. Our churches almost completely ignore it. It is the easiest and most effective way to "prove" that Jesus is God and that God is who he claims to be.

Let's get back to the "long time" for a second. If this "long time" lasts exactly as long as it did in the parable in Mark, then Jesus's return for his bride would take place sometime in the vicinity of 32+2006=AD 2038. I would say that is certainly unlikely, but the ominous signs all about us that seem to be similar to those presented in Matthew 24 could possibly be pointing to the soon return of Jesus. We just presented biblical evidence that according to God's own definition, Jesus has been gone a long time. When he does come, it will happen quickly, according to Jesus's own words.

Conclusion

Before Jesus came to earth it was impossible for anyone to be able to go to heaven. Nobody can enter heaven unless he or she is perfect in God's eyes. Jesus's blood sacrifice for people made it possible for them to be seen as perfect by God if they allow their sins to be covered by the blood of Jesus. While Jesus was on earth, his mission was to make it possible for man to get to heaven. It is not surprising then that much of what he taught had to do with what man had to do to be able to get to heaven. It is not surprising that every single one of the eighteen kingdom parables in Matthew had to do in some way or another with who would and would not go to heaven. Again, these kingdom parables are the last eighteen parables recorded in Matthew.

The fact that nearly every one of the kingdom parables deals with division, with separation of believers from unbelievers, with believers being rewarded in heaven and unbelievers being punished in hell should put an end to any thought among Christians that everyone is going to heaven. It simply is not going to happen. Based on a study of Jesus's parables, the majority of Jesus's teaching obviously focused on the separation of believers and unbelievers. Matthew 13:34 says that Jesus spoke to the crowd in parables; he did not say anything to them without using a parable. If he always used parables when he spoke to the crowds that followed him, then obviously he was always speaking to them about the division of believers from unbelievers, since nearly every one of his parables dealt with this topic. The Bible teaches very clearly over and over that Jesus is the only way to heaven.

The "long time" kingdom parable we just studied gives us an entirely new insight into the end-times that we had not previously encountered in this book. That is a possible date for the coming rapture of the saints. Earlier in this chapter, when we were studying Hosea's two-days-equal-two-thousand-years prophecy, we were speculating on possible parallels between the events surrounding the four thousandth year and the six thousandth year. This was largely based on the fact that there were parallels between the events surrounding the two thousandth and four thousandth years in history. In that case we concluded that the year AD 2038 was the most likely year for the rapture. Thus, we have one confirmation that we may be on to something.

In our search for clues about our key questions concerning the times of the coming fulfillment of the purpose of God's will, twin global resets and family reunions, we have just identified a very key clue.

One of the key points we wanted to make in this study of the kingdom parables of Matthew is that Jesus emphasized the study of Bible prophecy in his teachings in a huge way. Not only that, but in doing so, he always used very figurative language. Jesus is the author of Revelation as he points out in chapter 1 of Revelation. In that book, which is all about the final seven-year tribulation period and the Second Coming of Jesus, he also used the very same type of figurative language he used in his parables. We would like to emphasize that Jesus told his disciples in Matthew 13 that he never spoke to the people without using figurative language.

On our website we have about four hundred pages of commentary, charts, tables, and so forth concerning how to interpret the book of Revelation. One of the aids we created to do that was a Symbology Dictionary of about 140 words that seem to be used symbolically in Revelation and in the whole of the Bible, for that matter. That is available to anyone who is online at no cost.

Final Summary of What We Have Learned about the Kingdom of Heaven and the Kingdom of God

♦ When we began this study, we hypothesized definitions for the terms "kingdom of heaven" and "kingdom of God" based on our prior study. We said we would then test them by analyzing every situation in which these terms are used in the New Testament, with heavy concentration on the book of Matthew. We said we would look for any contradictions to these definitions. We further said that if we didn't find any contradictions that would give us confidence that our definitions were valid, as far as they went. We agreed that this would certainly not prove that they were complete, for they certainly must not be. We have completed the study and have not found any obvious contradictions. I certainly believe that I now understand much better what Jesus had to say about the kingdom of heaven and the kingdom of God. I hope that the same applies to the reader. Let us restate our proposed definition as we wrap up this study.

♦ The "kingdom of God" seems to be a term used to express the all-encompassing reign of God over all things in the mega verse through all of eternity past, present, and future. The kingdom of heaven seems to be the way in which we experience the kingdom of God while we live on the earth. Another way of saying that is that the kingdom of heaven is the kingdom of God as experienced on earth. We experience it or enter it in a spiritual sense as humans as soon as we are reborn in Christ and receive his Spirit within us. We will experience it in an entirely different way, in a physical sense, and in the millennium when we are on earth with Jesus while in our resurrected bodies. Thus, we might say that the kingdom of heaven has two phases, a spiritual phase and a physical phase. The ultimate kingdom we will inherit will be the kingdom of God in the unified heaven and earth of the new order from Revelation 21–22. According to Hebrews 12:25–29, that kingdom cannot be shaken. The author of Hebrews then tells us that because of that, we should be thankful and worship God acceptably with reverence and awe. What a glorious place that will be!

♦ Finally, we will repeat the simplified definitions for the kingdom of heaven and kingdom of God.

Kingdom of God: heaven, the place where God lives. This is the all-encompassing reign of God over all things in all places. In this context, it includes the kingdom of heaven.

Kingdom of heaven: Phase 1 is the kingdom of God as experienced on earth by believers through Jesus living within them through the Holy Spirit. Phase 2 is the kingdom of Jesus on earth in the millennium. Both phases are the place where Jesus dwells and reigns as God. Also, in Matthew 19:16–26, Jesus equates eternal life with the kingdom of heaven.

Clues from Jesus's Kingdom Parables in Matthew

- We have discovered just how important the use of prophecy was to Jesus in his ministry. In fact, in one of his eighteen kingdom parables in Matthew, he may be giving us a clue to the possible time frame of his coming rapture. This must be used in conjunction with a parable in Luke to be able to do this. While Jesus's kingdom parables are extremely enlightening in being able to understand end-time prophecy, they are generally non-specific in terms of the specific time frames. We may have found an exception.
- When taken with Hosea's prophecy, we may now have a very specific end-time scenario of eight key events spread out over a thirteen-year time period, starting with the rapture in AD 2038 and ending with the great family reunion in the seventieth Jubilee year in AD 2051, likely during the Feast of Tabernacles according to Zechariah 14. This would also be the time of the anointing of the new millennial temple.

Taking Stock of What We Have Learned and Providing a New Perspective on How We Will Proceed from Here

The end-time prophecies we have just finished presenting in Daniel and Hosea were extensive and numerous, with some already having been fulfilled to the very month and year. Our presumptive conclusion from that is that the remainder of the prophecies, including the end-time prophecies, will also be fulfilled to the very year. We will act on that presumption for the remainder of this book. For example, we may say that Jesus's Second Coming will take place in year "xxxxx." There are several other reasons for acting on this presumptive conclusion including the following:

- We are trying to determine whether our generation is a good candidate for fulfillment of the end-time scenario.
- The mathematical event patterns hidden in the Bible that we have unearthed will lead us to one very precise fit for the end-times taking place in our generation.
- We have demonstrated that a very similar fit for the end-time scenario has already taken place in both the two thousandth and four thousandth year periods, with the fits becoming better and more complete in each successive two-thousandth-year period. The third two thousandth year is the year 2041 in our generation. In fact, there are dual two- thousand-year patterns hitting our generation. The first is a Gentile pattern in 2041, and the second is a Jewish pattern in 2051, with both patterns being extremely good fits for the end-time scenario.
- In Matthew 24 Jesus tells us that we should be able to recognize the season of his end-time return but not the day or the hour. In each two-thousandth-year period in history, the event patterns point to a specific 200+10 year period that can be identified as the "season" for the events taking place in that time frame. That 210 year "season" in our generation is the period from AD 1844 to AD 2051.

This 210-year period represents dual two-hundred-year patterns with 40-, 50-, and 66.666-year patterns included in the two-hundred-year pattern sets. All then converge in the years AD 2041 and AD 2051. Major convergences of the patterns within the two-thousand-year pattern sets or patterns of 400, 500, and 666.66 years are also converging in these two years.

- The end-times are designed around God's chosen people, the Jews. We will see in the next chapter that the 210-year period surrounding the six thousandth year is apparently God's time for reapplying the Jews to God's "witness program."

- The punishment-event pattern set shows that our generation is the convergence time for all those patterns. This includes all punishment periods that have been assessed on all four variations of the Jewish nation along with the Jewish patriarchs dating all the way back to the flood. All these punishment periods are ending in our generation.

- Enoch was the sixth of eleven pre-flood patriarchs to be listed in the genealogies given in the book of Genesis. He was apparently born around the year 3454 BC and raptured to heaven without dying in about the year 3090 BC. A book supposedly written by Enoch is mentioned in the Christian Bible in Peter and Jude. The credibility of that book has been greatly reinforced in this generation with fragments being found among the Dead Sea scrolls and complete copies in other locations. The Essenes broadly used it in the inter-testament period. It contains a vast number of prophecies of future events taking place all across the post-flood period up to our generation. Ken Johnson of BibleFacts.org has written a book that contains not only an English translation of the original book of Enoch but also a commentary of the book. A vast number of Enoch's prophecies that have already been fulfilled with great accuracy up to our generation greatly add to its credibility. That all leads me to the prophecies that are of great interest to the topics of this book. I have purchased DVDs and listened to podcasts and TV interviews of Ken Johnson giving his interpretation of the prophecies in the book of Enoch. It is my understanding that his interpretations include the following things that pertain to the topics of this book, with each one confirming what we have presented in this book:
  o Creation took place over seven one-thousand-year periods.
  o There would then be seven one-thousand-year periods of mankind on earth.
  o The seven thousand years of man on earth would be broken down into periods of five hundred years and two thousand years, with each ending in a final one-thousand-year millennium with Jesus returning to earth at the start of the one-thousand-year period.
  o The end-times would take place in the years surrounding the six thousandth year after the end of the seventh one-thousand-year period of creation.

Again, we are going to change our perspective in the way we are going to write the rest of this book. Our perspective will change from simply trying to show that our generation is a good fit for the end-times to this new perspective. That perspective will be that we are already within the "birth pangs" leading up to the end-times and that the end-times will actually take place in our generation, ending in the year AD 2051.

While doing all this, we will still recognize that all our clues may just be leading us to another much more complex and complete but yet still-intermediate model of a soon-coming future two thousandth year. While recognizing this, we will still continue to look for other new clues that we are really in the actual end-times. In fact, we will find seven of those much more complex and complete clues in the next chapter. Buckle your seat belts for that!

However, even if we conclude that the end-time scenario is actually taking place in our generation, we realize there are many possible reasons why the fit for the end-time generation may be several months or even years in error.

Clues from Daniel's and Hosea's Prophecies and Jesus's Kingdom Parables in Matthew Can Help Us Answer the Five W's Associated with Our Subject Questions. What Are the Coming Twin Global Resets and Family Reunions, and How Are They Associated with God Meeting the Purpose of His Will, Bringing Everything in Heaven and on Earth Together in Unity under Jesus When Time Reaches Its Fulfillment (the End-Times, Possibly in Our Generation)?

Key Clues from Daniel's and Hosea's Prophecies and Jesus's Kingdom Parables In Matthew

From Hosea's Prophecies

- Hosea forecasts the return of Jesus to the Jewish people after a two-thousand-year exile period. This could be sometime near the end of the year AD 2044, the end of a seven-year period surrounding the year AD 2041.5, or possibly a time of great chaos and tribulation.
- We have finally found our first clues to possible time frames for the twin global resets and family reunions, and they are in our generation.

From Daniel's Prophecies

- **The Twenty-Three-Hundred-Days Prophecy:** We now know the exact time between two of the key events in the end-times: the Second Coming and the anointing of the millennial temple in Israel. The second date would be the time of a great family reunion on earth for God's family and thus the families of believers in Jesus.
- **Daniel's 7+62+1 Prophecy:** Daniel's 7+62+1 sevens prophecy leads us to both the first and second comings of Jesus to earth, with the first being very specific and the second being much more mysterious. We found several ways to use this

formula that would lead us not only to the end-times but also to the year AD 2041 and our generation.

- **Daniel's 1260+1260+30+45 Days=Years Prophecy:** We found an interpretation of the 1260+1260+30+45 prophecy that leads us to the Second Coming in AD 2045, which matches the other prophecies in Daniel precisely, and they are once more in our generation.

From the Kingdom Parables of Matthew

- We unearthed an extremely key clue in these parables. It was the apparent time frame of the coming rapture of the saints to heaven. In concert with Daniel's twenty-three-hundred-days prophecy and Hosea's two-days-equal-two-thousand-years prophecy, we can now speculate on the time frames of eight key dates in the thirteen-year period from the rapture to the great family reunion and the anointing of the millennial temple in Israel. Expecting that the rapture would result in a great family reunion in heaven would give us a prospective time frame for the first great family reunion, with the second being at AD 2051. Again, these are in our generation.

The 5 W's Report Card

CLUES FROM BIBLE PROPHECY THAT WILL HELP US BETTER UNDERSTAND END TIME EVENTS, THE UNIFICATION OF EVERYTHING UNDER JESUS, THE DUAL GLOBAL RESETS, DUAL FAMILY REUNIONS AND THEIR POSSIBLE TIE TO OUR GENERATION			
WHO	**WHEN**	**WHERE**	**WHAT EVENT AND WHY**
Jesus Israel	2045	Israel, whole world	**HOSEA'S 2 DAYS EQUALS 2000 YEARS PROPHECY:** This prophecy may focus on the return of Jesus to the Jewish people after a 2000 year punishment period, toward the end of a 7 year period surrounding the 6000th year. This would be in our generation.
Jesus	2045 to 2051	Mill Temple in Israel	**DANIEL'S END TIME PROPHECIES:** In the 2300 days prophecy we now have the time gap between two key end time events, the Second Coming and anointing of the Millennial temple. This would be the time of a great family reunion for God's people, and thus our families.
Jesus	2nd Coming In end times	Whole earth	**DANIEL'S 7+62+1 7'S:** Prophecy leads us to both the first and second comings of Jesus to earth, with the first being very specific and the second much more mysterious. We found several ways to use this formula that would lead us to not only the end times but the year 2041 in our generation.
Jesus	Second Coming 2045	Whole earth	**DANIEL 12 END TIME PROPHECIES:** We found an interpretation of the 1260+1260+30+45=prophecy which leads us to the Second Coming in 2045 which matches the other prophecies in Daniel precisely. This is in our generation.
Jesus and the raptured saints	From 2038 to 2051 AD	Earth Israel	**FROM THE KINGDOM PARABLES OF MATTHEW:** We now have good clues about the timeframe of all 8 key dates that are associated with the 13 year end time prophecy period from the rapture to the anointing of the millennial temple early in the 1000 year millennial period. It is in our generation.

The Angel of Death and Pandemic Codes

God's Use of Two Unique Means That Result in Extreme Chaos to Bring about the Purpose of His Will

What We Are Trying to Accomplish in This Chapter

On the back cover of this book, we asked a very important question: Will the Angel of Death and pandemic codes tie the end-times to our generation? Presenting the discovery of these codes and then answering this question will be the major topics of this chapter.

We have not yet encountered God using these codes. We said earlier that if we didn't encounter them in our general search for clues about the twin global resets and family reunions, we would make sure to reveal them later in the book. Well, we are there. We are reaching the end of our major research topics with our next major topic being to search for possible beginning-to-end event-pattern strings that God might be using to bring about the purpose of his will. We will call that God's "master template." Thus, we wanted to cover this one final key set of patterns before presenting the big picture God seems to be using to bring about the purpose of his will, to bring everything in heaven and on earth into unity under Jesus when time reaches its fulfillment. Thus, we will now turn to this very interesting and unusual set of event-pattern strings.

As we stated earlier in our chapter on order and chaos, creating events that will bring about great chaos can be extremely valuable in helping to bring about a change in order, even in large societies. Some believe such events are currently being created in our country with the hope that the ensuing chaos can be an aid to bring about a global change in our form of government. We certainly don't know whether that is the case, but we do know that God can use this technique to bring about global resets because we have historical evidence of that happening.

The great flood is the best example. Other examples are the destructions of first Israel, then Judah, and finally Judea. We have presented that evidence in earlier chapters. We also know that Bible prophecy tells us there are three more such global resets in the world's future. We presented two of them in the previous chapter. The first is the mid-tribulation event, in which the Antichrist declares himself to be the ruler of the world and demands to be worshipped as God. The second will take place at the Second Coming of Jesus, at which time he will suddenly become King of Kings and Lord of Lords of the whole earth. That reset will last for one thousand years and will then be immediately followed by the third global reset, a global reset described in Revelation 21–22. That is the event in which heaven and earth, or the physical and spiritual dimensions, will be reunited as one.

In this chapter, we will present two sets of events God may use to bring about great chaos with a resulting set of twin global resets leading to the purpose of his will finally being realized. The two means we will present in this chapter that God will use are the Angel of Death and the pandemic codes. Will we again find these patterns or codes converging in our generation? We will begin with the Angel of Death code.

The Angel of Death Super Code

The first Angel of Death pattern we discovered was one that used two of God's ominous numbers, one being a pattern multiplier and the other being one of the most prominent event time gaps, the tribulation-pattern time gap. These are the numbers 13 and 66.666. The product of these two numbers, 13x66.666=866.66 360-day years or 854.23 calendar years, turned out to be our Angel of Death event-pattern time gap. Much later in our study, we began to wonder whether there might not be some other pattern or set of patterns that involved the number thirteen. Our thought was to investigate whether God might have used many or all of his principal sequential time gaps in patterns involving the unusual number thirteen as a pattern multiplier. As usual, this must have been an inspired idea since it turned out to be the case for all God's principal two-digit sequential year patterns. The results are shown in the chart we place at the end of this discussion.

In summary, the chart shows that we initially found nine patterns, including patterns of event strings of thirteen multiplied by the time gaps used by each of our basic two-digit patterns. This included time gaps of 30, 40, 50, 60, 70, 80, and 90, with 200 and 66.666 years included as well. We found that all four key dates in the seventieth Jubilee period—2001, 2021, 2041, and 2051—each had at least five of the nine patterns converging on them, with the year AD 2051 having convergences involving all nine.

These Angel of Death pattern strings fall into two key categories as follows:

- Those that started in a year of either a global or otherwise very key time of reset for God's people and nations, which would include 4070 BC, 3873 BC, 2444/34 BC, 2296 BC, and 1442/38 BC.
- The other possible Angel of Death patterns may just have occurred as the normal thirteenth event in the sequencing of the basic two-digit event-pattern string spacing and were not necessarily Angel of Death events. We could call God's punishment, destruction, and Angel of Death patterns that don't start in the years of major resets "wildcard patterns." In the case of the full set of ten Angel of Death patterns, we would call the patterns that start in the years of major resets "important" patterns, while those that may or may not be real Angel of Death patterns may be simply "interesting" patterns.

We are just including the first group of patterns in this discussion since they are the ones most likely to actually be associated with large-scale death and chaos. These are the following patterns that are converging in the seventieth Jubilee period.

- The 13x30-year pattern would likely involve a new temple in Israel and some key new world leader. It began in 1438 BC just before the exodus. This would be the most credible Angel of Death pattern since it began at the very time of the original Angel of Death event, which precipitated the exodus event. It hit in the COVID-19 pandemic year of AD 2021. Wow!

- The second pattern was a 13x90-year Angel of Death pattern as well as a new season pattern. It was a twin to our first pattern, in that it started and ended in the very same years, 1438 BC and AD 2021; and the ninety-year pattern is actually a subset of a thirty-year pattern. Again, it hit the COVID-19 pandemic year.

- The next two pattern strings are also twins, in that they started in the twin fifty-year patterns associated with the great flood, the years 2434 and 2444 BC, and ended up in the twin dates of the twin fifty dates associated with the six thousandth year of man, AD 2041 and 2051. These pattern strings are really special because they are the product of the multiplication of God's pattern multipliers 7x10x13x5. This also turns out to be 13x350, 13x50x7, and 13x70x5. All result in 4,550 years, the time gap in 360-day years from the flood years to the years AD 2041 and AD 2051. Wow! Thus, we have our two new patterns, and they involve the basic event-pattern string time gaps of fifty and seventy years, with each being multiplied by the Angel of Death pattern multiplier of thirteen. The fifty-year pattern hits the year 1399, the year the Jews first entered their Promised Land and began counting off Jubilee years, on the way to the year AD 2051. Big surprise! As we saw above, this can also be viewed as a 350-year pattern. When we do that, it turns out that there are exactly thirteen periods of 350 years from the great flood until the year AD 2051. So we now have a tenth Angel of Death pattern.

- The fifth and last Angel of Death pattern we will present in this discussion is the original Angel of Death we first discovered in our research. This was a pattern that started in the year 1442 BC at about the time the plagues against Egypt first began. It proceeds to the year 587 BC when the Babylonian siege of Jerusalem first began and then proceeds to the year AD 1975. God will then administer another seventy-year period of testing of the Jews, which will finally end in the year 2045.00, the year of the Second Coming of Jesus in the end-time scenario we have postulated and exactly twenty-three hundred days before the year AD 2051.39.

What Is Unique about This Set of Pattern Strings
That Helps Us Answer Our Key Questions?

So, we can see several topics in the five patterns discussed above that could have significance to the possible fulfillment of the end-times in our generation. These include a rebuilt temple in Israel, a key new world leader, the possibility of a new season for God's people coming together, a major judgment for God's people that might take place, the end of a long period of testing that could lead to redemption coming to its end, and finally the possibility of some sort of plague or series of plagues taking place.

The full nine event pattern Angel of Death pattern set is shown on the following pages without further discussion. The reader can go to our book *The Angel of Death Super-code,* to find much more discussion on this pattern set.

Clues from the Angel of Death Super Code

- The Angel of Death patterns include several topics that would be critical to the possible fulfillment of the end-time scenario and thus the fulfillment of the purpose of God's will. These include a rebuilt temple in Israel, a key new world leader, the possibility of a new season for God's people coming together, a major judgment for God's people that might take place, the end of a long period of testing that could lead to redemption coming to its end, and finally the possibility of some sort of plague or series of plagues taking place.
- The fact that all ten Angel of Death patterns converge in the year 2051 may be a clue that this year would bring about a major reset in the way in which death relates to humans on earth. This may be related to a major global reset that has just taken place. That would be the last of the twin global resets that are a major topic of this book. The millennium may have just begun, and people are living for hundreds of years again. Most of those on earth may now be living in resurrected bodies that are eternal and immune from death.

Demonstrating God's Supernatural Use of Similarly Themed Events Taking Place Within
The Angel of Death Super Code Set of Patterns
(Event Dates Within the Chart Before 1844 AD are Pattern Ending Dates in Our Generation While After 1844 they Represent Pattern Starting Dates)

Fixed Term Event Date	13x30 =390 384.4	13x40 =520 512.54	13x50 =650 640.67	13x60 =780 768.81	13x66. =866.66 854.23	13X70 =910 896.94	13x80 =1040 1025.1	13x90 =1170 1153.2	13x200 =2600 2562.	Total No. in Pat'rns
4070.5					1910					1
3025.7	1972	2100	2100		2100		2100		2100	6
2444.2			2041			2041				2
2434.3			2051			2051				2
2296.3	1933				1975					2
2285.5	1943									1
2099.2		1903								1
2049.9		2051					2051			2
1990.8		2110					2110			2
1941.5	1903		1903	1903						3
1902.1	1943		1943	1943						3
1872.5	1972		1972	1972						3
1862.7	1982		1982	1982						3
1842.9	2002		2002	2002						3
1793.7	2051		2051	2051						3
1517.7	1943							1943		2
1507.8	1952				1910			1952		3
1438.8	2021							2021		2
1409.3	2051							2051		2
1350.1	2110							2010		2
1054.4	2021	2021		2021			2021			4
965.7	2110			2110			2110			3
719.3	1972	1844	1844		1844	1972			1844	6
709.4						1982				1
610.9			1952		1952				1952	3
591.2	2100		1972		1972				1972	4
587.9					1975					1
561.6					2002				2002	2
522.2		2041	2041		2041				2041	4

512.3		2051	2051		2051				2051	4
463.0	1844	2100	2100	1844	2100			1844	2100	7
325.0	1982			1982				1982		3
68.77		1982					1982			2
19.5 B			1903							1
1.23 A		2051					2051			2
30.8 A	1952		1952							2
70.23	1992		1992							2
129.4	2051		2051							2
135.94					1844					1
139.2						1933				1
1055.9					1910					1
1253.0				2021						1
1657.1	2041									1
1844.4	463/6	719/5	719/4	463/3	719/3			463/2	719/1	7
1903.5	1941/10		1941/6	1941/5						3
1933.2	2296/11					139/2				2
1943.0	2286/11		1902/6	1902/5				1517/3		4
1952.8	1507/9	2148/8	611/4		611/3		2148/4	1507/3	611/1	7
1972.5	3025/13		1872/6	1872/5	591/3	719/3			591/1	6
1975.8					2296/5					1
1982.4	1862/10	68/4	1862/6	1862/5		709/3	68/2	325/2		7
1992.23	70/5		70/3							2
2002.1	1842/10	2099/8	1842/6	1842/5	561/3		2099/4		561/1	7
2021.8	1438/9	1054/6		1054/4			1054/3	1438/3		5
2041.5	1657/1	522/5	2444/7		522/3	2444/5			522/1	6
2051.4	1793/10	2049/8	2434/7	1793/5	512/3	2434/5	2049/4	1409/3	512/1	9
2100.6	591/7	3025/10	3025/8		3025/6		3025/5		3025/2	6
2110.5	1350/9			965/4			965/3	1350/3		4
Total hits	38	19	30	20	22	10	14	14	15	182
Unique Patterns	14	8	11	9	8	5	7	7	7	74

The Pandemic Code and Its Tie to Our Generation, the Twin Global Resets and Great Family Reunions

An Introduction to Pandemics in General

This topic should be very familiar to anyone who is able to read this book. That is because nearly everyone living on the earth has been affected by it in some fashion or the other. In chapter 4 we presented a discussion of the ongoing battle between order and chaos. We certainly saw that in the years of the COVID-19 pandemic. It seemed there was chaos in nearly every facet of our lives, from the simple to the very complex, from simply buying groceries, going to school, having family get-togethers, and even leaving our homes to the more complex including things like getting health care, knowing what to believe about what was taking place, holding sporting events, being able to get inoculated, dealing with the deaths of loved ones including holding services, and so forth. The chaos was everywhere.

The bottom line is that pandemics are horrible events. This pandemic was made much worse by the conflicting information we were getting about how to deal with it. The general public still doesn't know what to believe.

There have been many pandemics of several different colors and sizes, so to speak, in the history of the world. One key thing that separated this latest pandemic from all previous pandemics is that humans couldn't have created previous pandemics on purpose. Humans created this one, and the agent that caused it was created in laboratories and paid for by public health organizations. The creation of the pandemic agent may have been well intentioned in hopes of being able to prevent future pandemics, or there may have been ill will involved. We don't know the answer to that question. There is much the general population still does not know about all this.

If ill will was the intention, then there are two general possibilities. It could have been done by humans exercising their free will, or it could have been inspired by forces for either good or evil in higher-dimensional spaces. We often call these higher dimensions the "spiritual dimensions." Another possibility is that all three were involved.

One conclusion we can reach with certainty by studying the huge number of equally spaced and similarly themed event-pattern strings is that there is no way they could have been conceived or enacted by any form of human effort alone. The event patterns must have been part of an extremely complex plan created even before the creation of the universe and the humans who populate it. The equally spaced and similarly themed event-pattern strings we presented earlier and certainly in our three previous books in this series show that recurring themes in history such as this one have taken place in perfectly spaced numerical patterns. We will show that major worldwide pandemics have occurred in just such patterns, and we will present our findings below.

Presenting the Details of Our Search for the Pandemic Code

We will now begin our discussion of the pandemic code. The pandemic was quite a topic of discussion in the years from 2020 through 2022 for very good reason. Everybody was affected by it in some way or another. Much of the discussion centered on how it got started and who was responsible for it. Unfortunately, there were few, if any, people who knew that Bible codes exist that can foretell these types of events. However, we have discovered two different types of Bible codes that hit the period 2020–2022. The first was a variation of the typical type of event-pattern string, and the second was a very large time gap punishment event-pattern string. We will present each of these below.

The Short Time Gap Event-Pattern String Converging in 2020–2022

We began our study by searching for the years when pandemics hit the world. We found three that occurred since the year AD 1900. These occurred in the years 1917–1920, 1968–1971, and of course 2019–2022. It didn't take long to determine that a thirteen-year sequencing pattern of 360-day years hit all these periods if we started in AD 2020 and used a pattern of 12.8 years, which is the calendar-year equivalent of thirteen 360-day years. We also discovered that a pattern of 4x12.8=51.2 years also hit all three of these periods.

We next decided to see whether this pattern hit the black plague or bubonic plague, which menaced Europe, and so forth in the years of about AD 1345–1355. Again the 51.2-year pattern hit this period in AD 1353. It looked like we had a winner. So where would we search next?

We decided to see if the 51.2-year pattern would hit the year 1438 BC when the original Angel of Death struck just before the exodus. No such luck this time, so we decided to see whether a pattern of 12.8 years would hit 1438 BC. Voilà! We found that a pattern of 270x12.8 hit the exact time that our patterns had set for the exodus. So, what might be significant about this hit? Well, it was the multiplier of 270 that caught our attention. Our previous studies had shown that there was a 270-year pattern of ominous activity surrounding each of the two thousand-year event periods. They all involved death, exiles, and tribulations for the Jewish people. All were full of chaos, a close partner with pandemics. We had also recently found a wall-to-wall pattern in our master template research that showed that there were six periods of 270 years taking place in a hidden but well-defined mathematical pattern that spread across the whole history of the world. Wow! So this was likely a good clue that we had a two-faceted code associated with worldwide periods of great chaos and pandemics. That wraps up phase one of our pandemic code search. Now for phase two.

The Long Time-Gap Destruction and Angel of Death Event-Pattern Strings Associated with the Year 2021.8

There are eight long time-gap punishment patterns we discovered in our book three, *The Angel of Death Super-code*, that all converge in the year AD 2021.8. However, we consider them too complex to present here since they might get us lost in the weeds, so to speak, and we want to keep things simple. The reader can go to our third book if he or she wishes to dig into these patterns. They seem to present events that would help set the stage for an end-time scenario to come together.

There are two sets of long time-gap patterns we do need to include in our pandemic code discussion, however. The first set is the thirty- and ninety-year Angel of Death patterns presented in the first major topic of this chapter. These two patterns both began at the time of the original Angel of Death event in 1438 BC and then converged in the pandemic year AD 2021. As we stated in that earlier discussion, these patterns would involve the likelihood of the following types of things taking place in 2021, the start of a season that would include very important events involving some very key new world leader and a new temple in Israel. Could this be the Antichrist and the new temple that are key parts of the prophetic end-time scenario? Only time will tell.

The second set is the forty-, sixty, and eighty-year Angel of Death pattern set that began in the year 1054 BC and then converged in the year AD 2021 during the pandemic years. The year 1054 BC was the year when the Jews first agreed to begin using kings to rule over them. That could possibly infer that the pattern end year of 2021 would be in the season when an entirely new type of leader would be ruling over them. The forty- and sixty-year event gaps in these patterns could infer that the year 2021 would in some way be in the season when exiles and punishment for past sins would come to an end for the Jewish people. The eighty-year time gap could infer that 2021 could be in the season when the Jewish people and possibly the whole world would soon have a very new type of beginning.

Other Interesting Insights in God's Use of Pandemics to Bring about the Purpose of His Will

At about four o'clock in the morning on September 1, 2022, God gave me a few additional insights into the pandemic code on the very day I was going to try to finish the section of this book on the pandemic code and the year AD 2021. I will present them below.

The first new insight had to do with a tie between the year AD 1.23 and the year AD 1971/72. This goes back to the eleven parallel events taking place during each two-thousandth-year period since the end of the seventh day of creation in 3873 BC. We presented them earlier in this book. One event we didn't include that could be a twelfth parallel event took place seventy years before the two thousandth year in each case. These would have been AD 1.23 and the year AD 1971–72.

The year AD 1.23 was when Jesus would have been two and a half years old, and *he and his parents returned to Israel from their self-imposed exile in Egypt* while in hiding from Herod, who wanted to kill the baby Jesus. Thus, we see Jesus bodily returning to Israel in this account.

First, the year AD 1971–72 was the time of the end of the 7x390-year punishment of Israel, which began at the time of the Assyrian destruction of Israel in 719 BC. That was an exile from God's blessings because they neglected keeping God's three Leviticus 26 commands as we pointed out in the king's scroll shown earlier in this book. That meant *God would be returning to them in Spirit* in the 1971/72 time frame. So we see that the *first parallel* is that God was returning to Israel in some way. What else was happening at this same time?

Second, God was starting a seventy-year period of testing the Jews after their 2,730-year punishment had ended. We remember that the original punishment could be accounted in two ways: seventy periods of forty or twenty-eight hundred years of exile and also seven periods of 390-year exiles, plus a seventy-year period of testing at the end, with both totaling twenty-eight hundred 360-day years. Both ultimately end in the year AD 2041.

Third, a pandemic had just come to an end. This was the Hong Kong flu pandemic. I remember it well because I first got it on October 14, 1969, and it was a whopper. I had health side effects that would recur every few years until I was miraculously healed from them twenty-six years later in 1996. These two years were both in the 13-/12.8-year cycle we addressed above. Was God using this pandemic and the chaotic world events surrounding it to prepare the Jewish people for the coming seventy years of testing that were always intended to lead to redemption?

Fourth, in the Six-Day War of 1967, Israel captured the Temple Mount and reunited Jerusalem. In 1971, during a rabbinical council meeting, the rabbis voted not to allow the Jewish people to use the Temple Mount even though they now controlled it. That likely means the Jews had just entered their final seventy years of testing by God but were already failing the test. So we see that the Temple Mount was finally back in Israel, but they wouldn't use it out of fear.

So what was the parallel event in AD 1.23? We already made the point that Mary, Joseph, and Jesus had just returned to Israel from their self-exile. When they got back, there was a lot of chaos taking place between the Jewish people and the Roman leaders who ruled Israel. Even though Herod was now dead, there was still much unrest taking place. Jesus could still be a target for the Roman-appointed leaders. Thus, even though they were now back in Israel, they were fearful and didn't feel safe, so they moved on and settled in Galilee.

Thus, the parallel events involved fear of taking part in events in their own country. Fear of causing chaos was involved in both cases. We tie this parallel set of events to the pandemic code only through the events in our generation, as we stated above.

Another interesting insight into God's use of pandemics in bringing about the purpose of his will involves the two four-hundred-year periods immediately preceding the six thousandth year. We have made the point several times in our four 2041 book series that the four-hundred-year event-pattern strings have been an ominous series of events for the Jewish people. We know that nine of the twelve dates in this series of events have hosted events marked by great chaos and exiles of various sorts. If we go back to the last two of these four-hundred-year events, we can see great chaos, death, and even a tie to the pandemic pattern. These two event dates were AD 1252 and 1647.

Let us examine this. AD 1252 was the year of the papal bull allowing the torture of the Jews to force them to become Christians during the Catholic Inquisition. Thus, for the next six hundred years, there would be utter chaos and death for the Jews all over the Roman Empire. During the black plague, the Jews were blamed for causing the plague. That was because they were the only people who didn't seem to contract the disease. It was due to their cleanliness and unwillingness to touch a dead body, but the Roman citizens didn't realize this.

We saw earlier that the 4x12.8=51.2 pandemic code hits the time frame of the black plague in AD 1345–1355. Guess what? If we go back two periods of 51.2 years from the black plague, we come to the time of the papal bull. That year is in the four-hundred-year pattern that started at the Tower of Babel in 2296 BC. If we go forward to the next four hundredth year after 1252, we come to 1647. Poland had been a safe refuge for the Jews for some time, but in 1647 they killed nearly one hundred thousand Jews. All these years have been ones of great chaos, fear, and death for the Jewish people.

Do we see the same type of thing for the Jews in the pandemic years of our generation? Is there any hope for them? The answer is a whopping yes! Let's look again at the years in our generation and see whether we can identify that hope. First, in the pandemic years of AD 1917–20, we saw that the British and French conquered the Ottoman Turks near the end of World War II. The result was that the British decided to allow the Jews to return to their original homeland and reestablish their identity as a nation. In the pandemic years of AD 1968–71, we saw that the Jews had just reclaimed their Temple Mount and reunited Jerusalem. In the pandemic years of AD 2019–2022, we saw key Islamic nations for the first time being willing to allow Israel to rebuild their temple on the Temple Mount. All these bode hope for Israel, but they are also keys to setting the stage for the end-time scenario.

This part of the pandemic code may be a bit sketchy in places, but there is enough to raise one's eyebrows.

Putting All Our Clues Together with Some Additional Insights to Reveal the Final Pandemic Code

The pandemic code involves a multiple of the two numbers God seems to associate with the Angel of Death and exiles or 4x13=52 years. The year associated with the Angel of Death was 1438 BC. 1438.8 is closely associated with exiles in two ways. First, it was the exact end of the four-hundred-year exile of the Israelites in slavery in Egypt. Second, it was the start of another exile, this one for forty years. It was an exile in a wilderness for forty years until they were allowed to inhabit their Promised Land because they had disobeyed God. It was also exactly nine periods of 13x30 years and three periods of 13x90 years until the pandemic of AD 2019–22. In God's mathematics, this could signify an event that would begin a new season for Israel involving a new temple, a new world leader, and a time involving death.

We have also seen how the number 270 associates the years 1438 BC and AD 2021 and that the 270 years are associated with the wrath of God. We also see that 3x90 and 9x30 both equal 270, thus tying all three of these patterns together.

Thus, we also infer that the temple, a major new leader, death, and a new season from above would all be associated with the coming "wrath of God." That could imply the "great wrath of the end-times." So, might the pandemic of 2019–22 usher in the final season of the end-times? It certainly fits in with all the other clues we have been gathering. Only God knows for sure.

We saw in the long discussion presented just above that chaos was present in most of the topics in some way or another. It seems that pandemics always result in chaos and death. Chaos is a tool God has often used to bring about his global resets. In these global resets, God has often had to punish his people for long periods of unfaithfulness. This punishment generally resulted in changes in lifestyle, which produced chaos for his people. In several of the instances where this took place in history, it involved the Jewish nations or patriarchs of the Jewish nations. There is another one coming soon that will again involve Israel and this time the whole world as well. According to Bible prophecy, this one won't involve one global reset but two resets, thus creating twin global resets.

The Pandemic Code

We can thus conclude from the discussion above that the pandemic code is composed of the following set of patterns:

- The 13x30 and 13x90 year Angel of Death patterns that began at the time of the original Angel of Death event in 1438 BC and converge in the pandemic year of AD 2021, bringing death and chaos with them. Since these patterns involve the number thirteen, which emphasizes pandemic-type events, chaos and death will be involved.
- The normal thirty- and ninety-year event-pattern strings, which again started in 1438 BC and converged in 2021 BC. These doubled down on the new leader and Jewish temple involvement in this period.
- Forty-, sixty- and eighty-year event-pattern strings and Angel of Death patterns that started at the time when Israel first began using kings to rule over them in 1054 BC and then converged in the year AD 2021, thus tripling down on the year being involved in a season when an entirely new type of leader would rule over them. This could be both the Antichrist and then Jesus just three and a half years later. The forty-, sixty- and eighty-year event-pattern strings could point to the end of exiles, the end of punishment for past sins, and an entirely new beginning for the Jews when they would finally recognize Jesus as their Messiah and begin worshipping him as their God. Again, this all points to the fulfillment of the end-time prophecy.

- A pattern of 270x13, which again spans the period from 1438 BC to AD 2021. That would indicate a good possibility of the year 2021 either hosting or at least being involved in a period that would include the "wrath of God."

There are multiple patterns involved that would make the pandemic code a "super code."

Clues from the Pandemic Code

- All three major pandemics in our generation can be tied to Israel being able to return to their homeland, regain their Temple Mount, and possibly rebuild their temple. Will this result in end-time prophecy being fulfilled in our generation?
- The last three four-hundred-year event periods have all hosted chaos, fear, and death for the Jews. Will the next four-hundred-year period, which ends in AD 2041, be the same? Could this be an end-time event?
- Events in 2022 may lead to the possible rebuilding of a temple in Jerusalem. Could this lead to the end-times?

Insights into How the Number Thirteen Is Used in God's Mathematics to Accomplish the Purpose of His Will

In this chapter, we have seen God using thirteen as the key number in both the Angel of Death and pandemic codes. If we want to understand how God uses the number thirteen in his mathematics, we must first investigate a few of the places where God used this number so we can analyze the outcome of these events to help us do this. We will thus pick four key places where God prominently used the number thirteen and analyze them. We will next present four of those events.

1. The original Angel of Death event: When this event took place, the Israelites had already spent four hundred years in Egypt as slaves. They had grown from the small family of Abraham's grandson Jacob to a huge throng of over 1.5 million people. God had long ago promised them a future country of their own in what the Bible refers to as the "Promised Land." It was now time on God's calendar for them to leave Egypt and go to claim this land as their own. The problem was that they were very useful to the Egyptians, who would not allow them to leave. God's solution was to send a series of plagues of ever-increasing intensity and harm to the Egyptians, capped by the ultimate plague. This was one in which the Angel of Death would kill the firstborn son of every family in Egypt. The only families the Angel of Death would pass over and not kill the firstborn were those who had sacrificed a perfect lamb and placed its blood on the doorposts of their homes. The only ones who knew of this were the Israelites.

   This is a model of the event that would take place about 1,450 years later when the ultimate, perfect Lamb, Jesus, would be sacrificed and would sacrifice his blood to allow forgiveness of all sins for those who would accept it. That would allow them to escape ultimate death and then one day go to their Promised Land in heaven for eternity.

This work of the Angel of Death was successful in allowing the Israelites to escape from Egypt and begin a journey to their Promised Land. The number thirteen was involved in the series of plagues in two ways. First, it appears from our patterns that the plagues began in 1442.1 BC. This date marks the beginning of the series of 13x66.666-year periods that would eventually lead to the time when the Jewish people would finally be forgiven and begin serving Jesus en mass. This would also end at the Second Coming of Jesus, which would result in the following:

- A horrible time for the enemies of God, those who do not belong to Jesus
- An incredibly good time for the friends of God, those who believe in and follow Jesus

2. The Battle of Jericho: This event took place forty years after the exodus event, when the Israelites first crossed the Jordan River into their Promised Land. The walled city of Jericho was their first obstacle in taking over the large land God told them to conquer and take as their own. Jesus made a pre-incarnate appearance to Joshua, the leader of the Israelites, and told him how to conquer the city. In his instructions, he told them it would take only seven days to conquer the city. He told them to assemble everyone in a certain order, with the Ark of the Covenant in the lead, and then to march around the city repeatedly in a very special way. They were to march around the city once a day for six days, and then on the seventh day, they were to march around it seven times before blowing their trumpets. This would end up with the walls of the city crumbling down. That would be a total of thirteen times around the city to achieve success. By the way, this is a model of the exact way God will enact the Revelation judgments. See our website for more on this. Anyway, the final result will be as follows:

- A horrible time for the enemies of God, the idol-worshipping people of Jericho
- An incredibly good time for the friends of God, the God-worshipping Israelites

3. The period from the rapture to the anointing of the millennial temple: This is the thirteen-year period we are presenting as our postulated end-time scenario for the end-times taking place in our generation throughout this book. This fits the end-time scenario Daniel presented in Daniel 12 in a very precise way. In this scenario, the rapture will take place in AD 2038 at the very beginning of the seven-year period of tribulation. AD 2041 will host the middle of the seven-year period when the Antichrist will go into the newly built temple in Jerusalem and declare himself to be God and the ruler of the world. AD 2045 will host the Second Coming of Jesus, judgments by Jesus, the deaths of the enemies of God, the banning of Satan to the Abyss, and so forth. AD 2051 will host Jesus's anointing of the millennial temple during Tabernacles. The millennium will likely begin at the Second Coming of Jesus since Jesus is said in Revelation to become King of Kings and Lord of

Lords of the whole earth at that time. Again, this whole period will last thirteen years with the following results:

- A horrible time for the enemies of God and Jesus, including Satan and all who follow him, both angelic and human
- An incredibly good time for the friends of God and Jesus, including believers in and followers of God and Jesus from all ages past and then present

4. This is the time of the convergence of the Angel of Death event strings in our generation and particularly in the seventieth Jubilee period spanning the years AD 2002.1 to 2051.4. This is the time frame when the vast majority of event patterns are converging. In general, the ending of these pattern strings seems to indicate the end of all periods of punishment for the Jewish people, the time of forgiveness for past sins for both Jewish and Gentile people groups, and the time for the fulfillment of many of the biblical prophecies of the end-times. Of course, this includes the Angel of Death pattern strings. These patterns converge in four separate dates in the seventieth Jubilee period, and we will present our interpretation of the consequences for each date below:

   - 2001–2: This is the start of a fifty-year Jubilee period, and the seven patterns that hit on this date may be indicative of the period rather than this particular year. The years when the patterns started seemed to host the deaths of very key leaders, a change in the key witnesses for God on earth for the next long period, and so forth. That fits the end-time scenario with the return of all believers to earth in resurrected bodies to be the witnesses for Jesus for the next one thousand years and with Jesus himself being on earth in bodily form to be his own witness.

   - 2020–21: The start dates for the five pattern strings converging in this period would indicate a time of being in a forty-year exile period and a time when a new type of leader would be taking charge of the world. This would indicate a time of great chaos and the death of the previous types of world leaders.

   - 2040–41: The six Angel of Death patterns converging on this date indicate first that the Jewish people will be allowed back into an area they were once residing in but had then been banned from living there. Second, a major new leader will allow them to rebuild a temple in Jerusalem on their Temple Mount. Third, this period will host the most disastrous period of destruction in world history. This will of course be accompanied by a huge amount of death all over the world.

   - 2050–51: This period will host the convergence of all ten of the Angel of Death pattern strings. The type of death these patterns forebode will be an entirely new type of death. First, it will be the end of death for a large number of those living in the millennium, since they will then be living on earth in eternal resurrected, glorified bodies that will never face death. Second, those then living on earth as humans will be living in a new type of paradise setting, with no pollution, no harmful drugs in the presence of miraculous healing miracles, and with much longer life spans, possibly living for hundreds of years. Third, it will be a period in which only those who survive the great disaster of 2041 will still be living, and all those will be certified believers in and followers of Jesus. Fourth, it will be a time when all the great pre-flood and post-flood patriarchs are again living on the earth in the newly expanded country of Israel. Fifth, it will be a time of preparation for living in the millennial period for the next one thousand years. Lastly, there will be a great new temple available in Israel. It will mark the death/end of a time when the Jewish people do not have a temple in Israel, the death/end to anyone having to wonder about the truth of Jesus and his true identity, a death to openly sinful practices of all types, and so forth. Finally, the period surrounding 2051 will have very identifiable features associated with it:

- ○ A horrible time for the enemies of God since they will be killed, judged, and banned from the earth. Those banned from the earth will be both Jesus-rejecting humans and all evil spirits, including Satan and his angels.
- ○ An incredibly good time for the friends of God and Jesus as they will be rewarded and given new positions on earth, serving Jesus for the next one thousand years

From what we have presented above, four examples from the Bible, we can see very clearly that we can now look at the number thirteen with an entirely new perspective. Since the world is basically evil and the home for evil, with Satan being the god of the world according to the Bible, our perspective of the number thirteen has been seriously flawed. In all four of the above examples, we see the very same message regarding this number:

- A horrible time for the enemies of God and Jesus
- An incredibly good time for the friends of God and Jesus

So we see that the way we should perceive the number thirteen is very dependent on our status with Jesus. If we are believers in and followers of him, our futures are incredibly bright, even beyond imagination. If we are not in tune with Jesus, the future is incredibly bleak, again even beyond imagination. Which camp are you in?

Thus, the number thirteen represents the *penultimate triumph of good over evil*.

Clues from the Way God Uses the Number Thirteen in the Bible

There are clues from the ways God has used the number thirteen in the Bible that point to the seventieth Jubilee period and the thirteen thousandth year after the start of the creation process being a good fit for the end-time scenario to take place.

Clues from the Angel of Death and pandemic super codes can help us answer the five w's associated with our subject questions. What are the coming twin global resets and family reunions, and how are they associated with God meeting the purpose of his will, bringing everything in heaven and on earth together in unity under Jesus when time reaches its fulfillment (the end-times, possibly in our generation)?

Key Clues from the Angel of Death Super Code

- The fact that so many Angel of Death patterns converged on the key years associated with the refounding of the state of Israel must indicate that these were very key years in God's plan to bring about the purpose of his will.
- The fact that all ten Angel of Death patterns converge in the year AD 2051 may be a clue that this year will bring about a major reset in the way death relates to humans on earth. This may be related to a major global reset that has just taken place. That would be the last of the twin global resets, which are a major topic of this book. The millennium may have just begun, and people are living for hundreds of years again. Most of those on earth may now be living in resurrected bodies, which are eternal and immune from death.

Key Clues from the Pandemic Super Code

- All three major pandemics in our generation can be tied to Israel being able to return to their homeland, regain their Temple Mount, and possibly rebuild their temple. Will these result in end-time prophecy being fulfilled in our generation?
- The last three four-hundredth-year event periods have all hosted chaos, fear, and death for the Jews. Will the next four-hundred-year period that ends in AD 2041 be the same? Could this be an end-time event?
- Events in 2021 may lead to the possible rebuilding of a temple in Jerusalem. Could this lead to the end-times? Themes or topics of events converging in 2021 may be associated with plagues such as the pandemic and other disastrous events that are tied to the coming of the end-time scenario.
- Both Angel of Death patterns and normal event-pattern strings of thirty, forty, sixty, eighty, and ninety years are all converging in the pandemic year of AD 2021. All these could point to the end-times with major new leaders, a new temple, the end of exiles, the final end of punishment patterns, a new start over, and a new season all taking place in the period following AD 2021.

The 5 W's Report Card

CLUES FROM THE ANGEL OF DEATH & PANDEMIC CODES THAT WILL HELP US BETTER UNDERSTAND END TIME EVENTS, THE UNIFICATION OF EVERYTHING UNDER JESUS, THE DUAL GLOBAL RESETS, DUAL FAMILY REUNIONS AND THEIR POSSIBLE TIE TO OUR GENERATION			
WHO	**WHEN**	**WHERE**	**WHAT EVENT AND WHY**
Jesus, all people on earth	In 1000 yr mill., in 2051	Israel, whole world	**ANGEL OF DEATH CODE**: The convergence of all Angel of Death patterns taking place in 2051 may infer that a major reset has taken place involving death, that the millennium has begun and Jesus is ruling the earth
All people on earth	2020-2022	Whole world	**PANDEMIC CODE**: Events in 2021 may lead to the possible rebuilding of a temple in Jerusalem. Could this lead to the end times? Themes or topics of events converging in 2021 may be associated with plagues such as the pandemic and other disastrous events that are tied to the coming of the end time scenario.

God's Master Template and the Global Reset Code

*The Master Template, Which Includes the Global Reset Code,
That God Is Using to Bring About the Purpose of His Will*

What We Are Trying to Accomplish in This Chapter?

We cited God's master template in the section just above. That master template may be the most convincing paradigm we could use to demonstrate that God is in control, that all major events on earth have been preplanned, and that implementation of this plan will continue until the purpose of God's will has been accomplished.

In this chapter, we will present that master template, which is composed of the seven most comprehensive event patterns God seems to have been using, and show that they all converge in the same years during the seventieth Jubilee period. This leads us to speculate that they may be leading us to the end-times including the fulfillment of a major part of the purpose of God's will.

Our Attempt to Discover God's Master Template

As we are finally preparing to attempt to gather all the pieces of information we have discovered in this now-four-book series, we will next try to isolate the bottom line and big picture from all the event patterns we have discovered. Our first attempt in doing that resulted in us attempting to isolate the most basic features of the patterns, the commonalities that applied to all the patterns, and finally the key features of the event patterns that seemed to be the most significant and important to God in bringing his grand purpose to a close. What we will present below was taken from our attempt to do just that.

That attempt resulted in a compilation we consider to be the seven most important and most encompassing pattern sets we had discovered. We called that compilation the "master template." To qualify, a pattern set had to begin at or close to the fall of man and continue until the eternal state of Revelation 21–22. These pattern sets would generally last for either seven thousand or seventy-two hundred years.

We will start with a subset of the set of patterns we have dubbed "equally spaced and similarly themed event-pattern strings." We already presented a description of basic event-pattern strings in chapter 5, but we would like to reveal a few additional details about the pattern strings and why many of them qualify to be part of the master template.

- **Their Purpose:** The bottom-line purpose for these event-pattern strings was for them to be a valuable tool God could use to bring about the purpose of his will, to bring everything in heaven and on earth into unity under Jesus when time reaches its fulfillment. God uses them to test, judge, punish, and reward his people according to how they have performed in meeting his stated requirements for them. Also, all major events have been and still are scheduled and carried out using these event patterns. God planned these events even before the creation of the world according to the Bible. That includes the fact that Jesus would come to earth; live a perfect life; set up a new much simpler criteria for meeting God's standards; and then die for the forgiveness of all the sins of mankind to make it possible for humans to qualify for eternal life in heaven.
- **Their Description:** This description will generally include details of the patterns not covered in chapter 5.
  - All pattern strings would be stated in 360-day years and would need to be converted to calendar years with a multiplier of .98565.
  - All the basic pattern strings started at the fall of man in 4070.5 BC for Gentile people groups and ten years later for those who would ultimately become God's people. They would continue for seventy-two hundred years until the eternal state.
  - After two hundred years, the patterns seem to indicate that God must have started counting a new set of basic pattern strings. This must have taken place at the end of the seventh one-thousand-year day of creation. This would be necessary, for there to be two sets of seven one-thousand-year periods, one involving creation with a final one thousand years of rest and the other seven thousand years for man on earth before the eternal state.
  - Nearly all event-pattern strings would start and end in dates in a ten-year sequence. The major exception would be the 66.666-year punishment pattern, which would always converge in each two-hundred-year pattern and be in a tenth-year pattern in those years but not so in the two intervening events.
  - Events occurring in the two hundredth and two thousandth years would generally host the most meaningful events since patterns of 40, 50, and 66.666 or 400, 500, and 666.66 would always converge in them. That means events of exile, judgment, and tribulation would all be in play. Many other intermediate event-pattern strings would also converge in these years, making them the most ominous events in history, and likely the future as well. The year 2041 is the six thousandth year and may be extremely eventful.
  - God judges his people in fifty-year periods, and if they need punishment, he uses the Gentile people to do that and applies it through Gentile event patterns starting forty years later.
  - These patterns were perfect predictors when understood and properly applied, both during biblical times and also after those times, all the way up to our generation; we have hundreds of examples to prove this.

- All the other pattern types we have discovered and presented, including the master template patterns, are really all take-offs from this basic pattern set, but they are still quite unique and extremely important in the way God is bringing everything, both in heaven and on earth, to a unified conclusion under Jesus the Christ at just the proper time, when time reaches its conclusion in God the Father's eyes (Eph. 1:8–10).

After we discovered this amazing hidden secret super code, so to speak, it became the principal focus of our 2041 series of four books. This book both summarizes many of the discoveries of the first three books and expands them quite extensively while also making them easier to read and understand. In this chapter, we will present what we feel are the seven most overarching ways God used his basic pattern sets to bring about the ultimate purpose of his will.

As an introduction to the master template, we would like to preview the highest level of the apparent plan we believe we have discovered. It is short and simple, and all the details provide a skeleton of sorts for the master template patterns to build on. This in itself is another convincing argument to prove the points we have been trying to make.

The Very Highest Level of the Template God Has Apparently Been Using to Accomplish the Purpose of His Will

We believe we have discovered seven separate very high-level patterns God seems to have been using to bring about the final purpose of his will. We will start here with what may be the very highest level of those seven patterns. This is the twin set of convergence patterns, the first two patterns shown on the chart. We call this set of patterns "God's Witness Pattern set." This turns out to be a pattern that uses the following formula:

2000+2000+2000+1000=7000 years further broken down into a pattern of:
(1600+200+200=2000)x3+1000=7000 years

In which the 200+200-year periods may also be viewed as 400-year periods.

We are now only a few years from the year 2041, the six thousandth year since the end of God's seventh one-thousand-year *day* of creation. In that template, God has apparently chosen three very special people groups to be his witnesses, the people he would use to familiarize himself to the people of the world in general.

Before presenting that template, we would first like to present the reader with a bit more information on the way God has apparently been using the two-hundred- or two-thousand-year event-pattern strings down through history. There is a set of these event-pattern strings that are separated by exactly ten years and flow together down through history with one assigned to the Gentiles and the other to the people group God is then using as his witness group on earth. The Gentile events always precede the witness events by exactly ten years. The Gentile set began at the fall of man, and the witness set began ten years later. Thus, we can see that there are in reality two sets of two-hundred-and two-thousand-year event pattern sets, and they are separated by exactly ten years all down through history. Since these two event pattern sets are so closely tied together, that means that taken together, these pattern events really last 210 and 2010 years.

We also see that there are really two key six-thousand-year events that are separated by ten years, the first for the Gentiles and the second for God's witness group. God would typically judge his Jewish witnesses in their fifty-year Jubilee judgment events and then use the Gentiles to inflict any required judgments on them in the Gentile fifty-year pattern set that would take place forty years later. We will see that the majority of the most important events turn out to be in the Gentile-pattern series.

The witness pattern is really an integral part of the twin-two-thousand-year witness/ Gentile event-pattern set so we did not show it as a separate pattern in the Master Template chart.

God's Witness Pattern

The Sixth and Seventh One-Thousand-Year Days of Creation:
The Last Two Thousand Years before the End of the Seventh Day

The large volume of event-pattern sets we have discovered in this four-book series has led us to believe man's fall took place in the eight hundredth year of the seventh one-thousand-year day of creation. If Adam and Eve were created at the very start of the sixth day, that means they spent eighteen hundred of their first two thousand years in a paradise-like place. This would have been a unified heaven and earth. They would have been expelled from this unified heaven and earth at the time of their fall to Satan's tricks that involved the first sin. At that time, God separated heaven from earth, and they were no longer unified as one. God left them with only one way to get back into heaven. That would be to go through a fiery sword that protected the only entrance to heaven from the earth. Symbolically, that means being *purified by the Word*, which means becoming sinless by accepting Jesus's sacrifice for sins (see Eph. 6).

That would mean that man had only one more two-hundred-year period until the end of his first two thousand years of existence. There are two very important facets to the next two hundred years. First, It seems that God began counting off periods of the time of man on earth at both the beginning and ending of this two-hundred-year period. If God had originally intended for man to have seven thousand years on earth before accomplishing the purpose of his will, then we can see that the fall occurring before the end of the seven thousand years of creation would result in there being two ways to count off time until the start of the planned eternal state when God would again place heaven and earth back into unity forever. There would be periods of seventy-two hundred years from the fall of man until the eternal state and seven thousand years from the end of the seventh day of creation until the start of the eternal state.

This two-hundred-year disparity can be seen as a period of transition. In his first eighteen hundred years, God was the one who would be familiarizing man with his requirements. In the last two hundred years, there would be a transition to man having to familiarize himself and his offspring with God's requirements for living. In this last two hundred years and then the next two thousand years, it will be up to the eleven great patriarchs of the pre-flood and early post-flood eras to do this familiarization process.

God's Witnesses in the First Two Thousand Years after the Fall of Man

In this two-thousand-year period from the fall until the time of Jacob, the grandson of Abraham, God used a group of eleven great patriarchs, including Adam, Methuselah, Enoch, Noah, and Shem. Noah was six hundred years old at the time of the flood, and he lived until the end of the two thousandth year after the fall of man. Shem was Noah's son, and like his father, he survived the flood on the ark. He was one hundred years old at the time of the flood and lived another five hundred years, dying when Jacob was fifty years old, just forty years before the two thousandth year after the end of the seventh day of creation in 1902 BC when Joseph was born to Jacob. Thus, we see the eleven great patriarchs were those who conveyed God's will to the people on earth during the first two thousand years, whether we start at the fall or the end of the seventh day of creation.

This two-thousand-year period was thus the period of the patriarchs. The transition from this period to the second two thousand years took place over the last four hundred years of the period from 2296 to 1902. Historically speaking, we can see the beginnings of the change starting in the first two hundred years of this four-hundred-year period. The key dates associated with this period are as follows:

2148/2138 BC
These are the birth dates of Abraham and Sarah. They were the parents of the key group of witnesses for God in the second two-thousand-year period. This change was then quickly hastened in the last two hundred years of this two-thousand-year period with the following events:

2089 BC
Noah died in 2089 BC, ten years after the two thousandth year after the fall.

1941 BC
Shem died in 1941 BC, which was 1960 years after the fall of man. Noah and Shem were the last two of the eleven original patriarchs.

2050 BC
The birth of Isaac.

1990 BC
The birth of Jacob.

1902 BC

By the start of the year 1902 BC, the two thousandth year after the end of the seventh day, it would then be up to the descendants of Abraham, Isaac, and Jacob to be God's key witnesses on earth, those who were supposed to make God's requirements of mankind known to the world.

Thus, we have seen a gradual transition from the patriarchs to the descendants of Abraham, Isaac, and Jacob, who would be known as the Israelites, Judeans, and Jews down through the years.

If we look at this from a historical perspective, we can see this process continuing for all three two-thousand-year periods after the end of the fall of man. We can see both of the two-hundred-year periods before the start of a new two-thousandth-year period hosting very important dates in each case.

God's Witnesses in the Second Two Thousand Years after the Fall of Man

This period of two thousand years went from the birth of Joseph in 1902 BC until the destruction of Jerusalem including the temple and the exile of the Jews to the nations of the world starting in AD 70. This was the two-thousand-year period when God used those he called his chosen people, the Jews, the descendants of Abraham and Sarah. This really started when Jesus, as the Angel of the Lord, made visits to Abraham, Isaac, and Jacob, making covenants with them and giving them special promises. This reached fruition during four hundred years of slavery in exile in Egypt. During this time, they became a nation of about 1.5 million people. God used Moses and the Angel of Death to extract the Jews from slavery in about 1438 BC. God gave Moses the TORH, the first five books of the Bible, in which he laid out his requirements for them. Again, see the king's scroll earlier in this book for many of the details. In this two-thousand-year period, God was using the Jewish people to bring his message to the people of the earth, those we call the Gentiles.

This two-thousand-year period was thus the period of God's chosen people, the Jews. Again there would be a gradual transition, this time from the Jews to the Gentiles over the last four hundred years, from 325 BC to AD 70. This transition would have two dimensions associated with it.

The first dimension involved a transition of the countries that would rule over the Jews during this period. The transition would begin with the Greeks, who ruled over Judea starting in about 325 BC until the Romans overtook Judea and the Romans gradually overtook Greece and Judea in the years from 62 to 29 BC. The Romans then destroyed Judea in AD 70, the four thousandth year after the end of the seventh day of creation. The Roman Empire then was the dominant empire in the world over most of the next two thousand years.

The second dimension in the transition involved a change within those who controlled the Jewish religious hierarchy. In the big picture, this may have been by far the most important transition. This took place in the inter-testament period. It began about four hundred years before the beginning of the four thousandth year, AD 70, sometime in the period surrounding the year 300 BC. That was about the year the Essenes came together as challengers of the ruling hierarchy, the Pharisees and Sadducees.

We discovered much about this period from Ken Johnson's YouTube video presentations. We will cite a few rather astounding discoveries Ken reported on his telecasts as we remember them.[3] Much to the astonishment of most of us, the original patriarchs apparently had access to writing utensils and means to store their history for the use of following generations. It seems that some of these writings were found as a part of the Dead Sea Scrolls. The Essenes apparently had access to the book of Enoch and made good use of it. Enoch was one of the original eleven patriarchs, the sixth from Adam. Enoch made many astonishing prophecies, several about a coming Messiah, including the dates when he would be on earth. It also includes dates concerning the coming end-times, and these have recently become available to us.

The Essenes thus were very much awaiting the coming of the Messiah and were not surprised when he did appear, apparently right on Enoch's schedule. During the time of Jesus, they apparently had a school that taught many of their beliefs. It seems that John the Baptist may have been an Essene, while Paul may have also gone to the school after his conversion. Anyway, they certainly were believers in Jesus and quickly merged into the early church movement, so to speak.

Meanwhile, the Pharisees and Sadducees didn't accept Jesus as their Messiah and Savior, so they were not part of the very important body of early-church Jewish witnesses for Jesus and thus for God. Since the Jewish ruling class and their followers as a whole didn't accept Jesus, he pronounced his seven woes on them as recorded in Matthew 23. This resulted in the destruction of Jerusalem and the temple, with the Jewish people being exiled in large numbers and completely losing their country, Judea, seventy years after AD 70. Thus, the transition from the Jewish people as the world's witnesses for God was transitioned to the Roman Empire and those who had become Christians.

The dates associated with this transition process are as follows:

325 BC

This is the start of the four-hundred-year period before the four-thousandth year in AD 70. The Greeks took control of Judah at that time after conquering the Persians, who had controlled Judah since about 540 BC.

127 BC

This is the year the Anno Domini calendar became the dominant calendar in the world. Also, this is the four thousandth year after the fall of man. This was two hundred years before the four thousandth year after the end of the seventh day of creation. The transition from the Jews to the soon-coming Christians was sped up by the Romans coming into great power in the world in this time frame. Also, don't forget the most important date of all.

2.5 BC

The birth of Jesus.

AD 70

This is the year of the destruction of Jerusalem and the temple as well as the time of the death of hundreds of thousands of Judeans, with the exile of thousands of other Judeans by the Romans.

God's Witnesses in the Third Two Thousand Years after the Fall of Man

The Jewish people failed miserably in meeting God's test concerning taking God's Word to the nations of the earth, so he sent his Son, Jesus, to earth to be born as a human and to do what no man could in presenting God's message to the world. Jesus was eternal in the past and the future, but he chose to come to earth to provide a certain way for humans to get to heaven. God's plan was conceived even before the creation of the universe. In that plan, he would give his Son, Jesus, a very special gift. That would be a companion, created in his own image. The whole universe and all the major events that have taken place were all preplanned to eventually meet the purpose of God's will. That will is a companion for Jesus, a bride that will eventually join him in *unity*, in marriage, after time reaches its fulfillment. That unity will be completed at the end of a one-thousand-year period on earth with his bride, when God will once more *unify* heaven and earth as one.

When the Jews refused to accept Jesus as their Messiah and God, the Jews were replaced by an entirely different people group, the non-Jews or Gentiles. It was then up to them to be God's witnesses, who would take the message of Jesus to the whole world, to make becoming part of the bride of Jesus a possibility for them as well. Paul said in Romans that the Jews are now in timeout; they are partly blinded, and this blindness will last until a future period we call the seven-year tribulation period. We are thus now in the third two-thousand-year period, the time when Gentiles are taking the message of God to the whole world.

This two-thousand-year period was thus the period of the Gentiles, with the Roman Empire being dominant for most of the period. The Roman entity responsible for taking the Word of God to the nations was known as the Catholic Church or the Catholics. Again, there would be a gradual transition getting its start with the Protestant Reformation in the early 1500s. The transition got a boost with the King James Bible, which became available in the early 1600s.

The bad treatment of the Jews by the Gentiles in general and Roman Catholics in particular over the last eight hundred years of this two-thousand-year period was horrific. This got a big boost with the papal edict in 1252, allowing Jews to be tortured during the Catholic Inquisition to force them to become Christians. This Inquisition would last for six hundred years, with it finally ending in the mid-1800s. This treatment was especially tragic in the last four hundred years, with millions upon millions of Jews being slaughtered. This treatment finally ended up with the world again recognizing the right of Israel to its original homeland and its right to become a nation once more in 1948.

This whole scenario may have been necessary to be able to make it possible for the end-time scenario to be fulfilled in the general time frame of the six thousandth year. For this to take place, the Jews would need a dominant protector nation to come to their aid when necessary. That leads to our third and last four-hundred-year transition period. That nation would be the United States. The seeds for this nation were planted in England with the lack of freedom of worship. This led to the founding of the United States, with the first colony being settled in Jamestown in AD 1607.

The hard part of this story to tell involves the 270-year period that surrounds each two-thousandth-year period. It always seems to end with an event full of chaos, death, and destruction taking place. This may simply be a coincidence, but it will be exactly 270 years from the year that ended up with the Declaration of Independence being signed, 1775–76, until the year 2041. That year will have more event patterns converging on it than any other year in the history of man on earth by far.

If this does take place, it will be a whopper. The transition would be for the world to be ruled over by God himself, in the form of Jesus, with his co-rulers being a combination of Christians and Jews, all those who have been followers of Jesus during all ages past. This period will then see the dual global resets and family reunions taking place in very quick succession, all ending in AD 2051.

Jews and Christians will be unified together with each other and with Jesus in a great unification movement. These three four-hundred-year periods are all part of the incredible four-hundred-year event-pattern string that started at the Tower of Babel and will end in 2041, lasting forty-four hundred years with a full nine of the twelve events associated with it being very key events for God's people.

Again, as was the case in the previous two-thousand-year periods, the four-hundred-year period that directly preceded this two thousandth year, the six thousandth year in this case, can be broken into two periods of two hundred years each, with the transition from the Roman Catholics to another new group gradually taking place.

The dates associated with this transition process are as follows:

1517/19

Two major events that affected Judaism and Christianity took place in this time frame. First, the Ottoman Turks captured Jerusalem and controlled the Holy Land until the British and French defeated them in World War I. Second, the Protestant Reformation took place. This would mark the birth of the era when Protestantism would gradually replace Catholicism as God's major witness for him in the world.

1647/57

Again, there were two major events taking place and affecting God's witnesses in the world during this time frame. First, Poland, which had long been a sanctuary for Jews during the Inquisition, changed their colors, so to speak, and began persecuting the Jews in this time frame. They killed nearly one hundred thousand Jews during this period. Second, England, which had years before banned Jews from living in their country, also changed their position and began readmitting Jews.

1844

This year marked what may have been the watershed event leading to the Jews being able to begin returning to their original homeland and settling there. This was the "edict of toleration" for Jewish people in the Ottoman Empire, the empire that owned and ruled over what had once been the Jewish Holy Land.

2041

This is the year that has gradually become the major focus of this four-book series since major event pattern after major event pattern has converged on it, with many that seem to point to it as a great fit for fulfilling a large number of biblical end-time prophecies. As a matter of fact, it is the key target of all seven of our highest-level master template patterns. It also has by far the most individual patterns converging on it of any other single date in history.

God's Witnesses in the One-Thousand-Year Millennium Preceding the New Order

The fourth period in the highest level of God's apparent plan lasts one thousand years. It is quite different in that Jesus will return to earth at the end of the third two-thousand-year period to save the earth from utter destruction. Jesus will now represent himself on earth for one thousand years and rule the earth from a huge temple in Israel. He will rule with an iron scepter, meaning that he will allow no nonsense. We, his followers, will rule with him according to Revelation.

By the way, during this period the Jews will be grafted back into the Tree of Life with Christians since they accepted Jesus as their Savior and Messiah en mass during the seven-year tribulation period. Jew and Gentile will all serve God as one in this time frame. The Jews will have a preeminence of sorts since Jesus will live with them in Israel, and people from all over the earth will be required to go to Israel during the Feast of Tabernacles to worship Jesus and celebrate life with him. That will be the greatest family reunion of all time, and it will be repeated year after year.

The Final Order: Eternity in a New, Unified Heaven and Earth

The millennium will end with the final judgments of all those who have not accepted Jesus down through the ages. After that we come to the eternal order of Revelation 21–22. Thus, we now see what the word *unified* means in the purpose of God's will stated in Ephesians 1. In the new order, the physical and spiritual dimensions will be merged or unified as one twelve-dimensional space. The word *unified* has two fulfillments. One is that we will be unified in marriage to Jesus for eternity, and the other is that we will then spend eternity on an entirely new earth-like place in a new heaven of sorts, with the two being unified as one. We will be in all twelve dimensions at the same time. Whew! There will no longer be a need for witnesses there will no longer be humans in the universe.

A Second Type of Witness in Each Two-Thousand-Year Period

Before concluding this topic, there is another facet of the witness pattern we discovered, and it may be equally important. The witnesses we discussed above were basically people groups God selected to represent him in the world. However, it appears that there is at least one other means that was very effective in accomplishing this over the many centuries.

This was the written word. We will look at that in all three two-thousand-year periods.

- **First Two Thousand Years:** There seems to be good evidence from at least a couple of sources that the pre-flood patriarchs could write, record things in some written medium, and pass it on from generation to generation. The Dead Sea Scrolls are said to have fragments of the writings of Enoch, the sixth from Adam. Complete copies of this text are said to exist and are now being translated into English. The Essenes claimed to have copies of this and various other antique documents. If that is true, these documents must have been on the ark and were then passed on down through the generations. I have gleaned much of this knowledge from the work of Ken Johnson, who reports weekly on his YouTube telecasts. Moses presented a genealogy of the patriarchs all the way back to Adam in Genesis. Would this have been Moses's source? It is also true that the Christian Bible presents clues in many places that the patriarchs already had God's commandments and his law before the exodus. In fact, we find that the patriarchs, including Noah, Shem, Abraham, Isaac, Jacob, and Job, were aware of God's commandments and his law.
- **Second Two Thousand Years:** If there was a written record of God's requirements in the first five hundred years of the second two thousand years, it must have come from the patriarchs in one way or the other. This could have included the writings of Enoch and others who died before the flood, or it may have been written by either Noah or Shem, who of course survived the flood. Noah was born six hundred years before the flood. After the five hundredth year of this period, the writings of Moses would have been available to the Israelites on scrolls. Genesis apparently dates to about 1438 BC and Deuteronomy to 1400 BC. The other Old Testament books and other books not recorded in the Bible but mentioned in the Bible would all have been written in the period from 1400 BC to about 425 BC. The bottom line is that there was a written record of God's requirements available to the Old Testament scholars and kings. Many were kept in the temples.
- **Third Two Thousand Years:** During the first five hundred years of this period, the Old Testament scrolls and many other writings were available in the temples and to various groups not associated with the temples, including the Essenes. Soon after the death of Jesus, the letters and documents that would become the Bible's New Testament started becoming available. After the canon was approved in AD 325, the whole of the Christian Bible would start becoming available. It may have been available only in Greek or Latin until the invention of the printing

press in the late 1400s and the Protestant Reformation a few years later, which ignited the translation of the Bible into English. For many years now, it has been the best-selling book in the world, and that continues to be true year after year, even to today.

Thus, we can easily see that there has nearly always been a second source of witness for God in the world. Its true availability to the masses would have depended on the motivations of the stewards of that written record.

We have just finished presenting our interpretation of one very key facet of the very highest level of the template God has apparently been using to accomplish the purpose of his will. We have discovered seven total event patterns in this overall template, and we will next present the full seven pattern sets of that master template. *It will be quite interesting to see how many of these seven top-level event patterns involve some form of a 2000/2000/2000/1000 scenario.*

Clues from God's Witness Pattern

- God's witness pattern, like so many of his patterns, relies on similarly themed events taking place that surround each two thousandth year after the end of the seventh day of creation. In this case, the events involve a gradual change in the identity of God's witnessing group. It evolved from the eleven patriarchs to the Jewish people and to the Christians; and finally in and after 2041, it seems that we may have a merger of Christians and Jews into one group; and it will remain constant over the next one thousand years after that. This points to the fulfillment of the biblical end-time scenario in the 2041 time frame with the dual global resets and family reunions taking place. This means the first step in meeting the purpose of God's will finally be fulfilled, that being Jesus and his bride being united as one. The final steps will take place one thousand years later. In this one-thousand-year period, Jesus will be on earth as his own witness.
- We also found that there is a second witness in each two-thousand-year period. That is a written witness, and it expands from period to period. The written witness in the first two thousand years was the writings of the eleven patriarchs. This transitioned to the Old Testament writings over the second two thousand years, and it then expanded to include the New Testament in the final two thousand years. Paul told us that we always need two witnesses.

Our Interpretation of What May Have Been the Seven Major Event-Pattern Sets in God's Master Template

An Introduction to the Master Template Chart

What we will be doing in this presentation of God's apparent master template is demonstrating how extremely precise, thorough, detailed, inclusive, and expansive God has been in the control of his interactions with humans to bring about the purpose of his will.

As we were nearing the end of our third book in this 2041 book series, *The Angel of Death Super-code*, we were led to ponder all the things we had discovered and written about over the previous six years with the goal of coming up with a master template God might have been using down through the ages. Our thought was that it would likely consist of all the event-pattern strings that covered the whole seventy-two hundred years from the fall of man in about 4070 BC to the postulated date for the start of the eternal state in AD 3037. We quickly came up with four candidates as follows:

- the standard equally spaced and similarly themed event-pattern strings
- the ever-present seventy-year testing pattern
- the wrestling match pattern, a sort of nonstandard event-string pattern
- God's punishment patterns, which had multiple starting and ending dates, with some covering the whole seventy-two hundred years.

As we were pondering this topic we received early-morning inspirations that led us to two other end-to-end patterns that are quite stunning. These were:

- the death, passover and new home pattern;
- the wrath-of-God pattern.

The discovery of these incredible patterns certainly gave us a confidence boost, a renewed confidence that we were on to something very important in this series of books. We will next present the master template chart, which covers a full eight pages with about one hundred historical dates included. We ask the reader to ponder the chart a bit and then go on to our discussion of each of the patterns in the pages following the charts.

The charts on the even-numbered pages contain the seven end-to-end patterns, while those on the odd-numbered pages straight across from the even-numbered pages contain descriptive material that will greatly aid in understanding the seven patterns. This information on the odd-numbered pages is as follows:

- The first two columns contain the historical dates of the patterns on the odd-numbered pages across from them. The dates in the first column are associated with our current 365-day-per-year calendar, while those in the second column are associated with the dates on a 360-day-per-year calendar, the one God has obviously always been using. We speculate that God does this to keep people on earth from being able to discover the event patterns he has always been using in his dealings with people on earth. Thus, we say that the patterns have been coded. If we peruse the dates, we see in the 360-year column that the vast number of dates end in tenth-year periods. That would make it easy for anyone using a 360-day calendar on earth to be able to recognize the pattern themes and thus be able to predict the years of future events. We included this column to make this point for the reader.

- The third column contains our initial estimate of the relative importance of each of the events based on a grading system we devised. A description of our grading system and how we applied it are contained at the end of this chapter and in Appendix B. We also discuss the qualifications we placed on this process and some additional corrections we felt were necessary to achieve a final grade for the very most important patterns. We eventually came up with a list of the top-twenty most important event dates in the whole seventy-two hundred years God may have in store for man on this earth.

- The last column contains a description of the events that have taken place or are speculated to take place in the dates shown. Speculation is based on the themes of the patterns that converge on those dates. This is based on the way God has used the pattern denominations in the Bible combined with the themes of the key historic events that have already taken place in key events within that pattern.

We have already presented several major features of the first two patterns, the twin two-thousand year convergence patterns. Of course, this included the fascinating witness for God feature of those patterns. We will begin with a short discussion of several other features of those convergence pattern sets. The reader might want to take the time to get acquainted with the set of charts before moving on to our detailed discussion of the patterns.

- Philip R. Herron -

The Master Template

That God Seems to Have Been Using to Accomplish
The Ultimate Purpose of His Will (Eph 1:9-10)

Date	General Purpose 2000/200 Convergence Pattern Set			Specific Purpose Master Template Event-Pattern Sets				
Key Event Years	Gentile 40/400G 50/500G 66.666G 666.66G 200G 2000G 2000FG	Witness 50W 200W 350W 2000W 2000FW 30W,60W 90W	Full Season 1800G 30G/60G 90G 600G 1750G 350G	Destruction, Punishment 360 390 430 Full Angel + 13x All	Wrath of God (700+700+ 600)X3 +1000= 7000 Yrs With 270	Global Reset Death, Passover, New Home 500 Yr Super Jubilee	Wrestling Match With God 2000f+ 7x600 or 6x700+ 1000= 7200 Yrs	Always Present 70 & 70x7= 490
4070.5	2000Fs		1800s	360s	600s, 700s	Reset Comb	2000Fs	70
4060.6		2000Fs 30,60,90					2000Fs	70
3873.4	2000Gs 666.6	New Witness	1750s 600					70
3863.5		2000Ws				3x500s Global Reset		70
3480	400		30	430s				70
3380	500			390s	700i			70
3025.7				6 Angel s 12x430s				70
2690.5	400				700e,600s 200+70s			70
2493.4	200		350		200			70
2444.1	50		30					70
2434.3		350 200, 66.6		13x50, 70 Angel s	200+70e Wrath	Global Reset		70
2385.0						3x500e, 2x500s		70
2296.3	400		1800	360				70x7=490
2286.5		30,60,90		13x30 Angel s 11x390s				70
2148.5	50		1750G, 30					70
2138.6	40	30, 50						70
2099.2	2000FGe 200		600	13x40,80 Angel s	600e,700s 200+70s		700,600Gs 2000Fe	70
2089.3		350 2000FWe	30				700,600Ws 2000Fe	70
2049.9	50			13x40,80 Angel s				70
2040.1		200						70
1990.8		30, 50						70
1972			30	9x430s				70
1941.5	40		90, 60	360				70
1902.1	2000G 666.66	30 New Witness		13x50,60 Angel s 10x390s	200			70

The Master Template

That God Seems to Have Been Using to Accomplish
The Ultimate Purpose of His Will (Eph 1:9-10)

Key Event Yrs on Man's 365 Day/yr Calendr	Key Event Yrs on God's 360 Day/yr Calender	Total No. of Master Patterns Converg Score w/o Bonus pts (App B)	Key Information to Help Identify The Significance of the Individual Pattern Events
			Description of the events taking place in the specified years Key for fixed term patterns: s=start of pattern, e=end date in pattern, i=intermediate event Key for General Purpose Patterns: F=Pattern starts at Fall of Man G=Gentile, W=Witness (First 2000 yrs=Patriarchs, Second 2000 yrs= Jewish people, Third 2000 yrs= Christians, Final 1000 yrs = Jews/Chr)
4070.5	4130	969	Fall of man at end of 800th year of the 7th 1000 year day of creation
4060.6	4120	566	Start of God's Witness event pattern strings 10 years after the Fall of man
3873.4	3930	1878	End 7th day of creation: start 7 1000 year days of man on earth before start of the eternal state of Rev 21-22
3863.5	3920	1351	Start of God's Witness pattern strings associated with the end of the 7th day of creation; Global Reset 1
3480	3530	569	Unknown event; 25 years before the birth of Enoch, 6th from Adam
3380	3430	172	Near time of the birth of Methusaleh, longest living human died at age 969
3025.7	3070	962	Birth of Noah, patriarch of the only righteous family left on earth at the time of the flood; he and his family of eight lived through the flood on an ark
2690.5	2730	165	260 years before the flood; start of God's typical 260/270 year period of testing of man before a serious punishment event
2493.4	2530	144	End of the 200th year in the 200+60/70 year period of severe testing
2444.1	2480	9	Gentile 50th year that always precedes a Jewish 50th year by exactly 10 years
2434.3	2474	1334	The great flood event that lasted a full year and covered the complete earth; recorded in history of nations around the world; Global Reset 2
2385.0	2419	140	End of the Jubilee year pattern associated with the Global Reset 2, the flood
2296.3	2330	924	The approximate time of the Tower of Babel event
2286.5	2320	189	End Tower of Babel Event; God punished the people of earth by confusing the languages so that different people groups would speak different languages, thus making it difficult for people to jointly conspire against God
2148.5	2180	166	The birth of Abraham, who would father both the Jewish nations through his son Isaac and Arabic/Muslim countries through his son Ishmael
2138.6	2170	16	Birth of Sarah, wife of Abraham and mother of Isaac
2099.2	2130	1211	Exactly 2000 years after the fall. Start of Gentile wrestling match with God over his true identity; start of the 200+70 year testing period for Jews
2089.3	2120	782	Death of Noah; start of Jewish 4200 year wrestling match with God over his true identity; would last 7 rounds of 600 years each. Start Jewish 2000 pattern.
2049.9	2080	623	Birth of Isaac, son of Abraham and Sarah and father of Jacob; Abrahamic circumcision covenant; destruction of Sodom and Gomorrah
2040.1	2070	64	Shem was 500 years old, 400 years after flood
1990.8	2020	9	Birth of Jacob, grandson of Abraham, father of 12 tribes of Israel thru sons
1972	2000	499	Abraham dies at age 175
1941.5	1970	97	Shem dies at age 600; last known survivor of the great flood
1902.1	1930	1947	Joseph born, 11th son of Jacob and father of one of the 12 tribes of Israel; sold into slavery in Egypt by his brothers; eventually his whole family came to Egypt due to drought and end up in slavery in Egypt for 400 years. Jews become the new witness for God in the world.

Date	General Purpose 2000/200 Convergence Pattern Set			Specific Purpose Master Template Event-Pattern Sets				
Key Event Years	Gentile 40/400G 50/500G 66.666G 666.66G 200G 2000G 2000FG	Witness 50W 200W 350W 2000W 2000FW 30W,60W 90W	Full Season 1800G 30G/60G 90G 600G 1750G 350G	Destruction, Punishment 360 390 430 Full Angel + 13x All	Wrath of God (700+700+ 600)X3 +1000= 7000 Yrs With 270	Global Reset Death, Passover, New Home 500 Yr Super Jubilee	Wrestling Match With God 2000f+ 7x600 or 6x700+ 1000= 7200 Yrs	Always Present 70 & 70x7= 490
1872.5								70
1862.7	40							70
1842.9		30, 200		13x30,50, 60 Angel s 390i				70
1836.4	66.666							
1833.1					200+70e Wrath			70
1793.7		50	30	13x30,60 Angel s 430s				70
1507.8	400							70
1442.1 (1448)	666.6 66.666					Global Reset		70
1438.8		Written witness	30	13x30,90 Angel s 390s		TORH Given as wrwitten witness		70
1409.2	500		90, 60	13x90 Angel s	700i		700G	70
1399.4		30, 350				2x500e, 3x500s	700W	70
1350.1	40	50	60					70
1054.4		350 200	90, 60	13x40,60, 80 Angel s 390i				70
1015.0	50	30, 60						70
1005.1		50						70
965.7	50		90					70
916.4	500 200		600					70
719.3	400	30		6 Angel s 70x40s 7x390s	700e,600s 200+60/80s Wrath		700G	70
709.4		350					700W	70
610.9		50	90					70
587.9	66.666							
561.6	40	50		13x66.66s				70
536.4								70
522.2	200		1800	13x40,200, 66.6 Ang s 360,430i	200			70

			Key Information to Help Identify The Significance of the Individual Pattern Event Dates

Key Event
Yrs on
Man's 365
Day/yr
Calendr
	Key Event
	Yrs on
	God's 360
	Day/yr
	Calendr
		Total No.
		of Master
		Patterns
		Converg
		Score
		w/o Bonus
		pts
		(App B)
			Description of the events taking place in the specified years
			Key for fixed term patterns:
			    s=start of pattern, e=end date in pattern
			Key for General Purpose Patterns: F=Pattern starts at Fall of Man
			    G=Gentile, W=Witness (First 2000 yrs=Patriarchs, Second 2000 yrs= Jewish people,
			Third 2000 yrs= Christians, Final 1000 yrs = Jews/Chr)

1872.5	1900	1	Isaac dies at age 180 Joseph becomes leader in Egypt at age 30
1862.7	1890	8	Jacob and family come to Egypt to buy grain; Joseph recognizes them
1842.9	1870	338	There was a new Pharaoh in Egypt who did not recognize Joseph and appreciate him and his family; he mistreated them and eventually put them into slavery in Egypt which would last for 400 years
1836.4	1863	70	Joseph and his family are now under tribulation in Egypt
1833.1	1860	65	The 400 year period of slavery began
1793.7	1820	597	Death of Joseph at age 110; This would be a year when several long event patterns involving punishment for the Jewish people would begin
1507.8	1530	71	A new Pharaoh came to power in Egypt; things get worse for the Israelites
1442.1 1448	1463	1078	1448 was the Jubilee year that began the period of the 3rd Global Reset; 1442 is associated with start of the plagues leading to the Exodus
1438.8	1460	1275	Year of the miraculous EXODUS from Egypt after the Angel of Death plague; Seven weeks after the Exodus God gave the Israelites the 10 Commandments and the information that would be in the TORH which began the 3rd Global Reset
1409.2	1430	187	The Gentile 50th year, a pattern in which a Gentile 50th year always precedes a Jewish Jubilee by 10 years and also follows it by 40 years
1399.4	1420	99	Jews enter Promised Land; start 50 year Jubilee celebrations; this was the year in the 500 year pattern that would end another Global Reset cycle
1350.1	1370	17	Joshua dies; starts period of judges ruling the Israelites
1054.4	1070	177	This was a Jubilee year in which the decision was made to begin using kings to rule over the Israelite nation; this would not work well since the vast majority of their kings would entertain idol worship in their nation
1015.0	1000	11	Period when King Saul was attempting to murder David
1005.1	990	8	David captured Jerusalem which became the capital of Israel & Judah
965.7	980	11	Jerusalem Temple construction started 480 years after the Exodus
916.4	930	154	Israel split at death of Solomon; Rehoboam, first king of southern kingdom of Judah died in this year. He was the first open idol worshiping king
719.3	730	540	The northern Jewish kingdom of Israel had been worshipping both YHWH and idols for many years; God punished them in this year by allowing the Assyrians to conquer them and exile their people for 7x390 yrs
709.4	720	28	Only dateable Jubilee in Bible; God supernaturally saved Judah
610.9	620	11	Jubilee year when the Assyrians fell to the Babylonians
587.9	596	7	Babylon destroyed Jerusalem/Temple; Exile from temple lasted 70 years
561.6	570	106	Death of Nebuchadnezzar, Babylonian ruler; God punished him for excesses
536.4	544	1	Persians, who had conquered Babylonians allowed exiles to return after 70 yrs
522.2	530	1079	Darius became the new Persian king; issued edict allowing the Jews to renew construction of a new Temple in Jerusalem; it would begin in 517 and be completed in 513; fear of neighbors would keep them from using it; mid 7200

Date	General Purpose 2000/200 Convergence Pattern Set			Specific Purpose Master Template Event-Pattern Sets				
Key Event Years	Gentile 40/400G 50/500G 66.666G 666.66G 200G 2000G 2000FG	Witness 50W 200W 350W 2000W 2000FW 30W,60W 90W	Full Season 1800G 30,60G 90G 600G 1750G 350G	Destruction, Punishment 360 390 430 Full Angel + 13x All	Wrath of God (700+700+600)X3 +1000= 7000 Yrs With 270	Global Reset Death, Passover, New Home 500 Yr Super Jubilee	Wrestling Match With God 2000f+ 7x600 or 6x700+1000= 7200 Yrs	Always Present 70 & 70x7= 490
512.3		30, 50		13x200, 66.6 Ang s				70
463.0		200	60	7 Angel s	200+60e	1X500		70
443.3	40			7x360s 36x70i 4x70e	200+80e Wrath			70
423.6	500	30	1750G					70
325.0	400	30	600				600G	70
167.3	40	50	90, 60	360i				70
127.8	2000F 200	30, 60			600e,700s 200+70s			70
118.1		50						70
68.77		30, 200						70
62.2	66.666							70
29.33	50						700G	70
19.5 BC		350	30				700W	70
1.23 AD								70
4.52 AD	66.666							70
11.1			90, 60					70
30.8	40	50 Jesus is New Witness				Global Reset Jesus		70
70.2	4000G 666.66		60		200 Wrath			70
80.1		4000W 30, 50		390i		3x500e, 4x500s		70
129.36		200	60					70
135.9	66.666				Wrath			70
139.2		30			200+70e			70
267.4	200						600G	70
326.4		350,200		430i				70
563.2	500				700i			70
858.7	400		600				600G	70
1055.9	500 200	30						70
1253.0	400		1800	360i,390i	700e,600s 200+70s			70
1262.9		30, 50						70
1302.3	50		1750					70

Key Event Yrs on Man's 365 Day/yr Calendr	Key Event Yrs on God's 360 Day/yr Calendr	Total No. of Master Patterns Converg Score w/o Bonus pts (App B)	Description of the events taking place in the specified years
			Key Information to Help Identify the Significance of the Individual Pattern Event Dates
			Key for fixed term patterns: s=start of pattern, e=end date in pattern. Key for General Purpose Patterns: F=Pattern starts at Fall of Man G=Gentile, W=Witness (First 2000 yrs=Patriarchs, Second 2000 yrs= Jewish people, Third 2000 yrs= Christians, Final 1000 yrs = Jews/Chr)
512.3	520	100	1st Jubilee year after Temple completion; signs indicate Jews were under close testing by God, that they were failing again and testing would continue
463.0	470	56	Artaxerxes becomes Persian King, very favorable to Jews; edict allowed Ezra to return with more exiles with more self-rule, Temple implements, etc.
443.3	450	241	Artaxerxes issued edict in 444 allowing Jews to rebuild their city and walls; this was completed in 443, but the Jews had apparently still failed God's test, thus Judah got another 7x40=280 yrs, Israel another 7x360=2520 yrs
423.6	430	229	End of the Old Testament period; exact middle of the 7000 years of man
325.0	330	112	Greeks conquered Persians in 431 and assumed control of Judah in this year
167.3	170	104	Seleucid king commits abomination in Temple leading to Hanukkah event in 163
127.8	130	791	Start of a 260/270 year period of intense testing of man by God before implementing a very serious punishment event; the events of 70, 129/135 AD
118.1	120	8	May have been the last time the Jews celebrated God's required Jubilee 50
68.77	70	65	Pharisees take greater role in the Sanhedron in the Temple
62.2	63	7	Romans take control of Judea under Pompeii; gradually lose their self rule
29.33	30	18	Romans conquer Greeks
19.5 BC	20	29	Jubilee; when Herod, an Idumean descendent of Esau, begins Temple upgrade
1.23 AD	1	1	Self exile of Jesus, family in Egypt ends; exile due to Herod killing babies
4.52 AD	4	7	Prophecy of scepter departing Israel fulfilled when Rome limits Jewish power
11.1	11.3	6	Jesus visits Temple with family at age 12; shows great knowledge already
30.8	30	2015	30th Jubilee at start of 3rd year of Jesus ministry, exactly 50 periods of 50 years totaling 2500 years since the flood; Jesus fulfilled all Jubilee requirement; Jesus' death in 32 AD would initiate the 4th Global Reset. The Christians would then become Jesus' New Witnesses on earth for the next 2000 years.
70.2	70	556	Year 4000, thus a 2000th year; Romans destroyed Jerusalem and the Temple, killing thousands of Jews and taking thousands of others into slavery in Rome
80.1	80	590	Mount Vesuvius eruption destroys 4 idol worshipping temples in Pompeii; This was in the 500 year Global reset pattern
129.36	130	66	Last Jubilee year in Judea; Bar Kokhba revolt would result in Judea's end
135.9	137	7	Romans defeat Bar Kokhba revolt; plow Temple mount; build Jupiter Temple
139.2	140	66	Total end of Judea as it is renamed Palestine
267.4	270	84	In Gentile 200/600 event patterns; Jerusalem changes hands, more freedom
326.4	330	578	Counsel of Nicaea, creed was developed; Canon agreed upon
563.2	570	81	Byzantium Empire wars coming to a close
858.7	870	111	Pope Nicholas issues Bull; Jews must register, wear badges, become Christian
1055.9	1070	135	The great schism takes place in the Catholic Church as the Catholic and Eastern Orthodox Churches split
1253.0	1270	620	Papal Bull permits use of torture during the Inquisition to force Jews to become Christians; lasts 600 years; Jews expelled from France
1262.9	1280	9	Muslims capture Jerusalem
1302.3	1320	165	Pope Boniface issues Unam Sanctum bull declaring papal supremacy over national leaders

Date	General Purpose 2000/200 Convergence Pattern Set			Specific Purpose Master Template Event-Pattern Sets				
Key Event Years	Gentile 40/400G 50/500G 66.666G 666.66G 200G 2000G 2000FG	Witness 50W 200W 350W 2000W 2000FW 30W,60W 90W	Full Season 1800G 30,60G 90G 600G 1750G 350G	Destruction, Punishment 360 390 430 Full Angel + 13x All	Wrath of God (700+700+ 600)X3 +1000= 7000 Yrs With 270	Global Reset Death, Passover, New Home 500 Yr Super Jubilee	Wrestling Match With God 2000f+ 7x600 or 6x700+ 1000= 7200 Yrs	Always Present 70 & 70x7= 490
1351.8		30					700G	70
1450.1	200		600		200		600G	70
1517-19			90		200+70e Wrath			70
1607.8	40	50	90, 60	360				70
1647.2	400	30, 60	350					70
1657.1		50		13x30 An s				70
1844.4	2000F 200		60	7 Angel e	600e 200+??s			70
1903.53		200	60	13x30,50, 60 Angel e				70
1913.4		30						70
1933.1			30					70
1943.0	50	30		13x30,50, 60,90 Ange 10,11x390e 9x430e				70
1948.4		66.666 Flood						
1952.8		50		7 Angel e				70
1962.7	40		90, 60	360				70
1972.5		30		6 Angel e 7x390e				70
1975.8	66.666							
1982.4								70
1992.2	50		350, 30					70
2002.1	40	50 30, 60		7 Angel e 390e		Start 70th Jubilee		70
2021.8			60	5 Angel e 390e,430e				70
2041.5	6000G		600	5 Angel e 360e,390e	200, 1000s	Global Reset	4200Ge 1000s	70
2045						Global Reset		
2051.4		350 6000W New Witness	90	9 Angel e	4X500e, 2x500s		4200We 1000s	70x7=490
3027.2	7000 7200	200	1800 1750	360e	1000e		1000e	70
3037.0	500 200	30		360e	1000e	2x500e Global Reset	1000e	70

Key Information to Help Identify The Significance of the Individual Pattern Event Dates			

Key Event Yrs on Man's 365 Day/yr Calendr	Key Event Yrs on God's 360 Day/yr Calendr	Total No. of Master Patterns Converg Score w/o Bonus pts (App B)	**Description of the events taking place in the specified years**
			Key for fixed term patterns:
			  s=start of pattern, e=end date in pattern
			Key for General Purpose Patterns: F=Pattern starts at Fall of Man
			  G=Gentile, W=Witness (First 2000 yrs=Patriarchs, Second 2000 yrs= Jewish people, Third 2000 yrs= Christians, Final 1000 yrs = Jews/Chr)

1351.8	1370	12	Black or Bubonic plague in Europe kills about half of the population
1450.1	1470	167	Cardinal orders Jews register, wear badges; Jews expelled from Bavaria
1517-19	1540-42	68	Ottoman Turks capture Jerusalem; Holy Land controlled by Turks; Protestant Reformation takes place
1607.8	1630	104	Jamestown, 1st American colony; America becomes critical Jewish sanctuary
1647.2	1670	91	Polish massacre of nearly 100,000 Jews in the Inquisition
1657.1	1680	99	Jubilee year for Jews; England had recently made a decision to readmit Jews
1844.4	1870	1081	Critical Ottoman edict of toleration for Jews leading to future return to their home; Start of a 200+70 yr period of intense testing before punishment
1903.53	1930	248	Jubilee year marking end of 2nd Zionist Aliya, an organized immigration of Jews back to their original homeland
1913.4	1940	2	Start of WW1, which would lead to Jews getting original homeland back
1933.1	1960	2	Holocaust start, 1st concentration camp opened
1943.0	1970	870	The peak year in the Holocaust period, referred to as the final solution to the plan to rid the earth of all Jewish people, principally so that Satan could keep God's end time plan for him from taking place; About 6 million Jews killed, in the Gentile 50 and Jewish 40 year event patterns
1948.4	1976	7	Israel declares their independence as a nation; five Arab nations attack her to try to push her into the sea (Iraq, Egypt, Syria, Jordan, Lebanon)
1952.8	1980	372	1ST Jubilee after return; large immigration; 7 Angel of Death patterns hit
1962.7	1990	97	1st nuclear reactor comes on line in Israel; important to future defense
1971.5-1972.5	2000	366	Rabbis vote to not use Temple Mount acquired in1967; marks the end of the 7x390 year Assyrian exile with 70 yr testing following it ending in 2041
1975.8	2004	7	Start period of massive immigration to Israel from Russia
1982.4	2010	1	Israel's Operation Peace for Galilee war with Lebanon
1992.2	2020	26	Oslo 1 land for peace deal transfers Jericho and Gaza to PLO
2002.1	2030	382	Start of the 70th 50 year Jubilee period since 1399; year of the 7/11 attack on America; year when 7 ominous Angel of Death patterns hit; bad times ahead? Marks start ot the Jubilee period hosting the 5th and 6th Global Resets
2021.8	2050	773	Great convergence of patterns involving temple, new world leader; mid-point of the 2020-22 COVID 19 pandemic predicted by 5 Angel of Death patterns
2041.5	2070	4185	Year when both the Assyrian and Babylonian punishment periods end; year 6000 with over 100 pattern convergences, many ominous, 5 Angel of Death; patterns indicate it is a good fit for the mid-tribulation events involving the antichrist and the occurrence of the 5th Global Reset
2045		1000	May point to the Second Coming of Jesus to earth; this time as King of Kings
2051.4	2080	3407	Ends 70th Jubilee year with possibly major forgiveness coming; patterns may show some major new world leader and anointing of a new Temple in Israel; also the Jubilee period hosting the twin Global Resets and the time when the combined Jewish/Christian believer set becomes the new witnesses for Jesus on earth
3027.2	3070	2958	Ends 7000th and 7200th years of man; ALL MASTER TEMPLATE PATTERNS CONVERGE IN THIS YEAR!!; May be the end of the 1000 year millennium
3037.0	3080	3662	May be the year of the 7th and final Global Reset thus beginning the start of the eternal state of Rev 21-22

A Further Discussion of Each of the Master Template Pattern Sets

Describing Basic Event-Pattern Strings

This type of pattern was the principal focus of the first three books in this series. They are covered much more completely in those books, and we suggest that readers go to those books if they want to dig much deeper into this topic. We also presented this topic in chapter 5 of this book, so we will not present much of the material we have already covered. We will, however, go quite a bit deeper into the origin of, and God's use of, this type of pattern. In fact, we will start with that.

Why Would God Want to or Need to Use Patterns of This Type?

As we have seen over and over in this book, God had a reason to create our universe and the humans he designed to populate the earth. We have already covered this, but we will very briefly restate it. At some time before the creation of the universe, God decided to give Jesus a gift, a future companion created in his image. He wanted this companion to be one who would prove under very trying circumstances that he loved Jesus and would want to be with him forever. God devised a complex scenario he would use to bring this about over several thousand years (only several days on God's clock in heaven). This companion would be only a small subset, maybe 10 percent or so of all those who would ever populate the earth. They would have to pass difficult tests to become part of the companion of Jesus one day. One of the key parts of administering that test or set of tests was to personally inject himself into the affairs of humans regularly. The method for doing this involved a simple yet, at the same time, very complex set of equally spaced and similarly themed event patterns. These were defined in chapter 5, but we will now go a bit deeper into the way God is apparently using these patterns. We will present a few basics below:

- He uses a 360-day-per-year calendar to keep humans from recognizing what he is doing.
- He injects himself into the affairs of humans on earth in event patterns starting and ending in ten-year denominations. He uses the time gap specified in chapter 5 in this process.
- He makes great use of dual patterns separated by exactly ten years, and these would travel down through history together. The first set is associated with his interactions with those we refer to as Gentiles or non-Jews. The second set is associated with the Jewish people, the descendants of Abraham, called the "father of the Jews," and his wife, Sarah. These would be God's most basic pattern sets, the fifty- and two-hundred-year equally spaced event-pattern strings.
- God takes great advantage of the basic properties of mathematics in his dealings with his people on earth. He defines the topical themes of the time gap patterns in such a way that several of the just-right patterns converge in the key dates

enabling him to administer a process that will bring about the purpose of his will. In practice, we see that the greatest number of key patterns converge every two thousand years, with ever-larger convergences taking place in successive two-thousand-year dates. If we add together the BC date of the end of the seventh day of creation, 3873.4 BC, to the year 2041.5, we get 5,915 365-day years. If we multiply this by the conversion factor that converts it to 360-day years, 1.01455, we get 6000. This means that to God, 2041 is the six thousandth year on his heavenly calendar, and 2051 is the six thousandth year on his Jewish calendar. That, along with the fact that God has set up his punishment structure for his people in such a way that most of their punishment periods all down through history end in these two dates, means that there are far more patterns converging on these dates than in any other dates in all of history up to this point. In another one thousand years, we could make a similar case for the years at the end of the one-thousand-year period that follows the years 2041 and 2051, the dates 3027 and 3037. If the one thousand years following 2041/2051 are the millennium, then that would mean the eternal state starts in 3027/3037. We will present much more on this in a later chapter.

With that little bit of background, we will next continue our discussion of the seven Master Template pattern sets.

A Discussion of the Seven Master Template Pattern Sets

The Great Convergence Family of Pattern Sets

This is the immense set of patterns that have been the primary focus of these four books. These are basically the full and complete families of twin fifty/two-hundred-year sets of Gentile and Jewish equally spaced and similarly themed event patterns that span the whole seventy-two hundred years from the fall to the eternal state. The fifty-year patterns travel together down through time separated by exactly ten years with the two-hundred-year patterns doing the same, separated only by exactly sixty years.

We found three separate sets of event patterns that met our qualification to be part of the master template. The first two columns are the basic Gentile and Jewish fifty/two-hundred-year families of patterns. Since these two patterns are so integrally tied together and flow together all down through history we are viewing them as a twin pattern set rather than two individual pattern sets in the dialogue presented in this book. Thus we will be saying that the Master Template contains seven rather than eight pattern sets. As we can see from the column headers, the Gentile set of event patterns is much larger than the Jewish pattern set. As we mentioned previously, God judges his people, the Jews, every fiftieth year, called a Jubilee year. If the Jews met God's standards, they would receive rewards as shown in the king's scroll of chapter 5. If they failed God's test, he would use the Gentiles to punish them, typically starting forty years later in a Gentile 66.666- or 200-year event-pattern string.

This is God's general purpose family of patterns for interacting with his people. That is made even more obvious since a full 94 of the 102 dates in the master template chart are members of one or more of the event-pattern strings in this great convergence pattern family. We call it the "great convergence family" because one member of this family, the two-thousand-year pattern set, has by far the greatest number of patterns that converge on it. The 3x2000=6000-year pattern, which hits the year AD 2041, is again the convergence champion by a wide margin. Again, this family of patterns was the chief focus of our first three books in this series, so if readers would like to delve much deeper into a study of this pattern family, they can find that in our first three books. We also covered these event-pattern strings in chapter 5 of this book.

Our next pattern string is the third and final in the convergence pattern family. It is really a set of two pattern strings, the full season pattern strings. Again, these are wall-to-wall patterns, in that they transverse the whole history and future of humans on earth. These two patterns are based on the full time frame from first the fall of man and then the end of the seventh day of creation until the presumed start of the eternal state in AD 3027. The first is a pattern string of seventy-two hundred years, and the second is one of seven thousand years. If we divide each of these up into four quarters or presumed seasons for man on earth, we come up with pattern gaps of 1,750 and 1,800 years. The dates hitting in the 1,800-year pattern are as follows, with the three intermediate dates all involving major edicts issued by well-known world leaders:

- 4070 BC: the fall of man
- 2296 BC: the Tower of Babel incident with God issuing an edict that the languages of the world would be confused to keep mankind from conspiring against him
- 522 BC: when a new Persian king, Darius, issued an edict that allowed the people of Judah to rebuild the temple Nebuchadnezzar had destroyed in 586 BC
- AD 1252: when the Catholic pope issued an edict allowing the torture of the scattered Jewish people during the Inquisition to force them to become Christians
- AD 3027: the presumed start of the eternal state of Revelation 21–22

Thus, we see that these four quarters all involved key world leaders issuing edicts involving the Jewish people. We can presume that God issued edicts of a sort involving his people at the beginning and end of humans' time on earth. If so, then all five dates would involve very important edicts by key world leaders involving God's people.

The second wall-to-wall pattern in this family is the 1750-year quarter pattern starting at the end of the seventh day of creation in 3873 BC. The five dates involved in this pattern are as follows:

- 3873 BC: the end of the seventh day of creation and the start of the seven thousand years of man on earth
- 2148 BC: the birth of Abraham, father of the Jews
- 423 BC: the end of the Old Testament period and the start of the inter-testament period

- AD 1302: when the Catholic pope issues an edict claiming dominion over all Roman-controlled nations
- AD 3027: the presumed start of the eternal state of Revelation 21–22

Again, we can see a common theme in all five of these dates. They all represent the start of a new order of some sort for God's people. The bottom line of this master template exercise is that all these convergence patterns end up at the start of the eternal state of Revelation 21–22. In fact, looking ahead, we eventually see that all seven of the master template patterns end up at the same place, AD 3027. God had a plan when he created the universe, and in the end, it will result in the purpose of his will being fulfilled with full unity in every way, with a new global order and the greatest and largest family reunion of all eternity past taking place in AD 3027. Jesus, the Lamb who was killed even before the creation of the universe, will finally be united with all the members of his eternal bride. The purpose of God's will, to unify everything in heaven and on earth under Jesus when time reaches its fulfillment, will finally be fully accomplished.

Clues from the Great Convergence Family of Pattern Sets

- This is God's general purpose event-pattern set he uses in interacting with his people on earth. The most basic and most used patterns in this set are the two hundred- or two-thousand-year event-pattern strings. These patterns seem to be homing in on the seventieth Jubilee-year period from AD 2001 to 2051 and the years 2041 and 2051 in particular. These patterns fit the end-time scenario incredibly well, which would mean the fulfillment of God's ultimate purpose for his will to a large extent. It hosts by far the greatest number of key patterns with their topics including the following themes: the end of God's punishment sentences for his people, the forgiveness of the past sins of all of his people, the time of rewarding his people for their good acts, the end of death for many of God's people and longer lives in general for others, the grafting of the Jewish people back into the Tree of Life, the end of sentences of tribulation and exile for God's people, the beginning of a period of one thousand years of living on earth with Jesus as King of Kings and Lord of Lords in a paradise-like setting, and so forth.

God's Punishment and Destruction Pattern Set

The event-pattern sets included in this category were presented in some detail in chapters 6 and 8, so we will present only a brief overview of them in this section. We refer to these as punishment- and destruction-event patterns since the events that host these patterns started at the times when God must have finally decided it was time to punish his people for not keeping the three great commands. They are part of the king's scroll of Leviticus 26, which we included in chapter 5. We discovered that in his forbearance, God would wait for very long times of idol worship or other serious violations of his commands before punishing his people. We will present one amazing example of this.

In 591 BC, God told Ezekiel in chapter 4 that Israel had been seriously violating his commands for 390 years and Judah for another 40 years, totaling 430 years. In chapter 6 we saw how God administered these punishments, so we won't repeat them here. But we do see how patient God was with his people. When he did punish them, it was for a very long period, and he multiplied the punishment by seven according to Leviticus 26 since they'd had multiple warnings before he punished them. When he did punish them, it began with a great amount of destruction of both their capital city and temple in three cases.

We will next go to the Angel of Death event-pattern set. The only event patterns in this set that qualified for the master template are the 13x50, 13x70, and especially the 13x350 event patterns and then only with an asterisk. They fall a bit short of qualifying for seven thousand years in duration, but they are very important and miss only by a hair, so to speak. These patterns go from death to new life, from one major global reset to another, from the flood to the start of the millennium. This pattern spans at least 4,550 years and maybe 5,600 years. Let me explain. These 50-, 70-, and 350-year patterns may start at the rapture of Enoch to heaven. They hit the year 3459 BC, which is only fifteen years from the date we calculated for Enoch's rapture. That is close, but is it close enough?

We also included all the Angel of Death pattern dates on our chart. The 13x66.666 event pattern starts at the end of the seventh day of creation in 3873 BC and lands in AD 2041. The 360-event pattern starts at the fall of man in 4070 BC and spans the whole seventy-two hundred years until the start of the eternal state in AD 3027. Many of the punishment and destruction patterns span periods of thousands of years. Thus, we felt that this category of event-pattern strings deserved to be on our interpretation of God's master template.

The 13x350 Angel of Death pattern is an extremely important part of this pattern set. For that reason, we would like to present a bit more about this pattern. In fact, this pattern was not discovered until very late in our research. There are exactly thirteen periods of 350 years from the great flood in 2434.33 BC and the seventieth Jubilee year event in AD 2051.4. This is a colossal pattern because it is a pattern of all God's pattern multipliers—thirteen, ten, and seven—with God's Jubilee year event as an integer of five. Thus, it is a pattern of 7x10x13x5=4,550 years, the exact gap between 2434.33 BC and AD 2051.

The same pattern fits the gap between the Gentile fifty-year pattern exactly ten years before the flood, 2444.10, and the year of the apparent next great tribulation or AD 2041.53.

There are three gaps of 350 years from the flood to the start of the Jubilee pattern, when the Jews first entered the Promised Land in 1399 BC. It is then another ten gaps of 350 years until the seventieth Jubilee year in AD 2051. Our prophetic event-pattern strings have shown that this fits the time when Jesus will anoint the millennial temple, exactly twenty-three hundred days after the Second Coming from Daniel 8. It will also be the time of a grand reunion in Israel at the new temple, according to Zechariah 14. Thus, this pattern takes us from the flood to what appears to be the twin great family reunions, which are one of the main topics of this book.

If 2051 really hosts one of the great family reunions, then what is the significance of the Angel of Death pattern to this event? We will give a possible answer. We know from Revelation that when Jesus returns at the Second Coming, he will have his bride with him. The bride is composed of all people in history who had been believers in, and followers of, Jesus. They had gotten to heaven during a rapture event at the very first of the seven-year tribulation event. They were given resurrected, glorified bodies that are eternal, with no pain, sorrow, death, and so forth at the time of the rapture event. Thus, these saints will be on earth with Jesus for the next one thousand years in a paradise-like environment and will never again suffer death. Also, the humans who will still be on earth at that time will live very long lives, well over one hundred years, according to Isaiah. Thus, the great family reunion will be a time for meeting with Jesus at the Feast of Tabernacles event in the new temple in Israel and also a time for celebrating the end of death. Thus, we can see the connection to the Angel of Death.

Many of the Angel of Death patterns converge in years hosting huge periods of death. We can see that from the chart of the Angel of Death event-pattern string that is attached. In fact, this 350-year Angel of Death pattern is a "twin pattern." How so? The first 350-year Angel of Death pattern string above started at the flood and will end in the seventieth Jubilee event in AD 2051. The twin of this pattern will start ten years earlier in AD 2444 and also end ten years earlier, in AD 2041.

If this is indeed the year when the Antichrist enters the temple in Jerusalem and declares himself to be God, then it will initiate the worst catastrophe in the world's history, according to Jesus in Matthew 24. Thus, this is really an Angel of Death pattern in the normal way we use the phrase in our books. This would start the three woe judgments of Revelation 9. All the details of the scenario being painted in Revelation of this seven-year period are included on our website. Our site contains hundreds of pages of commentary, plain language interpretations, a symbology chart, many other charts, and so forth.

Clues from God's Punishment and Destruction-Pattern Set

- This is a special case pattern, in that it goes wall to wall, uses the patterns in the general purpose set, and utilizes the punishment pattern strings, but it also mixes the strings with other testing and punishment features that make it unique. Many of the patterns end in AD 2041, our target date, but this does seem to be the end of the physical destruction of cities and countries on earth. In that regard, it would signal the end-time scenario. However, a unique feature is that this pattern set may also contain God's use of his final judgments of many of the people on earth, both dead and still alive. The sheep-goat judgment, the Daniel 12 Jewish judgment, and other special-case judgments take place as part of the end-time scenario. That ties these judgments to the AD 2041 time frame. The judgments are wall to wall because the first judgment start time was apparently at the end of the seventh day of creation in 3873 BC. There were exactly four periods of 360 years, this time on our 365-day calendar, until the end of the great flood in 2433 BC. Also, there will be destruction of a sort taking place in AD 3037, at the end of the millennium, when the Great White Throne Judgment will take place (Rev. 20). The barrier between the physical and spiritual dimensions will be destroyed, and the two will merge together. Thus, this is a wall-to-wall judgment pattern that hits hard in AD 2041, according to our interpretation of God's pattern set.

The Wrath-of-God Pattern Set

This is a pattern of three sets of 700+700+600=2000-year event patterns starting at the fall of man sixty-two hundred years ago. The three six-hundred-year patterns within these sets always have a 200+60/70/80-year event sequence that begins at the very start and end of the six-hundred-year patterns. Since there are three two-thousand-year periods and thus three six-hundred-year periods, that means there would be six of the 200+60/70/80-year periods. These six 260/270 or 280-year periods host the very most significant periods of death, tribulation/chaos, and exile/chaos in the history of God's people on earth. Thus, we have dubbed this the "wrath-of-God pattern set."

As we can see from the master template chart, the six historical dates when these punishment periods ended were very serious events for God's people as follows. All the below dates are the 200+70-year dates except for AD 2041, which is a two-hundredth-year date. As we can see from the master template chart, some of the greatest "wrath" events took place in the two hundredth year and others in the 200+70-year event.

2434 BC: the time of the flood
1833 BC: the start of the four-hundred-year Israelite exile in Egypt
443 BC: the start of the 7x360-year exile of Judah/Israel
AD 139: the start of the total exile of Judea from their land
AD 1517/19: the Protestant Reformation and when the Ottoman Turks captured Jerusalem
AD 2041: the year when patterns point to the Second Coming and so forth

These are six of the most important events in the history of God's people, with all hosting an event when great changes were taking place. Again, this event-pattern set covered the whole time from the end of the seventh day of creation until the start of the eternal state. A chart that depicts the whole scenario for this pattern set and much more extensive discussion is included in the section on the master template in our book three in this series, *The Angel of Death Supercode.*

Clues from the Wrath-of-God Pattern Set

- In the third two-thousand-year period of this pattern, the 200+70-year period started in AD 1844, and the two-thousandth-year event is centered in AD 2041. We have shown that the biblical end-time scenario fits this time frame quite well. If that turns out to be the case, then AD 2041 will be the year when the three-and-a-half-year period dubbed the "great tribulation" will start. In Matthew 24 Jesus called this period the period of the greatest wrath in history. If that is the case, then AD 2041 will be in the center of the twin global resets and great family reunions.

The Global-Reset Pattern Set, the Crown Prince of All Pattern Sets

This event-pattern set has turned out to be the most important of any pattern set we discovered in the nearly ten years of our research leading to the writing of this four-book series. It is so extensive and multidimensional that we will wait until the end of this chapter to present it.

The Great-Wrestling-Match Pattern Set

We termed this pattern "man's wrestling match" with God over his true identity. God apparently changed the narrative of this wrestling match at the death of Noah exactly two thousand years after the fall in 2099/2089 BC. Thus, these are again twin Gentile/Jewish patterns. At this change in narrative or global restart of sorts, God's focus became the Jewish people, those he termed his "chosen people." This wrestling match between the Jews and God would apparently last for forty-two hundred years and end at the start of the one-thousand-year millennium. It would last for seven periods of six hundred years and six periods of seven hundred years. Again, this is a twin, and they will end in the same twin years of AD 2041/2051.

Thus, we have additional confirmation about our postulated scenario that surrounds the AD 2041/2051 period. This topic was covered extensively in our book three, *The Angel of Death Supercode*, and the biblical model upon which it is based was presented in chapter 3 of this book. We have already confirmed the clues we need. The intermediate events hit by these patterns are shown on the master template chart above along with the details of the events taking place in those years.

Our idea that there might be a wrestling match event-pattern string was inspired by a wrestling match recorded in Genesis 32. We will next present a small part of the narrative describing the original wrestling match presented in our book three, *The Angel of Death Supercode*, to help readers better understand this pattern and its great significance to God's people.

Background to Aid in Understanding the Wrestling-Match Pattern

The Jewish people are the descendants of Abraham, a biblical character first introduced to us early in Genesis, the first book of the Bible. This is important because the complete Old Testament concerns God's interactions with Abraham and his descendants, the Israelites or the Jewish people. The Jews descended from Abraham's son Isaac and then Isaac's son Jacob. Jacob had twelve sons, who became the twelve tribes of Israel. Abraham was born in 2148 BC, Isaac in 2049 BC, and Jacob in 1991 BC.

How the Jews Became Aware That YHWH Was Their God and What He Required of Them

The fall of Adam and Eve took place in 4070 BC, and they would have been thoroughly familiar with God and his requirements for them.

Before the flood, the average age at death of those described in the Bible was 910 years old. Adam lived for 930 years, and Methuselah, who died in the year of the flood, lived 969 years. They would have overlapped by about 240 years, so Methuselah would likely have also been well aware of YHWH and his requirements. Noah overlapped Methuselah by six hundred years, so he would likely have known about YHWH and his requirements from Methuselah. Noah and Abraham overlapped by almost sixty years, so Abraham could have become aware of YHWH and his requirements from Noah.

We know that Noah knew YHWH and his requirements for two reasons. First, God spoke to him often before the flood and gave him specific directions about building the ark, including who to take on it and when to do so. Second, we know that as soon as the ark landed, Noah built an altar and made a sacrifice to YHWH.

A second way we know Abraham knew YHWH and his requirements is because the Angel of the Lord made several visits to earth to give messages to Abraham and make covenants with him. There is great biblical evidence that this was the second person of the Trinity or the one we know as Jesus. He also visited both Isaac and Jacob to confirm his covenants and so forth.

What Is Our First Clue That the Jewish Nation Would Have a Lifelong Wrestling Match with the True Identity of YHWH?

There is a record of the Angel of the Lord visiting Jacob in Genesis 32. A very strange event took place during this visit. The Angel of the Lord had a night-long wrestling match with Jacob. The wrestling match lasted all night, and the Angel of the Lord couldn't free himself from Jacob's grasp. He finally injured Jacob's hip to free himself. After the match was over, the Angel of the Lord gave Jacob a new name, Israel.

This wrestling match was a prophecy of the facts that Jacob would become the father of a large nation that would be named Israel, that their whole lifetime would be lived in a time of darkness, and that throughout the whole nighttime of their existence, the Jewish people would wrestle with the true identity of their God. This had many facets to it, as we will see as we move on.

Wrestling During Their Slavery in Egypt

Jacob, his sons, and their families went to Egypt during a drought to buy food from the Egyptians. This went well for thirty years until a new Pharaoh placed them in a life of slavery in Egypt, which lasted four hundred years.

During this time, the twelve sons and their families grew into a large group numbering well over a million people. During this time of growth and slavery, they unfortunately became too well aware of the idols the Egyptians worshipped. Many of their number became quite confused during this time about the identity of the true God. The question seemed to be this: is YHWH the only God, or are these idols also true gods? Thus, their lifelong wrestling match over the true identity of God began. It had its birth in Egypt.

Wrestling during the Forty Years of Desert Wandering after the Exodus

YHWH supernaturally brought forward a man named Moses whom he used to lead the children of God out of their four hundred years of slavery in Egypt. The event hosting the coming out of Egypt was called the "exodus." God supernaturally parted the Red Sea to allow the Moses-led Israelites to escape from Egypt during the night.

Not long after the exodus, the Jews found themselves wandering in a large desert. After their long primer of studying idol worship in Egypt, YHWH apparently felt the strong need to reintroduce himself and his requirements to the Israelites.

God called Moses to meet him on a mountaintop, where he would give Moses a huge download on who he was and what the requirements of his people would be. This included the Ten Commandments and much of the information contained in the Torah. This meeting lasted forty days.

During the forty days Moses was on the mountain, the people returned to their idol worship when they crafted a golden calf to worship. Moses was disgusted, but the wrestling match was already in full bloom. The people groups who lived in the areas in which they were wandering were all idol worshippers, and the Israelites had several interactions with them in the forty years of wandering. Many of the Israelites would have had trouble understanding the true nature of the idols and would have wrestled with the idea that they might be real gods even though Moses gave them regular instruction concerning the true God, YHWH, and his requirements for them.

Wrestling Concerning Idols While in the Promised Land

In the year before the Israelites crossed the Jordon River into the Promised Land, the Israelites were camped at the foot of a mountain beside the river, waiting for God to allow them to cross. During this year, Moses was expanding Leviticus 26 into the whole book of Deuteronomy and teaching it to the Israelites. This book repeated God's three great commands, his blessings for keeping them, and his punishments for violating them over and over again. God wanted to be certain the Israelites knew his identity and requirements very well before he would give them their land.

The land was inhabited by seven idol-worshipping tribes, and God knew they would be a huge problem for the Israelites. Thus, he told them to destroy these tribes one by one, sometimes telling them to kill every man, woman, child, and even their animals. He wanted them to destroy all evidence of their idols before the Israelites could be tempted to worship them. The Israelites failed to do this to God's liking. The result was that the Israelites often found themselves worshipping the idols of these people groups.

After about 350 years, the Israelites were finally allowed to have kings over them. This made things much worse, especially when the third king, Solomon, became king. He became very powerful and wealthy, and he was the envy of all the neighboring countries. The result was that the kings and leaders of these countries wanted Solomon to marry their daughters and so forth. He did so in the extreme and ended up with six hundred wives and three hundred concubines. Guess what they brought with them? Their idols. As a result, most of the kings of Israel and several of those of Judah became idol worshippers.

The idol worship in this period became extreme, even to having idols throughout the temple in Jerusalem as recorded in Ezekiel 8–11.

After repeated warnings from God through his prophets and many visits by the Angel of the Lord, over about seven hundred years, God finally allowed his northern kingdom of Israel to be destroyed and the people exiled to foreign lands. This exile lasted over twenty-seven hundred years. About 130 years later, he allowed the same thing to happen to the southern kingdom of Judah. This exile of the southern kingdom had three phases to it, and God allowed the Jews to return to their homeland and rebuild their temple before the end of the Old Testament period.

After the return of Judah from exile and the rebuilding of their temple in Jerusalem, the idol worship decreased significantly. YHWH finally assumed a much more prominent place in their worship. However, the Israelites wouldn't give up their wrestling match with the true identity of God, as we will see. What would the next wrestling match be about?

Wrestling with the Law During the Inter-testament Period

With YHWH finally assuming the most prominent place in the religious life of the Israelites, the next really big question would then be this: Since YHWH is our God, how can we be certain we are not violating his requirements concerning how we live and how we worship him? The Israelites had a good starting point since they still had the written record of the laws and so forth recorded in the Torah, the five books of Moses. They also had the inspired writings of the other Old Testament authors.

Thus, the next wrestling match became a wrestling match with the law. A very high-level look at the results would seem to indicate that this may have taken two paths. The first resulted in a set of rules that interpreted the laws to the nth degree. The idea was to go to great lengths to make sure that the laws were kept to God's satisfaction. The second was an even more extensive set of interpretations that would provide a way around keeping the details of the law without irritating God.

How can we tell whether God was pleased with the result of this wrestling match with his intentions when he gave them his initial law?

Wrestling with the True Identity of Jesus While He Was on Earth

God personally came to earth and lived as a Jew for about thirty-three-and-a-half years. He had several reasons for doing so, the principal of which was to provide salvation for mankind and to provide a way for humans to get to heaven despite being sinners. However, while he was here, Jesus gave the Jews an answer to their question about what he thought of their interpretation of his law. He deplored it and said so very plainly to the Pharisees on several occasions.

In large part, the Jewish leaders rejected Jesus's answer to our question and even more importantly rejected his claim about being their God and Messiah.

The Jewish rejection of Jesus resulted in him and his ministry being accepted by huge numbers of Gentile people groups the world over. This split resulted in huge animosity emerging between the Jews and those who became known as Christians. This animosity spread to many other large people groups besides the Christians. The Jewish people became by far the most generally hated people group on earth.

This rejection of Jesus finally resulted in the nation of Judea being destroyed and the Jewish people being again exiled all over the Middle East and the Roman Empire. Paul said in Romans 11 that God blinded the Jews in part from being able to recognize the real, true identity of Jesus as their God. He further said that in the end-times this blindness would be removed and that the Jewish people would be saved, their nation returned to them, and so forth.

Wrestling with Christians and Muslims During Their Exile from Their Land and Country from AD 135 of Our Generation

As a result of the Jewish people rejecting Jesus, they ended up exiled in nations all over the world, especially in Europe and the Middle East for over eighteen hundred years, from AD 135 up until the 1900s. They were called "Christ Killers" and hated throughout this entire period. They were especially the target of the Catholic Church and the Inquisition. They were forced to wear badges identifying themselves as Jews, required to register, and pressed to become Christians or face severe torture, deportation, and all sorts of terrible persecutions. Millions were killed or executed over these eighteen hundred years.

Still, despite all this, the wrestling match continued. The Jews continued to cling to YHWH and his law but to reject Jesus as God.

When Will This Wrestling Match Finally Come to a Close?

As we presented in the first book of our series, the Christian Bible indicates that this wrestling match will end during a future seven-year period of great tribulation described in Daniel 9:24–27, Revelation, and several places in the Christian Bible.

One of the goals of this series of four books is to make all of this much more widely known and to probe history through the use of the event patterns we have discovered to see whether we can get some clues about when this might take place.

Clues from the Great Wrestling Match

- Many Jewish people and national and religious leaders have been wrestling with the true and complete identity of God for forty-two hundred years. The same goes for Gentile people groups and the two matches run together separated by exactly ten years. The match lasted for seven periods of six hundred and six congruent periods of seven hundred years. It started exactly two thousand years after the fall and will apparently end in 2041 and 2051, all within the twin two-hundred-year pattern set.
- These matches end in the same time frame as the twin global resets and family reunions.

The Ever-Present Pattern Set: Families of Seventy-Year Patterns Converging in the Seventieth Jubilee Period

God's two great event-pattern effect multipliers are the numbers seven and ten. The number seven is God's Leviticus 26-defined punishment period multiplier, and the number ten is God's general multiplier for all his sequential-year patterns. The number seventy is the product of these two pattern effect multipliers: 7x10=70. Thus, we might expect the final year in a pattern with a multiplier of seventy to host an event that would lead to some ominous conclusions that would yield the realization of God's original goal in his plan to choose the ultimate bride for Christ.

We see the most incredible event patterns using the number seventy converging every ten years and leading up to and including every tenth year in the seventieth Jubilee period. They culminate in the final two ten-year events in the seventieth Jubilee period, the years AD 2041 and AD 2051.

This category of events was presented in our book two as topic four in chapter 4. We have placed a slightly revised version of the pattern chart below. We will first present a summary of the key insights we can learn from the chart and suggest that the reader read these first and then go to the chart and ponder it a bit.

1. There are seven total seventy-year patterns shown in the chart. All the patterns are related to God's testing of the Jewish people. The patterns are unique in that the testing events are separated from each other by exactly ten years, and they recycle each seventy years.
2. All seven of these seventy sequential-year date patterns are converging in our generation in the seventieth Jubilee period. All started at different dates in ancient history, but after the last of the seven sequential-year date patterns started in 1990.8 BC, these seven patterns continued all the way into our generation, separated by

exactly ten God years. This is evident if we go to the year AD 2051 in the birth of Abraham pattern on the left in the chart below and track to the right from column to column. We progress from 2061 to 2051, 2041, 2031, and so forth as they go from pattern to pattern, separated by exactly 9.8565 years. Incredible! This means God is continually testing us and particularly the Jews in seven different ways all the time, and he has been doing so since 1990 BC.

3. If we take an even broader perspective on this seventy-year pattern set, we can see that it really began at the fall of man in 4070 BC. It seems that God first began his testing of his people in increments or patterns of seventy sequential years. He seems to have started a new seventy-year pattern in every tenth year over the next seventy years, resulting in a total of seven different seventy-year patterns that would continue for the next seventy-two hundred years or until the start of the eternal state in AD 3037.

4. There are about one hundred different event dates in the chart below that cover the sixty-two-hundred-year period from the fall to the Jubilee year after the six thousandth year or AD 2051. This covers all the key event dates for the Jews or God's people in the sixty-two hundred years that fall in the ten-year sequence. If we add the event dates that fall in other dates between ten-year increments, we add about another forty or so dates that are in our database for a total of about 140 event dates. That would mean that about 16 percent of all dates falling in ten-year increments on a 360-year calendar would be key dates for God's people during the sixty-two hundred years. It would also mean that about 2 percent of all dates in the sixty-two hundred years would be key dates for God's people.

5. These seven seventy-year patterns are all tied to the births of Abraham, Isaac, Jacob, and Joseph; and/or to the long-term exiles and major tribulations of the Jewish people. This clearly shows the great focus God has on the seventieth Jubilee period and on our generation.

6. These patterns host both very good and very bad events for God's people.

7. The major point we wanted to make about this family of patterns is that there is a separate seventy-year testing pattern God is using every tenth year in and surrounding the seventieth Jubilee period. All patterns start at some very key date in Jewish history and involve the very birth years of the four key Jewish patriarchs or the land in which they were residing. We will next present the chart.

8. Thus, we can see that this set of patterns qualifies to be a part of God's master template.

The Ever (Always) Present Pattern
The 7 70 Sequential Year Date Patterns Acting in Our Generation
Every 10 Years
(Chart Reads from AD to BC)

PATTERN 1 Birth of Israel as a Nation 1399.4 BC	PATTERN 2 Birth of End Times? 2041 AD	PATTERN 3 Birth of Joseph 1902 BC	PATTERN 4 Birth of Isaac 2049.9 BC	PATTERN 5 Births of Shem, Jacob 3025, 1990.8 BC	PATTERN 6 Births of Sarah, Moses 2138, 1517 BC	PATTERN 7 Birth of Abraham 2148.5 BC
2051.4	2041.5	2031.7	2021.8	2012.0	2002.1	1992.2
1982.4	1972.5	1962.7	1952.8	1943.0	1933.1	`1923.2
1913.3	1903.5	858.8	1883.8	1253.0	1657.1	1647.2
1844.4	1351.6 AD	99.8	1607.8	632.1	1450	1302.3
326.5	29.3 BC	30.8 AD	1262.9	80.1	622.2	267.4
119.5	167.3	522.2 BC	1055.9 AD	11.1 AD	139.23	129.4
50.5 AD	443.3	591.1	325.0 BC	127.8 BC	70.23	60.5 AD
19.5 BC	512.3	1005.1	463.0	610.8	1.23 AD	423.6 BC
709.5	719.3	1350.1	1015	1438.8	68.77 BC	561.6
916.4	926.3	1833.1	1842.9	1990.8	965.7	1872.5
926.3	1409.2	1902.1	2050.9 BC	3025.7	1517.7	1941.5
1054.4	1478	1971.1		3440 BC	1793.7	2148.5
1399.4	2099.2	2040.1 BC			1862.6	2286.5
2089.3	2444.1 BC				2138.6	2493.4
2296.3					3450	3390
2434.3 BC						
3814.2	3824.0	3833.9	3843.7	3853.6	3863.5	3873.4

Clues from the Ever-Present Set of Seventy-Year Patterns

Every tenth year all down through history is part of one of God's seven seventy-year testing patterns. This testing will end at the rapture events in the years surrounding the six-thousandth year or in the 2041 time frame and in the seven-thousandth-year time frame at the end of the millennium for those who receive glorified bodies at the final judgment in that time frame.

The Global Reset Code: The Crown Prince of God's Master Template

Setting the Stage for "Cracking" the Global Reset Code

We will next set the stage that will enable us to crack the global reset code by presenting several pieces of important information that will be necessary to know and understand to crack that code.

- The God of the Christian Bible is and always has been in control of the most important events in all history. This is an absolute truth and is proven by the fact that the key events in history for those deemed to be God's chosen people group have taken place in a perfect set of patterns from the creation of humankind all the way to this generation. This covers sixty-two hundred years.
- These patterns occur as event-pattern strings, and each individual pattern set exhibits the very same general theme, outcome, and timing from beginning to end.
- God's original event-pattern strings began with two events separated by ten years at the fall of man in 4070 and 4060 BC. The event-pattern string starting in 4070.5 BC was associated with a people group we call Gentiles. This word is generally defined to be "anyone who is a non-Jew" or non-Jewish. However, for our purposes we will modify how we use that term as follows: For the period of the first two thousand years after the fall of man, we will use that term to refer to those people groups who would be in opposition to the things of God. After the first two thousand years, we will revert to the classic definition of Gentile. The second event-pattern string started in 4060 BC and was associated with the people group called God's *chosen people* or simply *God's people*. This would be those people groups who would be chosen by God to be his representatives or his witnesses on earth who were to make his will known to all people. This would start a seventy-two-hundred-year period of mankind on earth. The event patterns also show that God began counting the same set of patterns once more two hundred years later at the end of the seventh one-thousand-year day of creation. Again, there would be two starting points, 3873 and 3863 BC, as before. These event patterns included the critical fifty-year "judgment" patterns and two-hundred-year "convergence" patterns. This would be the first of seven coming "global resets." As we will see later, this event marked the first of seven total global resets that would take place in mankind's time on earth.
- God would implement the "master template" cycle of 2000+2000+2000+1000 years, totaling seven thousand years for mankind on earth until the beginning of the eternal state. In the two hundred years before the end of each two-thousand-year period and the first seventy years of the following two-thousand-year period, God would gradually change the identity of his "chosen people" set, those who would be his witnesses on earth for revealing himself and his requirements for them. This would occur as follows:
  - The first two thousand years: the original patriarchs

- ○ The second two thousand years: the Jewish people
- ○ The third two thousand years: the Christians
- ○ The final one thousand years: a merger of Jewish and Christian people sets into *unity* under Jesus during the millennium, with each people group also keeping its own identity

Collection of More Information to Help Us in Our Search

To further set the stage to help us discover the global reset code, we must next make certain we have identified and understand both the historical resets that have already occurred and those prophesied to occur from Bible prophecy. Thus, we will next present a description of all those resets. Remember, we are still in the data-collection phase of our search for the global reset code.

A Description of Both Historical and Future Global Resets

Descriptions of the Four Previous Global Resets

The global resets we are describing are those with "eternal consequences" initiated by God. They do not include "minor" resets initiated by humans. In the whole history of the world, there have been only four true global resets. These have included the following:

- A two-stage reset involved first the fall of man in 4070–4060 BC when humans were transitioned from a unified heaven and earth to just living solely on a physical earth. Second were the years 3873–3863 BC, which would mark the end of the seventh one-thousand-year day of creation and the start of the seven-thousand-year period, which will end with the return of the eternal state of Revelation 21–22.
- This is the great flood in the years 2434–2433 BC when humans had a completely new start, with all humans living on the earth being destroyed by water except for one family, the family of Noah.
- The period of the exodus of the Israelites from Egypt in 1438 BC included the next seven weeks when God gave the Israelites, and really the whole world, a set of written rules, which they were to follow all their days. This included a list of rewards for keeping the commands and punishments for not keeping them; it also gave humans knowledge of the afterlife and so forth.
- The final historical global reset took place with the birth (2.5 BC), life, and death (32.25 AD) of Jesus. This gave humans a definitive way to eternal life in heaven because Jesus died to pay for their sins. This made it possible for any humans who would accept him to have full forgiveness for their sins, resulting in a free pass into heaven at their death. It would be the only way to get into heaven.

We have identified three more global events described in biblical prophecy, and they have not yet occurred. These are most clearly described in the books of Daniel and Revelation. In fact, the last two chapters in the Bible, Revelation 21–22, are all about the final global reset. We will now describe those three final global resets.

Descriptions of the Three Still-Future Global Resets

- The first of the twin global resets will take place in the coming seven-year period of tribulation on the whole earth. The first will involve the Antichrist coming to power as the ruler of a one-world government over the whole earth. The Antichrist will come to great prominence at the beginning of the seven-year period when he is able to negotiate a peace treaty after a nuclear exchange that involves Israel. Three and a half years later, he will reach a level of power over the whole world that leads him to believe he is God, and he thus goes into a newly built temple in Israel and declares that he is God and demands humans to worship him over the whole earth. This involves requiring all humans to take the mark of the Beast, implying full worship of him as God. The end-time scenario we have been postulating in this book points to this reset taking place in AD 2041.5.

- The second of the twin global resets will take place at the Second Coming of Jesus to earth at the end of the seven-year period of tribulation. Jesus will destroy the Antichrist and his kingdom, hold a series of judgments, throw Satan and his evil angels into the Abyss for one thousand years, renew the destroyed earth, and set up his kingdom on earth for the next one thousand years, during which he will rule as King of Kings and Lord of Lords. This reset will mark the end of all Satanically inspired and man-made religions on earth. It will also mark the end of the Catholic Church and Protestant denominations since there will now be only one church, the one headed by Jesus himself. The worldwide government will be a theocracy. The end-time scenario we have been postulating in this book points to this reset taking place in AD 2045.

- The seventh and final global reset will take place at the *start of the "eternal state"* of Revelation 21–22 at the end of the one thousand years. The final judgments of all those who have rejected God and Jesus through all ages past will take place, with all being thrown into first the lake of fire and then outer darkness forever. Jesus will then finalize the purpose of God's will when he creates a unified new heaven and new earth, with all physical and spiritual dimensions being united under Jesus. There will no longer be people in human bodies since all will then have glorified, resurrected bodies for eternity. There will no longer be evil, death, sorrow, tears, and so forth, since all will now live forever together with the Father, the Son, and the Holy Spirit in unity and perfection for eternity. The end-time scenario we have been postulating in this book points to this reset taking place in AD 3037.

We didn't discover the global reset code until we had finished the master template and the last couple of chapters in this book. We were in the final review of the book when we believe God revealed this incredible code to us. That required rewriting much of this chapter, and we thank God for that. That is because we hadn't found a global reset event-pattern string that satisfied us. When we finally recognized the real pattern, we were incredibly overwhelmed by it. We hope it does the same for you! With all of the above background now in view, we will next present what we found to be the first dimension of the global reset code, the global reset event-pattern string.

The Global Reset Code;
The First Dimension of the Code, The Event-Pattern String

The event-pattern string we found was based on the use of God's fifty-year Jubilee judgment pattern along with a 10x multiple of that pattern, a five-hundred-year pattern. We will next express some of the characteristics of this incredible pattern string:

- The five-hundred-year pattern string would start at the end of the seventh day of creation in the twin ten-year periods that mark that event. These twin events were separated by exactly ten God years with the first beginning the set of patterns that would always be used in God's interactions with Gentiles and the second in God's interactions with those he called his "chosen people" or "his witnesses." These were the years 3873.37 and 3863.5 BC. The second of these dates is where the five-hundred-year global reset event-pattern string began. That would make it a pattern string concerning the way God would interact with his chosen people all down through history.
- All seven of the global resets would take place within the very last fifty-year Jubilee judgment period within one of the five-hundred-year periods in the pattern string.
- The number of five-hundred-year periods between global resets is a descriptor of the characteristics of the event and/or the whole period following the upcoming reset.

In the following chart, we will describe how this has worked in every case.

The Global Reset Event-Pattern String Chart

50 year Jubilee period hosting the Global Reset	No. of 500 year periods Since the last reset Event	The theme of the Global Reset event and/or period based upon the number of 500 year periods until the next Global Reset. These themes are always consistent with the way that God used these numbers throughout the Bible. Since the basic spacing is 500 years each Global Reset would involve a MAJOR JUDGMENT of God's people.
3863.5 BC 4070.5 BC	0 The fall of man	This date was 10 years after the end of the 7th 1000 year day of creation and marked the start of a new 7000 years for man on earth. Thus it was a major global reset. Man was no longer in the personal presence of God. Actual fall was in 4070 so 4070 and 3863 are a sort of combo global reset for mankind.
2434.33 2385.0	3 The great flood	The 50 year Jubilee period that would host the second global reset was the period between the great flood and the next Jubilee year in 2385 BC. The 3 500 year periods preceding this reset would mean that this reset would involve some new leader for the people of the world. There would only be one family, that of Noah for the restart. Nephilim and other world leaders had been destroyed in the flood.
1448.7 1399.4 BC Key date 1438.8	2 Exodus and God giving Moses the 10 Commands, etc.	This 50 year Jubilee period hosted several important events including the plagues that led to the Exodus, the Exodus itself, God giving the Law to Moses, the 40 year exile in a wilderness leading to the Israelites being able to enter the Promised Land and then the Battle of Jericho and the actual entrance into the Promised Land. The two 500 year periods preceding these events may have indicated that God would marry the Jewish people in 1438 at the time of his giving the law to Moses, as in 1+1=2. He would then divorce them for unfaithfulness exactly 2 periods of 500 years later in the events of 463 BC when it became clear that the Jews had not passed God's tests for them. This is taken from the Book of Hosea which also indicates that God will remarry the Jewish people in the end times when they return to him in masses.
30.8 AD 80.1 Key date 32.25	3 Death of Jesus:	This 50 year Jubilee period started in the 3rd year of Jesus' ministry when he was 30 years old in 30 AD. It had been 3 periods of 500 years since the last global reset. One striking thing about the above set of numbers is that all of them are multiples of 3 which would hugely heighten the emphasis in this period of the huge importance of the key new leader and the Temple of God. Jesus was that new leader, the leader of all Christians of all ages. The temple would refer to believers in Jesus becoming the place where the Spirit would live in the future. The end date of this 50 year period, 80 AD, also was related to temples, since in that year Mt Vesuvius erupted resulting in the complete destruction of four idol worshipping temples demonstrating God's great disdain for such practices.
2002.1 2051.4 Twin Global Resets 2041, 2045	4 Rapture, great tribulation, Second Coming of Jesus, Mill Temple	This 50 year Jubilee period turned out to be the 70th Jubilee year period since the time that the Jews first began celebrating Jubilee years in 1399 BC. This period has been the principal focus of this four book series and the period when the vast number of event pattern strings are converging. This period in our generation turns out to be a good fit for the occurrence of the end time scenario. The fact that it will be 4 periods of 500 years since the last global reset may point to the fact that those periods were all characterized by exiles for the Jewish people from the blessings of God for their rejection of Jesus. It may also point to the likelihood that the 70th Jubilee period may host a horrible time of exile, tribulation and death. Near the end of this period Jesus would become Crown Prince of earth.
3037.0 AD	2 Start eternal state	This year is not only the end of another 2 periods of 500 years since the last global reset but also the very ending year of the 7000 years of man on earth since the end of the 7th day of creation as well as the end of the 1000 year millennium under the Kingship of Jesus from our speculative end time scenario. The number 2 in God's mathematics points to two unities converging into one unity as in 1+1=2. That could point to the time of the eternal state when the physical and spiritual dimensions become unified again, just as Rev 21 indicates. See the last chapter for details in the end time scenario.

The fact that the global reset event-pattern string and all the master template event patterns have taken place in an absolutely perfect mathematically organized manner right up to this very year is unchallengeable. It is absolute proof that we know who *is* in control and who is *not* in control. The important question is, what will each of us do with this knowledge?

The Discovery of a Second Dimension for the Global Reset Code

We have just completed presenting the global reset event-pattern string for the global reset code. As we were analyzing the seven global reset events, we were looking for any unique themes that defined each of the events that might also be part of the global reset code. We hit the jackpot as we were studying the third global reset. It took place in the events surrounding the exodus event and involved the Angel of Death. It involved death, a Passover, and a new Promised Land for the Jewish people. It also involved the number thirteen. Might the other six global reset events also involve these types of events? An analysis of those six events quickly showed that all six also involved death, a Passover of some sort, and some new land for God's people in some way. A few also involved the number thirteen. Thus, we had discovered a new dimension to what would be the final global reset code. We will next define that new dimension in some detail.

The Second Dimension of the Global Reset Code;
The Passover, Death, and New Home (or Promised Land) Theme

We have just finished presenting the first dimension of the global reset code. We saw that the global reset code is an event-pattern string with time gaps of multiples of five hundred years between events. In this case, the events are the seven major resets that either have already occurred or will one day occur on earth.

We have also pointed out that the events have a second extremely important theme associated with them. This theme is that each event involves three very important features. These are first death in some very significant way; second, a very important Passover event of some sort; and third, a Promised Land of some sort—a new residence, so to speak, that either is or will be available to God's people. We will now begin presenting that second dimension of the global reset code.

The First Death, Passover, Promised Land Event (3863 BC)

The five-hundred-year event pattern associated with the death, Passover, or Promised Land dimension began in the year 3863 BC, which would mark the end of the seventh one-thousand-year day of creation and the start of the seven-thousand-year period, which will end with the return of the eternal state of Revelation 21–22. This Passover event from living in a unified heaven and earth to being confined solely to earth, a new home, a new Promised Land, would introduce several hardships for humans. They would be faced with living in an environment featuring certain death, physical separation from God, a new requirement to work endlessly to provide for their own needs and the needs of their family, along with many other new challenges. Death hadn't been part of life in the paradise mankind had been living in before their fall to temptation led to sin, which led to being banned from living with God in the eternal paradise in heaven. Thus, it is obvious that this event involved a massive global reset, a passover from one environment to a totally new one, the entry of death into the lives of humans, and an exile into a vastly less desirable place, a land promised to them if they did not keep God's rules while they were in God's paradise. In this dialogue a passover would be a sudden major change in or passing over from one type of living environment to another vastly different living environment for God's people on earth.

The Second Death, Passover, Promised Land Event (2434–2385 BC)

The second death, Passover, and Promised Land event took place in the Jubilee-year period starting with the great flood in the years 2434–2433 BC, when humans had a completely new start with all humans living on the earth being destroyed by water except for one family, the family of Noah. The five-hundred-year event pattern hit the end of this Jubilee-year period in 2385 BC. The great flood featured both great death and a Passover from living in a near paradise with constantly moderate temperatures, no storms, plentiful food, very long life spans, and so forth.

Before the flood, people had to face the reality of the ever-increasing threat of a menacing, Satanically created population of evil giants. After the flood, they would face a very different environment in a greatly changed world, their new Promised Land. Humans would face many new challenges in this new home of sorts including having to completely start over with one small family, facing much quicker deaths due to much shorter life spans, many new weather-related challenges, having nothing to do their work except for what had been on the ark, and so forth. Initially, their only contact with God would be through prayer and the writings of other patriarchs who preceded them, including Enoch. Thus, we can see that this involved a massive global reset for God's people.

The Third Death, Passover, Promised Land Event (1448–1399 BC)

The third earth, Passover, and Promised Land event took place surrounding the exodus of the Israelites from Egypt in 1438 BC. The exodus included the original death, Passover, and Promised Land event. This event involved the Angel of Death in a ploy to get the Egyptians to allow the Israelites to leave their four hundred years in slavery and go to the Promised Land God had said he would give them. The ploy involved the Israelites placing the blood of an innocent lamb on their doorposts. The night the Israelites did this, the Angel of Death visited Egypt, *passed over* the homes of those who had placed the blood on their doorposts, and then proceeded to kill the firstborn of all who had not done so, namely the Egyptian families.

The great death that accompanied this for the Egyptians led to a quick escape for the Israelites from Egypt. This led to them being able to take a long journey to their Promised Land. Seven weeks after the exodus, God gave the Israelites, and really the whole world, a set of written rules they were to follow all their days. It included a list of rewards for keeping the commands and punishments for not keeping them; it also gave humans knowledge of the afterlife and so forth. Thus, we can see this was a global reset for God's people. The five-hundred-year event pattern hit the year 1399 BC, the year the Jews first entered their new Promised Land. That Jubilee period started in the year 1448 BC, so this period encompassed the exodus and the original Bible-recorded death, Passover, and Promised Land event of 1438 BC.

The Fourth Death, Passover, Promised Land Event (AD 30–80)

The final historical global reset took place with the birth (2.5 BC), life, and death (AD 32.25) of Jesus. This gave humans a definitive way to eternal life in heaven because Jesus died to pay for their sins. This made it possible for the sins of any human who would accept him to have full forgiveness for their sins, resulting in a free pass into heaven at their death. It would be the only way to get into heaven. The fifty-year Jubilee pattern that encompassed this global reset began in AD 30.8 when Jesus reestablished God's Jubilee requirements for man and ended in AD 80.1, the year hit by the five-hundred-year event pattern.

What we are about to reveal is incredible to the highest order! The year AD 30.8 was the start of Jesus's third year of ministry, and it marked the start of the thirtieth Jubilee period counting from 1399 BC. It was also precisely twenty-five hundred years after the very start of the great flood in 2434.33 BC. It was also two thousand years since the death of Shem, fifteen hundred years since the start of the exodus adventure, one thousand years since the Jubilee year directly following the completion of the original Jerusalem temple, and five hundred years after Artaxerxes's decree allowing the Israelites to return to their homeland with more self-rule and the return of the original temple implements for worship. Whew!

This would also have been the Jubilee year when Jesus made the decision to allow the destruction of Jerusalem, the temple, the nation of Judea, and the exile of the Jewish people for two thousand years for not accepting him as their God and Messiah. That two-thousand-year period ended in 2001/02, the start of the seventieth Jubilee year, marking forty fifty-year periods of exile from God. That is one of the principal reasons we feel that the complete return of the Jewish people en mass to worship Jesus will take place during this seventieth Jubilee period. That is a principal reason for the end-time scenario that patterns point to possibly taking place in the last ten years of this fifty-year period. This may be the penultimate Passover/death/Promised Land event. Jesus's death for our sins gives us a path to a free *pass over* into heaven, the ultimate Promised Land, at the time of our death; thus, it allows us to live throughout eternity in the promised paradise of heaven. Thank you, Jesus!

The Fifth Death, Passover, Promised Land Event (AD 2001–2051)

The first of the twin global resets will take place in the coming seven-year period of tribulation on the whole earth. The first will involve the Antichrist coming to power as the ruler of a one-world government over the whole earth. The Antichrist will come to great prominence at the very beginning of the seven-year period when he is able to negotiate a peace treaty after a nuclear exchange that involves Israel. Three and a half years later, he will reach a level of power over the whole world that leads him to believe he is God and thus goes into a newly built temple in Israel and declares he is God and demands that humans worship him over the whole earth. This involves requiring all humans to take the mark of the Beast, implying full worship of him as God.

The end-time scenario we have been postulating in this book points to this global reset taking place in AD 2041.5. The reign of the Antichrist will last three and a half years, according to the prophet Daniel. In our postulated end-time scenario, this will be the years AD 2041 to 2045, in the seventieth Jubilee period of our generation. It will be a time of death, Passover, and fulfillment of the promise of God that this will be a horrible new land for the people of the world. It will involve death since Jesus called this time the worst tribulation in the history of the world, with Zechariah and Revelation pointing to possibly two-thirds of all people on earth being killed. It will represent a Passover from freedom to tyranny for the people still on the earth, from a land inhabited by many millions of Jesus-loving and serving people to one inhabited by only Jesus-rejecting people. It will thus fulfill the time of a horrible existence in a land promised to exist for the people of the world in the book of Revelation.

The Sixth Death, Passover, Promised Land Event (AD 2001–2051)

The second of the twin global resets will take place at the Second Coming of Jesus to earth at the end of the seven-year period of tribulation. Jesus will destroy the Antichrist and his kingdom, hold a series of judgments, throw Satan and his evil angels into the Abyss for one thousand years, renew the destroyed earth, and set up his kingdom on earth for the next one thousand years. During that period, he will rule as "King of Kings and Lord of Lords." This reset will mark the end of all Satanically inspired and man-made religions on earth. It will also mark the end of the Catholic Church and Protestant denominations, since there will now only be one church, one headed by Jesus himself. The world-wide government will be a theocracy.

The end-time scenario we have been postulating in this book points to this global reset taking place in 2045 AD. The Second Coming of Jesus will represent a second massive global reset only three and a half years after the reset involving the Antichrist. It will again involve death, a Passover, and a new promised land.

Death is involved in that the millennial period will begin, and people will be living for hundreds of years, thus delaying the onset of death. The world will also be inhabited by all of the saints of all ages, who will be living in resurrected, glorified bodies that will never face death. They are eternal. It will represent a Passover from a world ruled by fallible humans to one ruled by the infallible Jesus. It will be in an entirely upgraded earth, a paradise of sorts. It will represent a time when the Jewish saints of all ages will finally be living in the whole of the Promised Land for the very first time. The Jewish people had never reached this full boundary of the land God promised them about forty-one hundred years ago.

The Seventh Death, Passover, Promised Land Event (AD 3037)

The seventh and final global reset will take place at the start of the eternal state of Revelation 21–22 at the end of the one thousand years. The final judgments of all those who have rejected God and Jesus throughout all ages past will take place, with all being thrown into first the lake of fire and then outer darkness forever. Jesus will then finalize the purpose of God's will when he creates a unified new heaven and new earth, with all physical and spiritual dimensions being united under Jesus. There will no longer be people in human bodies since all will then have glorified, resurrected bodies for eternity. There will no longer be evil, death, sorrow, tears, and so forth, since all will now live forever together with the Father, the Son, and the Holy Spirit in unity and perfection for eternity.

The end-time scenario we have been postulating in this book points to this global reset taking place in 3037 AD. This will be at the end of the one-thousand-year millennial period. At this time, all unbelievers of all ages past will be resurrected, judged, and then *passed over* into the lake of fire and outer darkness. Meanwhile, all believers of all ages will *pass over* into the eternal state of Revelation 20–21. This will be an eternity in a new heaven and new earth, the fulfillment of the final eternal Promised Land, where we will be living with God forever. This will mark the final end of death and mark the start of eternal life. Wow!

We will next present the second dimension of the global reset code. The first dimension was presented earlier in this section.

The Global Reset Code;

The Second Dimension of the Code, Death, Passover, New Home Theme

The global reset events have a second extremely important theme associated with them. This theme is that each event involves three very important features. These are first death in some very significant way; second, a very important Passover event of some sort; and third, a Promised Land of some sort—a new residence, so to speak, that either is or will be available to God's people.

We are finally ready to crack the global reset code.

Cracking the Global Reset Code

The global reset code involves massive world-order-changing global resets that God will impose on the people of earth. They always occur in the last Jubilee period of a five-hundred-year event-pattern string that began in 3863 BC, ten years after the end of the seventh one-thousand-year day of creation. They all involve events producing death, a Passover event, and some new Promised Land for God's people. They were all necessary for God to ultimately be able to meet the purpose of his will: "to bring everything in heaven and on earth into unity under Jesus when time reaches its fulfillment."

Clues from the Global Reset Code

- There have been seven events in history that have resulted in a sequence of first death, then a Passover of some sort, and finally a new home for those involved in the event. The 2041–2051 time period may host just such an event. If so, then it would be the twin global resets and family reunions that are the subject of this book. Incredibly, all seven of the Passover/death/new home events are part of one of God's incredible global resets which bring key means into play that are very important in God's plan to bring about the purpose of his will.

An Analysis of the Master Template Chart to Identify the Most Important Events in the Complete Seventy-Two Hundred Years Since the Fall of Man

We would next like to take a close examination of the complete master template chart to see whether we can identify the most important past and yet future events in the whole seventy-two hundred-year period speculated for mankind on earth. To do that, we had to first construct a scorecard to use in evaluating the importance of each event in each pattern included in the master template. We did just that, and it is included at the very end of this book in Appendix B. The scorecard is a mathematical algorithm based on my total familiarity with the event-pattern strings in the master template and my experience as a professional systems analyst. This is only one of many schemes we could have devised to evaluate the importance of the patterns to God in meeting his ultimate purpose in the end-times.

We used the scorecard to evaluate each of the approximately one hundred dates in the master template chart. The results are shown for each date on each second page of the master template chart. Those are the pages in the chart that give the descriptions of the events taking place on each date. We will next list the top twenty dates in this evaluation on the chart presented below. We will ponder the results after first showing the chart.

The 20 Most Important Events in the Master Template Chart
Based Solely Upon the Combined Scores of All of the Patterns
Converging on Each Date in The Master Template Chart
(The "Pattern" Chart)

Event Date	Total Score	Event Taking Place in the Pattern Year
2041 AD	4185	1- Speculated pattern shows date for mid-tribulation
3037 AD	3662	2- Speculated pattern shows rapture of the saints
2051 AD	3407	3- Speculated pattern shows anointing Millennial Temple
3027 AD	2958	4- Speculated scenario shows Great White Throne Judgment
30-32 AD	2015	5- Jubilee year in 3rd year of Jesus' ministry; a global reset at time of Jesus crucifixion in 32 AD
1902 BC	1947	6- 2000th year after the end of the 7th day of creation; Joseph born
3873 BC	1878	7- End of 7th day of creation on Gentile calendar
3863 BC	1351	8- Start Witness patterns 10 yrs after 3873
2434 BC	1334	9- Year of start of great flood; a global reset
1438 BC	1275	10- Year of Exodus; a global reset
2099 BC	1211	11-2000th year after fall; start wrestling match
1844 AD	1081	12- Ottoman edict of toleration for Jew; opens way for return to land
522 BC	1079	13- Darius decree allowing temple rebuild in Judah
1442 BC	1078	14- Start of great plagues resulting in Exodus
2045 AD	1000	15- Speculative year of Jesus' Second Coming
4070 BC	969	16- Year of the fall of man
3025 BC	962	17- Birth of Noah, patriarch of Abraham
2296 BC	924	18- Tower of Babel incident
1943 AD	870	19- The peak year of the Holocaust period
127 BC	791	20- 2000 Years after the fall of man, 200 years before 70 AD

The numerical values shown in the master template chart for each event reflect the sum of the relative importance of each of the patterns that converged in that event date. After initially pondering the above chart, we realized that we had left out one very important factor in the way in which we had calculated the importance of each event. That was the fact that about 10 percent of the events took place at times when either Jesus or the Father made an in-person visit to earth or was dealing with humans in face-to-face situations. Because of that fact, we felt it necessary to construct two separate listings of the most important events included in the seventy-two hundred years of man on earth. Thus, we devised a scheme to add "bonus" points to each event that so directly involved Jesus or the Father in person. The values of those bonus points were added to the results shown in the above chart and are also reflected in our scorecard in Appendix B. Thus, we reconstructed the chart by adding the bonus points to the events directly involving either Jesus or the Father God on earth and will show it below.

The 20 Most Important Events in the Master Template Chart Based Upon Two Key Factors Using the Scorecard of Appendix B:

These Factors Were the Combination of the Pattern Convergence Score in the Chart and the Bonus Points Added for Events During Which Jesus Was on Earth and the Event Originator (The "Bonus" Chart)

Event Date	Total Score	Event Taking Place in the Pattern Year
30-32 AD	7015	1- Jubilee year in 3rd year of Jesus' ministry; a global reset at time of Jesus crucifixion in 32 AD
2045 AD	6000	2- Speculative year of Jesus' Second Coming
2041 AD	4185	3- Speculated pattern shows date for mid-tribulation
3037-38 AD	3662	4- Speculated pattern shows rapture of the saints
2051 AD	3407	5- Speculated pattern shows anointing Millennial Temple
3027 AD	2958	6- Speculated scenario shows Great White Throne Judgment
4070 BC	1969	7- Year of the fall of man
1902 BC	1947	8- 2000th year after the end of the 7th day of creation; Joseph born
3873 BC	1868	9- End of 7th day of creation on Gentile calendar
3863 BC	1351	10- Start Witness patterns 10 yrs after 3873
2434 BC	1334	11- Year of start of great flood; a global reset
1438 BC	1275	12- Year of Exodus; a global reset
2099 BC	1211	13- 2000th year after fall; start wrestling match
1844 AD	1081	14- Ottoman edict of toleration for Jew; opens way for return to land
522 BC	1079	15- Darius decree allowing temple rebuild in Judah
1442 BC	1078	16- Start of great plagues resulting in Exodus
3025 BC	965	17- Birth of Noah, patriarch of Abraham
2296 BC	924	18- Tower of Babel incident
1943 AD	870	19- The peak year of the Holocaust period
2089 BC	781	20- Death of Noah; start wrestling match with God

We would next like to conduct a comparative analysis of these two charts and make a few comments about our key findings.

- First, nineteen of the twenty event dates are common to the two lists. The only one that is not the same is the twentieth event in both charts.
- Seven of the first eight events in the bonus listing involve direct contact between Jesus and his people on earth. The same can be said for five of the first eight in the "pattern" chart.

- Eight of the twenty events in both charts involved direct contact with either Jesus or the Father God with humans.
- The master template chart contains what God's patterns point to as the most important events for his people in the seventy-two hundred years of man on earth, and these twenty patterns seem to be at the top of that list of one hundred events, according to our personal analysis. Thus, we should be able to conclude that the most important events in the seventy-two hundred years of man on earth were those involving direct contact with either Jesus or the Father God.
- The patterns in this chart were the most important event-pattern strings God has apparently been using to bring about the purpose of his will for both himself and mankind. These patterns are prophetic or predictive, and they have proved to be absolutely perfect predictors of events for 5,980 years now. Should that not indicate that the same will hold for the next 1,020 years? If so, we now know the expected themes of the coming events in both the short and long term. Are we ready for this? It certainly seems that over 90 percent of the world is not.

What other factors would make us believe that these twenty events are really among the very most important events in the whole of the speculated seventy-two hundred years of humans on earth? We will next list several of those factors:

- They are all in God's master template, the vehicle he seems to be using to accomplish the purpose of his will from Ephesians 1:7–11. That is to bring everything in heaven and on earth into unity under Jesus when time reaches its fulfillment.
- The patterns continue throughout the whole of human existence.
- These patterns principally concern God's chosen people, those who eventually choose Jesus as their savior. All these events are key milestones in some way that lead to both the identity of those who will be in the finally chosen group and the time frame of when God's purpose will finally be fulfilled.
- There is great evidence that each of these events was preplanned, even before creation.
- We know the identity of the one who was the author of these patterns. God said in Isaiah 41 and 46 that he and only he is in charge of world events. He said he is the author of Bible prophecy and that every one of his prophecies would be fulfilled with absolute accuracy. We have an immense amount of history to verify this. We will further expound on this below:
  - There were over three hundred detailed prophecies concerning Jesus's first coming to earth, and all were fulfilled precisely in every way.
  - About 80 percent of all Bible prophecies have already been fulfilled, again with absolute accuracy.
  - With this being the case, we certainly would expect the remaining prophecies to be fulfilled. These are principally end-time prophecies.
- There is much more to the Isaiah 41 and 46 passages we would like to present in making this argument. For example, God said he proves himself, who he is,

through Bible prophecy. He further challenged all the false gods to do this and said they would all fail. He said he is the only one who knows "the end from the beginning." This meant that at the very beginning of man on earth, he already knew what would take place at the very end of time. That is exactly what these event-pattern strings are. They were designed in the beginning at creation, and they have been taking place exactly as planned all down through history until the pre-planned end-time is reached. Thus, we can see that the future is already "history" to God.

- These master template patterns were all prophetic in nature and were hidden in the Bible in event codes. We have discovered these codes, and they are the key topic in this four-book series.

- The master template actually contained seven pattern "sets." Each set often contained several different individual event-pattern strings that would all converge in the same events. Thus, there were in reality many more than seven patterns involved. For example, the two-thousand-year pattern contains at least nine separate event patterns. That greatly magnifies its importance.

How God does all this and still gives humans "free will" to make their own choices is a real mystery to us. An argument could be made that in light of the large event database contained in the Bible, along with the six thousand years of history since the end of the creation process, to not believe the God of the Christian Bible is the originator of the event patterns we are presenting is irrational. Why anyone who knows this information doesn't believe it is so difficult to understand; possibly the best explanation could be from what the Bible says in 2 Corinthians 4:4. There it says that God allows some to be "blinded" to the truth by Satan. In other words, God allows Satan to put blind spots in the minds of many people.

We will say in conclusion that by every measure we have used throughout these four books, it appears that the future dates of 2041 and 2051, along with the end of the millennium dates of 3027–37, appear to be among the most important dates in history.

Clues from the seven sets of event pattern strings in God's master template can help us answer the five w's associated with our subject questions. What are the coming twin global resets and family reunions, and how are they associated with God meeting the purpose of his will, bringing everything in heaven and on earth together in unity under Jesus when time reaches its fulfillment (the end times, possibly in our generation)?

Key Clues from God's Master Template:

God's Witness Pattern

- God's witness pattern, like so many of his patterns, relies on similarly themed events taking place surrounding each two thousandth year after the end of the seventh day of creation. In this case, the events involve a gradual change in the identity of God's witnessing group. It evolved from the eleven patriarchs to the Jewish people and to the Christians, and finally in and after 2041, it seems that we may have a merger of Christians and Jews into one group. It will remain constant over the next one thousand years after that. This points to the fulfillment of the biblical end-time scenario in the 2041 time frame, with the dual global resets and family reunions taking place. This means that the first step in meeting the purpose of God's will finally be fulfilled, that being Jesus and his bride being united as one. The final steps will take place one thousand years later.

- We also found that there is a second witness in each two-thousand-year period. That is a written witness, and it expands from period to period. The written witness in the first two thousand years was the writings of the eleven patriarchs. This transitioned to the Old Testament writings over the second two thousand years, and it then expanded to include the New Testament in the final two thousand years. Paul told us that we always need two witnesses.

The Great Convergence Family of Pattern Sets

- This is God's general purpose event-pattern set he uses in interacting with his people on earth. The most basic and most used patterns in this set are the 200/2000 year event-pattern strings. These patterns seem to be homing in on the seventieth Jubilee year period from AD 2001 to 2051 and the years 2041 and 2051 in particular. These patterns fit the end-time scenario incredibly well, which would mean the fulfillment of God's ultimate purpose for his will to a large extent. It hosts by far the greatest number of key patterns with their topics including the following themes: the end of God's punishment sentences for his people, his forgiveness for the past sins of all his people, the time of rewarding his people for their good acts, the end of death for many of God's people and longer lives in general for others, the grafting of the Jewish people back into the Tree of Life, the end of sentences of tribulation and exile for God's people, the beginning of a period of one thousand years of living on earth with Jesus as King of Kings and Lord of Lords in a paradise-like setting, and so forth.

God's Punishment and Destruction Pattern Set

- This is a special case pattern, in that it goes wall to wall, uses the patterns in the general purpose set, and utilizes the punishment-pattern strings, but it also mixes the strings with other testing and punishment features that make it unique. Many of the patterns end in 2041, our target date, but this does seem to be the end of the physical destruction of cities and countries on earth. In that regard, it would signal the end-time scenario. However, a unique feature is that this pattern set may also contain God's use of his final judgments of many of the people on earth, both dead and still alive. The sheep-goat judgment, the Daniel 12 Jewish judgment, and other special case judgments take place as a part of the end-time scenario. That ties these judgments to the 2041 time frame. The judgments are wall to wall because the first judgment start time was apparently at the end of the seventh day of creation in 3873 BC. There were exactly four periods of 360 years, this time on our 365-day calendar, until the end of the great flood in 2433 BC. Also, there will be destruction of a sort taking place in AD 3037 at the end of the millennium, when the Great White Throne Judgment will take place (see Rev. 20). The barrier between the physical and spiritual dimensions will be destroyed, and the two will be merged together. Thus, this is a wall-to-wall judgment pattern that hits hard in 2041 according to our interpretation of God's pattern set.

The Wrath-of-God Pattern Set

- In the third two-thousand-year period of this pattern, the 200+70-year period starts in AD 1844, and the two-hundredth-year event is centered in 2041. We have shown that the biblical end-time scenario fits this time frame quite well. If that turns out to be the case, then AD 2041 will be the year when the three-and-a-half-year period dubbed the "great tribulation" will start. In Matthew 24, Jesus called this period the one of the greatest wrath in history. If that is the case, then 2041 will be in the center of the twin global resets and great family reunions.

The Global Reset Code

- Seven events in history have resulted in a sequence of first death, then a Passover of some sort, and finally a new home for those involved in the event. The 2041–2051 time period may host just such an event. If so, then it will be the twin global resets and family reunions, which are the subject of this book. Incredibly, all seven of the Passover/death/new home events are part of one of God's incredible global resets, which bring key means into play that are very important in God's plan to bring about the purpose of his will.

The Great Wrestling Match

- Many Jewish people and national and religious leaders have been wrestling with the true and complete identity of God for forty-two hundred years. The same goes for Gentile people groups, and the two matches run together separated by exactly ten years. The match lasts for seven periods of six hundred and six congruent periods of seven hundred years. It started exactly two thousand years after the fall and will apparently end in 2041 and 2051, all within the twin two-hundred-year pattern set.

- These matches end in the same time frame as the twin global resets and family reunions.

The Ever-Present Set of Seventy-Year Patterns

- Every tenth year all down through history is part of one of God's seven seventy-year testing patterns. This testing will end at the rapture events in the years surrounding the six thousandth year or in the 2041 time frame and in the seven-thousandth-year time frame at the end of the millennium for those who receive glorified bodies at the final judgment in that time frame.
- These events will all host the final three global resets and family reunions.

The 5 W's Report Card

CLUES FROM GOD'S MASTER TEMPLATE THAT WILL HELP US BETTER UNDERSTAND END TIME EVENTS, THE UNIFICATION OF EVERYTHING UNDER JESUS, THE DUAL GLOBAL RESETS, DUAL FAMILY REUNIONS AND THEIR POSSIBLE TIE TO OUR GENERATION			
WHO	**WHEN**	**WHERE**	**WHAT EVENT AND WHY**
Jesus, Jews, Christians, 11 Patriarchs	2041/51	Whole world	**GOD'S WITNESS PATTERN:** God used a different set of witnesses to help accomplish the purpose of his will in each 2000 year period; the last two were combined into one at the end of the third 2000th year. This implies that 2041/51 will host the marriage of Jesus with his bride in fulfillment of God's purpose. Unification!
God, Jesus, Jews, Christians, Satan Antichrist, God's angels, Satan's angels, all people	Fall to Second Coming of Jesus, centers on 2041-51	Israel, whole world	**THE GREAT CONVERGENCE FAMILY:** It hosts by far the greatest number of key patterns with their topics including the following themes; the end of God's punishment sentences for his people, the forgiveness of the past sins of all of his people, the time of rewarding his people for their good acts, the end of death for many of God's people and longer lives in general for others, the grafting of the Jewish people back into the tree of life, the end of sentences of tribulation and exile for God's people, the beginning of a period of 1000 years of living on earth with Jesus as King of Kings and Lord of Lords in a paradise like setting, etc. All of these shout; end times are here, including the twin global resets and family reunions.
Israel, whole world	70th Jubilee, 2038-51	Israel, whole world	**GOD'S PUNISHMENT AND DESTRUCTION PATTERN SET:** God's Punishment patterns for his people and many of the final judgments for his people seem to be ending in our generation, and particularly in 2041/51. This signals the end time scenario with fulfillment of God's purpose, the twin family reunions and global resets.
Jesus, Satan, antichrist, all people	2041	Israel, whole world	**THE WRATH OF GOD PATTERN SET:** The great wrath in the final ominous 270 year period seems to center around the year 2041. If so that would signal the time of the twin global resets and family reunions.
Jews, Christians, All people	7 dates spread all across the 7200 years	Whole world	**THE GLOBAL RESET CODE:** There have been 7 events in history that have resulted in a sequence of first death, then a Passover of some sort and finally a new home for those involved in the event. The 2041-2051 time period may host just such an event. If so then it would be the twin global resets and family reunions that are the subject of this book. Incredibly, all 7 of the Passover/Death/New Home events are a part of one of God's incredible Global Resets which bring key means into play that are very important in God's plan to bring about the purpose of his will.
Israel, whole world	2100 BC-2041 AD	Whole world	**THE GREAT WRESTLING MATCH:** Both Jews and Gentiles have been wrestling with the true identity of God for a 4200 year period that will end in the year 2041, the end time period hosting the twin global resets and family reunions.
Jesus, whole world	2038-51	Whole world	**THE EVER PRESENT SET OF 70 YEAR PATTERNS:** It appears as though God has seven separate testing pattern event strings that he has been using to test his people ever since the end of the seventh day of creation. He appears to be using seven separate patterns, one starting in every tenth year after 3863.5 BC and continuing until the start of the eternal state. These patterns hit ever tenth year in the 70th Jubilee period. Thus they could be a factor in the end time scenario if it occurs in our generation.

The Thirteen Year End-Time Scenario and Great Family Reunion Codes

Presenting Our Postulated End-Time Scenario

In this book, we have accumulated a large number of clues in several search areas. We have basically come up with some level of confirmation for one of the five or so end-time scenarios most often postulated in Bible prophecy circles. Those scenarios are all described on my website for those who might be curious about them. The scenario our accumulated clues seem to be pointing to is termed the pre-tribulational, pre-millennial end-time scenario.

We will next present our version of that scenario, which is somewhat modified by our accumulated set of clues. We will add additional information we have personally accumulated over the last thirty years from our studies of Bible prophecy, certainly including the book of Revelation, to our approximation of the coming end-time scenario presented over and over, often in bits and pieces, throughout the Bible. This scenario ends with the culmination of our search for the time when the purpose of God's will can be accomplished. We see that it coincides with the time of the twin global resets and great family reunions. Will this take place in our generation?

We will call this scenario the thirteen year end-time scenario. We could also refer to it as a code since discovering it required us to look for many pieces of information that are hidden in prophetic topics throughout the Bible to piece it together in the proper way.

Our Interpretation of the End-Time Scenario Presented in the Christian Bible

Key Events in the Years Immediately Preceding the Seven-Year Tribulation

One of the most ominous things we learn from 2 Thessalonians 2 about this time is that the secret power of the lawless one, the evil one, will be already at work in the world before the end-times begin. We also learn from this passage that there will be a great falling away from God during this period. That is obviously taking place in a major way in the United States and Europe, certainly fueled by the technology explosion forecast by Daniel 12 and the accompanying social media expansion, which takes away from having time for the things of God. We have also seen a well-orchestrated effort, largely hidden, by anti-God forces to take control of the education curriculum and accompanying textbooks to mold the minds of young people to accept the humanistic agenda. Jesus addressed these pre-tribulation years in Matthew 24. One point he made is that there will be great fear over what is approaching in the heavens. He may be referring to an asteroid. This is happening at this very moment in time with the apparent close approach of the asteroid Apophis in the Easter season of 2029. It will approach earth again in 2036. Might this be the asteroid of Revelation?

Another interesting thing about the approaching years is that the secular world is well aware that conservative Christians are expecting the end-times to take place in the next twenty or so years. They may have a plan to explain the rapture away with a false agenda. We are being told for the first time that aliens have visited the earth in the past and that we have the corpses of aliens who have crashed on earth in spacecraft. Might their thought be that they can explain away the rapture with the idea that Christians will be simply abducted by aliens?

The last pre-rapture situation we will present is the very secretive plan by a large number of influential world leaders to use chaos of various kinds to help bring about a new unified global reset consisting of a one-world socialistic government. This may have had its roots in the 1960s, and it is now hitting warp speed since the early 2000s. Those doing this don't know that they are playing right into God's hands. We see that this is necessary to create the agenda that precedes the start of the seven-year period. It is necessary for God to meet the ultimate purpose of his will, which is a central theme of this book. Finally, in Matthew 24, Jesus calls the approaching seven years the worst disaster in history. Nobody should want to be left behind at the rapture, which we will discuss next.

Event 1, Scene 1: In the Clouds above Earth and in Heaven Where the First of the Great Family Reunions Will Take Place

It appears from our clues that the end-time scenario will last thirteen years. It will start with a _rapture_ of all living believers in and followers of Jesus. This will result in the first of our _great family reunions_. The Father God, Jesus the Son, the Holy Spirit, and God's whole family will be united in the same place for the very first time. Luke 17 says that events surrounding the rapture will be just like those before the flood and the destruction of Sodom and Gomorrah, in that they will come without notice for the residents of earth and will occur at the very start of the big occasion.

When this rapture takes place, Jesus will proceed from heaven to earth and bring with him all those believers who were already in heaven as spirits. Jesus will first give all these spirits glorified bodies and then call for all believers on earth to come and meet him in the clouds, where he will then give them the same type of glorified, resurrected bodies. This is all described in 1 Thessalonians 4. The glorified bodies are described in 1 Corinthians 15, starting in verse 51, and in Philippians 3:20–21. These bodies are eternal and can function equally well in spiritual and physical dimensions. Jesus will take these resurrected saints back to heaven with him for the next seven years.

During this seven-year period described in Daniel 9:24–27 things will be quite different in heaven and on earth. First, the seven-year period of tribulation will take place on earth. In heaven Jesus will be with his bride, the church, for the first time. A second rapture will also take place during the seven-year period. This will be a rapture described in Revelation 11 of those the Antichrist killed. It seems that this will take place at the end of the fifth trumpet judgment about six to twelve months after the mid-tribulation. Revelation 7 says this will include an uncountable number of souls who will come out of the great tribulation. In heaven this will be a glorious time of ceremony, ending in the marriage supper of the Lamb described in Revelation 19. At the same time, Jesus will multitask and direct the seal, trumpet, and bowl judgments of Revelation taking place on earth. At the end of the seven years, Jesus will return to earth with his army of angels and his bride at the Second Coming of Jesus to earth.

Event 1, Scene 2: On Earth at the Start of the Seven-Year Period of Tribulation

Meanwhile, on earth the seven-year period of tribulation will start soon after the rapture of the saints to heaven. Two horrible events will start the tribulation and seem to come in quick succession. There will seem to be an attack on Israel involving nuclear weapons, which will be quickly followed by a similar counterattack. An asteroid will also hit earth in the same general time frame. It will hit either the Mediterranean Sea or the Indian Ocean with catastrophic results. There will be huge damage to sea life and loss of the ships on the body of water. At the same time, both events will cause huge clouds of poisonous material, including radioactive material, to rise to the upper atmosphere, where they will spread over a band of the sky. It will encircle the complete earth in a band that covers one-third of the sky from north to south. This debris will gradually fall to earth over the next seven years with dramatic results in the fresh water, vegetation, and so forth. These will be huge health hazards, and the effects will be disastrous.

Event 1, Scene 3: The Rise of the Antichrist

Soon after the nuclear exchange involving Israel, an unlikely leader of a small country will come forward with a peace plan that is quickly enacted. This leader will turn out to be the one we call the Antichrist. Revelation 17–18 seems to refer to him as being a Nephilim. Genesis 6 refers to the Nephilim as being on earth just before the flood; they were the likely reason for the flood taking place. It seems that they were aliens of sort, beings crafted by evil angels using the eggs of women and fertilizing them with angelic genes to some way create a hybrid being. They were huge, strong beings that met the purpose of Satan and his following angels but were not in God's plans. The Bible tells us that Satan wants to be God just like the creator God, whom the Jews call YHWH. The Nephilim were apparently all over the earth at that time, so God needed a worldwide flood to destroy them.

It turns out that Satan attempted this same trick once when the Israelites were in their Promised Land, but God crafted another plan and rid the earth of them once more. It does seem that this type of behavior is taking place on earth once more; we have been reading reports of women being abducted, sometimes taken on spaceships, and having eggs stolen from their bodies. Books about these encounters abounded in the 1980s.

I read several of these books but remained quite skeptical about these supposed aliens and UFOs in general. I was an amateur astronomer and spent large amounts of time since my mid-teens studying the heavens with my telescopes. I have personally seen two exploding bolide meteors, but I have never seen anything in the heavens I couldn't understand and explain. As a Bible teacher for well over thirty years, I personally had two different women in the early 2000s tell me they had had encounters with evil angels. One was abducted, and the other was raped. So I really don't know what to think about this, but it does seem to fit the Biblical narrative.

Anyway, this supposed Nephilim Antichrist will gradually become the most powerful leader on earth, and by the middle of the seven-year period, he will be ready to act as we will see next. Anyway, there is a possibility that there may currently be Nephilim on earth posing as humans, but we cannot recognize them as yet.

Event 2: The First of the Twin Global Resets; the Antichrist Assumes Control of the Whole Earth and Declares Himself to Be God

This is the *first global reset* since for the first time there will truly be a one-world government on earth with one ruler, the Antichrist, in this case. He will go into the recently built temple in Jerusalem and declare himself to be the god of the world, demanding that all people serve and worship him as God. Over the next five months, he will institute the *mark of the Beast.* He will do so by using the evil angels Jesus allowed Satan to release from the Abyss. Satan had recently been kicked out of heaven and sent down to earth in the third trumpet judgment, with his fall described in Revelation 12.

These are the evil angels who created the Nephilim in the years before the flood, those God had punished by sending them to the Abyss, as recorded in Jude. These angels are sent out to visit everyone on earth to enact the mark of the Beast. They are given five months to do their work. They apparently start with the two witnesses and one hundred forty-four thousand Jews. We know this because they show up in heaven in Revelation 14 and will be raptured there. These evil angels must not get very far in visiting the other people in the world because we see in Revelation 12 that Satan takes them with him to go to the Jews in hiding In Jordan to kill them.

Thus, we can see that they do not even get to Jordan. On the way, God intervenes and returns them to the Abyss. As these evil angels are canvassing the people of earth, they are allowed to torture those who are not believers in Jesus to force them to take the mark. They are not allowed to torture those who have become believers in Jesus after the rapture, but they are allowed to take them to prison in Israel if they refuse to take the mark. God warns Christians in Revelation 13 to go to prison if they are charged but warns them not to take the mark of the Beast at any cost. After their ill-fated campaign to go to Jordan to kill the Jews in hiding, Satan and the Antichrist will return to Jerusalem, go to the prison where the Christians, including Christian Jews, are being held, and kill them by beheading them as reported in Revelation 11. Satan's goal is to kill all Jews remaining on earth to keep God from accomplishing the purpose of his will, which will result in Satan and his angelic followers being cast into the lake of fire. These events will be immediately followed by a huge earthquake, which institutes the sixth trumpet judgment, a huge woe judgment that sees tremendous death on earth.

Event 3: The Second Coming of Jesus to Earth, Which Enacts the Second of the Twin Global Resets

Just before Jesus's return at his Second Coming, there will be a repeat of the first six of the trumpet judgments, this time called "bowl judgments," all in quick succession, and then be followed up by all three sets of seventh judgments: the seal, trumpet, and bowl judgments. This will be the greatest catastrophe to ever hit the earth, even including the great flood. The last act in this series of judgments includes Jesus returning to earth with his army of angels and his bride. This thus ends with the *second of the twin global resets.* The seventh trumpet judgment recorded in Revelation 11 says that at this time Jesus will become *King of Kings and Lord of Lords* over the entire earth. This will then bring in the millennium, during which Jesus will reign for one thousand years in a renewed paradise like earth. Soon after the Second Coming, there will be two judgments, the sheep-goat judgment of Matthew 25 and the Jewish judgment of Daniel 12 which will be the judgment of Jews to determine who will be allowed to enter the millennium.

Event 4: The Anointing of the Millennial Temple, Which Includes Another Great Family Reunion

This event will take place exactly twenty-three hundred days after the Second Coming of Jesus, as recorded in Daniel 8. The temple will be built after the Second Coming as part of the refurbishment of the earth, which will literally be destroyed in the seven-year period of the tribulation. It will be a huge temple, one-half mile square with huge kitchens on each of the four corners, as described in Ezekiel 40–48. Zechariah 14 says every nation of earth must send its people to visit Jesus at the temple every year during the Feast of Tabernacles. The first such great meeting will be just 6.2 years or twenty-three hundred days after the Second Coming. It will result in *another great family reunion, and it will take place early in the millennium.*

During the one thousand years, there will be millions of humans still on earth, but there may be as many or more living on earth who are the resurrected saints now in their glorified, resurrected bodies. These bodies are like the body Jesus had after his resurrection, according to Philippians 3:20–21. Thus, we will still be able to eat, drink, and enjoy all the amenities of a good life during the millennium. We will also have many hugely upgraded senses and abilities. We will likely be able to communicate with Jesus telepathically, disappear and suddenly reappear in a distant place, and so forth. The whole period between the rapture and the anointing of the millennial temple will be thirteen years. The dates we postulated for the key events in the study of Hosea and Daniel are as follows:

- 2038 for the rapture and the start of the tribulation
- 2041 for the middle of the tribulation period, when the Antichrist declares himself to be God
- 2044.98 for the Second Coming
- 2051 for the anointing of the millennial temple

If this whole scenario actually plays out in our generation, then the following reflects the situation on earth in the year 2051:

- Israelites are now forgiven after being punished twenty-eight hundred years.
- Judah's people are now forgiven after 2,520 years.
- Judeans are now forgiven after two thousand years.
- Jesus is now on earth as King of Kings and Lord of Lords.
- Satan and his cohorts are now in the Abyss with no power or contact with humans.
- All unbelievers are in Hades, awaiting their final judgment.
- The earth is now a paradise once more.
- Jesus is ruling with an iron scepter; no unholy behavior will be permitted.
- Resurrected saints of all ages will be on earth in their glorified bodies and will use their rewards from Jesus as they live, serve, and enjoy paradise for the next one thousand years.
- Humans will still be on earth, but all must honor Jesus; they will live much longer lives, with one hundred years seen as young.
- The Jews will live in a much-expanded Promised Land and will be the center of activity on earth.
- There will be a grand reunion of people from all countries each year during the Feast of Tabernacles.
- This celebration will take place in a huge, new temple a few miles north of Jerusalem and it will be about one-half mile square with four huge kitchens, with one on each corner of the facility.

What About the Jews? What Is Likely the Most Significant Aspect of the Great Tribulation Period for Them?

- Jesus is the life, including symbolically the "Tree of Life."
- The book of Romans says the Jews were broken off from the tree when they rejected Jesus.
- Christians were grafted in as they accepted Jesus.
- The book of Romans says the Jews were the natural branches, and they can be easily grafted back in.
- This grafting currently happens one at a time as the Jews accept Jesus.
- They will be grafted back in en mass during the seven-year tribulation period.
- That is the real purpose of the seven-year tribulation period.

- We will then all be one big, happy family; and a great family reunion will happen shortly after the Jews are grafted back into the Tree of Life.
- Jews were blinded, in part, as punishment for idol worship in the Old Testament so a new people group could be grafted in. The blinding will be removed in about AD 2041 when the end of their punishment period has been reached.

Israel and the Jewish people have certainly been one of the major focuses of this four-book series. It is obvious they have also been God's focus ever since he made them his chosen people in the latter part of the first two-thousand-year period of humans on earth. In our first two books of this series, we had chapters late in the books that dealt with *the antidote for anti-Semitism.* It certainly appears that the Jews will once more be *the apple of God's eye* in the whole of the one-thousand-year millennial period.

Are There Other Possible Fits for the 13 Year End Time Scenario in Our Generation?

One of the major purposes of this four-book series has been to demonstrate that the current generation could be a good fit for the thirteen-year end-time scenario. We are homing in on our generation because Israel became a nation once more in 1948, and Jesus seemed to be saying in Matthew 24 that the generation that saw this happen would live to see the end-time scenario fulfilled. This scenario was laid out in detail in Daniel 8, 9, and 12; and it was repeated in other chapters in Daniel, too. He told us over and over in various ways that the scenario would last for thirteen years. He concentrated on four specific events and clearly told us the specific time gaps between the events. These are the events we placed in our thirteen-year scenario. What we did in this chapter was simply look for four dates in our event-patterns database in our generation that fit this specific scenario. However, after doing this, we felt that we should look for other possible fits we could find that might also fit the scenario. We found a couple of others that weren't quite as obvious but could also possibly be God's chosen pattern. In this book, we will consider our original thirteen-year end-time scenario to be our chosen scenario, but we certainly don't know which, if any, of the scenarios that might take place in our generation might be "God's" chosen scenario.

Are there any contraindications to "our" postulated thirteen-year end-time scenario being the proper end-time scenario? Might the "long time" parables we presented earlier point to the Second Coming of Jesus rather than to the rapture? If so, the whole scenario would then move back seven years and thus begin in the 2030–31 time frame. The rapture is a "free agent," so to speak. In fact, the rapture could move even further back in time. It seems that it will occur either very near the start of the seven-year tribulation period or at some time before that start, perhaps even a few years before the start of the tribulation period. That means we could already be in the window when this event will take place.

The whole scenario of moving back seven years would lead us to the following new end-time scenario:

2030–31: the rapture

2034: mid-tribulation

2037–38: the Second Coming of Jesus; judgments would take place.

2038–45: the seven-year period (Ezek. 39) when Jewish people will use supplies left from the totally destroyed armies that attacked them to sustain themselves while they rebuild their infrastructure

2041: the end of all Jewish punishment patterns; the construction of the new millennial temple will begin.

2044: the end of the twenty-three-hundred-day period; Jesus will anoint the newly completed millennial temple.

2051: the first Jubilee year celebration in Israel's vastly enlarged country; at this time people from all over the world will visit Jesus in Israel for the first great family reunion during the twenty-three days of the Feast of Tabernacles.

During the whole seven-year tribulation period and in the judgments immediately following it, all unbelieving people on the whole earth will be removed from the earth. The whole earth will be very desolate. The cities will be abandoned with the streets and buildings completely empty except for a few Christians who survived. One might ask, "What prophecy will this fulfill?" Revelation says that during the one thousand years of the millennium, all Jesus's followers of all ages will be on earth with him. Guess what they will inhabit and what they will be doing. Revelation 20 says Jesus's followers will not only be on the earth with Jesus but also reign with him. They (we) will be very busy rebuilding the infrastructure, teaching new believers (see Revelation 4) about Jesus and his requirements for them, setting up the new governmental structure in each of the countries, and otherwise doing what Jesus assigned to them. We will have supernatural strength, senses, skills, and communication abilities in our new resurrected bodies. Wow! I suspect that things will be ready all over the earth to allow the people from all nations to be able to attend the great family reunion during the first Tabernacles celebration in the new millennial temple.

This is all a bit speculative on my part, but it could fit into a possible end-time scenario, in my opinion. The one thing it certainly does is make it possible for the rapture to take place at any time between now and the time of the seven-year period of tribulation if it takes place in our current generation.

The Great Family Reunion Code and its Relationship with the Whole Set of End Time Judgments

The existence of several great family reunions has been one of the principal topics of this book. We have been searching for them as we have gone throughout this book. However, we didn't have enough information to allow us to discover a code associated with the reunions until we finished chapters 8–9, where we presented the existence of the patterns associated with the number thirteen, the code associated with the global resets and finally the thirteen-year end-time scenario earlier in this chapter.

Throughout this book, we have been referring to "twin" family reunions. *Twin* means there are two separate sets of family reunions. The first set includes four family reunions that will take place during the tribulation period, including the seventy-five-day period immediately following it, and the other is associated with the Feast of Tabernacles reunions that will take place yearly starting at the anointing of the millennial temple. This will take place yearly thereafter all during the one thousand years of the millennium. Thus, there are four distinct reunions and one yearly repeating family reunion we will be discussing here.

One of our major discoveries in understanding the timing of these family reunions was that they often seemed to take place at the time of end-time judgments. Thus, we will next present the judgments associated with the end-time scenario presented above and then show the great family reunion that seems to be associated with each of the judgments.

First, all the judgments and great family reunions will take place during the thirteen-year end-time scenario. The first two will take place in heaven and are associated with two separate raptures of God's saints to heaven, and the last three will take place on earth at or soon after the Second Coming of Jesus. Seemingly, a quick judgment will take place first and then be immediately followed by a great family reunion in each of the first four events. There will be two key aspects to each reunion, in that they will each involve a reunion of two separate families: first, the family of God; and the second, the family of each individual person. The order of the fifth is somewhat different as we will see later when we present it in detail.

We will next list the five separate events and then present a discussion of each along with their separate great family reunions in some detail.

1. The general rapture and associated judgment seat of Christ
2. The great tribulation resurrection and rapture of the two witnesses, one hundred forty-four thousand, and new believers with their associated judgment seat of Christ
3. The sheep-goat judgment of all living survivors of the seven-year tribulation period
4. The Daniel 12:1–3 resurrection and judgment of all then-dead Jews of all ages past
5. The Daniel 8 anointment of the millennial temple and its associated judgment of all those nations who do not attend

Before presenting the detailed discussion of the five great family reunion events with their associated judgments, we would like to present our understanding of a couple of definitions of the *holding places* God has been using down through history for certain groups of fallen angels and the spirits of humans before their judgments.

Hades

This is currently the place where the spirits of the dead are sent if their names are not written in the Book of Life. This place is described in Luke 16:19–31. That passage describes two holding places. One is referred to as "Hades" and the other as "Abraham's bosom." Hades, a place of torment, is described as being very hot and without any comfort from the heat available. This place will exist until the completion of the Great White Throne Judgment at the end of the millennial period when it will be destroyed because it will no longer be needed.

Abraham's bosom was the place where the spirits of those whose names were written in the Book of Life were sent at the time of death from their bodies. There was a great chasm between the two places, and it was impossible to go from one to the other. Hades is described as being in the lower area of the physical world, but it certainly is just a spiritual place, likely the spiritual area associated with the three-dimensional physical earth.

Heaven is said to consist of three levels, with each likely having three dimensions associated with it. Ephesians 4:7–10 may be saying that "Abraham's bosom" was initially in the lower earthly spiritual regions since it says that at his death, Jesus went to this place and took its residents on high and gave them gifts. This was possible because Jesus's death for the sins of his people made it possible for them to finally be seen as perfect and qualified for eternity in heaven. Thus, this place likely no longer exists since it is no longer needed.

The Abyss

This is the holding place for evil angels who have gone over God's boundaries set up for them, apparently sometime shortly after they were created. Jude 6 says that the pre-flood angels who left their abode in heaven, came to earth, and crossed God's boundary conditions for them were being held in this place. They were apparently the angels who created the Nephilim of Genesis 6, a half-breed angel/human alien of sorts.

Second Peter 2:4 uses another term for a similar place or possibly the same holding place, called "Tartaros," which says it was the place where evil angels who sinned in the pre-flood era were being held for judgment in chains of darkness. Other scriptures tell us the Abyss is the holding place for evil spirits and evil angels including Satan and the Antichrist. These scriptures dealing with those who are in the Abyss include Revelation 9:1–6, 11; 11:7; 17:8; 20:1–3; Jude 1:6; Luke 8:31.

We will now continue with a discussion of the five judgments in the thirteen-year end-time scenario.

The General Rapture and Judgment Seat of Christ

This rapture is described in 1 Thessalonians 4:13–17 and 1 Corinthians 15:51–53. This judgment associated with raptures is called the "judgment seat of Christ" in 2 Corinthians 5:10. It is a judgment of all believers in Jesus to determine the extent of the rewards each individual believer will receive that he or she will take with him or her into both the millennium and then later into eternity. The way the judgments will be carried out is presented in 1 Corinthians 3:8–15. One of the rewards everyone will receive is a huge upgrade in capabilities provided by the new resurrected and glorified bodies (Phil. 3:20–21).

At the end of the seven years, they will return to earth with Jesus at his Second Coming. They will then live on earth with Jesus and serve him for the next one thousand years. This rapture represents phase one of the first great family reunion. In reality, it will be the first in-person "union" of God and Jesus with their eternal family. It will also mark the first reunion of the newly raptured believers with their loved ones, who have already been in heaven as spirits.

The Fifth Seal Judgment Resurrection, Rapture, and Judgment for the Two Witnesses, One Hundred Forty-Four Thousand, and Newly Believing Jews and Gentiles Whom the Antichrist Recently Killed

The forces of the Antichrist will round up the two witnesses, one hundred forty-four thousand believing Jews, and all new believers in Jesus into a large prison in Israel. Before they are miraculously resurrected and raptured to heaven, the Antichrist will behead them in view of the whole world in some way. The Antichrist will kill them because they will refuse to take the mark of the Beast, meaning that they all refuse to honor the Antichrist as their God. This event will take place about six to twelve months after the mid-tribulation during the fifth seal or trumpet judgment. It will mark the second great family reunion in heaven.

Again, this resurrection and rapture will involve a judgment. This judgment is presented in Revelation 20:4. See Revelation 6:9–10; 7:9; 11:7–12; 20:4.

The Sheep-Goat Judgment of All Living Survivors of the Seven-Year Period of Great Tribulation on Earth (Matt. 25:31–46)

The sheep-goat judgment will take place soon after the Second Coming of Jesus to earth at the end of the seven-year tribulation period. He will immediately become King of Kings and Lord of Lords of the whole earth at that time (Rev. 11:15). When he comes back, he will have with him his army of angels and his new "bride." The first thing he will apparently do is "speak the word," and the armies of Satan and the Antichrist will be defeated. He will throw Satan into the Abyss, where he will be bound for one thousand years (Rev. 19–20). He will then have two quick judgments to conduct before beginning the task of placing the destroyed earth back into a paradise-like condition. The first judgment will be the sheep-goat judgment of all those humans still alive on earth after the terrible tribulation of the last seven years (Matt. 25:31–46). Other key characteristics of this judgment include the following:

- Jesus will be the one and only judge in this judgment.
- All who have become true believers in Jesus will be told to enter the millennial kingdom "prepared for them since before the creation." That means God already

had the key features presented in all four of our books strictly laid out before he created the universe and the humans who populate it.

- Nonbelievers in Jesus were told in the judgment to go directly to the "lake of fire," where their physical bodies will be destroyed and their spirits sent to Hades, awaiting the final Great White Throne Judgment at the end of the millennium.

The Daniel 12:1–3 Judgment of All Then-Dead Jews of All Ages Past

This judgment is described in Daniel 12:1–3. The characteristics of this judgment as Daniel described it included the following:

- This judgment takes place when Michael, the protector angel for the Jewish people, becomes active once more. His last recorded activity was in the Old Testament times. He was quite active during the lifetime of Daniel, in the years 620 to 535 BC. His next recorded activity will take place in Revelation 12 during the midst of the seven-year tribulation period when he will battle Satan and his angels in heaven, defeat them, and throw them down to earth as the "stars" recorded in the third and fourth trumpet judgments. This will be very near the mid-tribulation when the Antichrist will declare himself to be God and ruler of the earth from the new temple in Jerusalem (Dan. 9:24–27, especially 26–27).
- Those Jews who have their names written in the Book of Life will receive their resurrected bodies at the general rapture seven years before this Daniel 12 judgment. They will also be part of the Daniel 12 judgment in the following way. At this judgment, these Jews will receive their earthly rewards, which will be used over the next one thousand years. Each tribe will be given a section of land to call their own for the next one thousand years. Ezekiel 40–48 describes this in detail. One of David's rewards will be that he will be their shepherd and prince (Ezek. 34:23–24).
- All dead Jewish people of all ages past will be judged. Jesus, the judge, will already be on earth and will stay there for the next one thousand years. Those whose names are found written in the Book of Life will be judged, given their rewards, and allowed to then live on earth with Jesus in the whole of their Promised Land for the next one thousand years. Those not listed in the book will be sent to either outer darkness or back to Hades, the place where they were already abiding after their deaths, to await the Great White Throne Judgment one thousand years later. We see in Psalm 69:28 that God was already using "books," including the Book of Life, to record the deeds of people on earth in the Old Testament period.
- The end of Daniel 12 says that the second half of the tribulation period will last three and a half years plus another seventy-five days. It further says that those who reach the end of the seventy-five days will be blessed. This very likely means that the judgments will take place in this seventy-five-day period and that those who survive them will be "blessed" and be able to live in a paradise with Jesus on earth for the next one thousand years in their Promised Land of long ago.

- Matthew 19:8 says that at the renewal of all things, the twelve original apostles of Jesus will be set on twelve thrones and judge the twelve tribes of Israel. That will be at this judgment and possibly also at the Great White Throne Judgment one thousand years later. The judgment presented in Revelation 20:4–6 may include Jewish people who die during the millennium, and thus the twelve apostles will again be judges. Revelation 20 mentions that there will be thrones present at that judgment for those who will be judging. Will these be the apostles?

The Judgment and Punishment of the Nations That Do Not Attend the Yearly Feast of Tabernacles Celebration during the Millennium

Understanding this judgment and the punishment of the nations by Jesus during the millennium will require understanding a few facets of the coming millennium including the following:

- At the Second Coming of Jesus, he will immediately become "King of Kings and Lord of Lords" of the whole earth and will rule earth with an iron scepter (Rev. 19:14–16; 17:14; Zech. 14:9).
- During the whole one thousand years of the millennium, Jesus will require the nations of the world to come to the millennial temple in Israel each year during the Feast of Tabernacles to worship him.
- Those nations that don't do this will be struck by plagues, such as droughts (Zech. 14:16–19).

All this will obviously require that Jesus make judgments each year and follow them up with punishments when necessary. This will likely start twenty-three hundred days after the Second Coming (Dan. 8:13–14). All this will obviously result in yearly "reunions" of both the family of God and individual earthly families. It will be a whopper each year!

The Final Judgments, Those Taking Place at the End of the Millennium

Bible prophecy and the scholars who interpret it often refer to the scenario which begins with the general rapture, the seven year tribulation period and the Second Coming of Jesus as the start of the Biblical end times. These end times also include the whole of the one thousand year millennium which follows them as part of the end times. The millennium also ends with a set of judgments as we will see below.

The millennium will end with the final judgments of all those who haven't accepted Jesus down through the ages. After that, we come to the eternal order of Revelation 21–22. Thus, we now see what the word *unified* means in the purpose of God's will stated in Ephesians 1. In the new order, the physical and spiritual dimensions will be merged or unified as one twelve-dimensional space. The word *unified* has two fulfillments. One is that we will be unified in marriage to Jesus for eternity, and the other is that we will then spend eternity on an entirely new earth-like place in a new heaven of sorts, with the two being unified as one. We will be in all twelve dimensions at the same time. Whew!

The Great Family Reunion Code

We have finally accumulated enough information to assemble the Great Family Reunion Code. We needed to present the lagge number of end time judgments conducted by Jesus, all of which resulted in great reunions, before we could put the code together. So we are finally ready to do that. So what then is the great family reunion code we have been mentioning in this book? Well, it is a bit different from the other codes but still has a very distinct pattern to it. We will list those distinct features below:

1. They all take place or start in the thirteen-year end-time scenario.
2. They all take place when Jesus calls some set of his followers to come to him.
3. They all take place when Jesus either pays a quick visit to earth or has begun residing on earth.
4. They all take place in rapture events, judgment events, or Jewish feast events.
5. There are five of these events taking place in three categories as follows:
    a. The general rapture
    b. The witness rapture
    c. The sheep-goat judgment just after the Second Coming
    d. The Daniel 12 judgment of all then-dead Jews
    e. The event hosting the anointing of the millennial temple by Jesus

Every "code" has some common feature associated with it. For the family reunions, that common feature is this: every time Jesus conducts a judgment in the thirteenth-year end-times scenario, there is a resulting great family reunion. We could say that, in short, this is the great family reunion code.

The "ET" Scenario, AD 2041

In book one of this series, we mentioned that we would call this series of four books either the "2041 Series" or the "ET 2041 Scenario Series" without much explanation. We did say that "ET" would stand for both the "end-times" and "extraterrestrials." We also said we would wait until we had laid all the groundwork for understanding this before we explained what we meant by this phrase and that we would explain it in the latter part of book four. Well, we are there, and we have laid out much of the groundwork, so we will now explain ourselves.

First, "ET" stands for "end-times" since throughout this fourth book, we have been trying to determine whether the end-times can be shown to be a good fit for our generation.

Second, AD 2041 is within our generation, and a huge number of the event patterns that seem to be pointing to the end-times are converging in that year. Thus, the "ET" scenario is a good fit for the year AD 2041.

Third, "ET" stands for "extraterrestrials" since the book of Revelation may well be indicating that extraterrestrials will play a very big part in the end-time scenario in two different ways. We will explain each one.

- First, in the middle of the seven-year period of the tribulation, there will be a war in heaven between Michael, the archangel of Israel, and the forces of evil, Satan, and the large group of angels who follow him. This is documented in Revelation 12. Michael and his forces will overcome Satan and his forces, and will throw all of them down to earth in the third and fourth trumpet judgments. Thus, there will be "extraterrestrials"—in this case, angels—on the earth for a period of about three and a half years. They will be allied with the Antichrist and intent on killing every Jew on earth to keep God from being able to reach the purpose of his will, which includes the destruction of Satan and all who serve him. The outcome is shown earlier in this chapter in the end-time scenario.

- Second, there are indications in Revelation 17 that the Beast or Antichrist will be an extraterrestrial. He is called *the one who once was, is not now, but will again be.* One way of interpreting this is that he will be a Nephilim, a hybrid human/ angel. These Nephilim were first presented in Genesis 6, and their introduction to the earth and their work on it is likely a major reason for the great flood. Thus, the Antichrist may himself be an alien, a Satanically created half-breed, so to speak. If you would like to know more about these beings, you can go to my website, Proofthruprophecy.com, and find them discussed much more thoroughly under the topic "Angels: Good and Evil." They are also a common topic of prophetic books and on *Prophecy Watchers* on YouTube, TV, and so forth.

Thus, this is another interesting piece of evidence we can use in our case to show that our generation is a good fit for the end-times or ET scenario.

A huge amount of information about the end times that makes this 13 year end time scenario much easier to understand is presented on my website, www.proofthruprophecy. com under the header Revelation studies.

A Compilation and Analysis of All of the Assembled Clues

A Compilation of Our Clues from throughout This Book

We would next like to present a compilation of all of the clues we have compiled from the topics included in this book that should help us much better understand the five *w's* connected to the purpose of God's will. These topics include the coming dual global resets, dual great family reunions, the pandemic code, the Angel of Death code, the master template event patterns, and how all these play into the possibility that the end-time scenario appears to be a good fit for our generation. After presenting the clues, we will discuss what we have learned and then present our bottom line.

A Compilation of the Key Clues that We Have Discovered From Study of the Apparent Ways that God Has Been Interacting With His People on Earth for 6000 Years

Clues From All of Our Patterns that Will Help Us Better Understand End Time Events, the Unification of Everything Under Jesus, the Dual Global Resets, Dual Family Reunions and their Possible Tie to Our Generation			
CLUES FROM THE PURPOSE OF GOD'S WILL FROM EPH1:8-10			
WHO	**WHEN**	**WHERE**	**WHAT EVENT AND WHY**
Jesus & church	End times	Heaven & on earth	**EPHESIANS MYSTERIES**: When the purpose of God's will is fulfilled both in heaven and on earth; this must be the end times; (WHY) To bring everything into unity under Jesus.
Jesus & church	End times		**EPHESIANS MYSTERIES:** The marriage of Jesus to the church, his bride, those who accept him; to unify Jesus and his bride as one.
CLUES FROM 7 PROPHETIC OLD TESTAMENT MODELS			
WHO	**WHEN**	**WHERE**	**WHAT AND WHY**
Jesus			**MODEL: ABRAHAM'S SACRIFICE OF ISAAC:** Jesus sacrifice was necessary for him to one day be able to claim his bride

Jesus			Jesus will not be on earth again until he comes to claim his bride.
Jesus	End times post trib		**MODEL OF JOSEPH:** Jesus will become a very high ranking leader on earth after a 7 year period of tribulation.
Jesus		Israel	**MODEL: JOSHUA:** Jesus will one day oversee rebuilding of the temple in Israel as both king and high priest.
Jesus & Israel	End times		**MODEL: WRESTLING MATCH:** In the end times Israel will finally acknowledge Jesus as Messiah and God.
Jesus & church			**MODEL: JEWISH WEDDING CUSTOMS:** They model the church as the bride of Christ: Thus we see the whole family of God, of Jesus, including all of our family and friends who are or were believers in Jesus all being a part of the GREAT FAMILY REUNION of the end times.
Jesus & church			**MODEL: JEWISH WEDDING CUSTOMS:** They model the church as the bride of Christ: Thus we see the whole family of God, of Jesus, including all of our family and friends who are or were believers in Jesus all being a part of the GREAT FAMILY REUNION of the end times.
Jesus & church			**MODEL: JOHN 14:6 BURIED IN 1 JOHN;** 1 John emphasizes over and over that the only way to heaven is thru becoming a part of the bride of Christ.
Jesus & bride	End times	Israel	**MODEL: BATTLE OF JERICHO AS A MODEL OF REV:** Just as winning this battle provided passage into the Promised Land for the Israelites so to do the Revelation judgments take us to the new Promised Land, also in Israel.

CLUES FROM THE BATTLE BETWEEN ORDER AND CHAOS

WHO	WHEN	WHERE	WHAT EVENT AND WHY
		On earth	**CHAOS AND TRIBULATION:** Chaos often accompanies events used by God to bring about the purpose of his will.
Jewish people	7 yr trib period	Israel, world	The 7 year tribulation period creates great chaos and death which will aid in bringing about the final redemption of the Jewish people. We have had several events in our generation that have hosted great chaos and death. Might this point to our generation being a good fit for the end time scenario?

CLUES FROM THE BASIC PATTERN STRINGS & KINGS SCROLL

WHO	WHEN	WHERE	WHAT AND WHY
Jews	2051?	On earth	**THE KING'S SCROLL:** This scroll introduces us to our first event pattern string; a judgment string that will converge for the 70th time in the year 2051.

Jews		In the nations	The Jews will fail God's tests miserably and he will exile them to the nations, which will involve great chaos for them. He will re-gather them one day in a great family reunion.
Jesus, All believers	In end times	Whole world	**DANIEL'S 70 7'S:** Daniel gives us a formula for calculating the year of Jesus Second Coming to earth. Daniel's clues lead us to believe that the Second Coming will be closely followed by the 1000 year millennium.
Jews, all people	2041, 2051?	Israel, whole world	**BASIC 200/2000 EVENT PATTERN STRING:** These patterns involve great chaos for the Jewish people as a result of exiles, tribulations, terror, etc. They all will end in a whopper of an end time event.
Jews, whole world?	2041	Israel, whole world?	Both basic and mega event pattern strings of 50 and 500 year judgment enforcement, 40 and 400 year exile and 66.666 and 666.66 tribulation all converge in the year 2041. Could this forebode a period of serious end time chaos?
	2041		The year 2041 may also be the 13x1000 or 13,000th year since the beginning of the creation process. 13 is God's pattern multiplier pointing to serious punishment events. Could this be such a year?
Jews	2051	Israel, all over world	The year 2051 may also be a very significant year for the Jewish people since it is their 70th Jubilee judgment period since they first entered their Promised Land in 1399 BC. Might there be a clear tie between the events of 2041 and the judgments made in this year?
	3027 AD	Whole world	COMPLEMENTARY 30/60/90 EVENT PATTTERN STRINGS: The super season that covers the whole period from the fall to the eternal state contains 20x90=1800 years. It may end with the eternal state in 3027 AD after 4 full seasons.
CLUES FROM DESTRUCTION AND PARALLEL EVENT PATTERNS			
WHO	**WHEN**	**WHERE**	**WHAT EVENT AND WHY**
Israel, Northern Kingdom	Ends in 2041	Israel	**ASSYRIAN PUNISHMENT PATTERN:** Punishment for all Northern Kingdom Israelites for 390 years of idol worship will end in 2041 AD.
Judah, Southern Kingdom	167 BC, Ends in 2041 AD	Israel	**BABYLONIAN PUNISHMENT PATTERN:** Punishment for those of the southern kingdom of Judah was enacted in two phases. A first phase ending in the Hanukkah event in 167 BC. The second phase took place after they were overtaken by the Romans and ultimately destroyed. Their punishment was apparently for 2000 years and will end in 2041.

Israel	Ends in 6000th year, 2041	Varies with years, ends in Israel	**11 PARALLEL EVENTS IN THE 3 2000TH YEAR PERIODS:** There are 11 events in a 270 year period surrounding the 2000th, 4000th and 6000th years in history that are parallel, with all 11 pairs separated by exactly 2000 years and with all pairs thematically tied together. These events all culminate in 2041, the 6000th year, and all involve exile and great persecution for the Jewish people.
Israel	End Times	Israel	These events also parallel the theme of end time events from Bible prophecy.
Israel	Ends in 2041 AD	Israel	**PARALLEL EVENTS IN KEY MILESTONE YEARS:** The maga-400 year exile and 666/66 year tribulations are both punishment patterns and both converge in 2041.
Israel	Ends in 2041 AD	Israel	**ROMAN DESTRUCION OF JUDEA PATTERN:** This is the 4000th year, when Jesus first coming to earth took place. The Jewish people had corporately rejected him as their Messiah and God. Jesus apparently enacted a 2000 year judgment of 50x40 years on them in 32 AD from Matt 23 which started in 70 AD and will end in 2041.

CLUES FROM DANIEL'S PROPHECIES, HOSEA'S PROPHECIES AND THE KINGDOM PARABLES OF MATTHEW

WHO	WHEN	WHERE	WHAT EVENT AND WHY
Jesus Israel	2045	Israel, whole world	**HOSEA'S 2 DAYS EQUALS 2000 YEARS PROPHECY:** This prophecy may focus on the return of Jesus to the Jewish people after a 2000 year punishment period, toward the end of a 7 year period surrounding the 6000th year. This would be in our generation.
Jesus	2045 to 2051	Mill Temple in Israel	**DANIEL'S END TIME PROPHECIES: In the 2300 days prophecy we now have the time gap between two key end time events, the Second Coming and anointing of the Millennial temple. This would be the time of a great family reunion for God's people, and thus our families.**
Jesus	2nd Coming In end times	Whole earth	**DANIEL'S 7+62+1 7'S: Prophecy leads us to both the first and second comings of Jesus to earth, with the first being very specific and the second much more mysterious. We found several ways to use this formula that would lead us to not only the end times but the year 2041 in our generation.**
Jesus	Second Coming 2045	Whole earth	**DANIEL 12 END TIME PROPHECIES: We found an interpretation of the 1260+1260+30+45=prophecy which leads us to the Second Coming in 2045 which matches the other prophecies in Daniel precisely. This is in our generation.**

Jesus and the raptured saints	From 2038 to 2051 AD	Earth Israel	**FROM THE KINGDOM PARABLES OF MATTHEW: We now have good clues about the timeframe of all 8 key dates that are associated with the 13 year end time prophecy period from the rapture to the anointing of the millennial temple early in the 1000 year millennial period. It is in our generation.**
CLUES FROM THE ANGEL OF DEATH AND PANDEMIC CODES			
WHO	**WHEN**	**WHERE**	**WHAT EVENT AND WHY**
Jesus, all people on earth	In 1000 yr mill., in 2051	Israel, whole world	**ANGEL OF DEATH CODE:** The convergence of all Angel of Death patterns taking place in 2051 may infer that a major reset has taken place involving death, that the millennium has begun and Jesus is ruling the earth.
All people on earth	2020-2022	Whole world	**PANDEMIC CODE:** Events in 2021 may lead to the possible rebuilding of a temple in Jerusalem. Could this lead to the end times? Themes or topics of events converging in 2021 may be associated with plagues such as the pandemic and other disastrous events that are tied to the coming of the end time scenario.
CLUES FROM THE MASTER TEMPLATE			
WHO	**WHEN**	**WHERE**	**WHAT EVENT AND WHY**
Jesus, Jews, Christians, 11 Patriarchs	2041/51	Whole world	**GOD'S WITNESS PATTERN:** God used a different set of witnesses to help accomplish the purpose of his will in each 2000 year period; the last two were combined into one at the end of the third 2000th year. This implies that 2041/51 will host the marriage of Jesus with his bride in fulfillment of God's purpose. Unification!
God, Jesus, Jews, Christians, Satan Antichrist, God's angels, Satan's angels, all people	Fall to Second Coming of Jesus, centers on 2041-51	Israel, whole world	**THE GREAT CONVERGENCE FAMILY**: It hosts by far the greatest number of key patterns with their topics including the following themes; the end of God's punishment sentences for his people, the forgiveness of the past sins of all of his people, the time of rewarding his people for their good acts, the end of death for many of God's people and longer lives in general for others, the grafting of the Jewish people back into the tree of life, the end of sentences of tribulation and exile for God's people, the beginning of a period of 1000 years of living on earth with Jesus as King of Kings and Lord of Lords in a paradise like setting, etc. All of these shout; end times are here, including the twin global resets and family reunions.

Israel, whole world	70th Jubilee, 2038-51	Israel, whole world	**GOD'S PUNISHMENT AND DESTRUCTION PATTERN SET:** God's Punishment patterns for his people and many of the final judgments for his people seem to be ending in our generation, and particularly in 2041/51. This signals the end time scenario with fulfillment of God's purpose, the twin family reunions and global resets.
Jesus, Satan, antichrist, all people	2041	Israel, whole world	**THE WRATH OF GOD PATTERN SET:** The great wrath in the final ominous 270 year period seems to center around the year 2041. If so that would signal the time of the twin global resets and family reunions.
Jews, Christians, all people	7 dates spread all across the 7200 yrs	Whole world	**THE GLOBAL RESET CODE:** There have been 7 events in history that have resulted in a sequence of first death, then a Passover of some sort and finally a new home for those involved in the event. The 2041-2051 time period may host just such an event. If so then it would be the twin global resets and family reunions that are the subject of this book. Incredibly, all 7 of the Passover/Death/New Home events are a part of one of God's incredible Global Resets which bring key means into play that are very important in God's plan to bring about the purpose of his will.
Israel, whole world	2100 BC-2041 AD	Whole world	**THE GREAT WRESTLING MATCH:** Both Jews and Gentiles have been wrestling with the true identity of God for a 4200 year period that will end in the year 2041, the end time period hosting the twin global resets and family reunions.
Jesus, whole world	2038-51	Whole world	**THE EVER PRESENT SET OF 70 YEAR PATTERNS:** It appears as though God has seven separate testing pattern event strings that he has been using to test his people ever since the end of the seventh day of creation. He appears to be using seven separate patterns, one starting in every tenth year after 3863.5 BC and continuing until the start of the eternal state. These patterns hit ever tenth year in the 70th Jubilee period. Thus they could be a factor in the end time scenario if it occurs in our generation.

The Bottom Line of All Our Clues

We have presented a large set of thirty or so topics that deal with God's plans for his creation and how he will bring it to a close. We have collected a large quantity of clues in each of those topics that have given us many things to ponder concerning what God has in store for the world in his end-time scenario and when it might all come about. We have seen an incredible similarity in the bottom line of the clues from topic to topic, with all leading us to the same set of conclusions. The topics we studied to arrive at our conclusions include the following:

- A broad outline of God's complete plan for mankind as presented in the book of mysteries, Ephesians, and the early parts of Colossians
- Seven prophetic models that help us better understand what God has in store for us in the end-times and how to understand God's techniques that have a secret, somewhat hidden flavor to them
- A study of chaos, one of the techniques God often uses to bring about his purposes along with one example of this, the use of pandemics along with a secret code that reveals their timing
- How God uses mathematics and order to bring about the fulfillment of his purposes including a study of the ways God has used mathematical patterns strung together to produce events with extremely well-preplanned themes in them with the exact timing that fits his plans for mankind. We call these equally spaced and similarly themed event-pattern strings, and we presented several examples.
- A demonstration of how God gave his chosen people a very well-organized set of guidelines for living. These guidelines included a list of rewards he would provide them for keeping his rules for living. He also gave them an extremely detailed description of the punishments for not keeping his rules as well as how long they would last. We presented several examples of how these punishments were applied, when they started, and when they would end. This was all part of the king's scroll of Leviticus 26, which we presented earlier.
- How God has used prophecies presented in the Bible to first warn his people and then how he had to punish them for not heeding his repeated warnings. We presented seven detailed prophecies, in addition to the one presented on the king's scroll above, that led to the end-time scenario and God's plan for man being fulfilled, with our generation having a good chance of being the time for that fulfillment.
- Seven very high-level mathematical techniques God has been using to bring the fulfillment of his will to a conclusion in the exact time frame he chose even before creation. We call this God's "master template," and we presented the details of each of these seven techniques. All the other techniques we have presented fall into these seven high-level techniques.

Again, the bottom lines of all the clues were consistent, and they led us to the following conclusions:

- The vast majority of the who's, the individuals and groups involved, fit into a very short list: Jesus, Israel, the Jewish people, Christians, and the whole world's population.
- The when, the time frame of the end-times, was consistently in the seventieth Jubilee period in general and in the last thirteen years in particular, with the dates AD 2041 and 2051 appearing over and over in the clues.
- The location was either Israel or the whole world.
- The clues gave many specifics, and they were all in cahoots, so to speak.

We are left with only two choices about the timing of the end-times and when they will finally appear, whether in this current seventieth Jubilee period that is wrapping up the current two-thousandth-year period or in some future two-thousandth-year period. We have voiced that opinion several times in these books, and the clues overwhelmingly enhance that conclusion, in our humble opinion.

We will tabulate the results below in each category.

Who

- 18: Jesus
- 12: the Jewish people
- 9: Israel
- 9: the whole world
- 5: all believers
- 5: the church
- 2: the Antichrist
- 1: God, Judea, Satan, God's angels, evil angels, raptured saints, the patriarchs

When

- 11: AD 2041
- 10: AD 2051
- 7: end-times
- 3: AD 2038
- 2: AD 2045, the Second Coming
- 1: seven-year tribulation, post-tribulation, AD 3027, millennium, seventieth Jubilee, AD 2020–22

Where

- 21: the whole world
- 18: Israel
- 1: in heaven and on earth

Why and What

Presenting the why's and what's required us to first analyze all of the comments in the five w's report cards compilation presented above and summarize what we find. After doing that the answer to both the why's and what's became a bit clearer. We found that every one of the topics in the long list that we presented above was very important in God's plan to bring about the purpose of his will at exactly the proper time as presented in Eph 1:8-10. In order for us to more completely understand the why's and what's we must know more about what God originally had in mind when he created the universe and the humans who populate it. Therefore we will next present our understanding from the Bible of the reason for that creation. Once we know that the why's and what's will become much clearer. The end purpose of all of this is really very simple, but God used an incredibly complicated process to bring it all together at precisely the proper time. That purpose was just this:

- At some time in the distant past, apparently about 13,000 years ago God came up with a brilliant idea; to give his companion, the one we call Jesus, a gift, a future bride of sorts.
- Everything that has taken place in the whole history of the universe is a part of that plan.
- The very reason that you, I and everyone else have been on this earth is for one and only one very important reason; to determine precisely who will and who will not be a part of that future bride.
- In this four book series we have simply discovered and are presenting a large number of the techniques that God has been using to bring about the process of creating that bride.

Throughout this book, we have been searching for clues to help us answer a very important question: *Is our generation a good fit for the Bible's end-time scenario?* It turns out that the end time scenario includes the very time when Jesus will come to earth to finally claim his bride for all of eternity future. The above summary of the accumulated clues provides a resounding answer to that question. That answer is yes, yes, yes—far beyond dispute!

CHAPTER

12

Current Indications That God Might Be Choosing Our Generation to Enact His End-Time Scenario

How the Global Reset Code Can Help Conservative Christians Understand What Is Currently Taking Place in the World Today, Even in the USA

Since that topic fits right into the main agenda of this book, the coming God-enacted dual global resets, we decided we needed to add that topic to this book, one that would provide additional understanding about a human-conceived global reset many believe is already in the early stages of enactment.

Hidden Factors That May Be Driving the Liberal Agenda That Baffles Conservatives

Environmental protection is one of the major items currently driving the agenda of many of the leading countries in the world. I personally agree with this agenda item. That is because it is one of the three most important laws God first gave the Israelites in Leviticus 26. If it is one of God's three most important commands, then I must align with it. This is presented in the king's scroll, shown and discussed earlier in this book. I should say that I agree with the agenda but not necessarily with the way it is currently being implemented.

Let me move on to what I currently see going on in the world and how it ties into the agenda of this book, the coming dual global resets and family reunions. What I will say is thus from my perspective as a scientist in the areas of mathematics, physics, and astronomy; and as a self-taught theologian with a focus on Bible prophecy.

Let me now more completely explain my main agreement with this agenda.

First, it starts with world population growth. I will next present a table that shows this growth over the last two thousand years. It will reveal the real reason for why all of us should be concerned. We will present an analysis of this information after the table.

World Population Growth Rate Doubling Chart

Demonstrating Major Contributors to the Coming Environmental Pollution Crisis			
Date AD	World Population (Million)	Number of Years to Double Population	Comments
1 AD	200		
1000	400	1000	
1500	460	3500	Black Plague in 1346-53 killed about ½ of world population
1800	1000	250	
1925	2000	125	Man made pollution quickly increasing (coal, oil, gas for power)
1975	4000	50	Pollution of environment accelerating
2020	8000	50	Controls implemented but effectiveness of some is questionable
2070	16,000	50	Things would be getting scary!
2120	32,000	50	Situation for environment would be out of control unless there are great advances to protect it

Analysis of the Population Growth Rate-Doubling Chart

Major Contributors to the Environmental Crisis Include the Following

- The population-doubling rate
- An increased need for power, transportation, and so forth, with the major sources being polluters
- The conversion of forest land to agricultural land to feed the huge population

Man's Answers for Controlling and Eliminating the Crisis Include the Following

- Attempting to foster a major global reset to establish means for greatly controlling or even greatly reducing the population
- Creating a one-world government that could demand and enforce while controlling any means of resistance from the population
- Using methods that are clearly marginally effective rather than investing in massive efforts to seek new, not-yet-discovered, and major improvements for providing energy, power, and so forth
- Taking advantage of situations that cause chaos, events such as riots, wars, and so forth

God's Proven Methods for Controlling This
Type of Crisis Include the Following

- Global resets that would greatly reduce worldwide population including the following:
  - The great flood
  - The black plague
- Many types of events that produce chaos to meet his purposes

These types of events have kept the population rate down so God can bring about the purpose of his will at exactly the time he originally planned.

We notice that man has tried to mimic God, in that he often tries to use means that are similar to those God uses. The major difference is that God never fails while man seldom succeeds. Also, man is often being controlled by forces of evil, even being manipulated by forces of evil. Satan, the one the Bible calls the "god of this world," controls these forces.

In the chart we presented above, we attempt to show that overpopulation of the planet is certainly one of the most important contributors to environmental pollution, if not the most important contributor, as long as world conditions remain in their current state. The chart also shows at least two factors that could result in reducing this burden on the environment. We started the chart in AD 1 a little over two thousand years ago. We chose that date because the world population was a nice round two hundred million people or so. We chose the next date because it was the date when the population had doubled to about four hundred million people. We continued this trend in choosing our dates. We used information from "World Population in Wikipedia" while preparing the chart.[6]

We see that the number of years it would take for the population to double was at first being drastically lowered first from 1,000 years to 250 years, then to 125 years, leveling off at 50 years, and then remaining constant at about 50 years. There was only one outlier, that being the years from AD 1000 to AD 1500. In that period the doubling rate dropped drastically to about thirty-five hundred years. What was the great contributor to that outcome? It was the black plague or black death pandemic between the years of about AD 1346 and AD 1353. In that period, about 50 percent of the population of Europe died, with similar conditions existing in many other parts of the world. Thus, we can see that one thing that can cause a huge drop in world population is a worldwide pandemic. In this five-hundred-year period, the overall number of years that would be needed to double the world population would be a whopping thirty-five hundred or so.

This event and one other event that resulted in a huge drop in world population, the great flood, were events mankind had no control over. However, things have changed greatly with the currently approaching period of overpopulation of the whole world. We can now see the effects our lifestyles are having on the environment. In a few parts of the world, humans are recognizing this and trying to take steps to correct and control it.

When God created the earth and its environment, he left it with an automatic system for cleansing itself and keeping the environment in a steady state, so to speak. This involved the rain cycle, which is a cleansing system for the atmosphere, and so forth. Another part of this self-cleansing process involves plant and tree life ingesting air, using the carbon dioxide, and then releasing oxygen into the atmosphere; while humans ingest air, use the oxygen, and then release carbon dioxide back into the atmosphere, keeping things in proper balance. However, mankind's lifestyle is currently disturbing this God-made balance, which could result in a potential future environmental catastrophe. So what can humans do to stop this problem before it really gets out of hand? I will briefly state what I see taking place in both the areas of mankind's fixes and then the only real solution, one God has already planned and may soon implement. You will likely be surprised.

The great surprise is that two major factors will be used to try to produce the desired results: population control and a new form of worldwide government to enforce it. An even bigger surprise is that both mankind and God are planning to use the same two factors.

Let me explain.

Population Control

Man's Plan

- Use abortion and pills, and promote confusion between the sexes. This would include a *change* in the very nature of many of those populating the earth.
- Institute a one-world form of government with one ruling body and one overall leader. This would allow for a worldwide enforcement agency and the ability to make it economically difficult to have and raise children. It could also enforce a limit on the number of children per family with penalties for not abiding by the limits.

God's Plan

- Institute a change in the very nature of many of those populating the earth. This will take place during the one-thousand-year millennium when the majority of those living on earth will have resurrected, glorified bodies that are incapable of bearing children; they won't need oxygen or produce waste.
- Institute a one-world form of government, in which Jesus will be the one and only ruler, acting as King of Kings and Lord of Lords. The very nature of the earth will be changed to the form of a near paradise, with absolutely no form of environmental pollution possible.

The reason man's solution for environmental pollution problems is so similar to God's is just this: Satan is *the ruler of the earth at the present time*, and he is always trying to mimic God in every way he can as he attempts to achieve his primary goal, which is to become God himself. There are many examples of this in the Bible, including the modeling of the Trinity in Revelation 16, which is composed of Satan, the Antichrist, and the false prophet.

Thus, we see another great example of the use of the primary topics of this book: God's ultimate purpose, his plan for mankind, and the use of global resets taking place here.

The real bottom line of this book is just this: *God is in control, and the purpose of his will is to be realized in the end-times whenever they take place.*

Why Would God Choose Our Generation to Accomplish the Purpose of His Will? What Are Some of the Obvious Signs That Point to This Taking Place?

There are several reasons why this generation makes perfect sense as the one God would choose to accomplish the purpose of his will. Again, that purpose is to finally produce the bride of Christ for all eternity. This bride will be all of those throughout all history who have had their names written in the Lamb's Book of Life. That means they chose to believe in and follow Jesus. Some of the reasons Jesus would choose our generation for the end-time scenario and some of the clues that it could be coming soon are listed below.

- We are fast approaching what appears to be the six thousandth year since the end of the seventh day of creation. Ken Johnson of Biblefacts.org has recently prepared an English translation of the book of Enoch, apparently written several hundred years before the flood. My understanding is that this book seems to say that the Bible's seven days of creation were actually seven one-thousand-year "days." It also seems to be saying that the seven thousand years of creation will be followed by seven thousand years of man on earth before the eternal state of Revelation 21–22 is realized. It also seems to be saying that these final seven thousand years will be broken up into three two-thousand-year periods followed by a final one-thousand-year period with Jesus making two appearances on earth. One will be in the period just before the four thousandth year, and the second will be in the period very close to the six thousandth year. According to the research we have been reporting in this four-book series, that would be very near the year AD 2041. If that indeed is God's original plan, then we will certainly expect it to take place at precisely that time.
- God is all knowing, and he certainly knows that the earth is fast approaching a population-doubling crisis at this time in history. That would eventually produce a huge environmental crisis, a huge food shortage, the destruction of many species of life on earth, and so forth. In fact, it appears that many animal and plant species and so forth are already becoming extinct in some parts of the world because of the loss of forest land. Obviously, some supernatural intervention is called for.
- God has instituted punishment and forgiveness sentences for his people, which were spread all across the last forty-five hundred years. He has given the sentences in such a way that nearly all are ending or converging in or very near

the six thousandth year. That again would make this period the perfect time for Jesus to return for his bride. The event patterns associated with these sentences have been a major focus of this four-book series.

- Satanic activity on earth appears to be reaching gigantic proportions. The great flood was God's means to destroy Satan's work the last time it reached such proportions. That crisis was due to the evil angels producing a hybrid type of angel/human being that Genesis 6 called "Nephilim." By the time of the flood, there appeared to be only one family not polluted with the genetic seed of these evil angels. The same seems to be happening once more on earth if the reports we are hearing and reading about are true. God will again need to intervene to stop this activity. Daniel 12 says that in the end-times there will be a knowledge explosion, a technology explosion of sorts. That has happened in incredible proportions in this generation. It is unprecedented and may be due in large part to the reported angelic or "alien" intervention over the last eighty years or so.

- All this seems to be leading up to the great apostasy or falling away from God in the end-times forecast in the Bible in 2 Thessalonians 2 and 2 Timothy 3. It appears that the world is heading for a one-world government, and that wouldn't be possible without a falling away from God. Again, apostasy is one of the signs of the end-times spoken of in the Bible.

Without intervention, all the above factors will eventually reach disastrous proportions. Humankind may not be capable of doing this intervention successfully by itself. God has always known that the world would reach this situation at this very time. He had a plan for dealing with this even before creation. It is the end-time scenario we presented in chapter 10. That end-time scenario involved two massive global resets. Both involve situations that will cure the population-doubling problem. This whole scenario is covered extensively in the book of Revelation.

The first global reset involves the one who is called the Antichrist taking control of the whole world and declaring he is the God of the world. He will attempt to kill all people on earth who will not worship him as their God. This is described in Revelation as an uncountable number of people. The Antichrist will also precipitate a war that will result in massive death on earth. There will also be massive "natural disasters that end up killing billions of people around the world. If we calculate the statistics given in Revelation concerning the number of deaths from all these disasters, we easily come up with somewhere between one-half and two-thirds of all people on earth being killed in the seven-year period of tribulation.

The second of these global resets in God's end-time scenario calls for Jesus to return to earth and intervene in a situation that would end up with the world completely destroying itself without godly intervention. This intervention is called the "Second Coming of Jesus." The Antichrist together with Satan will assemble the whole army of evil angels along with a huge army from nations that are anti-Jesus with a plan for destroying the nation of Israel and all Jewish people. At his Second Coming, Jesus will simply speak the word, and all the evil angels along with Satan will be immediately banned to the Abyss for the next one thousand years.

The next phase of Jesus's Second Coming also involves a huge reduction in the number of people who will then be on the earth. This will be the sheep-goat judgment of Matthew 25:31–46, which involves all people still alive at the time of the Second Coming. All those who are not believers in Jesus and his followers will be immediately banned to Hades, awaiting their final judgment at the end of the next one-thousand-year period. This is the Great White Throne Judgment of Revelation 20. Again this will be a huge number of people.

Thus, we see that the only people still alive on earth to start the millennial period will be those who became followers of Jesus. When Jesus returns to earth at the Second Coming, he will bring with him the resurrected dead of all ages past who have been his followers. They will be in their new, glorified bodies, which will not be polluters of the earth in any way.

Finally, Jesus will supernaturally return the earth to its original pristine condition. Earth will be a true paradise for the next one thousand years. There will no longer be vicious animals, poisonous insects, unclean air, polluted water, violent people who will not be properly dealt with, openly sinful activities of any sort, homeless and hungry people, and so forth. A true paradise!

The problem is finally solved! Jesus will be King of Kings and Lord of Lords of the whole earth. Thank you, Jesus!

We listed and discussed many of the signs the Bible says will take place in the period just preceding the start of the period of great tribulation presented in Revelation. There are also many other unique and Biblically necessary signs that might point to this generation as a good candidate for the end-time scenario. We will list a few.

- Revelation indicates that an asteroid will hit the world during the seven-year tribulation period. For the first time in the history of humans on earth, we have a good candidate. That is the asteroid Apophis. It will make close approaches to earth in both AD 2029 and AD 2036.
- We have recently experienced the first worldwide pandemic with colossal consequences since the black plague of the period surrounding AD 1350.
- Nearly all the biblical signs that involve the nation of Israel are either in alignment or seem to be approaching alignment in the near future.
- The gospel of Jesus is now available to all people groups in the world for the first time in history.
- A one-world government is a requirement for the end-times, and there are powerful forces in the world that are trying to bring this about for the first time since the Tower of Babel forty-four hundred years ago.
- The technology explosion of Daniel 12 didn't arrive on earth until our generation. For the first time in history, we are seeing the feasibility of several key features of end-time prophecy being fulfilled. I will present these items with very little

explanation since this would get too deep for the intentions of this book. These items include the following:

- The means for implementing the mark of the Beast
- The means for seemingly bringing a fatally wounded person back to life. This will take place with the Antichrist, as presented in Revelation 13:12
- The means for creating a true one-world government with a plausible plan for implementing it
- The means for implementing a feasible system for tracing every person on earth, controlling all their financial transactions, and even reaching the possibility of reading their minds
- The means for access to higher-dimensional technology and possibly the beings that control them

This list goes on and on. It involves the use of a recent explosion in the use of artificial intelligence technology, having thousands of tracking satellites in orbit, the development of microchips that can house an incredible amount of information with great processing capabilities, and so forth.

- Israel had to be an independent nation again, living in the land originally given to them by God, and Jerusalem had to be their capital city once more. These details were fulfilled in 1948 when Israel became a nation once more and in 2018 when Donald Trump and the United States recognized Jerusalem as their capital. As I was writing this information about Israel becoming a nation once more, with its people returning after being scattered all over the world for about nineteen hundred years, I was led to the discovery of an incredible, new event pattern. I discovered that it was 1,950 calendar years from the birth of Jesus in 2.54 BC until the birth of Israel in AD 1948.37. That led me to search for other event time gaps of 1,950 years in the history of God's people. I was really amazed to find that there were at least twelve 360-days-per-year instances of God using such time gaps between important events as he was dealing with his people. These are shown below:
- The fall to the birth of Abraham
- The end of the seventh day to the death of Shem in witness pattern
- The flood to the Jubilee year one year after the completion of the rebuilt temple
- Shem's death to the start of Herod's temple
- Jacob's/Jesus's wrestling match to the death of Jesus
- The reign of Pharaoh, who enslaved Jews, to the Mount Vesuvius eruption in the Jubilee year
- Joseph's death to the Bar Kokhba revolt
- Jesus's birth to key events post World War I, leading to the rebirth of Israel
- The Jubilee year in Jesus's ministry to the first Jubilee year after the rebirth of Israel

- The destruction of the temple by the Romans in AD 70 to the failed trade of land for peace
- Mount Vesuvius to the start of the seventieth Jubilee since 1399 BC
- The Jubilee year of the start of the Bar Kokhba revolt to the last Shemitah of the seventieth Jubilee period

All this clearly points out that Israel is the "apple" of God's eye (Zech. 2:8). She will clearly be his focus in the coming seven-year period of great tribulation. That period will result in the Jewish people coming to believe in Jesus as their Messiah and Savior en mass. Believe it or not, but it is exactly 66.66666 times 66.66666 360-day years from the end of the flood in 2433.35 BC until the year AD 1948.37, the very time when Israel became a nation once more. Whew!

Does the Above Pattern Involving 66.666, the Flood, and the Year 1948 Conclusively Prove the Accuracy of Biblical Dates?

The Bible doesn't contain event dates, but it does have a vast number of genealogies and time gaps between key events. We can thus use well-established historical dates for a few biblical events to then establish the dates of other biblical events, assuming that the biblical information is accurate. We have done just that in this book. The date we established for the flood was derived in this way, and we have been using it for years, assuming it was quite accurate. The pattern cited above for the time gap between the year of the great flood's end and 1948 certainly proves to us that the dating information we have been using is extremely accurate. We will demonstrate why this is so.

- Israel became a nation once more in the year 1948.37 or May 15, 1948.
- In our date database, the flood began in 2434.33 BC and ended exactly one 360-day year later in 2433.35 BC.
- 66.6666 times 66.6666, or 65.710 in 360-day years, is 4,380.68 years.

Lastly, the time gap between 2433.35 BC and AD 1948.37 is precisely 4,380.72 years on a 365-day-per-year calendar.

That is a difference of a minuscule fifteen days. Wow!

The date 2433.35 was the very day Noah and his family departed from the ark. It represented a new start for mankind. We have seen throughout this four-book series that the complete history of God's chosen people, the descendants of Abraham, has been characterized by extremely long periods of tribulation and exile. This number 66.666 is God's number for tribulation, and thus this pattern is predictive of this proven fact. That pattern of tribulation will finally come to a complete conclusion during the coming thirteen-year end-time scenario. Anyway, my main reason for including this final pattern was to demonstrate that the one-hundred-plus dates we have developed from the Bible and used in our patterns are very likely highly accurate dates to a few months or so, in our opinion. It also might sway some skeptics who are reading this book. At least we hope and pray so.

Again, as we have said repeatedly, this doesn't apply to our speculated dates for the thirteen-year end-time scenario in our generation. It could be in any future two-thousandth-year time frame or whenever God otherwise chooses.

There have been many times since the end of World War I when prophecy scholars have gone far overboard in predicting the time of the end-time scenario. That was usually because something that could be interpreted as an end-time sign had taken place. They were all easily refuted, principally because there were a whole herd of signs of the end-times that must be occurring. That was never the case. However, this time seems to be much different because that whole herd of signs is either occurring or seems to be in their birth. These may be the birth pangs Jesus spoke about. That does not make it a certainty, but the probability is certainly much greater that it could occur in the next several years or so. This is the first time in my long life that every prophecy expert I am aware of is openly stating their belief that we are actually in the early phases of the end-times.

I have recently heard or read about several dates being mentioned for the time of the coming rapture, which will begin the thirteen-year end-time scenario. These dates include 2025, 2029, 2033, 2036, 2073–75, and so forth. A couple of these dates are associated with the asteroid Apophis and the fact that an asteroid hitting the earth seems to be part of the Revelation scenario early in the seven-year tribulation period. One is 2033 because it is two thousand calendar years after the year when some scholars believe Jesus was crucified. Another is 2073 because some believe it will be the six thousandth calendar year since the fall of man and so forth.

Any of these could be correct, but I have my doubts about any of them that use calendar years. That is because I find God to be incredibly consistent in every way. He does not seem to compromise. He uses 360-day years in the two major end-time prophetic books of the Bible, Daniel and Revelation. For that reason, I certainly expect him to use that calendar in all his dealings with his creation. That was my thesis throughout this four-book series, and the results have been incredible, in my opinion.

There are only a couple of cases where I found that God could have used calendar years, but they were the huge exception and may have been coincidences. The hundreds of patterns disclosed in these books are not coincidences. They are extremely precise patterns that never seem to fail. However, that certainly doesn't mean I completely understand God's intentions in his use of the patterns or that I am correctly interpreting them. I'm certainly not the creator or owner of the patterns presented in this series, but I know who their owner and creator is. He is the creator of all things and my personal Savior. There are certainly many things he may not want us to know and many things we cannot fully comprehend. Biblical end-time prophecy is one of those things. Since we cannot be sure of the day or time when Jesus will come for us, the best thing any of us can do is simply get ready and stay ready for the day when he will come for those who believe in and follow him.

I have presented my evidence for the possibility of the end-time scenario taking place in our generation. I now rest my case.

The Bottom Line for This Book and in Fact the Whole 2041 Series of Four Books

Likely the most important bottom line of this series of books was surprising in that it was not something we were looking to accomplish. The God of the Christian Bible is currently and has always been in complete control of the most important events in the history of the world, especially as they apply to those who honor him and recognize him for who he is. We saw that demonstrated literally hundreds of times in the incredible fulfillment of prophecies made in the Bible thousands of years ago. We also saw it in the dozens upon dozens of event-pattern strings that kept on occurring with the same themes being repeated over and over in patterns. The fact that these event patterns converge in the very most important years for God's people makes us double down on this conclusion.

Thus, it is very clear who is really in charge of the most important world events. As part of his end-time prophecies, we were able to put together a scenario that should be at least reasonably close to a match for what the real end-time scenario will be. As part of the somewhat-speculative end-time scenario, we have been able to come up with what we consider to be reasonable clues to help us answer the key questions with which we began this book. Those questions were associated with some very interesting and important events that will be part of that end-time scenario. A shortened version of those questions follows:

- What are the soon-coming twin global resets and great family reunions?
- Who is the Angel of Death, and what are the Angel of Death and pandemic codes? Are they associated with the timing of the global resets and family reunions?
- What was the "purpose of God's will" or his master plan that he conceived even before the creation of the physical universe?

We were successful in finding many clues that led us to answers for each of these questions, and they are all found in the end-time scenario we presented above. Most importantly, however, we discovered that the reason for God's creation of the physical universe and the humans who populated it was just this. God chose to give his "Son" or companion in the Godhead, the one we call Jesus, a very special gift. That gift was an eternal companion. That companion would be created in his image and be one who would grow to maturity over a period of several thousand years and become complete when "time reaches its fulfillment" according to Ephesians 1. The things we have been presenting in this four-book series describe the growing process for this eternal companion. We discovered that this growing process will apparently become complete at some date that is in years surrounding some two-thousandth-year period starting with the end of the seventh day of creation or 3873 BC from the information given to us in the Bible. So then, what does that have to do with us and our generation?

In a nutshell, it is this: the third two thousandth year after the end of the seventh day of creation will occur in approximately AD 2041, according to our detailed analysis of the timing presented in the Bible when matched with recorded secular history.

We discovered there was a series of major events taking place for God's people associated with the time frames surrounding the two thousandth and four thousandth years in history. That leads us to expect that another very important series of events for God's people will also take place in the six thousandth year or AD 2041. The big questions associated with this year are as follows:

- Will God's pattern of having major resets for his people be continued in the years surrounding the year AD 2041? If so, will it be another intermediate reset in the same vein as those of 1902 BC and AD 70, or will it be the final target in God's plan, the period when time reaches its fulfillment?
- If it is another intermediate year, what type of reset might we expect? We really don't know, but if so, the event would likely involve events that would set the world on a slightly different path that would aid in the final reset being some multiple of two thousand years in the future. We will not speculate on that.
- If this is the two-thousandth year when time reaches its fulfillment, as stated in Ephesians 1, then we should expect the world to continue on the path it already seems to be on. The events of the last 180 years are certainly following the end-time scenario as we have clearly shown throughout this book. If it continues, then the next major event we would expect will be the rapture of the saints to heaven. In the meantime, leading up to the rapture, we should expect a continuation of the growing apostasy in the world in the events that could lead us closer to a one-world government and an increase of catastrophic events around the world.
- Finally, if our generation is really the time when the end-time scenario will be fulfilled, then our patterns lead us to the following incredible pattern:

Jesus's Second Coming will take place at the beginning of the seven-thousandth-year period after the end of the seven-thousandth year of creation. It will be in Daniel's seventieth-seven-year period and in the last seven-year Shemitah period in the seventieth Jubilee period since the Israelites first entered the Promised Land in 1399.4 BC. Wow!

The bottom line of all this is that neither we nor anyone else on earth really knows. Only God really knows. The only advice we can give is that we don't know, but with the signs being what they are, we should all get ready and stay ready in case this is the period when time will reach its fulfillment.

How to Get an Invitation to All Three of the Upcoming Great Family Reunions

It is very simple: just get on board the cruise ship called "Salvation," which is bound for the glory land. See my website for how to get a free invite.

Appendix A

Key Event Dates in the Whole History and Future of God's People

Presenting Our Date Charts

We will now begin presenting our date charts. We will present them in five separate charts just as we developed them over twenty years from 1997 to 2017. We developed each chart for a specific purpose: to aid us in the studies we were conducting at the time. Each chart has its own unique format, and the specific type of information varies from chart to chart due to the nature of the study we were engaged in when we developed the chart. That is why there isn't just one large comprehensive date chart. You will understand this as you study the charts.

We will now begin presenting our five date charts. We developed our first chart in 1997. We wanted to develop a timeline all the way back in ancient history from the exodus to the fall of man. Fortunately, the Bible contains all the information necessary to do this. The challenge was finding all the clues that allow one to do this since they are spread over several Old Testament books and chapters within the books. Putting these charts together turned out to be a fun journey for us.

CHART 1: Establishing Key Dates in the Period Between the Fall of Man and the Death of Solomon Using Information in the Torah and 1 Kings

EVENT OR BIRTH DATE (Solar) BC	AGE AT BIRTH OF SON OR GAP TO EVENT	AGE AT DEATH (see note)	NAME OR DESCRIPTION OF EVENT
4068(70.5)	130 (128)	930	Adam Genealogies in Gen 5:3-32
3940	105 (104)	912	Seth
3836	90 (89)	905	Enosh
3747	70 (69)	910	Kenan
3678	65 (64)	895	Mahalalel
3614	162 (160)	962	Jared
3454	65 (64)	365	Enoch was raptured; he did not die
3390	187 (184)	969	Methuselah
3206	182 (179)	777	Lamech
3025	500 (493)	950	Noah
2532	(100) (99)	600	Shem (100 yrs old 2 years after flood)
2434			Flood end (Adam to flood 1660/1636 years)
2434.3	35 (34.5)	438	Arphaxad, Gen. after Shem, Gen 11:10-26
2400.4	30 (29.6)	433	Shelah
2370.8	34 (33.5)	464	Eber
2337.3	30 (29.6)	239	Peleg
2307.7	32 (31.5)	239	Reu
2276.2	30 (29.6)	230	Serug
2246.6	29 (28.6)	148	Nahor
2218	70 (69)	205	Terah
2149	100 (99)	175	Abram born, Gen 17:17 (Flood to Abram 290/286 years)
2089-90			Noah dies
2050	60 YR GAP	180	Isaac born, Gen 25:26, 35:28
1991	130 GAP TO 1863	147	Jacob born, Gen 25:26, 47:28
1941.5			Shem dies
1902		110	Joseph born (17 when he entered Egypt)
1863	430 GAP TO 1438	147	Jacob 130 as he/sons enter Egypt, Gen 47:28

1833	**400 GAP TO 1438**		**400 years slavery in Egypt begins, Gen 15:13**
1518		120	**Moses birth, Deut 34:7; he died 1399-1400**
1438.8	**480 GAP TO 965**		**Exodus (430/424 yrs in Egypt, Exod 12:40)**
1399.4	**300 GAP TO 1097**		**Enter Prom Land; Num14:33-34, Jud 11:26**
965.7			**4th yr of Solomon; 480 yrs to Exod; 1 Ki 6:1, 2:11**
931			**Death of Solomon, 1 Ki 14:25**

Notes on Chart Concerning Dates of Torah Events

1. Additional scriptures are regarding the time the Israelites spent in Egypt: 400 years in exile (Gen. 15:13; Acts 7:6), 430 years total for the four hundred years' exile, and 30 years from the time Jacob's family entered Egypt until the exile in slavery started (Ex. 12:40, 41; Gal. 3:17).

2. These dates were calculated using information and figures given in the Bible. Starting with the fourth year of Solomon's reign in 965.7 BC, the Bible presents an unbroken datable chain of about thirty events leading all the way back to the fall of man. The information is presented in 360-day years, as are all ages, time gaps, and so forth throughout the whole sixty-six books of the Bible. Thus, we had to translate this information to calendar years by using a multiplication factor of .98565. This led us to the fall of man occurring in 4068 BC. Since all ages, time gaps, and so forth were given in whole years, that means our final result would likely be in error by about +/- five years or so. The evenly spaced, sequential date patterns we are presenting led us to the actual date for the fall of man being in 4070.5. Thus, our original date was apparently in error by only two and a half years.

3. How can we be certain that 4070.5 was the actual date of the fall? We will give a quick answer to this question. First, the information and dates in the chart very accurately represent what is shown in the Bible. That leaves us with two other questions. Why believe the Bible, and how accurate was the presumed starting date? One short answer suffices for both questions. We discovered a whole myriad of equally spaced date patterns that spanned both sides of the starting point, and they were all mathematically perfect on both sides of that date. This is obvious from the material we discovered and presented. If you want to see some examples, we suggest that you look at the wilderness and tribulation patterns. The number of key event dates on which these patterns converge is mathematical proof of their validity.

4. In Hebrew, Methuselah means "when he dies it shall come." From the above figures, it can be seen that he was 969 years old when the flood started. That is also the age when he died. Might that be another proof that these dates and ages are literally true?

5. The maximum age a man could live gradually decreased from 950-plus years before the flood to 120 years after the flood. That is one possible interpretation of Genesis 6:3. Under ideal conditions, humans can currently live to be about 120 years old. In King David's era, 1000 BC, people were living seventy to eighty years (Ps. 90:10).

6. Assuming a lifespan of seventy years, a generation of thirty-five years, and starting with one family, it would take ~3,500 years to reach the current world population of eight billion. According to the above, it has been ~4,400 years since the flood. In the sixteen-hundred-plus years before the flood, considering the life spans and good health conditions, there would have been millions of people on the earth at the time of the flood.

CHART 2: Approximate Dates of Selected Events Surrounding the Life of Jesus and the Origin of the Christian Church

DATE	EVENT
• 2 BC	Birth of Jesus, Likely during the Feast of Pentecost; 2 ½ yrs before 1 AD. No year 0.
• 27 AD	John the Baptist begins his ministry.
• 28	Baptism of Jesus at 30 years of age (Luke 3:23). Well confirmed date.
• 30.8	Beginning of 30th Jubilee year in Jesus 30th year in year 30 AD
• 32	Crucifixion of Jesus. Some scientific evidence to support this date.
• 32	Pentecost; 3000 accept Jesus- the Church begins (Acts 2).
• 33==>	Christianity/Church begin spreading outward from Jerusalem. Disciples maintain their base in Jerusalem for awhile, then gradually begin moving; John to Ephesus sometime after 51 AD, etc. James, Peter remain in Jerusalem.
• 34	Saul's conversion (Acts 9).
• 34-37	Paul in Arabia; takes 3 years preparing for his ministry (Gal 1:17-18).
• 37	Paul goes to Jerusalem to meet Peter and James for the first time (Gal 1:18)
• 44	Herod Agrippa dies (Acts 12); James (John's brother) is the first disciple martyred
• 45	James, Jesus' brother, writes his letter to the scattered Jews (Jas 1:1; Acts 8:1)-1st NT Book.
• 45-60	Periods of Paul's missionary journeys (also went to Spain in 64-65).
• 50	Matthew (Levi) writes the first recorded Gospel. See NOTE 1 below.
• 51	Paul's second visit to Jerusalem- meets Peter, James and John (Gal 2:1, 9).
• 51-52	Paul's 1st recorded letters (Thess, Gal).
• 60	Paul taken to Rome- jailed 2-3 years (wrote Col, Eph, Philemon, Phil).
• 61	James, Jesus' brother, killed in insurrection in Jerusalem.
• 65-67	Peter killed in Rome.
• 66-67	Paul back in prison in Rome- beheaded in 67.
• 66-73	Great Jewish revolt. Romans siege; destruction of Jerusalem and the temple in 70 AD.
• 85-97	John's books and letters written (from Ephesus and Patmos).
• 100-120	John dies; the only disciple to die a natural death (in Ephesus).

NOTE 1: Matthew (Levi) was one of the twelve disciples. He had been trained to be a tax collector by the Romans, and had to be adept at writing and record keeping. He certainly had the capability and the means to keep notes of what Jesus said during his public and private ministry (to the twelve). It's possible that his (or another disciple's) notes may have been copied and passed around. He wrote the

book of Matthew, the 2nd recorded NT book. Matthew, more so than any other book, is composed mostly of direct quotes of what Christ said. It's interesting to note the similarities and sometimes the same words used by Matthew, Mark, Luke and even James in their books.

NOTE 2: The precise dates of letters and books written in New Testament times are sometimes hard to determine. Authors at that time referred to events, rulers, etc. to date their writings rather than dating them directly. Luke 3:1-2 is a good example. This was true of both religious and secular writings.

CHART 3: A Chronological History of Israel (Approximate)
Based Upon Biblical & Historical Evidence
(These are calendar year dates converted from 360
day year dates always used in the Bible)

DATE	DESCRIPTION OF EVENT
4070.5 BC.	Approximate solar year date for the fall of Adam; start date for God's Gentile patterns
4060.6	Start date for God's "Witness" patterns: 10 years after the fall
3873.37	200 years after fall of man; start of 7 1000 year days for man
3863.5	Start date for God's Witness patterns that are associated with the 2000 year pattern set
2434	Approximate timeframe for the end of the great flood of Noah
2296-86	Approximate timeframe of the construction of the Tower of Babel event
2149	Birth of Abraham; Birth of Isaac was in 2050
2099	2000th year after the fall of man
2089	Death of Noah
2064	Birth of Ishmael to Hagar; God's promises to Hagar about future nations, etc.
	All when Abraham is 86; this happens 2006 years after the fall, a long time
2050	Destruction of Sodom and Gomorrah when Abraham is 99; God changes
	Abram to Abraham and makes his covenants with him, including circumcision,
	See Gen 16:1 to 21:5
2049.9	Birth of Isaac
1991	Birth of Jacob
1941	Death of Shem at age 600, the last known survivor of the flood
1902	Birth of Joseph; Year 2000 since 1st 1000 year day of man in 3873.37 BC
1863	Jacob and sons enter Egypt; Joseph is already there. Ex 12:40-41 says they will be there 430 years; 1863 − 424 = 1439 (1438.8). Bondage began 30 yrs later, 1833, Gen 15:13, Acts 7:6
1833	Jacob's family, the future 12 tribes of Israel, go into a 400 year period of slavery in Egypt.
1518	Birth of Moses
1478	Moses kills an Egyptian, flees to the desert, tends sheep, etc. for 40 years.

1442	Timeframe when the 400 year tribulation in Egypt is nearing its end
1438.8	Exodus under Moses. 1 Kings 6:1 says it was 480 (473) Years from Exodus to 4th yr of Solomon's reign; 1439 – 473 = 966
♥1399.4	Israelites enter the Promised Land; Battle of Jericho
♥1350-1050	Period of Judges; Joshua ~60 when entering Promised Land. Led Israel until death at age 110 in ~1350. Israel spent ~300 years under judges.
♥1054	Jubilee year ushering in the period of kings
1050-586	Period of Kings: Saul, David, Solomon first three kings, each approx. 40 yrs.
1010	David becomes king of Israel, reigns until Solomon in 971 BC.
♥1005	David conquers Jerusalem, assumes control of both Israel & Judah; Jerusalem becomes capital
966-965	Fourth year of Solomon's reign; Temple construction started 480/473 years after Exodus.
960-59	Solomon's Temple finished after 7 years ; 960 – 355 = 605 & 960 – 424 = 536 – another prophetic use of 430 & 360 year gaps between key events
931-30	Israel divided over taxes; north becomes Israel, south becomes Judah after death of Solomon in 931
916-15	Death of Rehoboam, first king of Judah in the divided kingdom realm Year 3000 since 1st 1000 year day
719.29	Israel exiled by Assyrians; not reinstated as a united nation again until 1948
♥709.4	Key Jubilee year, in fact the only dateable Jubilee year in the Bible, given as a sign by God that the Assyrians would not succeed in destroying Jerusalem, 2 Kings 19:29; Event involves King Hezekiah and prophet Isaiah being involved in this supernatural event
♥612-611	Babylonians conquer the Assyrians setting up conquest of Judah by Babylonians
606-605	Babylonians (Nebuchadnezzar) seize Judah; first exile to Babylon includes Daniel; Jeremiah prophesies that the exile will last 70 years (until 536), Jer 25:11-12, 29:10
587-586	Siege of Jerusalem and destruction of the temple and city by Babylonians. Last Jewish king until the millennial reign of Jesus.
♥562-561	Death of Nebuchadnezzar; leads to eventual fall of Babylon and freedom from exile for Judah
539-536	Persia (Cyrus) conquers Babylon in 539; Cyrus issues decree in 537-536 to let Israelites return to Jerusalem; end of 70 year desolation
536	Foundation of Temple in Jerusalem laid; protests by surrounding peoples leads to suspension

522	Darius becomes Persian king; allows Jews to renew construction of their temple
517	Reconstruction of the Temple proper begins; 70 year desolation of the Holy City ends (586-517)
♥513-512	A Jubilee year; the Second Temple is completed after 3 ½ years
♥464-63	Artaxerxes becomes King of Persia; He proves to be a key friend to those Jews still in exile
457-456	Artaxerxes letter to Ezra allowing return to Jerusalem and re-initiation of self rule for Jews
444	Artaxerxes decree of Dan 9:24-27; start date for prophecy of coming Messiah's death in 7x69 yrs
443	Rebuilding of city & walls begins per Dan 9; start date for 3rd Babylonian captivity punishment
325	Greeks (Alexander the Great) assume control of Judah and it becomes Judea
♥168-167	Maccabean Revolt follows "abomination of desolation;" Temple cleansed in 164-163 after Maccabeans defeat Seleucids, celebrate the first Hanukkah
♥69-68	Pharisees assume a major role in the Sanhedrin
63-62	The Romans (Pompeii) conquer Judea
♥20-19	Herod (an Idumean descended from Esau) begins remodeling and expansion of the Temple; 19 + 424 = 444-443 BC, another prophetic use of 430 year time gaps by God
2 B.C.	Jesus birth; conception during Tabernacles 9/11/03 BC, with birth during Pentecost in 2 BC
♥28-32 A.D.	Jesus earthly ministry (Rabbis had to be 30 yrs old); 30th Jubilee cycle began in 30.8 AD
66-73	Jewish revolt against the Romans; the temple and city are destroyed in 70 A.D
♥129-139	Jewish revolt, Jerusalem destroyed, plowed under; new city and temple to Jupiter built. Many Jews killed or exiled; area renamed Palestine (from Philistines). Last Jubilee 129
257	Wars between Romans and Sassanid's results in expanded religious freedoms for Jews
♥325-326	Council of Nicea; creed developed, canon agreed upon
♥622	Muhammad's Hegira to Medina
632	Muhammad's death
638	Jerusalem falls to the Muslims
677	Byzantines retake Jerusalem & part of Judea for a short time before losing it again to Muslims

858	Pope Nicholas issues Papal Bull requiring Jews to register, wear badges and become Christians
1099	Crusaders capture Jerusalem for the Christians
1252-53	Papal bull permits torture as part of inquisition – bad news for Jews; Jews expelled from France
♥1262-3	Egyptian Muslims capture Jerusalem
1302.3	Pope Boniface issues Unam Sanctum bull declaring papal supremacy over national leaders
1351	The Black or Bubonic Plague took place throughout Europe from about 1346 to 1351 with about one half of all Europeans being killed; huge numbers of Jewish people were killed from country to country because they were blamed for causing the plague, possibly because they seemed immune to it due to their sterile practices
1450.1	Jews expelled from Bavaria in the Inquisition; Cardinal orders all Jews to register and wear badges
1517	Ottoman Turks capture Jerusalem
1517-23	Reformation; Luther translating Bible into German
1544	Muslims seal the Eastern Gate because of prophecy Jesus will return via this gate
♥1607-8	Jamestown becomes first English colony in America, a critical future sanctuary for Jews
♥1647-56	Polish massacre of nearly 100,000 Jews as part of Inquisition; Jews readmitted to England 1655' Jubilee in 1656-57
1844-5	Ottoman edict of tolerance for Jews; Jews expelled from Russia; 360 yr Spanish inquisition ends
1879	Jewish immigration to Palestine begins; first new settlement of retuning Jews
1897-98	Official birth of the Zionist movement to recreate a state of Israel
♥1903	Jubilee year; end of 2nd Zionist Aliya , organized immigration of workers, etc. to original land
1917	British capture Palestine from the Turks in WW; issue Balfour Declaration
1919	Jews claim Palestine, Arabs claim Iraq, etc.
1920	Palestine placed under the British; Arabs riot and demand end to Jewish immigration
1942-3	Nazi holocaust peaks; the final solution
1947	Palestine divided into Jewish and Arab states; Jews accept, Arabs reject
1948	Israel declares independence; five Arab nations attacked; Iraq, Egypt, Syria, Jordan, Lebanon

1948-52	800,000 Jews expelled from Arab states flee to Israel, 650,000 Arabs flee from Israel and are placed in refugee camps by Muslims
♥1952	Jubilee year; huge effort to begin organized reclamation of land, planting huge number of trees
1956	Sinai campaign; Egypt blocks Israeli shipping; Israel captures Sinai, then withdraws.
1962	First nuclear reactor comes on line in Israel
1967	Egypt again blocks Israeli shipping in Red Sea; in Six Day War Israel defeats Egypt, Iraq, Syria, Jordan, capturing Sinai, Gaza, Judea, Samaria, Golan Heights; Jerusalem Reunited; Israel gives admin control of Temple Mount to Jordan.
1971	Rabbi Council votes to forbid use of Temple Mount despite it being under Jewish control
1973	Yom Kippur War; Egypt and Syria launch surprise attack on Israel; ask for cease fire in 3 weeks
1975-82	Period of mass immigration from Russia to Israel
1978-79	200,000 Jews immigrate to Israel from the Soviet Union
1988	PLO declares establishment of Palestinian state with Jerusalem as its capital
1992-93	Oslo I transfers Jericho and Gaza to PLO
1994	Peace treaty established with Jordan
1995	Oslo II transfers Bethlehem, Hebron, etc. to PLO
♥2001	This whole year represents the 69th Jubilee year counting from 1399.4 BC. The 70th Jubilee began in late 2001. Year of 9/11 attack on America signaling new set of Harbingers?
2041	Year when Both the Assyrian and Babylonian captivity pattern punishment of the Jews ends; Jews will then be finally totally forgiven for past sins of ancestors
♥2051	The next Jubilee year, the 70th since their beginning in 1399.4

♥ Dates marked by a ♥ indicate Jubilee years. God told the Jews in Lev 25 to start counting off 50 (49.2825) year periods after they entered the Promised Land in 1400 (1399.4) BC. These would be special years for the Jews. There have been 70 such periods since 1400 BC. 65 of the key dates in the history of the Jews of this timeframe are included on this chart. Since the Jubilee years are separated by 50 years you would expect there to be about a 1 in 50 chance for a random event to fall on a Jubilee year. You would expect about 1 to 2 of the 65 events to fall on a Jubilee year. However, almost 25 event dates fell on Jubilee years. That is incredible. That tells me that God was in control of history. His analysis was quite over simplified and a bit biased but it is incredible none the less.

CHART 4: Key Dates in Ancient Jewish History
From Solomon Through Abraham Including the Period of Judges
(God Year Dates Are Only Meaningful Wrt Solomon's Death In 931 BC)

God Yr Date BC	Cal Yr Date BC	Bible Verses	Event Taking Place Bible.ca was a ref. often used in this chart
922	909		Nadab is king
923	910		Jeroboam dies
924	911		Abijah dies, Asa king for 31 yrs
930	916-5	1 Ki 14:21, 31	Rehoboam dies at 58, Abijah is king
939	926	1 Ki 14:25	Shishak, King of Egypt, attacked Jerusalem
945	931	1 Ki 14:21, 11:42	Solomon reigns 40 yrs, dies, Rehoboam king
974	960		Temple completed after 6 years
980	966-5	1 Ki 6:1	Temple begun 480 years after Exodus in 4th year of Solomon's reign
984	970	2 Sam 5:4, 1 Chr 29:27	David reigned 40 yrs, died at 70; Solomon becomes king
988	974		Rehoboam born
993	979		Absalom insurrection and death at age 29
1004	990		Rape of Tamar
1015	1000		Solomon born
1020	1004-5	2 Sam 5:4-7	David plans for temple. David seizes Jerusalem
1020	1004-5		JUBILEE Yr 1005-04: Asahel killed by Abner
1025	1010	2 Sam 5:4, Acts 13:21	David becomes king in Hebron; Saul dies at 70 Jonathan dies at 57
1028	1013	1 Sam 25:1	Samuel dies at 90
1032	1017		Saul kills priests at Nob
1040	1025	1 Sam 17:50	David kills Goliath; anointed king at age 15
1055	1040		David born
1066	1051	1 Sam 13:1	Saul king at 30, reigns 40 yrs, Acts 13:21
1070	1054.42		JUBILEE Year: decision to allow kings in Israel
1082	1066		Jonathan born
1082	1066		Abdom dies
1090	1075	Jud 12:13-14	Elon dies, Abdom judges
1097	1081		Saul born
1100	1084	Jud 12:11	Elon judges for 10 years
1107	1091	1 Sam 4:15-18	Ark captured; Samuel called age 8; Eli dies 98
1107	1091	Jud 12:8	Ibzan judges
1113	1097	Jud 12:7	Jephthah judges

1113	1097	Jud 11:26	300 years after entering Promised Land
1118	1103		Samuel born
1147	1131	1 Sam 4:15-18	Eli judges
1167	1141		Deborah dies; 1201-1141
1205	1188		Eli born
1270	1251.55		JUBILEE Year: RamsesII and Ehud
1370	1350.12	Joshua 24:29	Joshua died at 110; JUBILEE Year
1420	1399.4	Exod 16:35	First Jewish harvest in Promised Land
1460	1438.81	Exod 7:7, 12:40-41 1 Kings 6:1	Exodus from Egypt, Moses 80 years old Israel's people begin 40 years in wilderness; end 400 yrs slavery, 430 yrs in Egypt (1862.6)
1462	1442	Exod 3:1-22	Israelite persecution grows; Moses preparation
1480	1459		Joshua born
1499	1478		Moses kills Egyptian, flees to the desert 40 yrs
1540	1518	Exod 2:2, 5	Moses born; adopted by Pharaoh's daughter Egyptians were killing Jewish babies.
1570	1547		Semite king Hyksos expelled as Egyptian ruler
1820	1793	Gen 50:26	Joseph dies at 110
1860	1833.1	Gen 15:13, Acts 7:6	Begins 400 years of slavery in Egypt, 70 years after birth of Joseph
1863	1836.4		66.6 yrs after Joseph's birth; begins tribulation
1870	1842.9		End 200 yr pattern period that began in 2040
1873	1846	Gen 47:28	Jacob dies at 147
1885	1858.7		End of the 7 years of drought and famine
1876	1862.6	Gen 47:9, 28 Ex 12:40-41	Jacob at age 130 enters Egypt with family. This was 430 years before the Exodus.
1890	1865.6		Year that the drought and famine began
1900	1872.5	Gen 35:28 Gen 41:46	Isaac dies at 180; year plentiful harvest began; Joseph is ruler in Egypt at age 30
1909	1882		Joseph placed in prison in Egypt
1912	1885	Gen 37:2	Joseph in Egypt at 17
1919	1892	Gen 32, 35	Jacob wrestles all night with God in Bethel, he is renamed Israel; prophetic of the nations' long nighttime struggle over the true identity of God
1930	1902.07	Gen 37:2	Joseph born
1970	1941		Shem dies at age 600
2005	1974.36	Gen 25:7	Abraham dies at 175
2020	1990.8	Gen 25:26	Jacob and Esau born
2042	2013	Gen 23:1	Sarah dies at 127
2064	2034.75	Gen 22	Abrahamic promise of large nation; world bless

2070	2040.04		Shem was exactly 500 years old
2079	2049.92	Gen 21:5, 19:37	Isaac Born; Ammonites and Moabites begin
2080	2050	Gen 16:1-21:5	Abraham 99; Sodom & Gomorrah are destroyed God's covenants with Abram, incl. circumcision
2094	2064	Gen 16:1-21:5	Abram 86; God's promises Hagar; Ishmael born
2104	2074	Gen 12:4,7	Abraham leaves Haran; Altar at Shechem
2120	2089.3		Noah dies
2170	2139	Gen 17:17	Sarah is born
2180	2148.48		Abraham born

Appendix B

The Scorecard for the Master Template Chart

Pattern No.	score		Pattern no.	Score
30	1			
40	7			
50	7	7X		
60	2	7X		
66.66	7	7X		
70	1			
80	14			
90	3			
100	14			
200	63	3X7		
300	10	10X30	350	17
400	70	10X		
500	70	10X		
600	20	10x		
666.66	70	10X		
700	10	10x70		
800	140	2x400		
900	30	3x300		
1000	140	2x500		
1750	157	1000+700+		
1800	280		2000FG	287
2000G	630	3x210	2000W	280
360	84	7X300+60	2000FW	280
390	91	7X		
430	497	7X	270	64
490	490	70x7		
ANGEL	91	7x13	30,50,70,90 66.666	All 455
4000	420	2X2000	200W	28
6000G	1890	3X2000	6000W	840
7000	2030	6000+1000	7000W	980
Global Reset	1000		New Witness	1000
Jesus Key	5000			

References

1. Grant Jeffrey, Armageddon; Earths Last Days; 1997 Frontier Publications, Inc
2. Yacov Rambsel, Yashue; 1196 World Publishing, Nashville
3. Dr Chuck Missler; Koinonia House
4. Wedding, Nelson New International Bible Dictionary, 1995, Thomas Nelson Publishers
5. Zola Levitt, A Christian Love Story, 1978
6. World Population History, Wikipedia.org

Cracking
the Twin
Global Reset Code

This book reveals how the process of
cracking the global reset code
led to discovering several
other secret codes.
Those codes reveal
hidden aspects of
the end-times.
These codes are
the pandemic code,
the Angel of Death code,
and the great family reunion code.
Will these codes tie coming end-times to our generation?

Printed in the United States
by Baker & Taylor Publisher Services